CARLYLE TILL MARRIAGE

LET us honour you not so much with passing praises as with our reverence, and so far as we can with our emulation, pondering in our hearts your words and acts, cherishing the features of your character. It is not that I would forbid the statues wrought in marble or in bronze; but the faces of men and these their likenesses are all alike frail perishable things, while the fashion of the soul is ever-lasting, not to be shown in matter or by the help of art, but in our lives.

TACITUS, ON AGRICOLA.

Yours faithfully,

T. Carlyle

Date, London, 1832. By Daniel Maclise. This is the best picture of Carlyle in his early days in London, when he was still dressing up to the " jemmy hat " Miss Welsh gave him in 1824. In January, 1871, William Allingham overtook him in King's Road, and joining in his walk was told about the artist :—" Maclise was a quiet, shy man, with much brogue. His drawing of me in *Fraser* had a very considerable likeness. Done from life in Fraser's back-parlour in about twenty minutes."

Miss Carlyle Aitken, a niece of Carlyle, says she used to hear him call this picture " the Dominie," a familiar Scotch word for a teacher.

[*front.*

CARLYLE
TILL MARRIAGE

(1795–1826)

BY

DAVID ALEC WILSON

LONDON
KEGAN PAUL, TRENCH, TRUBNER & CO., LTD.
NEW YORK: E. P. DUTTON & CO.
1923

3984

Made and Printed in Great Britain at
The Mayflower Press, Plymouth. William Brendon & Son, Ltd.

PREFACE

FROM 1890 to 1912 I collected for pleasure whatever could be known about Carlyle. In 1890 at Ecclefechan I inspected what had been the original of the cottage in *Sartor*, the home of his boyhood ; and at Middlebie sat by the bedside of a very old woman who wanted to tell me all she knew—her mother had been the midwife who brought Carlyle into the world. In 1895, when I returned to Ecclefechan, the cottage was demolished. What is visited now is the house where he was born.

To be as candid as Froissart, I must say what he said : " The true reason of my undertaking this book was for my own amusement." Besides, it seemed sad that human curiosity about one so important to the world as Carlyle would soon be in vain. So I started to make notes, recognizing they might some day be used for a " Life " :

> " For whatsoe'er we perpetrate
> We do but row,—we're steered by Fate."

My trade was official work in Burma, where Europeans die sooner than at home, and I could not begin to write a " Life " till after retirement.

In the house of Prof. C. E. Norton, near Boston, in 1895, when he urged me to write at once, I had to answer : " If I live to 1920 or so, a ' Life ' of Carlyle by me is sure to be written. If not, then Providence, whom it concerns, must find some other to do it."

" What is done in 1920 cannot possibly concern me— nothing will interest me then," he answered gravely.

The method of composition has been like that of the artist who began by elaborately drawing everything, and then struck out the most of it. When I retired in 1912, the

v

materials available about the European Confucius would
have filled fifty volumes of the common kind; and I
allowed myself ten years to reduce it all to a readable size.
Only the opening chapters deal with his surroundings. The
rest is Carlyle, and *not* " his times." To minimize footnotes,
his journal and his works and the published correspondence
of himself and his wife, and all the books published by
Mr. Froude, Prof. Norton and Alexander Carlyle are
generally taken as read. The recently published *Guide to
Carlyle*, by A. Ralli, makes it needless to give footnotes to
these. For controversy, see my own *Mr. Froude and
Carlyle* (1897), Mr. Froude's *My Relations with Carlyle* (1903)
and *The Nemesis of Froude* (1903), by Sir James Crichton-
Browne and Alexander Carlyle, and my own *Truth About
Carlyle* (1903), with a Preface by Sir James, a supplement
to the *Nemesis*, dealing with new evidence. To minimize
theology, the *Faith of All Sensible People* appeared in
1913, to show what is meant here by such an expression
and where Carlyle stood in theology. Suffice it to say
now that the essence of it is reverence for reality and
confidence in the enlightened conscience. For the comfort
of readers the dots of omission in quotations are generally
omitted.

Mr. Froude was rather the occasion than the cause of the
" slump in Carlyle " that has disgraced us for fifty years.
" Setting too good an example," said Benjamin Franklin,
" is a kind of slander seldom forgiven; 'tis *Scandalum
Magnatum* "—a libel on Grandees. That was one of the
reasons why the death of the great moralist was followed
by a carnival of obscenity, hardly ended yet.

In later volumes Mr. Froude shall be seen the dupe of a
knave. He was an English-clerical variety of Tartarin of
Tarascon, a very English compromise or blend of Don
Quixote and Sancho Panza, living in illusions. But he is
also a bore, and it is needless to do more than look at him
and pass. He tried to be an imitation Carlyle, but was
rather like a counterfeit. Nature and Newman together

were too much for him. He could not be sincere, and often deceived himself. Yet he must have known he was doing wrong when he made free use of the love-letters. Carlyle had searched for them in vain in order to destroy them ; and, failing to find them, left clear instructions which Froude received : " My strict command now is, ' Burn them if ever found. Let no third party read them : let no printing of them, or of any part of them, be ever thought of by those who love me ! ' " It is not strange that when Froude disregarded words like these, his conscience made him, if possible, more careless than usual. He was like a flustered apprentice-thief, rummaging among stolen goods with a dark lantern and trying to comfort himself by saying : " The master's dead ; he wouldn't mind—at least, he shouldn't."

In some such way he may have deceived himself into making the mis-statement that Carlyle wrote Memoirs " mainly autobiographical," and " made over to me . . . these with his journal and the whole of his correspondence . . . with unfettered discretion to use in any way that I might think good," inasmuch as he wished the ' Life ' " to be as authentic as possible."

The striking fact was that to the end Carlyle punctiliously ignored as Froude's business and not his whatever Froude was to write. It was by talk about Mrs. Carlyle and by enduring to hear him talk about her that Froude had won the favour of the " foolish, fond old man " ; and yet the letter he prints from her to himself (IV, p. 264) is palpable chaff ; and a clever Scotch maid of hers whom she treated confidentially told me Mrs. Carlyle showed her a letter from Froude and scoffed at him as hollow, and bade her observe him for the fun of the thing. The " master " knew nothing of that, and, recognizing the literary " tact " of Froude, put into his hands the task of condensing further a voluminous mass of selections from Mrs. Carlyle's later letters. He gave him all the profits for his pains, making him perhaps the best paid editor of that generation.

The biography was volunteer work undertaken long afterwards. In 1875 Carlyle had given all his manuscripts but some business papers to his niece. She gave away whatever she liked in whatever way she liked ; and in 1877 and afterwards, with her uncle's vague approval, let Froude take away on loan whatever he wanted. By and by, at her request, her uncle told Froude the papers were hers and to be returned to her ; but that was all. To be explicit, her uncle had told her to lend Froude what she thought would be useful, and, without troubling him further, she let Froude have " almost all I had," she said, " without my uncle's knowledge."

While accepting responsibility for everything here, I have to explain that I had many opportunities of discussing with David Masson and Sir Charles Gavan Duffy not only all they had written about Carlyle, but all the problems of his life. I have had many talks on similar lines with other " Boswells," Frank Espinasse and C. E. Norton, Alexander Carlyle, Frederic Harrison, Sir J. Crichton-Browne and some scores of others, including all the relatives discoverable who had known him.

In Canada, in 1895, I visited and stayed some days with his youngest sister, Mrs. Hanning ; and at her request read all the papers she had, burned one or two for the sake of others, not for the sake of Carlyle, and satisfied her the rest might appear. " Print, print ! " has always been the advice I gave when consulted, even when previous perusal was not offered. It was never repented. There never was anyone of whom it could be more safely said : " Whatever record leap to light, he never shall be shamed."

Thanks are due to Allen and Unwin and many other publishers of Carlyle Correspondence. C. E. Norton, who edited seven volumes published by Macmillan and Co., 1883 to 1888, told me that his work was made light by the help of Alexander Carlyle, whose name should have been upon the title pages. Mr. Carlyle had to come forward as editor himself in time ; and it is to him as editor and owner of the manuscripts, and to John Lane as publisher that thanks are due in respect of the later six volumes, 1903 to 1909; in addition to which Mr. Alexander Carlyle has published valuable correspondence of both Carlyle and Mrs. Carlyle in the *Nineteenth Century* and the *Cornhill* Magazines. He is now in his eightieth year, and for almost forty years he has devoted himself to the service of his uncle's memory with a fidelity surpassing that of sons, and like the filial piety Confucius praised. In particular his work on *The Love Letters of Thomas Carlyle and Jane Welsh* has finished the filthiest fiction of Mr. Froude as finally as *Oliver Cromwell's Letters and Speeches*, edited by Carlyle, has finished the fictions about Cromwell.

Of MSS. used and not yet published, unless so far as quoted here, five large collections must be mentioned.

(1) The Letters from Francis, Lord Jeffrey, to Carlyle and his wife, which Mr. Froude was not allowed to quote, were lent to me by the owner, Miss Empson, the granddaughter of Jeffrey.

(2) The Letters from Carlyle and his wife to Joseph Neuberg were lent to me by Mr. Neuberg's nephew, F. J. F.

(3) The John Forster Letters in South Kensington.

(4) The Letters and Note-books of Mrs. James Anstruther, for which, as well as for the knowledge of Miss Empson's treasures, I am indebted to her sisters, the Misses Anderson, Ayrshire.

(5) The Correspondence of T. C. and William Graham, of Burnswark, for which I am indebted to John Graham, of Philadelphia.

I must beg forgiveness here from many who will see with sorrow no use made of sound materials kindly supplied. There is space for only a small fraction of what was known.

In many cases the result of much enquiry is negative, and nothing could anyhow appear. For example, credible persons have told me of contradictory statements by Sir Richard Quain. These might be interesting to a biographer of Quain; but to a biographer of Carlyle the only result is that what Quain said conveys no knowledge. Contradicting oneself is an old way of keeping a secret.

On medical matters many footnotes may be saved by a few sentences here. Samson Gemmell, of Glasgow, was for more than twenty years an intimate of mine, and known to be and to be esteemed one of the most skilful doctors in Scotland. He was strangely incapable of quackery, although an eminent consultant and professor. If a specialist in anything, it was in matters of digestion. He was also a disciple of Carlyle; indeed it was he who first persuaded me to read Carlyle. He considered long and carefully everything ascertainable about Carlyle's health and his wife's, too, not only all that was in print, but a great deal more. The opinions he at last expressed were accepted by me both here and elsewhere. Many doctors familiar with the history of medicine in Scotland have corroborated, such as Dr. George S. Keith of Edinburgh, about Carlyle, and Sir James Crichton-Browne about Mrs. Carlyle; and, in short, there is no room for any serious differences of opinion. The facts are plain.

John T. Wells, of Ecclefechan, for many years a missionary in Edinburgh, assisted me with the results of exhaustive local researches he made in the seventies. Moreover, he and another missionary, to whom he introduced me, George McRobert, and Robert Cochrane, an Edinburgh author, were the most assiduous and successful of about a score of acquaintances who watched the Press for me with a zeal no press-cutting agency could supply for money.

The letters of Margaret Gordon and much else, far more than appears in the notes, we owe to Alexander Carlyle; but I believe I meet his wishes in saying that all the responsibility is mine. He has said all he could in the course of twenty-five years to dissuade me from writing a " Life " on the scale of Froude's. He agreed with Gavan Duffy in advising " something of the size of Garnett's." The experiences of his wife and himself at the hands of Froude have filled him with a natural horror of authorizing

PREFACE xi

anybody. And if I had been open to persuasion he would have prevailed. However, I do not want to supersede Garnett, but Froude, and my writing this " Life " is not a matter of calculation or argument ; it is a matter of instinct, the same kind of feeling that made many a brave boy lately " go over the top " in the dark, without being doped by rum or military rot, inspired to—do what he could. In the course of twenty-five years Alexander Carlyle has answered all my questions, and I am old enough to dispense with a sponsor. In fact, I am delighted to be " unauthorized " by anybody. I always discount authorized biographies myself. " I won't be authorized, and will be read."

Perhaps the most important of many helpers is a venerable friend who declines to be named. In his ninth decade he is mentally equal to his prime. He has read every sentence of this volume, and of those to follow, much of it several times, in order to indicate to me for omission or correction anything that might pain the pious. My single aim has always been to tell the truth, the whole truth and nothing but the truth, as pleasantly as possible ; but I feel that for success in avoiding offence, the credit is mainly his.

I regret to have to sign my own name ; but I must. Poetry or fiction may be anon., as the best of it often is ; but anonymity is as much out of place in history as in a court of justice. I went to London first in 1883 and never saw Carlyle. So I could only study him as he had studied Burns and Goethe, Frederick and Cromwell. But if a Boswell be defined as a disciple who makes soon a good record of talk he has heard, there never was a sage, not even Confucius himself, who had more or better Boswells. The earliest was Emerson in 1833, and this volume ends in 1826. It is mainly the work of multitudes of Boswells that has expanded the rest of his story into four volumes more, which may be expected at short intervals. All or any part of it may be translated into any language without payment. The sooner that is done, the better. If he had been better heeded, the wars that have taken place since he died might all have been avoided. He was scoffed at because he foresaw and foretold such horrors as have become familiar in Europe since 1914; and he cursed every war that took place while he lived. His life's work was to " hold the mirror up to Nature," and beckon his fellows to working instead of fighting, as the one way to make life in the world worth living. As the war-wearied Chinese learned from the wise —Confucius and others—to be rational and despise the killers, so may we wild men of the West be taught by Voltaire and Goethe, Carlyle and Tolstoy, to be ashamed of slaughter and abhor to fight.

His preaching of peace is none the less wise because it is also sometimes funny. By instinct he was fearless and pugnacious ; but the folly and wickedness of strife was the best lesson he learned from religion in his boyhood, and it was ratified on reflection and practised. In private life he was a peacemaker, and patient without weakness.

He spoke so freely on so many things that it is easy to find inconsistencies. They never troubled him, for logic was his servant, not his master, and his theory of the Universe was that there never can be any theory complete. It is stupid to doubt his sincerity. That is his supreme attainment. His philosophy had nothing new ; but he was the Rembrandt of writers ; and in the great pen-portrait gallery of his works there may here and there loom greater men than himself, but not one more amusing.

DAVID ALEC WILSON.

Ayr, 1923.

CONTENTS

BOOK III

APPRENTICESHIP (1818–22)

CONTENTS

BOOK IV

WANDERING YEARS (1822–4)

CONTENTS

BOOK V

ROMANCE (1824–6)

LIST OF ILLUSTRATIONS

BOOK I

ECCLEFECHAN
1795–1806

IN THE DAYS OF ROBERT BURNS

AS James Carlyle, a mason, was standing in Rob Scott's smithy in Ecclefechan, he heard someone saying—" There's the poet Burns." He went out to look, and saw a man of about his own age, like " a well-dressed farmer, walking down the village on the opposite side of the burn," which ran down the main street. He "was a strong-built, grave-looking man, dressed in riding gear, with his hat on the back of his head, lying on the nape of his neck, as if shaken there by riding, and left." [1] This might be in 1795.

Assuredly 1795 is the only important date in the history of Ecclefechan, for Thomas Carlyle was born there then, and Robert Burns, inspecting its distillery and many public-houses, was in that very year detained there by the snow.

ROBERT BURNS TO GEORGE THOMSON [2]

'ECCLEFECHAN,
7th Feb., 1795.

'MY DEAR THOMSON,—

'You cannot have any idea of the predicament in which I write to you. In the course of my duty as Supervisor I came yesternight to this unfortunate wicked little village. I have gone forward, but snows of ten feet deep have impeded my progress. I have tried to " gae back the gate I cam' again," but the same obstacle has shut me up within insuperable bars. To add to my misfortune, since dinner, a scraper has been torturing cat-gut, in sounds that would have insulted the dying agonies of a sow under the hands of a butcher, and thinks himself, on that very account, exceeding good company. In fact, I have been in a dilemma, either to get drunk, to forget these miseries, or to hang

---

[1] This last sentence is from the private notebook of Mrs. A. Anstruther, reporting Carlyle's words.
[2] Currie's *Burns*, IV, pp. 223–4.

3

myself, to get rid of them : like a prudent man (a character congenial to my every thought, word, and deed), I, of two evils, have chosen the least, and am very drunk, at your service !

' Do you know an air—*We'll gang nae mair to yon town* : I think, in slowish time, it would make an excellent song. I am highly delighted with it ; ' and so on, ending—' good night.

' ROBERT BURNS.'

In answering this letter, Mr. Thomson said it proved that " drunk or sober, your mind is never muddy " ; but many readers to-day might misunderstand it. " Drunk " was a word used loosely then for many conditions, ranging from drunkenness to the happy state of Tam o' Shanter, who was under the influence of liquor but not the worse of it.

In those days to be " as drunk as a Lord " was the fashion. Nobody supposed that Burns was uncharitable when on his deathbed he blamed the " Edinburgh Gentry " for teaching him the drinking habits which shortened his life.[1] Assuredly disease and crime were " not traceable to the drinking habits of the people." [2] Even brawls were seldom due to drink. From time immemorial the common drink of the country was a mild fermented ale, brewed freely in every village, country house or farm, and taken with their food. The original highland " quaich " was of wood and might hold a pint. The little silver " quaich," for whisky is comparatively modern.

However much the infinite thirst for beer which Tacitus ascribed to our forefathers survived elsewhere, in most of Scotland the Reformation and what followed it sobered the people,[3] and all was well in that respect until in 1725 the London politicians enforced a malt tax, and steadily

[1] See R. Chambers' *Picture of Scotland*, I, 307, footnote ; and, of course, Lockhart's *Life of Burns*, Chap. V, and Professor Wilson's Review of it, May, 1828.

[2] W. Hector's *Judical Records of Renfrewshire*, Second Series, pp. 141–2. This was typical of Scotland.

[3] See for what follows H. B. Graham's *Social Life of Scotland in the Eighteenth Century*, and in particular the footnote, II, p. 263, for the amazing growth of the consumption of spirits in the eighteenth century. Scores of other references might be given : e.g. Currie (1803) in his *Life of Burns*, I, 24–5 and note ; *On Scots Drink*, by Wm. Cramond, LL.D. (1895) ; Alexander Laing's *Lindores Abbey ;* and see Hume Brown's *History of Scotland*, III, pp. 150–2, 206–8.

persisted in picking purses in that indirect way, to get money to squander. The appetite of politicians for money is like that of fire for fuel. The absent-minded people could not muzzle their masters. If not as meek as sheep before the shearers, they were as stupid. To balk the excise, they took less and less of their wholesome ale, and eked it out with " spirits," a novelty to the common people, and cheap in the eighteenth century, when it was allowed to be distilled at Ferintosh with a nominal tax, and could be smuggled from elsewhere. The Porteous Riots were an incident in the protracted wrestle between the people of all classes and the politicians out of reach and diligent in evil-doing.

Unfortunately the " gentry," unable to guide the people against the mischievous tax on malt, took to the " fiery water " themselves, and so enhanced its natural attractions in a cold country where its bad effects were as yet not realised, not even by the most faithful of the clergy, who preached that whisky was " exceedingly hurtful both to health and morals," and exhorted the people to return to " good ale," [1] " the natural and wholesome beverage of the country." [2] But in cursing whisky, they coupled it with tea, because it was also a novelty then, and dear—which was a good ground of objection, but also shows how much they underestimated what whisky could do when it became a common drink. The lesson of Hogarth's happy " Beer Street " and deadly " Gin Lane " was unknown in the north. The middle classes were as heedless as the gentry, content to carouse, and the bulk of the clergy were too genteel to object at all. Many of them mimicked the gentry and became hard drinkers.

So Robert Burns had no more misgivings about becoming an exciseman than his contemporary, Tom Paine. Burns was the greatest victim of the drug ; but he praised it without suspicion. Thus the abuse of it as a daily drink grew worse and worse, till it became " the curse of Scotland." Such was the effect of London extortion. " Government " may be feeble to do good, but it is powerful to do evil. Any fool can start a fire, and any " Government " a war or a tax. So let us all join in the ancient prayer that " the High Court of Parliament may do no more harm."

[1] Sir John Sinclair's *Statistical Account of Scotland*, 1791-9, XVII, p. 438. (See James Murray's *Life in Scotland a Hundred Years Ago*, pp. 73-85 for more details conveniently collected about whisky, beer and tea.)
[2] *Ibid.*, XIII, p. 603.

As for Burns at Ecclefechan in 1795, we should recall the lack of better drink. A Chinese author once lamented the pitiable condition of Queen Elizabeth—the poor woman could not get a cup of tea ; and it was an expensive luxury, not likely to be obtainable in a hotel in Ecclefechan in 1795.

Burns died the next year, and it is remarkable that he continued to grow better to the end, as Shakespeare did. The letter mentioned as written " yesterday " in what we have just read enclosed the exquisite duet, " Let me in this ae night," a duet equal to many sermons upon how a young woman should behave. A few weeks before, in January, 1795, he had sent to the same correspondent the song— " A Man's a Man for a' That " ; and in the previous month, December, 1794, he had sent a perfect song of lamentation by man for woman—" My Nannie's awa'."

Robert Burns was only thirty-six when he walked down Ecclefechan, and James Carlyle when he came out of the smithy and looked at him was about a year older. In figure, features and complexion, the two men might have been brothers. In culture and language they were much alike ; but the mason was prejudiced. The exciseman was of ill-repute. James Carlyle looked indifferently at the stranger as a passing notoriety, and to the end of his life he never heeded any utterance of Robert Burns.

It was a pity. They had much in common. The family life which the poet celebrated, the sanctification of spontaneous love by fidelity, which breathes in the best of his songs, is the taproot of righteousness. Though Burns laughed in the Devil's face as a medieval nightmare, he revered his parents and cherished his wife and children as devoutly as a Chinaman and as well as the best of the saints ; while James Carlyle was as devoted to the oldest of civilised religions, woman-worshipping, as ever the poet was himself.

James Carlyle was the " leader of the fighting masons of Ecclefechan." His first wife had been a namesake and a distant cousin, Janet, the daughter of a farmer locally known as " Old Sandbed," after his farm, but like his son-in-law, a Carlyle, pronounced Kerl. The name is a mere variation in spelling of the town Carlisle. There never was any such " clan." In the second year of their marriage, the first wife of James fell sick of fever, and would let none but her husband cut her hair. He cut it, " feeling sure of contagion," and maybe wishing it. She died on 11th September, 1792 ; and " her long fair hair lay in his secret drawer " for the rest of his life. He never spoke of his feelings, or " only transiently with a historical stoicism." Why talk ? What could sympathy do ? What were these treasured tresses to anybody else ? " Only a woman's hair."

> " To me there needs no stone to tell,
> 'Tis nothing that I loved so well."

" Old Sandbed " took their baby home, his little grand-son John. The child remained with his grandparents. James Carlyle lived alone in his two-roomed dwelling, the upper part of the " arched house," which was all he needed. The ground floor he let to a baker, and his brother is said to have lived next door.

James had built both houses for sale in the ordinary way of business ; but the buyer would not or could not pay and tried by promises and threats and " lawyer's letters " to get a conveyance without payment in full. James never answered him nor his lawyer, but retained the property, which people said was " just like James."

II

THE WIDOWER'S WOOING

BY 1795 James Carlyle had been living alone for more than two years. Whoever lives on must be ready for changes, and healing time brings roses. In the farmhouse of Townfoot, John Bell's, near England, and nearer still to Ecclefechan, there was a servant called Margaret Aitken in formal documents, but better known to James Carlyle as Peggy—a slender little woman with the sweetest of tempers and features. Her father, John Aitken, had had a farm in Nithsdale, Dumfriesshire; but in 1795, the year when Warren Hastings was acquitted in London and the Directory came into power in Paris and Ecclefechan took its place in history, John Aitken was a bankrupt and working to do what he did at last—pay every creditor in full. In the meantime his daughter Peggy was serving at Townfoot. The farmer's wife was her aunt.[1]

By 1795 James Carlyle and Peggy were in love with each other, though different in much besides age. She was gentle and self-forgetful, as good women tend to be, a " real woman," with the sweet low voice of harmony, compared to which the finest orchestra is no better than a huge mechanical hurdy-gurdy. How she came to love the leader of the " fighting masons " remains a mystery. " When I say that I know women, I mean that I know I don't know them." But we must not mistake the facts. The masons of Ecclefechan were not rowdies. Scotland was then afflicted both by starving Irish in-comers reducing wages and raising rents, and by remnants of the vagabond gangs that, under many names, such as " Egyptians," had plagued it for centuries.[2] More savage than Red Indians, and not unlike the Thugs of India, they lived and bred like wild

[1] Statements of contemporaries in the 'seventies, in notes of J. T. Wells, and statements in 1903 and later to D. A. W. by John Grierson, Town Clerk of Dumfries, and great-grandson of John Aitken.
[2] See the *Second Discourse* in the *Political Works* of Andrew Fletcher, and Graham's *Social Life of Scotland*, I, 228-33, and II, 224-5.

beasts in the dens and caves, and haunted the dwellings of men. They gathered at fairs, marriages and funerals, like vultures round carrion, kidnapping children, blackmailing all who lived or worked in isolation, stripping lonely travellers, and sometimes murdering at large.

Severe enough were the laws against them, but enforced spasmodically. There were no police and few good roads. When farmers went to market in the eighteenth century, they carried loaded sticks or swords or pistols. The masons of Ecclefechan had often to work far from the village, and, having to choose between blackmail or self-defence, they became the " fighting masons," and made the country-side ring with laughter and applause at their exploits. " Pithy, bitter-speaking bodies, and awfu' fechters (fight-ers) " was the report of them, quoted by Easton, the last survivor, with a "radiant" face of triumph. Here is one fight as sample of many, not the best but the best authenti-cated.[1]

A party of about thirty gypsies was passing some scaffold-ing whereon James Carlyle and six or seven others were working. Some words were exchanged. The gypsies advanced in a mass, and James Carlyle and his men, " all at once " like soldiers doing an exercise, lifted their pails and poured a cloud of lime on the enemy. The gypsies rushed at the scaffolding. " Easton, Easton," shouted James Carlyle, " haul up that ladder my man, or the gypsy loon'll have us a' killed ! " The ladder was pulled up in time. The gypsies grasped and tugged at the poles, which stood firm, and stones flew on both sides like rifle bullets for nearly half an hour. Then the gypsies drew back, " many of them limping, and nearly all their swarthy faces streaked with red."

As good at working as at fighting, the masons prospered well. Arkwright and Watt were making Britain rich in spite of the wars, and there was plenty of building and re-building. " His men all liked him," said William Easton, speaking of his employer, James Carlyle. " He always paid the best wages in the district, and was a just man. If he had a tough job on hand, he encouraged us by extra pay. We were always eager to oblige him in any way. We never felt the day long. He worked alongside us, and made

---

[1] The late John T. Wells, missionary, Edinburgh, said he took it down from the lips of William Easton, who was in the fight. Easton in old age received a small annual pension from T. C.

the work light by his stories and jokes." The strangest thing of all is that he was little envied, though " his worldly success was quite wonderful for these days." Perhaps it was felt to be deserved.

Alone of the " fighting masons," he had become religious and objected to take pleasure in fighting ; but his religion was without fanaticism. He was saved from the bitterness of the " narrownebs " or bigots by his habit of reading and thinking for himself. There was a circulating library in the village and several villagers had books worth reading, which were studied by James Carlyle as closely as Howe's theology. Impatient of fiction, he was as reverent of facts as Oliver Cromwell, seeing in events the mysterious will of " Him that walketh on the wings of the wind " ; but such were the limits of his outlook that he never knew anything that shook his belief in his Bible. The result was a rare combination of mental activity and Christian faith, unconscious of a doubt.

Annandale was one of the " gardens of Scotland," and " the Garden of Annandale" was Hoddam Parish, wherein was Ecclefechan, the market town for a wide district. Though it had only eight shops and five hundred inhabitants in the seventeen-nineties, it had four hotels and twenty-two other " tippling-houses," [1] and from John o' Groats to the Land's End was known to drovers for its cattle fairs and monthly cattle markets, to say nothing of weekly markets for swine. There were also many weavers in the village. The Robert Peel who prospered by calico-printing in Lancashire, grandfather of the statesman, had come from Ecclefechan, and was a son of the " Robert Peal " who was buried there in 1749, aged fifty-seven.

There were more people than there are to-day employed in agriculture. Farms were small, and nearly everybody in the village had an allotment on which he grew potatoes, and in nearly every house there was a pig or two. The pigs of the village were pastured on the common as described in *Sartor*.

Though much has since been done to improve the land, there was less of it then sterilised for mere amusement, and the country sports were not monopolised by a class. The lairds were closer to the people than farmers are to-day, and nearly all the farmers were men who held the plough

[1] Sir John Sinclair's *Statistical Account of Scotland*, III, pp. 347–58 : 1792 ; and the *New Statistical Account*, 1842, IV, p. 289.

themselves and got much of the help they needed from their
families.

The principal novelty was one that recent improvements
in the roads had made possible—daily stage-coaches between
Glasgow and the south. Ecclefechan was the first station
north of Carlisle, and at 3 a.m. the mail from there stopped
to change horses, and at 6 p.m. the Glasgow coach did
likewise, going south.

The common people were more contented than to-day.
They sang and fiddled more, and with potatoes and pigs
to eke out the oatmeal, and with light beer in daily use,
they were probably better nourished. Assuredly their lives
were pleasanter. The rich were less arrogant and sophisticated than now, while supernatural Christianity survived,
and filled the vacant minds with beautiful dreams and
perpetual puzzles. " Life was argument in those days,"
declared a survivor. Like Milton's devils, " on a hill retired,"
the groups that gathered at the meeting-house door, or round
the big sycamore in the forum of the village, opposite the
Grapes Inn, were wont to " reason high "

> " Of providence, fore-knowledge, will and fate,
> Fix'd fate, free will, fore-knowledge absolute,
> And found no end, in wandering mazes lost ; "

and wished for none—their joy was in the fighting ; polemics
took the place of border battles.

An occasional word was the only contribution to such
talk that came from James Carlyle. What must be doubtful
did not interest him. One day two village theologians were
debating the details of the Resurrection, an impending
event which seemed as certain as the next year's spring and
summer. George Macivin and Robert Scott took that for
granted ; but George Macivin maintained that new bodies,
fresh and pleasant, would then be provided for the saints,
and Scott was arguing that the identical bodies which here
were worn would rise again, for all things were possible to
God, and so on. They might have talked till they were tired,
if they had not entangled James Carlyle in their debate.
He cut it short by saying—" I think a stinking clog of a
body like Robert Scott the weaver's would be very unfit to
inhabit those places ! "

Free as he was from even the fear of doubt about the
creed which had sufficed for Milton and Cromwell, he was
ready to comment on events in Scripture history as on other

events. The Bible was not exactly " like any other book "
to him ; but the difference was not magical. It was *quite
true ;* and other books were valued more or less according
as they came near to its standard.

The Rev. John Johnston, who preached in the little
thatched meeting-house which he attended, was his friend
from boyhood, and " beautifully combined the Christian
and the Christian gentleman." [1]

Their friendship was never interrupted ; but when James
was consulted about another and a very different pulpiteer,
departing for better pay, he cut short the doubts of the
elders by saying—" Pay the hireling his wages, and let him
go." [2]   A few such remarks explain the tradition that
sometimes " he said a thing and it ran through the country," [3]
and was remembered after many years. He once compared
a confused preacher to "a fly wading among treacle." [4]
He " loved a joke with all his heart " and " was full of
anecdotes," and told a story well. " It was a treat to hear
him," the gossips agreed.

This was a treat young Peggy could enjoy as often as he
came to Townfoot, and maybe it was in this way that, like
another Desdemona, she learned to love the speaker. Blithe
and merry herself, she was as fond of a joke as he, and
religion was another thing they had in common. Some said
it was love of her made him so pious ; for though no man can
ever know the heart of another, there is nothing to hinder
a guess, and every man must take himself for a common
measure of humanity. In saying James Carlyle was extra
pious to please Peggy, his coëvals were merely indicating
that it was what they would have been themselves. Assuredly
the success of his courtship was a legitimate wonder. The
girl herself was surprised to find she liked him, as it was
plain she did. His visits

" 'Tween the gloaming and the mirk,
When the kye come hame,"

were welcomed ; but not always in the same way. Sometimes blithe and sometimes shy, she received " Jimmy
Kerl " as the mood of the moment prompted her.

[1] T. C. quoted in *Life and Times of Dr. Lawson*, p. 27, by the Rev.
John Macfarlane.   [2] H. J. Nicoll's *Thomas Carlyle*, p. 237.
[3] See *Edinburgh Sketches and Memories*, by David Masson, p. 281,
footnote 2.
[4] " Tar," wrote T. C. in the Reminiscences, but John T. Wells produced
evidence to D. A. W. that in this instance "Tom's" memory was ques-
tionable. Treacle was the current report.

She confided to another girl,[1] that she was " unable to fathom him," and she " could not completely understand Jimmy." One evening, which may have been in this same winter (1794–5) of the great snow-storm, he came to the kitchen door, and Peggy opened it, wide enough to let her see who was there, but not enough to let one enter. The half-opened door was not a bad emblem of her heart at the moment. But this was a caller impatient of uncertainty. Putting his hand on the door he flung it open wide, but did not enter at once. " Now shut the door," said he, " in Jimmy Kerl's face." " Come in," said Peggy, and she told the other girl she had to let him know that she would take him.

[1] Who told her sister, who told Mr. John Wells, missionary, who told D. A. W.

III

THE FIRST TWO YEARS OF THOMAS CARLYLE

PEGGY was now twenty-three years of age ; and in those very weeks when Burns, shut up in Ecclefechan like a lion in a cage, was in such fiery haste, as if he knew his end was near, James Carlyle and Peggy were preparing to wed. They were married on 5th March, 1795, and lived at first in the " arched house." There Peggy's first, James Carlyle's second son, was born on Friday, 4th December, 1795. It is a safe guess that the women told the father the child was like him ; but in truth he was a thickset man, and as the mother herself said by and by, the baby was a " lang, sprawling, ill-put-together thing."

They named him Thomas Carlyle, and spoke of him familiarly as Tom [1] ; and when his mother was well enough to take sole charge of him herself, she confessed that she looked with equal alarm and admiration at the " big head " and " long and supple limbs." She was " almost afraid to wash him, lest she might hurt him," and feared and confessed her fears that he would never live to be a man. [2]

" Wee Jack," his elder half-brother, the firstborn son John, was living at the house of his grandfather, " Old Sandbed," but came often to his father's, and was much interested in the baby brother, Tom. The interest appears to have been reciprocated. " What ails wee Jack ? " was the first utterance of little Tom Carlyle—according to his mother. In August, 1797, before he was two years old, another baby brother was born, and named Alexander,

---

[1] John Carlyle of Langholm, son of Carlyle's brother James, said to D. A. W.: " Tam was never then heard of in Annandale south of Moffat."

[2] Told D. A. W. in 1895 by Mrs. Hanning, Carlyle's youngest sister, who had often heard it from their mother.

" Alick " or " Sandy." Then Tom began to enjoy a little more liberty, his mother being occupied with the new-comer ; and, clad in a gown of yellow serge and barefoot, like the rest, he was generally out of doors when not asleep, playing with the other children, and catching " beardies " or little fishes and "paidling in the burn" (toddling in the brook) that ran down the road.[1]

He made friends with the cat, it is said, as soon as he could crawl. His most alarming adventure in those days happened when he was less than two years old. " An uncle of mine," he said, " sent me the gift of a small wooden can—they called it a noggie (or noggin)—to eat my porridge from. That can had two bottoms and some small pebbles between that rattled—but this was a profound secret to me at the time, the source of the rattling. One day, finding myself alone in the kitchen with my noggie, I conceived the scheme of making some porridge for myself, and for the first stage I poured water into my noggie and set this on the kitchen fire to boil. After a little, however, it all suddenly blazed up, and out I rushed shrieking with terror—I was under two, I don't know how much. It must have been some months later, probably in 1798, that we moved from one house to another. A pathway and short cut led between the two, across a field known to the villagers as Pepper Field, because the owner was said to have made his fortune in the West Indies. I was allowed to suppose myself helping in the flitting, and I recollect very well carrying the nozzle of a watering-pot across Pepper Field, and blowing through it like a horn, feeling at the same time a great exaltation." [2]

The new house was the home of Tom's boyhood—the original of the " little orchard " and " roomy painted cottage" in *Sartor Resartus*. It has been demolished ; but in 1890 almost every detail of Andreas Futteral's dwelling-place could easily be recognised. It had been built for a double cottage, and the walls were as sound in 1890 as if newly built. It was then in a paved yard, which in 1798 had been a garden and orchard of apple trees [3] entered from the main road by " Matthew Murray's Close." [4]

[1] Statements of those who played with him, corroborated as to the Misses Little by a letter of his 19.9.1848.
[2] Told in October, 1877, to William Allingham. See W. A.'s *Diary*, pp. 256–7.
[3] Village traditions collected by John T. Wells, missionary, Edinburgh, who saw three of the apple trees himself still surviving in the 'seventies.
[4] Now " Carlyle Close."

To this house in 1798 James Carlyle brought his young
wife and little Tom and the baby; and there among the
apple trees she could work and tend her children, while
hearing and seeing of the fairs and the passing coaches and
the other village excitements as much as she liked, and no
more.[1]

[1] In local investigations, commenced in 1890, the notes of John T.
Wells, made in the 'seventies, were found perfect. Another sound enquirer
was James Routledge, quoted in Chap. X of H. J. Nicoll's *Carlyle*. Few
other "enquirers" had avoided bad mistakes, and many, including Hall
Caine, appeared to have been deliberately humbugged.

JAMES CARLYLE'S HOUSE IN A GARDEN

(Original of the cottage in " Sartor," as it was in 1870)

The home of James Carlyle from 1798 to 1815, as it stood about 1870 and remained till after 1890. The garden had been made a paved yard and the building used as a slaughter house for many years. Drawn by John T. Wells.

This was originally a double cottage. After some time James Carlyle used the second cottage, partly for sleeping rooms, partly for tools and materials. His grandson, John Carlyle of Langholm, a son of his son James, explained to D. A. W. in 1890 all he had heard about it from his uncle Thomas Carlyle, who once went over the building with him showing how each part had been used. The garden grew potatoes and had many apple trees.

Similarly in old James Carlyle's early married life, he occupied only the upper half of the " arched house," and let the ground floor to a baker. In short, he lived like other villagers, with no thought of " gentility."

IV

CHILDHOOD

A S none can know the feelings of another, autobiography
is the best of history, if it is sincere, and *Sartor
Resartus* the truest of Carlyle's writings. The explanations
needed are mainly such as that Diogenes Teufelsdröckh
is Thomas Carlyle, Entepfuhl means " duck-pond " and
Ecclefechan, Andreas Futteral and his wife the father and
mother of Carlyle, the miraculous gift of a child, its birth,
and so on.[1]

To complete the picture a few details may be added. He
had to notify his mother whenever the pig was among the
potatoes ; but it was friendship with a dog that first drew
public attention to him. His parents attended the " New
Licht " Church, the same which later became the " United
Presbyterian " and then the " United Free." The Ecclefechan congregation met in a little meeting-house, " rude,
rustic, bare." James Carlyle and his wife sat in the front
pew in the gallery, and so had to be helpless spectators of
an event that was talked about more than most of the
sermons. Tom might be three or four, too young to go
with his parents to church, but able to run about. One
bright summer Sunday he heard a dismal barking and
howling in the house of a neighbour, " Martha " Something,
who had gone to church with the others. He supposed the
dog was in distress, went to the meeting-house, and standing
in the open doorway, saw Martha inside and interrupted
worship by shouting to her loudly, " Matty, come home to
Snap." [2]

He always supposed himself " a still infant," but nobody
else ever did so. The most sincere of autobiographers, like

[1] See Appendix to the *Love Letters* edited by Alexander Carlyle, II,
pp. 365-6, etc., for the explanation of a mistake which caused this to
be doubted. Besides Wotton Reinfred there is another preliminary
sketch in a MS. in the Carlyle House describing " Duckdubs."
[2] Told by his sister Jean, Mrs. Aitken, to her daughter, Miss M.
Carlyle Aitken, who told D. A. W.

18

the rest of us, is unable to see himself as others see him·
As soon as he could walk, he found his way out of doors·
His mother thought him like quicksilver. She taught him
to read, he could never remember when, but he was not
a bookish baby. He relished the games of childhood as
much as any.[1]

He was induced to come home to supper by placing his
porringer upon the garden wall and the ladder handy for
him to mount to it. There he sat upon the wall and ate,
in full view of his mother, but forgetting her, watching the
swallows under the eaves, the men putting down their
tools, or the pigs trotting home. " One of the pleasantest "
of these early recollections was " the flight of the crows in
summer evenings far up in the sky, over Ecclefechan
village towards their home in Wood-cock-air."

One day he quarrelled with " wee Jack," his elder brother.
They were indoors. Jack was three years older, and may
have found it difficult to treat as an equal one who had been
a baby recently. Tom flung his stool at Jack and soon was
wildly weeping, partly because he had hurt his brother,
partly because he had broken his stool. His father comforted him. This was his earliest recollection of his father.
His tears came freely when he was excited in these early
years, though he quickly learned to control them, and in
the autobiography " seldom or never cried." He was
nicknamed " greeting Tom " occasionally by other boys,
nevertheless, and his quickness in resenting such a nickname
made his mother urgent in teaching him not to fight. The
unusual combination of readiness to strike and to weep
was remarked and discussed at the time. "He's as hard
as granite and as soft as a rabbit," said his bewildered
father.[2]

The only way to keep him quiet was to set him doing
something or answer his questions. If one did not do so,
he was soon in search of somebody else who would. When
recruiting parties came with drums, he asked the meaning
of the three big feathers and the words below them. He
was very early remarked to be an attentive listener, amazing
and amusing people by his capacity for mimicking and
reproducing whatever he heard.

---

[1] Tradition confirmed by Carlyle's *Notebooks*.
[2] Statements of the then apprentice to his father, William Easton, and
of Mrs. Milligan, then a girl beside him and some years his senior, confirmed
in various ways.

The smithy near their house was a favourite resort, combining the usual attractions of a smithy and the battles of words, when cronies came to argue with brawny old John Smail whom they commonly called " Reekie " (smoky). " Take either side ye like, an' I'll doon ye," said Reekie once, to the admiration of the boys who clustered at the door, and whispered and believed he used " to make a pudding for himself at Christmas time of horse-nails to keep his bones green." In struggling years to come Carlyle used often to quote an answer of " old Reekie " to a customer threatening to leave him. " How can I help it ? We must just do the best we can for a living, boy." [1]

No kindergarten could surpass such a village for opening the mind. Most of the weavers and labourers kept pigs, which " old Scott " tended on the common by day, and brought home in a herd every evening. In return for manure they were allowed by the farmers to use strips of land for potatoes or greens. Besides the arts and crafts to be seen in practice through the open doors there were passing coaches daily, and waggons, and many market days besides the annual fair, and fields and woods and streams around, and plenty of persons willing to answer questions. As soon as the new baby brother, Alexander, could run about, he was put in charge of Tom, and soon they became inseparable ; but " Sandy " was no more a drag on Tom than the hind wheels of a coach are a drag on the front wheels.

" Grandfather " was a wiry old man, who had now given up his farm and come to live in the village, supported by his sons. His wife had died when her grandson Tom was only six months old, but the old man survived for ten years longer, and, " sitting in his high-backed chair in the long winter nights," or under the sycamore in the summer evenings, had many a thing to tell and no more attentive listener than the new little Tom, who would sometimes be called on to repeat what he heard for the fun of observing his unintended imitations.

It was mainly in the evenings that Tom's father and other men of working age had time to talk. The living examples round him left Tom no room for doubt that the business of life was work, and a man's capacity for doing

[1] For corroboration of tradition, see William Allingham, *A Diary*, p. 226. The answer to a customer was quoted 24.12.1834 in a letter from T. C. to W. Graham, and in other places.

things and for knowing and speaking the truth the measure of his worth.

The " clogger " or maker of clogs was also famous for his skill in draughts, a " celebrated local " champion ; and he used to boast that he had often put his work aside and laid the draught-board on his lap for a game with little Tom. He said the youngster was a " tough " one, hard to beat ; and long afterwards declared he had been among the first to prophesy that " this will be a great man yet." [1]

In the bakehouse of Mrs. Jenny Lockhart, Tom and his brother watched her making for them little rolls, or " wee nods," and putting them into the oven where the dough was changed into bread. Her daughter Mary was affectionately remembered many years afterwards.

When he might be " perhaps not more than four," he encountered " one of my first tragedies." [2] Like Eve in Paradise, he was misled by tempters exploiting his curiosity. " I went into the house of two old women who were fond of snuff. I did not know then what snuff was. Their box seemed something wonderful to me. Either as a cruel jest or in utter foolishness, they bade me take a pinch, and I took, as they showed me how to do, a very big pinch indeed. A succession of explosions followed, and I thought my head was blown off." Like rain after thunder came a flood of tears, which neither sweets nor a copper coin could abate.

One fine summer evening that year (1800) he was running beside his father when they came to Mein Water, near where the Meinfoot bridge is now ; and crossing a pool his father lifted him against his thigh with his right hand and walked over as if " careless " of the weight, to the wonder of the child. " My face was turned rather downwards," he said afterwards. " I looked into the deep clear water, and its reflected skies, with terror yet with confidence that he could save me. He was very kind and I loved him." The danger passed, he asked—" What are these little black things, like penny rows (rolls) but far less ? " He meant what he seemed to create by rubbing his palms together, and his father explained it to him, concluding, " Your hands are not clean." In the same year his mother heard

---

[1] Tradition confirmed by Rev. John Wilson in his *Thomas Carlyle*, p. 32, quoting statements by the clogger.

[2] The best report of this, which confirms the rest, is in *Cope's Smoke Room Booklets*, No. 5, being "Thomas Carlyle—Table Talk." "The late William Maccall" is the authority for what T. C. said to him in 1872. For W. Maccall see *Espinasse's Literary Recollections*, pp. 247-55.

his father giving him a lesson in arithmetic—"This is the divisor," and so on. "He gave me quite a clear notion how to do," Tom always maintained afterwards.

"He'll forget it all," said his mother at the time. "Not so much as they that have never learned it," answered the father ; and soon after then, about the age of five, he was "admitted to the dignity of trousers."

His "first profound impressions in this world" were assigned by himself to the death of his baby sister (8.2.1801), when he was five. His "first passing glance at the spectre Death" was a "white-sheeted bed and small piece of elevation there, which the joiner was about measuring." His mother was weeping ; he burst into tears himself, not knowing why. He wondered to see his mother continuing to weep, inconsolable. In amazement he listened in the mornings to the dreams that visited her in the nights of sadness that followed. "For a long time she seemed to dissolve in tears—only tears. For several months not one night passed but she dreamed of holding her babe in her arms, and clasping it to her breast. At length one morning she related a change in her dream : while she held the child in her arms it had seemed to break up into small fragments, and so crumbled away and vanished," and she dreamed of it no more.[1] In the same year, an accidental glimpse of the ghastly pale face of his uncle John in his coffin was a new horror to the five-year-old.

The last two years of the eighteenth century and the first of the next were long remembered as "the dear years," and famine was abroad in the land when baby Janet died. To feel for the sorrows of others softens the sting of our own and helps us to realise—"what must be, should be." Oatmeal, the staff of life, was ten shillings a stone instead of less than two. Wages were only as usual, about a shilling a day, and Tom heard his father say he noticed the labourers go separately to a brook at the midday interval, and drink there instead of dining, anxious only to hide it, making no complaint.

One snowy day in these winters Tom was alone in the house, father and mother both absent, when an old man came to the door, "a Shetland beggar with a bad arm, pale, weary, worn and hungry, dripping with wet."[2] Tom

---

[1] Moncure Conway's *Thomas Carlyle*, pp. 28, 29.
[2] *Memoirs of Gerald Blunt*, by Reginald Blunt, p. 93. *Mrs. Brookfield and Her Circle*, by C. and F. Brookfield, II, pp. 435-6.

searched for food to give him and found none. The old man was turning away. Tom bade him wait, and drew a bench to the dresser, climbed upon it and lifted down his " penny-pig," an earthenware bottle with a slit for pennies. He broke it and handed the coppers in it, all his savings, about fourpence, to the poor old man.

" I never in all my life," he afterwards confessed, " felt anything so like Heaven as the pity I had for that man," [1] and to Dicky Milnes he said once, " I would give one hundred pounds now to have that feeling for one moment back again " ; which confirms Miss Martineau's observation that pity predominated in the character of Carlyle. [2]

[1] Wemyss Reid's *R. M. Milnes, Lord Houghton*, II, p. 479.
[2] In her *Autobiography*, I, pp. 378–82.

V

AT SCHOOL

EARLY in the new century Tom was sent to school, but not to the parish school in the village. Poor William Gullen was the teacher there, a "downbent, broken-hearted underfoot martyr," going about with rueful countenance. Most of the inhabitants, James Carlyle among them, preferred a livelier teacher for their children, though the fees elsewhere were higher.[1] A "severely correct young man," Tom Donaldson, had "come from Edinburgh College," and was teaching in the "Brick-house" at Ecclefechan, and to his school "our Tom" was sent. When he came home the first day he was asked, "Who was the nicest lassie?" "Jean Johnston," he replied at once, and wondered why they laughed. He was a "teacher's favourite" from the first. When Donaldson departed, he was sent to Hoddam school, a mile away, but better than the one at hand; and by 1802 the little boy of six was going daily to and from it through a long avenue of big old shady trees, "the kind beech rows of Entepfuhl."

He continued conspicuous in the village. In 1803, when he was seven, he was to be seen "perched upon honest Jamie Beattie's loom," and "yelling forth" the ballads of "Blind Harry with the voice of a sibyl to overcome the jingling racket of four shuttles and twice as many treadles," two for each loom. The listening weavers would hardly miss a word. It was a custom of theirs to have someone reading to them whenever possible, or to do it by turns themselves. The boy "reverenced" Blind Harry's hero, Wallace, but liked even better the squire, "the tight, little, true-hearted fellow, John the Graham."[2]

One day this summer there stepped into Hoddam school the eldest son of "Wull Beattie," the country carpenter, whose house and workshop adjoined it. "Wull" was "thrice-great as a ruling elder," and this eldest son of his

[1] The notes of John T. Wells.   [2] Unpublished letter.

had finished his college career and was now a licentiate of the Church. So as a matter of course he would be invited to examine the children, and doing so he noticed the mason's boy, and told James Carlyle that Tom was now " complete in English " and must " go into Latin " or " waste his time."

A *Ruddiman's Rudiments* was given him at once and he read it with the enthusiasm of a juvenile on promotion ; but the Hoddam teacher himself did not know Latin, or only knew enough to bewilder the boy. A son of the Rev. John Johnston took him in hand, and " pulled me afloat," said Tom. Let the tutor tell us what he was fond of telling by and by : " The boy, not yet eight years old, had been studying his Latin Rudiments with great industry, but his grammar and construction were in a chaotic state. After three months' drill, however, little Thomas succeeded in grasping the intricacies of both, and could translate Virgil and Horace with an ease that astonished me." [1] When the tutor returned to college, his father, the white-haired preacher to whom Tom listened on Sunday, occasionally gave the boy a lesson.

It was a happy day when he discovered some use for Latin, translating inscriptions found on Roman remains, which farming people had found and shown to him. Blatum, alias Blato-Bulgium, the only Roman station in Scotland whose name survives in the books,[2] was at Birrens or Burrens, the very place where once Carlyles had been farmers—a mile or two from Ecclefechan ; and digging for other purposes on the site of the vanished town, people were finding then stone figures and slabs, tools and axes. Farther away, two or three miles N.N.W. of the village, was the outstanding hill of Burnswark, with one of the best preserved Roman camps in Britain upon it ; and tho neither Tom nor any other saw the supposed sub-terranean passage, " big enough to drive a cart through," connecting camp and town, he did one day behold " with awe and wonder " the end of a small tunnel just unearthed. The historian of the locality [3] mentions only " one very curious gold coin found in the stream that runs through Ecclefechan, thicker than a guinea and bearing on it the head and superscription of Alexander the Great."

[1] W. H. Wyllie's *Thomas Carlyle*, pp. 37–8. This young Mr. Johnston was for many years a clergyman in Jersey City, New York, America.

[2] See Hume Brown's *History of Scotland*, I, p. 7, and footnote.

[3] The new statistical account of Scotland, *Dumfriesshire*, 1841, pp. 292–3.

Tom's mother encouraged him to read—she did not much care what. His father thought fiction sinful ; but it was some time before this appeared an irksome restriction, for what was fiction, what was fact ? For example, the *Arabian Nights* among his grandfather's books was read with enjoyment, but—was it true ? Not all of it, he felt sure. Tom was eagerly groping his way to a knowledge of reality. What he wrote of the childhood of Frederick was true of his own. " Fiction itself is either an expository illustrative garment of Fact, or else is of no value to him. Once for all, he has no pleasure in dreams, in parti-coloured clouds and nothingnesses. Better symptom of its quality (whatever *quantity* there be of it) human intellect cannot show for itself."

When the stream in the village street was covered, pious hands saved " that idle crag " mentioned in *Sartor*, a granite boulder in it, near the entry to Tom's father's house. But though " Teufelsdröckh " sat upon it, it seems doubtful whether ever Tom did. He was never seen sitting unless he was doing something. About the time he was beginning Latin, he reflected that the mail coaches were not like the moon, but like the carts—the work of men, and coming from and going to big cities along roads made by men. As he watched them pass he thought as many another has done that any road would lead to the world's end. It was probably after deciphering some of the inscriptions at Birrens that he reflected the little burn was running when the Romans were there.

His mother had babies to nurse, and little leisure. Tom moved about more and more freely after he began to go to school, and found the farmers and labourers as willing to explain things to him in the fields as the weavers were at their looms.

The home of the crows, the shady hill of Wood-cock-air on the other side of the River Annan, had from early days hung like a mystery before him ; but a boy able to go and come alone as far as Hoddam was not to be mystified for ever by a hill that was only a mile or so further away. He explored it one day so fully that he felt he knew all about it and need never examine it again. The river became familiar after he came to the school at Hoddam Kirk ; but he never forgot how wonderful it seemed at first sight— " running solemnly down with a slight rippling." [1]   He

----

[1] William Allingham : *A Diary*, p. 217.

examined the bridge with the critical eyes of the son of a mason.

" You may think yourself a big man in the world noo," said a labourer one day to James Carlyle, who was finding fault with his digging. " But I mind when ye were glad to catch eels for your dinner."

James looked at him with composure, recalling early days, and replied in the lingo of boys—" Thou muckle suggle " (slobbery simpleton), " thou couldest never catch ony eels."

The composure was characteristic. Eels were taboo for feeding there and then, and the sting of the taunt intended is explained to be in the meaning—" You were so poor that you had to eat the eels." It left James cool. Old Testament " culture " had this at least in common with Confucian and Indian, that it set free the soul and removed the shame that is the sting of poverty.

Ecclefechan Burn runs into the Mein on its way to the Annan River. Tom was proud in his early years of his skill in catching eels in the Mein, and his pleasantest recollections of the squat little parish school-house at Hoddam related to the mid-day interval, when " the hot cabin vomited forth its exulting population to frolic their gamesome hour beneath the clear summer sky. Of the boys, some arranged themselves for pitch and toss, some preferred marbles, others shinty " or rounders, played with balls and sticks; " the girls produced their skipping ropes, or set to pile their bits of crockery into a dresser ; in short, the whole green was swarming with a noisy throng of little men and little women, all bustling, all happy." [1]

At another time of the day, alone or with companions hushed, Tom once beheld a miracle of Nature, a pipit's nest and mother pipit fostering a cuckoo, and seeming proud of the size of the baby. It is what a naturalist in Scotland looks for and never forgets—the dainty, nimble little mother sometimes perching on the shoulder of the cuckoo and dropping food into its mighty bill. " An emblem of much that can be seen in human society," this particular observer used to say when he grew up, but he did not think of that at the time, any more than any other naturalist.

[1] T. C. in Cruthers and Johnson, *Fraser's Mag.*, January, 1831, p. 692.

VI

AT MARKET AND AT KIRK

THE " thriving and sweet little post-town of Ecclefechan [1] " was a lively place on its quietest days, being much addicted to open-air life. Every June the crowds from far and near that came to its cattle market made a rustic Vanity Fair, where showmen shouted, ballad-singers bawled, and men and women made service contracts for long terms, and horses and oxen, sheep and pigs, butter and pork and other necessaries, and things not necessary, were bought and sold.

Tom roamed about with Sandy at his heels, beholding the hurly-burly. One of the " shabby little " chap-books " in greyish-paper " which he bought,[2] *Reynard the Fox,* sank deep into his mind, illuminating better than newspapers events of the day. The wicked English Excise laws which made strong drink the curse of Scotland were only beginning then to show their worst effects. The fighting men when Tom was a boy were not always the alcoholic lunatics familiar afterwards, and he by and by delighted to " amaze the shovel-hatted " by telling what he had seen.

'The venerable John Johnston is my model of an Apostolic Priest; more Priestlike in his humble simplicity than Archbishops to me ; and more honoured too, for I have seen the Cuddylane Population (most brutal of the creatures of God) suspend their quarrelling and cursing till he had passed thro' them, and touch their hat reverently to him. Had it been the Archbishop of Canterbury with all his gilt coach-panels, they would have thrown dead cats at him.'[3]

The " Holy Fair " was held a few weeks after the other. It was less sacred than Sunday worship, as may be read in Burns, and Ayrshire was much more pious than Dum-

---

[1] Robert Chambers' *Picture of Scotland,* I, p. 210.
[2] Letter of 5.4.1832 to Harry Inglis, 1827.
[3] *Scribner's Magazine,* April, 1893, p. 422 ; and *Memoirs of Gerald Blunt,* by Reginald Blunt, p. 96.

friesshire. Hallowe'en no longer pretended to be anything
but fun, and fun or business was the function of the rest
of the fairs and festivals that dotted the year, and delivered
the drudges from monotony.

In the meeting-house on " The Lord's Day," Tom saw
and heard Mr. Johnston, in " white full-bottomed wig,"
expound the scriptures—earnest and erudite, a humble
Wycliffe, reproducing features of Chaucer's Clerk of Oxford
as well as of his Parson.

He used to watch fellow-worshippers too, and never forgot
some of " their heavy-laden, patient, ever-attentive faces."
On returning home he used to question his mother about
them.

Some wet plaids hanging up to drip caught his eye one
day. " The wearers of them must have come far. Who were
they ? " " Good weavers," he was told, " settled near
Carlisle, and walking from there all the way to the meeting-
house," which was impressive.

More commonplace were the worshippers from adjacent
Annan—Adam Hope, the teacher, and a squint-eyed
handsome boy, the tanner's son, Edward Irving ; " Wullie
Drummond with mournful goggle-eyes," and limping Joe
Blacklock, a " rickety " weaver, " with protruding chin."

" Rude, rustic, bare," was that thatched meeting-house,
" but there were tongues of authentic flame from Heaven,
which kindled what was best in one " and never went out :
for indeed the fire was here kindled in that little boy, who
was to complete the work of Knox and Buchanan and spread
the spiritual lightning which " burns but is not consumed."

Tom was eagerly attentive to the preacher, and the
complete fullness with which he could reproduce the sermon
when required attracted admiration. It was not odd ;
the custom was to exhort the children to attempt this—
a stimulant to the intellect hard to beat. But Tom's
unusual excellence was so much remarked that in discus-
sions on the sermon when disputes arose as to what had
been said, the cry was, " Where's Tom ? " or " Fetch Tom " ;
and when he came, his admiring elder brother used to say,[1]
he " never failed to quote any part of the sermon wanted."

[1] To his son, who, as an old man himself, Dr. Carlyle, told D. A.W. in
Toronto in 1895. Carlyle's youngest sister, Mrs. Hanning, told D. A.W.
she had heard her mother tell it ; and Thomas Carlyle, Brantford, Ontario,
Canada, said to D. A. W. he heard his father, Carlyle's brother "Sandy,"
tell it. It was also village tradition. Not one of all who told this to D. A.W.
knew he had heard it before.

VII

THE HOLY FAIR

A FEW weeks after the cattle fair and before the harvest began, the countryside gathered at Ecclefechan for "The Holy Fair." It was such as Burns has described in a poem surpassing any movie-show, presenting not merely the forms of men and women, but their thoughts and feelings. The crowd was too big for any building there. A portable pulpit was set up in the local Forum, the spacious place for meetings, traceable in many villages. Preacher succeeded preacher. The audience came and went as in a Parliament.—

> "Smith opens out his cauld harangues
> On practice and on morals ;
> And aff the godly pour in thrangs
> To gi'e the jars and barrels
> A lift that day."

What drew the crowd most easily was " tidings of damnation," as when a Rev. Russell's

> "Piercing words, like highlan' swords
> Divide the joints and marrow ;
> His talk o' Hell, where devils dwell,
> Our very ' sauls does harrow '
> Wi' fright that day !
> A vast unbottomed boundless pit,
> Filled fu' o' lowin' brunstane,[1]
> Wha's raging flame, an' scorching heat,
> Wad[2] melt the hardest whun-stane ![3]
> The half-asleep start up wi' fear,
> And think they hear it roaring,
> When presently it does appear,
> 'Twas but some neebor[4] snoring
> Asleep that day."

From kings to beggars then, the common crowds believed in Hell and Heaven, and James Carlyle was like his neighbours in his creed ; but his openness of mind and reverence

[1] Flaming brimstone.　　　　[2] Would.
[3] Basalt.　　　　[4] Neighbour.

30

for facts were uncommon ; and he wanted warrant in
scripture for theological dogmas. It was probably some
time soon after the death of his little daughter Janet that
bereaved mothers, perhaps his wife beside him, were being
agonised by pulpit assurance of certain damnation for
children, unless they were saved by some hocus-pocus.
James Carlyle rose and was going away. The preacher
paused as if in tacit rebuke. James turned and faced him,
shaking his fist, and this is what, for half a century afterwards, the people said that he said—" Ay, ye may thump
and glower [1] till your een [2] start frae [3] their sockets, but
ye'll no' gar [4] me believe sic stuff as that." [5]

[1] Stare with flashing eyes. Some reporters said " stare "—translating.
[2] Eyes.   [3] From.   [4] Make.
[5] Notes of John T. Wells ; and see an article by James Routledge
quoted in H. J. Nicoll's *Thomas Carlyle*, p. 238. Mr. Hunter, the head
master of the school at Moniaive, told D. A. W. in 1918 that he had heard
the story many years ago.

VIII

"THE RIGHT SORT" AND OTHERS

ECCLEFECHAN was never a village of saints. The Reformation was almost as slow in reaching the Borderers as the Highlanders. Superstition was slipping away, but the only puritanism appreciated was that of animal nature, seldom wrong in sexual matters but prone to strife. The " man in honour " there was the drinker and the hunter, and above all the fighter. No Irishman was ever more sincere in cursing the English nor readier for a row than the Borderers.

When fighting is profitable its attraction is irresistible, but the profit had long been out of it here. Not even the Highland raid into England in 1745 had drawn the Borderers —their leaders knew better. But there were many who loathed the ways of peace and objected to work. Some enlisted, and some who did not enlist were rowdy at home and smashed the "windows of the meeting-house" for one item, to see if that would not make somebody come out and fight. But when James Carlyle went about enquiring of one and another—" Did you do it ? " and would not say what he was going to do, there was nobody said—" I did it." [1]

" You can't be sure of him," they explained. " He is a very conspicuous Christian, marshalling his family into the front pew of the gallery every Sunday ; and he's honest and pays well and doesn't quarrel and all that ; but what if he thought he should hit you ? " That was the awkward question. Somebody had been all but killed by him—defending a brother who had got into a row. His brothers were not religious at all, and remained his partners and the best of his friends, and they could always rely on him when they were in a corner. " A real Christian should not be like that," said the Border rowdies, who never missed an opportunity of roundly declaring James was not a Christian at all—in

[1] Notes of John T. Wells.

32

some ways. He did not seem to heed them. "Indifference
to Public Opinion" was his settled habit, imitated by his
son.

Life was variegated then, as it used to be in medieval
Europe, and will be and continue again—when we return
to social health, to common sense and the use of "the
measuring square"—the rule to do to others as they should
to us. That is impossible when the public wealth, the
bounties of nature and the profits of inventions and
monopolies, are allowed to be grabbed for private gain.
In Ecclefechan, when Tom was growing up there, men of
all sorts spoke freely together, and only evildoers were
taboo to any. The very snobberies did not hurt.

What may seem, but was not, inconsistent with this was
that people felt no more difficulty than Dr. Johnson in
showing whatever outward deference to rank was usual,
and James Carlyle himself bared his head and addressed as
"Your Honour" Sir William Maxwell or any other laird
who was usually so addressed. This could not be done with
self-respect to-day—the custom has ceased. It ceased so
soon that a modern representative (son or grandson) of
that same Sir William, calling on a son of James at Cheyne
Row in working hours, was unable to obtain admittance,
and departed angry.[1] Presuming on his rank, he had called
at the hour which suited himself and without an appointment.

Except perhaps among the criminals and beggars, there
was little if any of that "hail fellow, well met" impromptu
intimacy now common among mere acquaintances who feel
"on a level"—a dangerous and often a degrading thing.
Even a labourer would have resented familiarity from a
stranger, tho the stranger were a Duke. This "reserve"
has been much misunderstood. Far from being a family
trait of the Carlyles, as one has said, this modest self-
respect was visible in various parts of England and almost
universal in Scotland then. It is still familiar there, and
in many other places where people know how to behave.
It has been seen [2] among Arabs, Indians and Chinese, and
was nowhere more beautiful than among the Burmese
before the English spoiled them. It is part of Carlyle's
gospel of silence, inconceivable to many critics.

As for "oor Tom," he was specially fortunate in being

[1] Language credibly reported unfit for publication.
[2] By D. A. W.

D

neither rich nor poor. He was never in want ; and no man
ever put on a false face to flatter him. Thus he grew up
familiar with the realities of the daily lives around him, and
this made him safe from the delusions that beset noble-
minded men, whose experience has been more restricted.

" Poor but honest " is a touching phrase, importing
sympathy with those who are tempted to lie because they
are poor. But nowhere is truth easier than in a working
village. Tom's father and neighbours were all doing what
was useful and none of them needed to hold his head down,
and few of them did.

A conspicuous figure in the meeting-house when Tom
began to attend it was old David Hope, who lived on a
little farm on Solway shore, a mile or two east of Annan.
He was tall and straight, " very clean always, brown as
mahogany and with a head white as snow." He seemed
to be " the picture of gravity and pious seriousness," and
was made memorable to " our Tom " by a familiar story.
In Hope's locality the harvests were late and often hard to
save, when all-day rains continued week after week, and
gain or loss for the farmer depended on intervals of a day or
two, " during which the moments are golden." On one such
morning old David was in haste to be afield. The breakfast
porridge was speedily dispatched. Then as the Bible was
opened for family worship, somebody came in crying—
" Such a raging wind has risen : will drive the stooks [1]
into the sea if let alone ! "

" Wind ? " answered David. " Wind canna get ae
straw [2] that has been appointed mine. Sit down, and let
us worship God."

[1] Sheaves of corn.   [2] Wind cannot get one straw.

IX

THE TAILOR AND THE LAWYER

LONG afterwards Carlyle was speaking about the badness of London bricks [1] to the same effect as he has written, and " whole streets of scamped brick-and-a-half shells," not meant to last. " A seventy-seven or ninety-nine years' lease seemed to satisfy people in London ; but in Scotland, in his young days, folks liked to build on freehold ground, unrestrictedly their own." In short, though he did not say so, the bad building of England is a consequence of its bad laws. What Carlyle went on to say was :—

'An old tailor used to come to our house in Matthew Murray's close at Ecclefechan, in order to " make down " my father's clothes into quasi-new suits for my brothers and myself. The wages paid to the tailor were a shilling a day and his victuals. I well remember his arriving in the morning, and fetching with him a round sod of turf, about as large as the top of a little table. This he placed on the floor, stuck a stick into it, with a notch on the top, which held a candle like a vise, and there the tailor sat on the floor from morning to night and worked away.

'This man, by dint of great industry and saving, had amassed a little money, and his special ambition was to become a laird, by purchasing the house in which he lived ; but it so happened that the owner of the house, who had also made his money in the same slow, sure way, wanted to drive a hard bargain and obtain a good price for it. So negotiations went on for four years, more or less, between the two high contracting parties, as if it had been a treaty between two of the great European Powers.

'At length the matter so far took shape that a meeting was held, at which each was represented by a lawyer and a draft deed was produced. On its being begun to be read

---

[1] 13.8.1869 to A. J. Symington. *Personal Reminiscences of Carlyle*, by A. J. Symington, pp. 101–7.

aloud, " I, John So-and-So " (the names were given, but
the reporter forgot them) " hereby agree to let, lease, etc.,
for 999 years," the tailor at once struck in with, " What
is that you say about letting and leasing ?   I tell you what
it is.   I'll ha'e naething adae' (nothing to do) with the
transaction ava' (at all) unless I can buy the house out
and out to a' eternity ! "

' The one lawyer, seeing they had got a character to deal
with, gave a knowing look to the other, who represented
the tailor, and, anxious to expedite business, said, " Well,
now, suppose we add a 9 figure to it, and then see how it
reads : ' I, John ——, hereby let, lease, etc., for 9999 years.' "
And with great difficulty, after much persuasion,' said Carlyle, 'they at length got him to entertain and accept of
these amended terms.'

And he might have added, the tailor spoke of this freely,
at the expense of the lawyers—with reason enough.   It
seemed a proof of the depravity of the fellows to be so fond
of lying that, even when it was needless, they insisted on
saying one thing and meaning another.

X

INDOORS AND OUT

TOM'S mother was a willing worker. By evening her tasks were done, and she used to sit and read the Bible aloud while her husband sat and smoked. Last scene of all each night, James "took the book" and read some chapters more. They sang a psalm and prayed spontaneously in no fixed form. Hypocrisy and formality were as far from them as from the earliest Christians.

Best of all was the affection which filled the house, impalpable like electricty or vital heat, but all-pervading. True it is that Tom by and by wrote of his father, revealing himself :—

'Though genuine and coherent, "living and life-giving," he was nevertheless but half developed. We had all to complain that we durst not freely love him. His heart seemed as if walled in ; he had not the free means to unbosom himself. My mother has owned to me that she could never understand him ; that her affection, and (with all their little strifes) her admiration of him was obstructed : it seemed as if an atmosphere of Fear repelled us from him. My heart and tongue played freely only with my mother. He had an air of deepest gravity, even sternness. Yet he could laugh with his whole throat, and his whole heart. I have often seen him weep too : his voice would thicken and his lips curve while reading the Bible : he had a merciful heart to real distress, though he hated idleness, and for imbecility and fatuity had no tolerance.'

Which merely shows that the affection binding James Carlyle and his family together lay deep down, beyond the reach of words.

Many a night Tom's mother, as she lay awake, was disturbed by Tom and Sandy upstairs in their bedroom fighting with the pillows. Sometimes she endured the affliction, as mothers can. At other times she could not. " James ! James ! James ! " Poor James Carlyle had to bestir himself. " Go up and wallop them, do you hear ? Wallop them well, make them quiet."

James had to obey. It was a common experience. He went upstairs, and with stern words brought down his hand heavily—upon the bedclothes. He always took care there was plenty of padding between the little sinners and his hands, and made as much noise as possible. When he had thrashed the bedclothes till mother was satisfied, father returned downstairs, and Tom and Sandy, half choked with laughing and want of air, emerged unhurt. They always felt it would be mean and ungrateful to father to make a noise after that, and lay as still as they could. The sounds of suppressed laughter may have sounded like sobs to their mother. At any rate she did not suspect till many years afterwards what really used to happen on these occasions.

It was only when kept awake that she was sometimes querulous. She was never one of the dismal sisters who make the world dull. She was busy about her housework by day, but cheery all the time, and fond of fun, " jocose " say the witnesses, the whole of her life. Her example of willing work and cheerfulness must have been a fine element in her children's education. The idea of duty was so early planted in their minds that obedience to what was right became instinctive, and their teachers found thrashing was never needed. But it cannot be denied Tom figured in a fight described in an American magazine in 1898.[1] The deposition of the principal sufferer seems to have been recorded by a grave divine. Nobody but those directly concerned observed it at the time. Tom had a quarrel with some other boys, and torn between inclination to fight and obedience to his mother, who was always forbidding it, he shed tears, and his enemy cried—" See greetin' Tom ! " Tom then struck out. Some hurt must have been done, for in old age the boy he struck was still complaining of it. The other boys rejoicing to join one side or another, there was a general fight. In the middle of it, when Tom, aged nine, was defending himself like a hero of Homer against several contemporary champions, his brother Sandy, aged seven, and short for his age, though sturdy, dashed in to help him,

[1] *Atlantic Monthly*, February, 1898, corroborated by letters.

and " with little fists like walnuts rained rapid blows on the enemy." [1]

Tom was " tall for his age," said one who was a big girl then, observing him. [2] " Slender like his mother, and sallow-coloured, but strongly built and active. Many a time I have seen him trotting along the street by the side of his father, as if listening with eyes and ears to every word that was said." Which may explain another trifle noticed—" his talk was like a man's." He was by all accounts a " great reader," but coëvals noticed only that he had no trouble with lessons ; and once, but only once, he was seen " in the fields poring over a book."

The villagers gathered in the summer evenings in the open " place "—the younger men and women dancing to the fiddle, the children playing, the women talking among themselves, and the men, especially the older men, sitting together under a sycamore tree, big and old enough to be a landmark, debating the eternal conundrums of theology, and telling the latest news of the wars, with older stories of the two veteran Scots Greys, the sole survivors there of twenty who enlisted for the German wars in 1742. Even such common topics as the weather, crops and taxes, were at times discussed with breadth of sympathy and outlook. In the words of Burns—

> " They lay aside their private cares
> To mind the Kirk and State affairs :
> They'll talk o' patronage and priests,
> Wi' kindling fury in their breasts ;
> And tell what new taxation's comin',
> And ferlie at the folk in Lon'on."

" Ferlie " means to express wonder, and conveys a feeling of pity or contempt—the natural sentiment of any man of sense discussing the doings of " governing men " in Europe then or now. Tom listened eagerly and noticed that his father often thought the criticisms just, but also confined his speech to matters of fact, or what could or should be done on the spot—" wholly a man of Action," " with Speech subservient thereto."

It was not fear that kept James silent. He did not fear the face of man. But his business was to work with his

---

[1] The fight in Lochmaben described in *James Burn, the Beggar Boy* (1882, Hodder & Stoughton) pp. 55–6, may have concerned a cousin of T. C. but certainly cannot have concerned him.

[2] Mrs. Milligan, examined by John T. Wells.

hands. He had "no call" to instruct politicians. Little Tom perhaps might ! He had noticed his little Tom, and spoke of educating him.

The general opinion was in favour of his doing so. Even unbelievers there had a notion that Knox might be right in thinking every scholar an addition to the riches of the Commonwealth. Besides, men valued each other in old Scotland for what they were to a degree incredible to us now, and the discovery of a promising boy among them rejoiced the hearts of many more than his relatives in Ecclefechan.

There was much to be said on the other side, however. Many a son of equal promise had been only a sorrow to his family. " Educate a boy and he grows up to despise his ignorant parents," said James Bell, earnestly dissuasive ; but if Tom had gifts more than common, what then ? The sinfulness of leaving high talents unused was clearly present to James Carlyle's mind. Long afterwards he told his son what Bell had said, and added—" Thou hast not done so. God be thanked for it ! " Meanwhile, he faced the risk.

Mrs. Carlyle seems to have been passive in this. It was James Carlyle " exclusively " who decided Tom must have " education " ; and everyone that knew him agreed he " was always a very strict old body, and could bide no contradiction." Whatever was said, and, if " Peggy " did not approve, it is extremely unlikely she was silent, it was settled that Tom was to be educated, and his father proceeded to do his part in that matter with the same thoroughness that he did his other work.

Education enough Tom was to get, and give himself ; but he always gratefully felt that he owed more to his father's example than to anything else ; and when difficulties faced him and flesh and blood seemed weak, " I'll gar (make) myself do it, as my father would say," Tom whispered to himself. His father's force of will was only part of what the son was imitating. To work, and work with a conscience, he also learned like reading, so early that he could never remember how, and he remarked of his father, with the admiration which makes imitation easy—" he never spoke of what was disagreeable and past "—let bygones be bygones, in short, and heeded the " might-have-beens " as little as any other dreams. He " delighted to hear of all things that were worth talking of ; the mode of living men had, the mode of working, their opinion

virtues, whole spiritual and temporal environment. His
habit of intellect was throughly free and even incredulous."
His reading was not restricted to the Bible and books of
theology. He assimilated Smith's *Wealth of Nations* and
other up-to-date books, such as *Macartney's Embassy* (to
China)—which he never forgot, so much had the Chinese
astonished him. Napoleon, too, was specially interesting
to him ; but as for spiteful country clatter and the super-
stitions current then and there, " Long may we remember,"
said his son, " his ' I don't believe thee,' his tongue-paralys-
ing, cold, indifferent ' Hah ! ' "

One of the best of the blessings Burns conferred on his
countrymen was teaching them to laugh at all the stock-in-
trade of necromancers, from spooks and spirits to the poor
old Devil himself. The lesson went home ; but it took a
generation or two. In many a big house or " Castle " the
laird's children were trembling at shadows at which Tom in
the village laughed. James Carlyle's lucky children were in
advance of their contemporaries—to say nothing of ours.

While thus teaching his children to think at large, he
never doubted the fundamental dogma of Heaven and Hell
awaiting us at death—as credible as China or London or
any other places known only by repute.

The horrors of Hell appeared to be beyond discussion.
The shortness of life should be ever present to people of
sense. " If I live," " if I be spared," were always implied
and often said in talk about the future by James Carlyle
and many of his contemporaries. The easy rejoinder,
" If you're dead, we'll not expect you " is only pat in talking
without thinking. And Walter Scott, soliloquising in his
diary,[1] when his wife died, remarked another custom of
his common neighbours which seemed to him worthy of
his imitation—to remember the departed and not " strangle
natural feeling by way of avoiding a painful sensation."
" My wife that's gone." " My brother that's gone."
" Generous and manly " seemed the custom to Scott ; and
to children in Ecclefechan then it was as much a matter of
course to hear such words tenderly spoken as to hear the
music of the birds in the spring.

[1] Lockhart's *Life of Sir Walter Scott*, VIII, p. 340.

XI

TALES OF THE ELDERS

WHEN Tom was a boy, the Londoners had forgotten how all their shops were shut in a fright when Prince Charles and his Highland raiders were in the Midlands; but the folks round Ecclefechan were still talking of it after sixty years, as if it had happened yesterday. The people were rooted in the soil, and hardly heeded the tides of the ocean of time—they counted by generations.

Few families had been longer in Annandale than those who were named from the town of Carlisle, "as old as Solomon," they said. Of their connections with the Bruces, let this suffice, that a sister, Margaret, of the Robert Bruce of Bannockburn was the wife of "Sir William de Cairlyle" and the mother of the first Thomas Carlyle in history, who seems to have been too young to be with the rest at Bannockburn; but lived to meet a common fate, "died fighting," at Neville's Cross long afterwards.

Vain is it to object that our Carlyle was like other men— the son of his mother as well as of his father, and so as much an Aitken or Gillespie or Bell as a Carlyle. No doubt, and it is well to remember that. But of Jesus Christ Himself Matthew and Luke provide a pedigree through his father only; and the pedigree or even parentage of his mother, Mary, is never mentioned nor missed.

According to the genealogists, the grandfather of " our Tom " was descended from that ancient William who married Bruce's sister, through Robert,[1] second son of John Carlyle, first Baron of Torthorwald. The " baronial house " was, of course, descended from the eldest son, and was at last represented by an entirely different " Thomas Carlyle," a nominal " advocate " who went about pamphleteering as an Irvingite Apostle. As a " double-goer," perplexing strangers in foreign parts as well as at home, the

---

[1] See note at end of chapter.

" Apostle " was occasionally an innocent, inadvertent nuisance to " our Tom."

Nicholas Carlisle, an antiquary who was also assistant librarian to King George III, came into Annandale gathering details for his quarto—*Collections for a History of the Ancient Family of Carlisle*, and seeking an interview with " our Tom's " father, James, discovered him working in a field with a brother. They discussed antiquities there and then and sundry other things. It has always remained a perplexity how Carlyle knew the private way of George III in selecting books for his library. The care of the dull but honest King for books that were good was a fact Carlyle often quoted to his credit. But how did he know it ? The likeliest guess is—through his father from the aforesaid Nicholas, who would know it at first hand.

What nobody then could see was that a son of this insignificant mason and farmer was the one Carlyle of consequence in history. But for Mr. Carlyle of Waterbeck, who lent the work of Nicholas to our Carlyle in April, 1842, and half a century afterwards to one of Carlyle's biographers,[1] and supplemented it with MS. notes, the most inquisitive reader could never know the genealogy about which James himself, and his son, " our Tom," and the rest, felt as Dr. Johnson did about what Lord Marchmont was willing to tell of Pope—" If it rained knowledge, I'd hold out my hand, but I would not give myself the trouble to go in quest of it."

James was the son of Thomas Carlyle of Brownknowe, and of Mary Gillespie ; and his father was the son of John Carlyle of Burrens and Isabella Bell. That John Carlyle was the son of Thomas Carlyle of Burrens, who was the son of a Carlyle of Burrens whose Christian name is uncertain, but is given in one pedigree as John. His father was Alexander Carlyle of Supplebank, who was the son of Thomas Carlyle " of Banks," who was the the son of Thomas Carlyle " of Banks," who was the son of Robert Carlyle of Pettenaine and Margaret Weir his wife. That Robert Carlyle was the second son of John Carlyle, first Baron of Torthorwald, by his wife Janet, and that John's father, William, was the grandson of the grandson of the William of Cairlyle or Carlisle, " de Karleolo," who married Margaret Bruce, sister of Sir Robert of Bruce, the King Robert of Bannockburn, who gave as a kind of dowry, perhaps, or royal wedding

[1] D. A. W.

present, " et Margaretæ sponsæ suæ, sorori nostræ caris-
simæ " (and to Margaret his bride, our dearest sister) the
lands of "Crumanstoun," which we need not pause to
identify. Like other lands the Carlyles had, and the
Torthorwald title itself, these may now be among the
multitudinous possessions of the last Buccleuch who gave
himself the trouble to be born.

It is needless to dwell on departed cousins in distant
generations. The only ancestor prominent in " our Tom's "
family tradition was one of the Carlyles at Burrens, probably
the one whose Christian name is doubtful. It must have
been soon after the Union of the Crowns that men from
Cumberland came to his farm on the track of stolen cattle ;
and though he was innocent, they " hanged him on the spot,"
in the sight of his weeping wife and crying children. " A
perpetual gift of the little farm was made to the poor
widow as some compensation. Her children and children's
children continued to possess it " till " the Duke " and his
lawyers grabbed it as usual. Americans who have thought-
lessly resented Carlyle's curses on Lynch Law might have
understood them better if they had known that little bit
of family tradition. It was not quite history. In Pennersaughs, as in other graveyards, the sandstone lettering does
not last long. The farthest ancestor " our Carlyle " named
as his was his great-grandfather, the last John Carlyle of
Burrens, who died there in 1727 at the age of forty.[1] His
widow removed to the nearest village, Middlebie, with her
two children, Tom, a boy of five, and Frank, a baby about
a year old. In seventy years' time that little boy was our
" Grandfather Tom " in Ecclefechan, and baby Frank was
back in the village; "the Captain of Middlebie " they
called him now, for he had long commanded a revenue
cutter that cruised in the Solway ; but by this time he was
unwieldy and old, retired on half pay.

The families of the two old brothers, living in adjoining
villages, had long been stiffly strangers, through " some
misunderstanding." Both men were far beyond threescore
and ten, the elder past eighty, the younger about seventy-
six, when little Tom was standing by and saw a cart from
Middlebie come over roads of the roughest to the door of
his grandfather. " The Captain " had heard his brother
was dying ; and being unable to walk, had had himself
lifted, armchair and all, into the cart, and came to visit

[1] See Tombstone, Pennersaughs, by Ecclefechan.

him. Broad-shouldered and grim of feature, he seemed terrible to his brother's grandson, " our Tom," whose father helped to carry the visitor in his chair upstairs to grandfather's room, where " the two old brothers saluted each other, hovering over the brink of the grave." In about twenty minutes the chair was seen descending—the captain was replaced in the cart and jolted homewards, and was seen no more. He died in August, 1803. His face haunted little Tom for more than sixty years, appearing a " prototype of Smollett's Trunnion." The full meaning of what had happened the child could not understand till older ; and his immediate questions filled a day or two.

His grand-uncle, he learned, had been a shoemaker at Middlebie in youth, and gone into England " to travel for work and insight " ; but falling among gamblers in his drink, had lost his cash, and getting into difficulties, enlisted on a man-of-war. There was a mutiny on board. He quelled it, for which he received promotion, and so came to command the revenue cutter, an exciting job on the Solway then, as appears from Scott's *Guy Mannering* and other evidence.

The adventure of the poet Burns in 1792 [1] was almost current news in Tom's boyhood, and must have been discussed in his hearing. A smuggling brig, well armed, with " four carronades," was caught on a shoal in the Solway. Burns led the boarding party, sword in hand, and the smugglers surrendered. At the auction of the brig and her stores, he bought the carronades and sent them to the French Convention as a mark of his admiration. It is a well known story that they were stopped at Dover, the English Government preparing to make war. At the theatre in Dumfries in October (1792), " the Caledonian Hunt being then in town," a crowd of gentry watching *As You Like It* interrupted " Miss Fontenelle " and other star performers by calling for " God Save the King." When it was sung, " we all stood up uncovered," all " but Burns," said " a gentleman of birth and talents " to Allan Cunningham, and the harmony of worship was spoiled by " a great tumult, with shouts of ' Turn him out ! ' and ' Shame, Burns ! ' " By reason of these events, Mr. Mitchell, the collector who was official superior of the exciseman Burns, had to write to him in December that he was blamed " as a person disaffected to Government " and that he was

[1] J. G. K. Lockhart's *Robert Burns*, Chap. VIII.

ordered by the " Board " to " enquire into his political conduct."

If there had been a scamp among his immediate official superiors, the gentry who " reported " his " disgraceful behaviour " might have had their way—he might have been dismissed ; but luckily there was goodwill to him in the department and he was represented as insignificant. So he was merely admonished that it was his business to act and not to think—for which he was grateful.

Much has been said of these events. What remains to be noticed is that the real reply of Burns is in the song he sent to Edinburgh in January, 1795—" A Man's a man for a' That," a " Marseilleise " of all mankind. Much of the thunder of Carlyle was like a sequel to the poet's intellectual lightning, for excepting only his father, Burns was his earliest hero and the best beloved, and not even his father's disapproval diminished the boy's adoration of Burns.

NOTE UPON GENEALOGY

Robert Carlyle, the second son of John the first Baron of Torthorwald, is erroneously called illegitimate in some new peerages, the editors supposing so because he was once called " natural " ; but in this instance, as in many, " natural " did not mean illegitimate, but " own " son, as distinguished from son-in-law or stepson.

John Carlyle, the first Baron, had three wives, and at least one of them was a widow when she married him. In 1917 when D. A. W. had given up as insoluble the petty question of the legitimacy of that faraway Robert Carlyle, he visited Dumfries again and the Antiquarian Society there, and G. Macleod Stewart demonstrated to him the error of the later Peerage editors by contemporary documents, which seemed conclusive. He owes to Mr. Macleod Stewart these references, R.M.S., No. 2337 dated 27th January, 1497, and 2799 of 25th August, 1504 ; and a perusal of a letter from T. Carlyle, Cheyne Row, Chelsea, to Col. T. Carlisle, R.A., dated 3rd February, 1870, beginning : " I certainly am not the representative of the late Lord Carlisle. By all evidence that exists, I descend," etc., as in text, a conclusion reached separately by D. A. W. in 1897.

See *Douglas's Peerage of Scotland*, Wood's revised edition of 1813, Vol. I, pp. 306–9. See also the huge quarto of 1822, *Collections for a History of the Ancient Family of Carlisle*, by Nicholas Carlisle, F.R.S., etc., Assistant Librarian to King George III, Fellow and Secretary of the Society of Antiquaries of London. It was supplemented by MS. genealogies by Gracie of Dumfries and others, verified in 1897 by D. A. W. so far as then possible, from stones in Pennersaughs and other graveyards.

It must not be supposed the Carlyle family was odd in being able to trace its ancestry. On the contrary, Carlyle's father heeded this less than his neighbours. More than half the farmers in the lowlands of Scotland could then have told almost as much about their ancestors as the utmost research has enabled D. A. W. to discover about the Carlyles. The fixture of the population led to this, and it is only ending, not quite ended yet. In Ayrshire there is a family tracing itself back for over 500 years, and all workers, not a parasite among them, mainly farmers ; and there is another man living in Ayrshire whose grandmother was born in the adjoining shire of Lanark, in a house where her people had lived 400 years. In another shire a farm is soon to be vacated by an old bachelor whose ancestors have been tenant-farmers there for 280 years. Such things used to be common, and Sir Walter Scott was fond of dwelling on them.

When even common folk are thus enabled to think in genera-tions, they may see or at least suspect what otherwise only wide study and exceptional intellect can discern—the justice of " Heaven " or Nature. That is the " Fact of Facts," which underlies all Science and Philosophy, and though too little known in Europe and sometimes doubted in the idol-caverns of our universities, it is almost a tradition in civilised Asia and a commonplace in China. However absurd humanity may be, Nature makes no mistakes. Things are what they are, and the consequences will be what they will be, and effects follow causes as the night the day, as sure in morals as in chemistry.

So great a blessing is such knowledge that one should have patience with any way of learning it and blame not those who seem to linger overlong in looking backwards. There is small danger of many doing that too much to-day. When fumbling over pedigrees in Frederick, Carlyle must have felt among familiar things. The feudal fooleries of Central Europe must often have reminded him of the country bumpkins of the old home land ; and the greatest truth he had to teach, that Righteousness is a law of Nature, was a living tradition around him as a child. It was the best tradition of old Scotland, purified by persecution and delivered from bondage to the letter, the sorest of all slaveries.

XII

GRANDFATHER AND CARLYLE OF BRIDEKIRK

THE grandfather of "our Tom" had spent some seasons in England when young. He was a carpenter, and found work in Lancashire; and "skated along the Westmorland and Cumberland Lakes" on his way home one winter. His mother's house in Middlebie was his till he married Mary Gillespie, and then he took the farm of Brownknowe by Burnswark Hill, and for the rest of his active life was a farmer, as his father and grandfather had been.

He never quite ceased to handle the tools for woodwork; and in his old age in the village his little grandson and namesake, "our Tom," has helped him to grind them; but in those days of wooden implements a carpenter turned farmer could easily "keep his hand in." Once, at least, and maybe often when he had barley for sale, he carried it on horseback to Annan. By one means or another he raised his rent, and then he used to lock the money away, not to be touched whatever the need. The well-doing wife with her four sons and three daughters did the rest. They had to scramble for their food—the very meal was sometimes scanty, and the boys who knitted and thatched for hire were cunning in hunting the hares—" like wild Indians, from Necessity." They sold the skins at sixpence each to buy clothes. But farms were small then, and they really were no worse off than most of their neighbours, so that Carlyle was surprised to have to confess that neither his father nor any of his uncles saw anything to complain about. In the words of Burns—

> " How it comes, I never kent yet,
> They're maistly wonderfu' contented;
> And buirdly chiels, and clever hizzies,
> Are bred in sic a way as this is."

48

Their father spent most of his ample leisure hunting and carousing with his cousin, Adam [1] Carlyle, the laird of Bridekirk, across the Annan River, beyond Wood-cock-air Hill, as you go to Annan town. Bridekirk was many years his senior and the hero of the borders then. " He was a man of great strength and activity," and " you could hear his voice from a hilltop for miles around."

A fox-hunt then was a gathering of men and dogs to keep down the vermin, driving them out of hiding and killing them whatever way was easiest. The hares and other ground game were caught in the same way, often at the same time. Another country pleasure now monopolised was the spearing of salmon. To attend the laird in hunting was often specified as a service included in the rent of a farm.

There was a hunting air current said to have been used by the Annandale spearmen at Bannockburn, to keep time when they stepped forward shoulder to shoulder to meet the astonished English cavalry. Burns made a song for the tune—we know it as " Scots Wha Ha'e." And a generation before him, Bridekirk set words to it which were sung all over Annandale.

> " The cock's at the crawing,
> The day's at the daw'ing,
> The cock's at the crawing,
> We're o'er lang here !

> CHORUS
> " Bridekirk's a-hunting,
> Bridekirk's a-hunting,
> Bridekirk's a-hunting,
> The morn an it be fair.

> " Will thy dog or my dog (repeat twice)
> Catch the nimmle hare ?
> " Up and down yon bonnie lea (repeat twice)
> On the banks o' Wood-cock-air."

Other verses named men and dogs in ways that set the table in a roar for reasons mysterious now—the jokes are vanished like the foam of their ale—

> " There's Gingler and Gowler,
> And Tingler and Towler,
> And thy dog and my dog,
> And a' will be there."

[1] William, son of Adam Carlyle, according to the antiquarian, Nicholas Carlisle ; but T. C. was less likely to be mistaken and was explicit in talk to a nephew, Thomas Carlyle, Brantford, Canada. Mistake was easy as he was commonly called Bridekirk.

E

" A jest's prosperity lies in the ear of him that hears it."
After a hard morning in the open air and a good dinner,
men were easily amused. Here is a glimpse of the " Lady
Bridekirk," as they styled the wife of the laird. She was
not a breeder. No child of theirs succeeded them; but in
other ways she was a successful wife.

Her husband had many cousins. One who was a parson
in Prestonpans came visiting in native Annandale in the
summer of 1733, in company with an eleven-year-old son
and two more divines, the Rev. Robert Jardine of Lochmaben, and a " Mess John Allan " who " lay in their route
and was their constant butt." The boy, of course, remembered best this summer-morning call and told about it when
old. He had become the Rev. Alexander Carlyle, a famous
leader of the " Moderates," and called " Jupiter."—[1]

' The laird was gone to Dumfries, much to our disappointment ; but the lady came out, and, in her excess of kindness,
had almost pulled Mr. Jardine off his horse ; but they were
obstinate, and said they were obliged to go to Kelhead ;
but they delivered up Mess John Allan to her, as they had
no further use for him.

' I had never seen such a virago as Lady Bridekirk, not
even among the oyster-women of Prestonpans. She was
like a sergeant of foot in women's clothes ; or rather like an
overgrown coachman of a Quaker persuasion. On our
peremptory refusal to alight, she darted into the house like
a hogshead down a slope,' meaning that she wobbled from
side to side but went very quick and straight. She
' returned instantly with a pint bottle of brandy—a Scots
pint, I mean '—twice the capacity of our modern " quarts "—
' and from it she filled almost a bumper. After a long grace
said by Mr. Jardine—for it was his turn now, being the
third brandy bottle we had seen since we left Lochmaben—
she emptied it to our healths, and made the gentlemen
follow her example ; she said she would spare me as I was
so young, but ordered a maid to bring a gingerbread cake
from the cupboard, a luncheon of which she put in my
pocket.' The old man acting as recording angel had
forgotten apparently how the wealth of gingerbread rejoiced
him at eleven !

' This lady was famous, even in the Annandale border,
both at the bowl and in battle : she could drink a Scots

[1] *Autobiography of the Rev. Alexander Carlyle*, pp. 22–4.

pint ' (⅜ of a gallon) ' of brandy with ease ; and when the men grew obstreperous in their cups, she could either put them out of doors or to bed, as she found most convenient.'

Which makes one doubt the report about her drinking a bottle herself. Many a laird's wife was skilful in shuffling the bottles, replacing one three-quarters full by another nearly empty that seemed the same, a kindly trick to make the men be moderate. At any rate, when Thomas Carlyle of Brownknowe was coming about, by which time she would be turned fifty and thicker than ever, but not so fleet of foot, she liked him none the less because he was " not a drinker " and held by table beer.

He was one of many young fellows who imitated her " magnificent " husband. This one went so far that he was known to wear a sword at Ecclefechan fairs, instead of merely carrying a loaded stick, such as contented most farmers and drovers, and once in a market-brawl when some man he was chasing disappeared behind the door of a public-house and held it shut, he thrust his sword through the door, which was then opened, and disclosed a man with a hideous wound, which stopped the squabble. However, the fellow recovered,[1] and we may hope that he was like the jovial King Christian of Denmark and "lived to be often beaten after that, and had many moist years more."

[1] Notes of John T. Wells. Statement by old John Bell of what he heard said by his father who saw the fight.

XIII

BRIDEKIRK AND THE "FORTY-FIVE"

LISTENING to his grandfather, Tom heard many tales; and never forgot a description of Glasgow as grandfather saw it—the streets deserted by nine o'clock and no sound but the singing of psalms from house after house. Perhaps the most interesting experience he heard from him was about the "forty-five"; but what was said appeared "too brief and indistinct" to the curious youngster, who began to put questions in all directions, till at last his genial uncle Frank sat down beside him one day to quiet him and delighted him with the details he wanted; and then the boy was always ready to repeat it in his turn—which may be called the first of his historical performances. Here is the best report[1] of what Tom used to tell:—

'The Highland army retreating from Derby was coming north and on this side of the border met Bridekirk on horseback. He seemed a person of consequence, and was wearing a sword, as all gentlemen did then. "Prisoner," he was told, "give up your sword." He replied that he would never give it up, but as they were the stronger party, they might *take* it. So he had to go with them; and his wife sent for grandfather and sent him after them to "try to get speech" of her husband.

'Grandfather went in pursuit, and getting in advance of the army climbed a high gate-post, and sat there watching them pass and saw Bridekirk and hailed him, asking—"What can be done for you?"

'"Nothing can be done," was the reply. "I do not think my life is in any danger. We are going to halt at Dumfries. Tell my wife to send me clean linen there by one of the servants."

'Grandfather did as bidden, and was entreated by the

---

[1] Thomas Carlyle of Brantford, Canada, son of Alexander C., brother of T. C., wrote it soon after hearing it from the lips of his uncle, T. C., and showed it to D. A. W. and gave him a copy, 1895.

anxious wife to go to Dumfries himself to "do whatever you can think of "—" at least to get speech of him again," said she. So he went to Dumfries and saw the Highlanders there, ragged and bare-footed many of them, and looking tired. They gathered in the open streets round fires, over which they were busily roasting slices of beef or mutton stuck on the ends of their pikes and cut by their dirks from freshly slaughtered carcases beside them.

'Grandfather's shoes were good; and he had to say "No" as politely as possible to repeated offers to "niffer brogues" (exchange shoes). At last one stalwart wild-looking clansman who was barefoot asked him to "niffer brogues"; and receiving "No," he swore great Gaelic oaths and drew his dirk and was actually coming close to grandfather when Lochiel and other chiefs came by, on the way to a Council of War. Lochiel demanded the cause of the disturbance, and bade the man sheath his weapon and go, which he instantly did in a very cowed way.

'Grandfather went after the chiefs and tried in vain to get admittance to the big room in the hotel where they were. He had a talk with the sentry, a Highlander with drawn claymore, who would not let him pass; but on hearing what his business was, the sentry remarked to him,—" It won't be long till your friend finds the weight of his body hanging from his neck. What do you think he did in the presence of our King the other day? When the rest were drinking 'Success to Prince Charlie and his Cause!' he not only refused to join, he rose up alone when the cheering was done and drank: 'Confusion to the Pretender!'" (This happened in the hotel at Annan.)

'Grandfather looked through the door, which was partly open, as the man was speaking, and he saw the chiefs striding from side to side in an excited way The decision was to continue the retreat. Bridekirk was let go at Glasgow; and at Culloden, Cumberland won over them his only victory, and gained the title of "Butcher." He had only been "Bungler" up to then.'

The sequel to this adventure was so well known that it would commonly be talk about it which made men wish to hear the story. The Highlanders had made war like gentlemen in spite of hunger and cold. It was a beautiful thing for the chiefs to tolerate the insult from Bridekirk, and send him home unhurt. Cumberland, on the contrary, continually behaved like a common German royalty, scandalising Europe by his cold-blooded brutality and thus providing Tom Paine with one of his best arguments for fighting out the fight for Independence in America. The French Government protested in vain.[1] His own officers were ashamed. It may be true, as they say, that Wolfe on the battlefield refused to obey a " royal command " to finish a wounded man ; and what there is no room for doubt about is that when the " Butcher " returned and was told of the courage of Bridekirk, worth regiments in its effect at the time, he sent for " the hero of the borders," and even, according to Nicholas Carlisle, the Royal librarian and historian of the Carlisle family, " offered to relieve Bridekirk's estate of its heavy debt " ; but " to the great grief of all his relatives," Bridekirk would not speak to the " Butcher." The learned Nicholas, a royalist by trade, sentimentally speculates as to fine motives ; but there is small room for speculation. Nobody doubted the motive at the time. The people were singing a new song to an old tune. It may have been Bridekirk's own—he made many a song, they say. Assuredly he must have heard this one often and joined hilariously in the chorus. The air of " Highland Laddie " is still familiar. Here are the best words ever sung to it, none the worse for smelling of the Middle Ages :—

> " I ha'e been at Crookie-Den,[2]
> Bonnie laddie, Highland laddie !
> Viewing Willie and his men[3]—
> Bonnie laddie, Highland laddie !
> There our foes that burned and slew—
> Bonnie laddie, Highland laddie !
> There at last, they gat[4] their due,
> Bonnie laddie, Highland laddie !
>
> " Satan sits in his black neuk,[5]
> Bonnie laddie, Highland laddie !
> Breaking sticks to roast the Duke,
> Bonnie laddie, Highland laddie !
> The bloody monster gave a yell,—
> Bonnie laddie, Highland laddie !
> Loud the laugh gaed[6] round a' Hell !
> Bonnie laddie, Highland laddie ! "

[1] Voltaire's *Louis XV*, Chap. XXV, p. 165.
[2] The hottest part of Hell, where the Devil's cauldrons are. Crookie is a humorously tender form of the word " crook," a pot or cauldron hung by a chain and hook over a fire.
[3] Meaning William Augustus, alias Cumberland.
[4] Got.　　　　[5] Nook : corner seat by a fire.　　　　[6] Went.

The poor border laird, " the Hero of the Borders," who feared not Prince Charlie at the head of his army, and declined to shake hands with Cumberland when Cumberland was conqueror, and would take no money from such a royalty although his estate was in debt, had more than distant kinship in common with our Carlyle. Let us salute the shade of the frank and brave, the right sort of man, as he passes from our sight for ever.

Towards the end of the year 1805, Tom used to say,[1]
" a neighbour woman was in one evening talking with my
mother about the war and the fleet, and what great things
were supposed to be at hand ; the next day she came in
and said all their speculations had been vain, a tremendous
battle had already been fought, and the French and Spanish
fleets were smashed to pieces, and—Nelson was killed.
I had more grief for his death than joy for the victory."

Curiously blended with such sentiments were his boyish
love and respect for the poet Cowper, and about this time
began the enthusiastic admiration for Burns which lasted
all his life ; but neither now nor later would his father
heed the writings of Burns. However, he let the boy talk
as he liked, and the rest were soon in chorus with him,
everybody saying ditto. Their father heard them in silence,
with a face as unrelaxing as the Sphinx. It is said Tom was
particularly fond of reciting Burns's "Death and Dr.
Hornbook."[2] If James enjoyed it he gave no sign.

Americans have told of his youngest son long afterwards
that when they gushed to him about coming to Ecclefechan
for hero-worship, he merely said, " It's a gey (very) harmless
occupation." This has been guessed [3] to be an echo of some
remark of his father's about Tom's worship of Burns.

About 1805 Tom heard his grandfather say to his father
in a tremulous palsied voice—" Thou hast been a good son
to me." Grandfather died on 10th January, 1806, aged
eighty-four. Then Tom was clad in black for the first time
in his life, and at the wake was set to read aloud a religious
book. " He was a good reader," said one who was there,
and young enough to notice him, which the grown-ups
hardly did.[4] " What do you mean by that ? " " To listen
to him was as if he was thinking all he was reading and
telling it to you. There was a kind of sing-song, but not so
marked as his mother's when she was reading. In him you
hardly noticed it more in reading than in talking."

By this time Tom was rising eleven. The old farmer,
David Hope, familiar in their meeting-house, had a nephew,
Adam, attending it who was "English Master" in the new

[1] W. Allingham, *A Diary*, p. 305, etc.
[2] Village tradition. See also *Thomas Carlyle*, by Rev. John Wilson (1881), pp. 11–12.
[3] By D. A. W., who talked things over with John C. of Langholm, the son of that James, who seemed to think the guess likely.
[4] Notes of John T. Wells, quoting a girl Milligan, some years older then Tom.

Academy at Annan, six miles away ; and an aunt of Mrs.
Carlyle was the wife of " Bailie " Waugh, a shoemaker and
magistrate there. So Tom's mother consented to let him
stay with her aunt from Monday to Friday every week ;
and on a bright May morning (26.5.1806) James Carlyle
walked to Annan with Tom trotting at his side, as described
in *Sartor;* and then it may have been that he said what
the boy certainly heard him say—only the date is doubtful—
" Tom, I do not grudge thy schooling, now when thy Uncle
Frank owns thee to be a better Arithmetician than himself,"
which must have helped to make the boy conceited.

James left him at Waugh's, at the east end of the High
Street. The Academy was near the bridge at the west end,
so that his daily walks to and fro were through the wide
main street which was the Forum or Market-place. One of
the first sights he saw there survives in *Sartor*—" A little
dog, in mad terror, was rushing past ; for some human imps
had tied a tin-kettle to its tail ; thus did the agonised
creature, loud-jingling, career through the whole length of
the Borough, and become notable enough. Fit emblem of
many a Conquering Hero," and so on. The reflections
were later. The sight would be now (1806).

Launched among bigger boys, he found them thoughtless
animals, " rude, savage, natural " men in miniature ; and
he enjoyed the week-ends at home more than the days at
school, especially when father or mother took him to
Dumfries, as they sometimes did. His mother once lost
him in the crowd there, and when she became anxious
went in search and found him in the graveyard, sitting by
a stone in which he was interested.

She knew where to look for him another time, for he went
to it afterwards also. The first time he went may have
been 1806. He had found the gate locked and climbed
over the wall and searched about in the grass, reading with
interest the tombstones of the Covenanters, till suddenly
thrilled by the sight of the one he was looking for. " There
it was," he used to say, " in the midst of poor fellow-
labourers and artisans "—a flat stone with " Robert
Burns on it and the dates." In 1879, more than seventy
years afterwards, he said—" It was the most impressive
experience of the kind I have had in my life." [1]

[1] W. Allingham, *A Diary*, pp. 282–3 ; H. J. Nicoll's *T. Carlyle*,
p. 132 ; W. H. Wyllie's *T. Carlyle*, p. 40 ; J. H. Balfour Browne's *Forty
Years at the Bar*, p. 136, etc.

BOOK II

FROM BOY TO MAN
1806–18

I

SCHOOL AT ANNAN

(1806–9) [1]

THE border town of Annan had been a citadel against the English in the Middle Ages ; and the children could show a visitor the " sword-well," where gentlemen returning from killing the English used to wash the blood from their weapons. They had an uneasy feeling that they had fallen on duller days, though Austerlitz was 1805, and Jena this year (1806), and the commonest news was news of war.

On the Borders boys were extra fond of fighting ; and all the harder was the fate of " our Tom " when his mother, sending him to Annan, made him promise and pray for strength to fight no more. George Borrow tells what happened to himself when brought from the peaceful south and sent to school in Edinburgh. [2]

' " Scotland is a better country than England," said an ugly blear-eyed lad, about a head and shoulders taller than myself, the leader of a gang who surrounded me in the playground, on the first day. " Scotland is a far better country than England, in every respect."

' " Is it ? " said I. " Then you ought to be very thankful for not having been born in England."

' " That's just what I am, ye loon ; and every morning, when I say my prayers, I thank God for not being an Englishman. The Scotch are a much better and braver people than the English."

' " It may be so," said I, " for what I know—indeed, till I came here, I never heard a word either about the Scotch or their country."

---

[1] The notes of John T. Wells supply the reminiscences of the boy Maconachie, son of the cooper and librarian ; he was at school then and told much of T. C.

Alexander Tweedie, builder and poet, and his friends, Mr. Cuthbertson, editor, and a nonagenarian, Mr. Anderson, gave D. A. W. a full and complete history of Annan and its Grammar School or Academy.

[2] George Borrow's *Lavengro*, I, pp. 98–100.

' " Are ye making fun of us, ye English puppy ? " said the blear-eyed lad ; " take that ! " and I was presently beaten black and blue.

' I held my peace, and silently submitted. This was enough ; from an object of persecution I soon became one of patronage. The Scotch are certainly a most pugnacious people. Every noon there was at least one pugilistic encounter, and sometimes three. In one month I witnessed more of these encounters than I had ever previously seen under similar circumstances in England.'

The fate of " our Tom " was different, for he did not " submit." He had been a boy and an equal at Ecclefechan. His hands were now tied, but not his tongue ; and one of his victims was still complaining in old age,[1] declaring he had been " a cantankerous loon " ; and on sight of his *Reminiscences* apostrophising him :—

" Ah, Tom, Tom, that is just like you ; ye were aye sair afflicted with the big head, aye bragging about yourself and a' belanging to you." He added—" None of us liked him. He was aye saying biting, jibbing (gibing) things." But the witness confessed he was biassed, for " they had fought and Tom Carlyle had given him a sound thrashing." Which would be in the second year of Tom's schooling or later.

Indeed, it was likely Tom was biassed himself by abstaining from fighting till his second year. He wrote in 1866 :—

' Mythically *true* is what *Sartor* says of his schoolfellows, and not half of the truth. Unspeakable is the damage and defilement I got out of those coarse, unguided, tyrannous cubs, especially till I revolted against them. I had never been so wretched as in that school (for) the first two years of my time in it.'

He never suspected how much he was provoking the others. He disliked the lessons as much as they did, but learned them because he was bidden ! This made him a teachers' favourite from the first, and he " almost loved "

[1] *Atlantic Monthly*, February, 1898 ; the Contributors' Club : the actual writer, a clergyman, and the witness whose words he repeats, a deacon of his church in North Illinois. Another writer spoke of the refusal of the man to give his name because he had confessed to the beating, which shows the witness's good faith.

the Englishman Morley who taught mathematics. As if that were not bad enough, he talked back instead of begging mercy when refusing to fight, and had the impudence to object to other boys being cruel to animals or beggars, as if that were his business, as if he were entitled to give orders! The older boys when appealed to sometimes "took his part for a moment," which angered his contemporaries more than ever. So he soon learned enough of human nature at first hand to see the double meanings of his favourite classic in cheap "grey paper," *Reynard the Fox;* and much of what he wrote of Wotton Reinfred is likely to be true of himself:—

'They flouted him, they beat him, they jeered and tweaked and tortured him by a thousand cunning arts. He could only answer with his tears. He knew not what to do. For he was a quiet, pensive creature, that loved all things, the very cat.

'His mother became doubly dear. He knew no joy till he started homewards on Fridays, and leaving the pavement of the burgh behind him, could resign himself among shady alleys and green fields to a thousand dreams, which fancy was already building for him. In the future he was by turns a hero and a sage, in both provinces the benefactor and wonder of the world ; and would weave a history for himself, of dainty texture, resuming it day by day, and sometimes continuing it for months. The past was beautified. The ever-memorable *Arabian Nights*, which was "devoured," made a queer mixture with his mother's theology, but he was aware of no contradiction and watched over his words and actions with even an over-scrupulousness. His little prayer came evening and morning from a full heart, and life, in the thought of the innocent boy, seemed little else than a pilgrimage through a sacred alley, with the pinnacles of the Eternal Temple at its close. Beyond the region of material usefulness religion was the only study profitable to man.'

Which explains his perseverance in refusing to fight. Nobody but himself supposed he had much to suffer. He was boarding with his grand-aunt Barbara. She had been fond of his grandmother, her sister Margaret, from whom she had parted six years ago near Dumfries. He used to hear her "almost daily" muttering and weeping about her "dear Margaret," and their parting "at the dyke-end, sae

F

little thinking it was for the last time." He made no complaint to her, nor to her shoemaker husband, " Bailie " Waugh, a " living Hans Sachs," whom he admired for veracity and hatred of injustice even to a dog. Once his own father came into the schoolroom, and finding the teacher out sat down beside him and asked—" Are you all well ? " He said—" Yes," and complained of nothing.

What hurt him the most was the intangible habitual hostility which makes human beings whose better nature is to help each other revert to the savagery of cats or fishes ; but he was wideawake and evaded most of the intended torments. One of the commonest was a kick or blow from behind ; but that had to be a surprise, and nothing was farther from the mind of a big boy tormenting him in 1807, and turning away with jeers. " Our Tom " took off his clog then and went after him, and at the right moment dealt him with the clog a stroke from behind that sent him sprawling into " a convenient mass of mud and water." He came out in a state of consternation which filled Tom with holy happiness ; and then there was peace.[1] Tom had no more scruples about the duty of self-defence, and was persecuted no more. It was like him to be slow in learning that—*sure but slow*.

If fighting was the mother's pet aversion, the father's was fiction ; and yet by the time Tom was defending himself, he had learned to love the romances of Smollett. The business of John Maconachie, the cooper, was making barrels for the West Coast fishing trade ; and several boys attending the Academy boarded at his house. His pleasure was in his circulating library, used by boys and masters and many others. There used to be informal gatherings at Maconachie's to discuss the books, which his son declared " included every important biographical, historical and geographical work then published," to say nothing of fiction.

" Tom Carlyle came twice a week from the first," said Maconachie, Junior, by and by ; and assuredly he took out the first volume of *Roderick Random*, and " was inconsolable " because he could not get the second. He had to be content with *Humphry Clinker*, and liked it so much that he said after sixty years—" To this day I know few writers equal to Smollett. Nothing by Dante or anyone else surpasses in pathos the scene where Humphry goes into the smithy made for him in the old house, and whilst he is heating the iron, the poor woman, who has lost her husband

[1] *Thomas Carlyle*, by Moncure D. Conway, p. 30.

and is deranged, comes and talks to him as to her husband.
' John, they told me you were dead. How glad I am you
have come!' And Humphry's tears fall down and bubble
on the hot iron." [1]

Another book read then which left its mark upon him
was Robertson's *Charles V.* It " opened new worlds of
knowledge, vistas in all directions." To history James
Carlyle had no more objection than to mathematics.
But " fiction " ? Was Tom to make no better use of his
education than to stuff his noddle with stories as silly as
those of lassies gabbling at the wells ? This was as bad as
ranting after Burns, and Tom was now a big boy, soon to
be a man. Many a pious father on less provocation has
fallen into foolish orders, which lead to deceit. Happily
the convictions of James were controlled by conscience of
the right sort. " My conscience is not so," said Queen
Mary to Knox, and was answered—" Conscience, Madam,
requireth knowledge ; and I fear that right knowledge ye
have none." James was content to see his son was working
well. Indeed, there is no evidence that he ever ratified his
wife's prohibition of fighting, which was fortunate. " When
my father frowned," Tom used to say afterwards, " the
universe was darkened for me." [2] Both father and mother
agreed to trust their boy, and neither about the fighting
nor the reading of fiction was there ever any need for
concealment.

It may seem more surprising that from the age of eleven
Tom smoked tobacco openly without rebuke. [3] Snuff was
fashionable. Ladies objected to smoking. But among
the people it was common with both sexes. Tom's mother
would sometimes join in a whiff ; and he saw his father
giving tobacco " by way of over-and-above " to some old
women who had been gathering potatoes for him, and heard
him tell of seeing a heap of smuggled tobacco burned at
Langholm—" Dragoons were ranged round it with drawn
swords : some old women stretched through their old
withered arms to snatch a little of it, and the dragoons
did not hinder them."

[1] *Ibid*, pp. 31–2.
[2] *Literary Recollections*, by F. Espinasse, pp. 206–7.
[3] This was reported by William Maccall, as said to him by T. C., in
Thomas Carlyle—Table Talk (Liverpool, *Cope's Smoke Room Booklets*,
No. 5.) David Masson was consulted about it in 1896 and told D. A. W.
he had heard something to the same effect and believed it. W. Maccall
we agreed was a good witness. Corroborated in William Allingham, *A
Diary*, p. 237.

Many of the clergy, like Spurgeon, "smoked to the glory of God." An elder smoking on the way to church would put out his pipe as he entered; but light it in the porch as he departed. The fragrance of it pervaded the vestry. In the *Gospel Sonnets* of Ralph Erskine (1726, etc., approved by Isaac Watts and George Whitefield), there was an old hymn with additional verses of his own which is quoted in *Sartor*.[1]

THIS INDIAN WEED

" This Indian weed now withered quite,
Tho green at noon, cut down at night,
    Shows thy decay,—
    All flesh is hay :
Thus think and smoke tobacco."

And so on for four verses, whereof this is the best—

" In vain the unlighted pipe you blow ;
Your pains in outward means are so,
    Till Heavenly fire
    Your heart inspire :
Thus think and smoke tobacco."

Both in praising tobacco and in cursing the politicians who taxed it, picking people's pockets, Carlyle meant what he said ; but he was saying ditto to his father all the same.

It is as likely to have been at home as at school that Tom learned to smoke. He seldom was a day in Annan when he could be at home.[2] A sister afterwards said he was unusually obliging to mother and sisters, a "willing messenger always" and ready to "go with them and carry bundles" wherever required.[3] Which did not interfere with school at all. He regularly returned to Annan with his pockets stuffed by his mother with home-baked bannocks.[4] He had much to do and learn there both in and out of school.

[1] *Sartor Resartus*, I, Chap. III. See footnote 4, p. 59, Barrett's Edition ; and *The Erskines*, by A. R. MacEwen, pp. 46–50.
[2] Abundantly proved. One item of evidence was a statement to D. A. W. in 1895 by Thomas Graham, Draper, Ecclefechan, whose father John Graham came and went with T. C.
[3] Told by Mrs. Austin his sister : *Autobiography of Moncure D. Conway*, II, p. 190.
[4] *Thomas Carlyle*, by W. H. Wylie, p. 21.

II

ANNAN LESSONS

(1806–9)

ONE market day there was a bust of Shakespeare on the board of an Italian shouting " Images ! " in the main street.[1] A woman among the crowd who gathered read the lines inscribed—" The Cloudcapt Towers " and so on. " Shankespeare " was her rendering of the name. These lines from the *Tempest*, among the best of Shakespeare's, were the first Tom read, and always afterwards he loved to quote them. The thought in them—" We are such stuff as dreams are made of "—has long been a proverb in China. But it thrilled Richter, and must have seemed strange doctrine in Annan and impressed the boy, like a glimpse of the stars through the church windows.

To boys from the country, the harbour and the shore were an attraction. He became expert in " sailor-knots." In learning to swim, at the common bathing-place " at the back of the hill," he got into deep water, began to sink, and shouted for help. He felt he was drowning, and never forgot it. He saw nothing but the sky, and a line of Virgil was running in his head—" Et sale tabentes artus in littore ponunt " (and laid their limbs upon the shore a-dripping with salt water). A man pulled him out by the hair of his head. His mother made him promise never to venture into deep water again.[2]

As for books, he " devoured " all he could get. In a bundle of old numbers of the *Belfast and County Almanack* he found mathematical conundrums which he worked out for himself,[3] a kind of thing encouraged by teachers then. He

[1] W. Allingham, *A Diary*, p. 247.
[2] Referred to in a letter, 31.7.1832. What is here told is what T. C. told to Mrs. A. A. Anstruther on 10.9.1878, when escorting her from the hotel at Annan to the Railway Station. For additional details in *Thomas Carlye* by A. S. Arnold, p. 8, Mr. Arnold gives no authority, and on local enquiry D. A. W. could not find corroboration.
[3] W. Allingham, *A Diary*, pp. 205 and 216.

learned arithmetic well, and algebra and geometry, as well
as " English " and geography, French and Latin, and even
the Greek alphabet. Whatever was taught he learned and
stored away on trust, so to speak, though seeing as yet no
use for most of it.

He afterwards regretted [1] that he had never been taught
music, believing his defective sense of rhythm, which made
the best of his verses mechanical, was due to this omission ;
and he was still more emphatic about drawing.   He
hankered to learn it when at school, but never could.[2]

One bright afternoon in 1808, he was one of a class doing
Latin lessons under the rector's eye when Adam Hope,
the English master, entered and introduced to the rector
Edward Irving, an Academy boy who was now a " distinguished student." Though supposed to be preparing lessons
and not listening at all, the boys were eagerly attentive
to the visitor ; and fifty-six years later Tom remembered :—

' Irving was scrupulously dressed, black coat, ditto tight
pantaloons in the fashion of the day ; and looked very neat,
self-possessed and enviable : a flourishing slip of a youth ;
with coal-black hair, swarthy clear complexion ; very
straight on his feet ; and, except for the glaring squint
alone, decidedly handsome. We did not hear everything ;
gathered in general that the talk was all about Edinburgh,
of this professor and of that, and their merits and methods
—wonderful world up yonder : and this fellow has been
in it, and can talk of it in that easy cool way !—The one
particular I clearly recollect was something from Irving
about new doctrines, by somebody (doubtless Leslie),
" concerning the circle " ; which last word he pronounced
" circul," with a certain *preciosity*, which was noticeable
slightly in other parts of his behaviour. Shortly after this
of " circul," he courteously made his bow ; and the interview melted instantly away.'

Becoming ashamed of his handwriting, Tom tried to
improve it, doing several pages daily. A note in French
in a school-book [3] is dated " Annan Academy, 1809," the
last year he was there, and shows progress in more than
handwriting. He had learned to think in French, which

[1] To David Masson, who told D. A. W.
[2] See conversation of April, 1851, with Woolner and W. B. Scott.
[3] *Chelsea House Catalogue*, Item 15 (4), and *Some Personal Reminiscences of Carlyle*, by A. J. Symington, pp. 27–8.

made him familiar with forcible language, and strengthened the example of his father's emphatic way of talking. By one means or another he early began to deliver himself from the monotony of English and Scottish understatement, which makes much of our literature like the bleating of sheep. While thinking in French, the boy was also thinking for himself, and by no means as a Frenchman. 1809 was the year of Wagram and Corunna :—

'Why is the French language so universally studied ? The English is more nervous, the Italian more musical (douce) as well as more easy to learn. Why, then, is the French generally read and spoken ? I confess I cannot determine why. Still, one should remember that it is perhaps in truth a little more fashionable (un peu convenable à certaines bagatelles qu'on a nommé élégantes), and that for a long enough time the French have had the goodness to teach the fashions to the poor barbarians of the rest of Europe, and that the gentlemen of the Great Nation have said so often that their language was the best in the world that we English have at last admitted it—poor fools that we are (que nous sommes pauvres sots !)'

III

A STUDENT

(1809–10)

ON a dark, frosty morning (7.11.1809) when Tom was nearly fourteen, James Carlyle and his wife walked through the village with him and another boy a few years older, Tom Smail, and saw them start to walk to the University of Edinburgh. Smail had been there before and was to find lodgings for both ; and they put Tom " in the charge of a very decent man who was driving two carts of potatoes up to Edinburgh," and who let the boy when he was tired " lie on the potatoes " under " some sort of covering." [1] Thus they passed through Moffat and climbed out of Annandale in the daylight. In passing Erickstane Hill, Tom looked back and saw the last of Burnswark ; and went aside to look at the hollow where Annan springs. A mile or two further on was the source of the Tweed.

Tom was full of hopes that bespangled like a rainbow the tears of separation ; but he had " very small respect " for Smail, " knowing him to be of no scholarship or strength of judgment," and finding him wearisome, " with nothing to say when questioned." Smail stalked on ahead and whistled. On the third day they started with only twenty miles in front of them, and entered Edinburgh between two and three. They found lodgings in Simon Square behind Nicolson Street, and after a hasty meal hurried out to make the most of the short winter day, and see the wonders of the High Street.

They saw St. Giles High Kirk and the Luckenbooths (or " Lock-up ") and entered Parliament House itself— the " Westminster Hall " of Scotland. It was full of busy crowds, judges in red velvet sitting in the various elevated seats on one side, advocates in black gowns and wigs eagerly speaking, striving to be audible above the noises ; while " wildly plangent lamentable sounds " pierced the ear at

---

[1] W. Allingham, *A Diary*, p. 279.

intervals, from the " Criers of the Court," perched up aloft, " like swallows in their nests." A little daylight came through the big windows, and candles were burning here and there. Among the leading lawyers, John Clerk's face impressed the boy—" a grim strong countenance with its black far-projecting brows and a look of great sagacity."

In a day or two he was attending the Latin and Greek classes. In the dimly lighted Latin classroom Professor Christison was unable to distinguish him from a bigger Carlyle, " the worst Latinist of all my acquaintance," said Tom, who was vexed. Before Christmas, at the funeral of Dr. Adam of the High School, Tom was one of the boys who " hung on by the railings outside." Another day he was going down Leith Walk towards the sea. In front of him a " solid quiet-looking countryman " was going in the same direction, when suddenly faced and stopped by a drunken sailor, who needed the whole breadth of the foot-path and wanted to fight. " Go to Hell ! " said the sailor. " 'O'd man," said the other gently, as if pleading a prior engagement, " I'm gaun to Leith," and passed on evading the sailor, followed by Tom who was full of admiration.[1]

The pugnacity seen by Borrow in an Edinburgh play-ground had a verbal vent at college in meetings of " Debating Societies." The reports of " speeches " by our Tom are mythical—neither his nor any other boy's palaver survives ; but long afterwards he told Moncure Conway, discussing the " Survival of the Fittest " :—" What they call Evolution is no new doctrine. I can remember when Erasmus Darwin's *Zoonomia* was still supplying subjects for discussion, and there was a debate among the students whether man was descended from an oyster or a cabbage. I believe the oyster carried the day." [2] Carlyle's recollections are confirmed by Samuel Smiles, who was then a bright boy running about Haddington, one Dr. Welsh the family doctor. He came to Edinburgh as a medical student and attended the lectures of Dr. Fletcher, and tells us : [3] " When the works of Darwin afterwards came out, I felt that Fletcher had long before expounded very much the same views," as Charles Darwin would be sure to know, when he came to Edinburgh as a student in 1825.

[1] David Masson's *Edinburgh Sketches and Memories*, pp. 228–9.
[2] Moncure Conway's *Thomas Carlyle*, p. 84. There are references to these societies in letters of T. C. which came to light after D. Masson had written his *Edinburgh Sketches*.
[3] *Autobiography of Samuel Smiles*, p. 35.

In an earlier draft of what is in *Sartor*, it is said of the university : [1] " Spiritual liberty was admitted in its broadest sense. He was left to choose his own society and form his own habits, and had unlimited command of reading. What a wild world rose before him as he read, and felt, and saw, with as yet unworn avidity." He found " solitude exasperating. A keen and painful feeling of his own weakness, added to a certain gloomy consciousness of his real intrinsic superiority, rendered him at once suspicious and contemptuous of others." Most of his classmates felt the same.

It was probably this year that he read Adam Ferguson's *History of the Roman Republic*. He always praised it, and must have been influenced by its example of accuracy, subordinating style and opinions to " facts." Sallust he also read ; and while his theory of heroes is implied in the Bible and Homer and Plutarch and many authors, his exposition of it is anticipated and may have been suggested by a fine passage where Sallust says the greatness of Rome was achieved by the supreme qualities of a few great men. [2]

He continued to read Latin for a long time, and found Tacitus as interesting as Virgil had been at school, but never cared much for Horace—" too egoistic and light in the touch." For several years he tried to esteem Cicero better than he ever could and decidedly liked him, perhaps for the same reason as Luther did, because Cicero was a good man who had done and suffered much.

The gradual discovery that the best of both Cicero and Virgil was taken from the Greeks may be why he said little about them by and by. At this time Tom was contrasting with admiration Cicero's book on duties addressed to his son with the only book of the sort in English, *Chesterfield's Letters to His Son*, which Croker praised as masterpieces, while Dr. Johnson said : " they teach the morals of a whore and the manners of a dancing master." The boy Carlyle was more reasonable than either. He reprobates the " pitiful disposition " of Chesterfield, " the flattery, the dissimulation and paltry cunning he is perpetually recommending " ; and yet with a blend of candour and irony in the style of Swift declares : " His directions concerning washing the face and paring the nails are indeed very praiseworthy," and might well be " printed " in " large type " for the use of schools.

[1] Wotton Reinfred, pp. 20–1. (*Last Words of Thomas Carlyle*, Longmans, 1892.)   [2] *Catiline*, Chap. 57.

The patron of Croker was in trouble this year (1809). As a son of the third George Guelph who was King of England, he had been made Duke of York and Commander-in-Chief of the English Army, and was now removed from his military job because a woman of his had been detected dealing in army promotions. In Hanover they had " elected " him Bishop of Osnabruck when he was one year old, for the same good reason the English had had for making him Commander-in-Chief—he was the son of his father ; and it may be added that his family influence saved him after all and he was reinstated ; and contemporary flunkies raised in his honour the " Duke of York Column," still standing in the Mall. Carlyle used to declare a pit-shaft would have suited him better—the great scandal of 1809 left its mark on his memory.

He had no sympathy for the " honoured guests " of Edinburgh " Society," the exiled Bourbons, accommodated with cheap lodgings in Holyrood Palace from 1796 to 1810. The only Scottish institution he ever thanked aloud was the Advocates' Library ; but he seems not to have had access to it till 1819. He resorted to private subscription libraries ; and the books he took from that of the university this session included a volume of Gibbon and Hume's *England* and Robertson's *Scotland ; Cook's Voyages* and John Byron's *Shipwreck in Patagonia ;* the *Spectator* and *Congreve's Works*, the *Arabian Nights* and *Gil Blas*, and three successive volumes of Shakespeare.[1]

Returning home in April (1810), Tom met his father on the road outside the village. James had been ill this winter, but was now convalescent, and walking out " with a red plaid about him " had taken the road to the north on the chance of meeting his son. The summer was spent at home. In 1810 the stripling of fourteen taught mathematics to a Major of over six feet, " and a very apt scholar I found him,"[2] said Tom, in boasting of it. That might not be till November, when back in Edinburgh

[1] David Masson's *Edinburgh Sketches*, p. 231.
[2] *Memories of a Long Life*, by Col. Davidson, C.B., p. 307.

IV

THE STUDENT'S AWAKENING

(1810–11)

RETURNING to Edinburgh with two others, he reached Moffat about 1.11.1810 ; and there they were joined by two more students, one of whom was a thick-set, sagacious fellow, Thomas Murray, on his way to college for his first session, but four years older, nearly nineteen, having been teaching school for more than three years to scrape together the few pounds needful. He tells us : " Young Carlyle was distinguished at that time by the same peculiarities that still (1849) mark his character—sarcasm, irony, extravagance of sentiment, and a strong tendency to undervalue others, combined, however, with great kindness of heart and great simplicity of manner. His external figure, though then only about fifteen years of age, was similar to what it now is—tall, slender, awkward, not apparently very vigorous. His provincial intonation was then very remarkable, and it still remains so ; his speech was copious and bizarre. With this gifted and ingenious person I lived on terms of affection," as abundant letters survive to show.[1]

His classes this year were Logic, Greek and Mathematics ; and in the last, Professor Leslie remarked his ability and recommended him to anyone enquiring for a tutor in algebra or geometry. Whereby " an old gentleman in Princes St." [2] became a pupil of his this year or next apparently.

From the University Library he took much more than what related to classwork, such as Locke's *Essay* and Reid's *Inquiry into the Human Mind*. The other books included *Voyages and Travels ; Scotland Described ;* a volume of Smollett and four of Fielding ; the Abbé Barthélemy's *Anacharsis ;* and a volume of *Don Quixote*.[3]

[1] From a small book privately printed in Dumfries, 1911, *Autobiographical Notes* (Etc.), by Thomas Murray, Edited by John A. Fairley, of which a copy was kindly given to D. A. W. by Janey M. Fairley.
[2] *Literary Recollections*, by F. Espinasse, p. 207.
[3] David Masson's *Edinburgh Sketches*, p. 233.

The summer of 1811 was spent in Ecclefechan. Success in obtaining pupils enabled him to take the coach between Edinburgh and Moffat, to hurry over the bleak monotony of the Upper Tweed Valley :—

' Alick used always to escort me as far as Moffat when I was going away, in my student days,' he said to Alick's son afterwards,[1] 'and to meet me at Moffat, when I was returning, and accompany me home. Once I had not been able to leave Edinburgh at the time arranged. I asked a passenger who was going to tell Alick to wait. He promised to do so but forgot. So Alick went home and was not at Moffat when I arrived. I got tea at the house of a minister ; who advised me in walking home to spend a night on the way and sleep at the house of a farmer, a friend of his.

' I walked on and came to the farmer's house. He seemed a churlish, insulting sort of a man. I spoke of things that might interest him but it was of no use. He remarked at last : " Those who do not do any work have no right to be a burden on those that do." I thought to myself, well, the night will be dark indeed if I remain under your roof. I waited a little, however, and then rose, and took my hat and bade him " good night." Then he made a great ado about my leaving at that time of night, but I stepped out into the darkness and walked away. The stars were looking down silently, village lights twinkling far-off and the hills looming weirdly. I reached the cottage of a shepherd and his wife, a decent old couple, who made me very welcome to stay. I happened to ask what sort of man that farmer was, and the shepherd answered, " Man, he's just a dirt ! " '

One day a subscription was requested from Tom's father towards " blinds " for the meeting-house windows. " What!" cried James. " You want siller to shut God's blessed licht out o' his ain house ? No, no, I'll give nothing for sic a purpose. If you had wanted more licht, it would have been a different matter, and I might have given you a subscription." [2]

Though Annandale is fair and fertile, the mountains that stand around and shelter it are near ; and so an occasional

[1] Thomas Carlyle, Bieldy Knowes, Brantford, Ontario, Canada, who wrote it down when he heard it, August, 1878. See *Mr. Froude and Carlyle*, p. 296.
[2] W. H. Wylie's *Thomas Carlyle*, p. 16 : confirmed by J. T. Wells.

storm sweeping across the valleys is not strange. Yet it is nearly always a surprise.

In the midst of one a man greeted James Carlyle—" Here's a fearful day, James ! " and he repeated for many years the answer—

" Man, it's a' that. It's roaring doon our glen like the cannon of Quebec." [1]

James had once undertaken to build at " Cleugh Brae " a weir in a narrow gorge, where the stream was apt to become swiftly a torrent after rain. On the day the wall was finished his man Easton saw him take a parting look at it and heard him say as if half to himself—" That will stand now through time and eternity." Scarcely was he home at Ecclefechan before the wind rose and rolled up dark clouds from the sea, and there was a deluge of rain—not a common downpour, but what is called a "water-spout." So next morning early James called Easton to go with him and they returned together to the newly finished wall. " The plaster had not had time to dry," said Easton, with sadness still in his voice after sixty years. " The wall was burst. He looked long at the ruins, and said as he turned away—' Well, well, I'll never swear by the elements again.' " [2]

Even such a wall as that was his religion. Already the waters were out ; and though to James it still seemed fit to stand " through time and eternity," the son of James was now to go forth to examine for himself, and find the doctrine of his father a dream.

What set him on enquiry was the discovery that men he respected were careless about it. [3] He asked his mother this summer (1810) :—

" Did God Almighty come down and make wheelbarrows in a shop ? " Which made her lie awake for hours, praying and weeping bitterly. [4] The next enquiry was a natural one for any healthy boy in the country who happened to read the " Song of Solomon,"—" What can be the meaning of it ? " And on hearing from her the orthodox fiction, which only the simplest of females can believe,—" How is it known

[1] Told to James Routledge in 1872 by the gentleman who heard it. See *Thomas Carlyle*, by Moncure D. Conway, pp. 17-18.
[2] Notes of John T. Wells.
[3] Statement in conversation to David Masson, in the course of a talk on Edinburgh men ; and repeated to D. A. W. by Masson. Corroborated by Dr. J. Beattie Crozier, repeating to D. A. W. talk with T. C. on this : and see his book, *My Inner Life*, p. 388.
[4] W. Allingham, *A Diary*, p. 253.

that it is symbolical, representing Christ and the Church ? "
Which shocked her beyond bounds. The sight of her horror
made him say no more. " I saw I must not," he said
afterwards, "and so I shut up my thoughts in my own
breast." [1]

This may have helped to make his next journey to
Edinburgh more dreary than usual. He seems to have been
alone after Moffat, and so it may have been this very year
that he had in mind when telling [2] how " after travelling
all the day, with no company save the great dumb monsters
of mountains, he rested at a wayside inn, and lay down to
sleep that night ' the most miserable being under God's
heaven,' " in his own imagination.

Assuredly he had to pay in full the penalty which Nature
exacts from the young whose brains have been bandaged
by " principles " which cannot be verified ; and when he
now returned to Edinburgh his mind lay open like a raw
wound to the humbug and sophisticated indifference to
truth and goodness pervading, like its smoke, that
" wretched infidel town." The offset for which he might
have been more grateful was less hypocrisy. The revival
of religion to keep the poor content came later. Intellectuals
were as rational as the philosophers of Paris, and almost
as frankly pagan. So many were pagan, however, without
being intellectual, that the prejudices of the boy remained
in favour of the pious ; and for years to come, as he had to
confess, he was reading *Evidences of Christianity* " with the
greatest desire to be convinced, but in vain." [3] He
never " revolted " against Christianity ; only, reluctantly
and gradually, disbelieved it.

[1] W. Allingham, *A Diary*, p. 268, reporting talk of 1878, and a letter
of 16.6.1875 from Mrs. Anstruther of Ballikinrain to her sister.
[2] *George Gilfillan*, by R. A. and E. S. Watson, p. 76.
[3] W. Allingham, *A Diary*, p. 232.

V

STUDENT LIFE (continued)

(1811–12)

THIS year Carlyle took Professor Brown's Moral Philosophy in place of Logic. Brown was much admired, and some budding preachers copied his " affected feminine delivery " ; but it nauseated others,[1] and none more than Tom, who heeded him little and afterwards spoke of " Missy Brown " as " a finical man—who used to spout poetry." [2]

This was his third year of Greek. Three years of steady work at it, twice afterwards resumed for months and often intermittently, ensured him a better grasp of it than usual. He was faithful to the traditions of the elders and had no misgivings yet about the value of Latin and Greek. He paid in full his tax to " contemporary stupor."

He was as well off as the average student, and had thrifty habits. Avoiding amusements which " pulled him down," he clung to the best he knew of the lads from his own locality, and had rare success in making friends of the right sort. After the first two years, he saw little of Smail, but a great deal of James Johnstone, several years his senior, whose diligent accuracy in book work he admired and imitated. Another able to teach him something, though nearer his age, was Robert Mitchell. Then there was a humorous fellow called Hill, who signed himself Peter Pindar ; Thomas Murray and Clint, and one Donaldson, " as careless, good-natured a being as ever breathed the air of this world," to say nothing of a musician, Andrew, nameless except as the " son of catgut," and " good honest Davie Graham," who took to the practice of physic.

It was remarked of " our Tom " that even then he " abhorred all affectation." The young men from the country were often aggressively rustic. As they could not

---

[1] *Autobiography of Sir Robert Christison*, p. 45.
[2] David Masson's *Edinburgh Sketches*, p. 235.

afford to be dandies, they jeered at those who could,
" affecting to be unaffected "; but that must have been
less of a pose with Tom than the rest, or they would not
have credited him with extra sincerity. He took a great
deal of walking exercise, and bathed in the sea whenever
possible. He was uncommonly clean, and too tidy, active
and wideawake to pass for a typical " Divinity." He lounged
like the rest in the booksellers' shops ; but he was never
mistaken for a " Book in Breeches."

Executions were public. The first man he saw hanged
was a Liddesdale Borderer, Armstrong, convicted of horse-
stealing. Through the boy's eyes he can yet be seen. " He
was a strong man, grimly silent. His body spun and twitched
horribly. I saw it before my eyes in the dark and in daylight
for weeks. At last I drew the horrible figure on paper as
exactly as I could, and thenceforth it ceased to haunt me." [1]

Another time it was an " old woman, a mere old wrinkled
wretched bundle." She was said to have killed a bastard
of her son. She cried—" You *cannot* hang me ! " The boy
through whom we look and listen explained this to himself
by recalling—she was " reputed a witch." [1] Perhaps she
merely meant—" You cannot have the heart to hang a
poor old woman." But they did.

There were gangs of footpads infesting Edinburgh. Once
they hit Carlyle, but only broke his hat, and ran away.
He saw three of them hanged.[1]

The Law Courts which supplied the gallows and filled
the jails were open also, and more exciting than now, for
Scotland was then a litigious country. Frequenting the
courts, where lawyers crowd "with gabble loud to argue
for a fee," Tom soon was familiar with the leading
champions, but he was not awed by any. He recognised
the good points of several, and particularly a dainty little
man he was to know better by and by, Francis Jeffrey,
who had "uncommonly bright black eyes " to match his
close-cut hair, and seldom wore a wig. Sitting behind and
listening, Tom would notice the jerk of his hair, and then,
he said, " I knew his brow was puckered, and his eyes
looking archly, half-contemptuously out, in conformity to
some conclusive little cut his tongue was giving."

Jeffrey's boldest flight he must have heard reported.[2]
Defending a clergyman accused of drunkenness before the

[1] W. Allingham, *A Diary*, pp. 219, 220.
[2] *Life of Lord Jeffrey*, by L. Cockburn, I, pp. 179–84.

G

General Assembly, on failing to shake the evidence, Jeffrey extenuated the offence.—" Is there a single reverend gentleman in the House who can lay his hand on his heart and say that he has never been overtaken by the same infirmity ? " Shouts of " Order " and loud demands for apology and rebuke interrupted the orator, who stood till the uproar subsided and then went on " with a half-innocent, half-cunning air,"—" I beg your pardon, Moderator—*it was entirely my ignorance of the habits of the Church.*" There was a general laugh and full forgiveness. He had been paying them the compliment of assuming they were all " gentlemen," and not ashamed to be as " drunk as a Lord."

Tom was now turning eagerly towards studies that promised to supply something he could be sure of. 1811–12 is the likeliest date for what was told " about 1869 " by a Dr. Nicholson, returning from the West Indies. " I was a student with Mr. Carlyle at Edinburgh in lodgings along with another, the whole three in the same bedroom. Carlyle took the *dux* prize in the mathematical class and the other bedroom companion the second. I observed that while Mr. Carlyle seemed to master the subject without much effort or application, the other had laboured at his problems with desperate zeal, sometimes sitting up all night at the task."

This being repeated to Carlyle, he corroborated the witness, whom he remembered and described, but added :—

" Nicholson was greatly deceived if he thought I mastered mathematics with ease or that it did not cost me much exertion. I laboured most intensely, and have gained nothing worth speaking about without the hardest of labour."[1]

In truth he had found then what boys want—an example. Conspicuous among the crowd, the figure and career of John Leslie were beckoning him, and Tom was trying to follow in his steps.

[1] *Observations on the Public Affairs and Public Men of England*, by David Buchanan, Sydney, 1871. Quoted in *Thomas Carlyle*, by W. H. Wylie, pp. 59–60.

VI

JOHN LESLIE

JOHN LESLIE was born in 1766,[1] the son of a cabinet-maker in Fifeshire. He took to mathematics like a duck to water, but his aversion to Latin was great. Though destined for the Church, he turned aside from it, and received from appreciative seniors, Adam Smith among them, such patronage as he in turn was giving now. He maintained himself as a tutor in Staffordshire, and for years abroad in Virginia, Germany and Switzerland, Norway and Sweden. What he was paid for a translation of *Buffon* is said to have laid the foundation of his pecuniary independence ; but it was mainly by thrift that he was able to devote his time to his favourite studies. Before 1805 he had invented his " Differential Thermometer " and obtained the Rumford Medal for discoveries about heat. In that year Professor Playfair was transferred to the Chair of Natural Philosophy, and Leslie became a candidate for the vacant Chair of Mathematics. But it was profitable enough to be coveted by many. So the " Moderate " party in the Church found a clergyman good enough for it, and by meetings public and private, by libels and abuse, they tried to make the Town Council elect their man, though no one disputed Leslie's superiority in Mathematics and Science. In writing about heat, however, he had referred politely to David Hume's theory of Causation, and this was made the excuse for calling him an infidel.[2]

The Town Council elected Leslie, and even in the Synod his enemies were defeated, as the Evangelicals saw in the case an opportunity to defeat the " Moderates."

In July, 1810, a few months before Tom entered his class, he made his most brilliant discovery, freezing water and even mercury itself by his air-pump, which makes us all his debtors to-day. He not only knew his subject, he

---

[1] Macvey Napier's *Memoir of Leslie ;* and Blackie's *Biog. Dict. of Eminent Scotsmen,* VI, pp. 416–25, etc.

[2] Lord Cockburn's *Memorials of His Time,* pp. 200–11.

knew whatever books could teach about it from the beginning. History was his favourite relaxation. He was a living encyclopedia of anecdotes, and had such knowledge of all sorts of antiquities that it was said you might talk with him all day without suspecting his special line. Least of all would that have been suspected from his style, which friends occasionally found too warm and metaphorical, feeling it strange, like tropical heat in east-windy Edinburgh. He must have influenced Carlyle in many ways. He had him three years in his classes (1810–13), and was the only professor Carlyle always spoke of " with real gratitude and affection " ;[1] but without any blinking of reality. There was no Mrs. Leslie to study appearances. The tidy boy could not help seeing that the clothes were slovenly which Leslie thought smart, and the hair dyes not manipulated with the same success as the scientific experiments—streaks of pink and green were among the youthful black.

Leslie was prosperous now and growing rich. But " the Worldly Hope men set their hearts upon turns Ashes." He thought himself young and engaging long after nobody else thought so. " There are as good fish in the sea as ever came out of it—I'll find a young wife yet," said another like him to a younger friend, and was answered,—"Yes, of course, but remember, the bait goes bad."

So busy a man had little lesiure for " Society," and when he did go into company, the women, " punctilious " in their " flats and narrow closes," shrugged their shoulders and voted him too careless and abrupt. The girls said his teeth projected too much. It was not for want of use. He loved his food so well that even in his forties his knees were unsteady under the weight they bore and his chin was multiplied. He was no hero to behold ; yet a good observer [2] at Jeffrey's dinner-table admired his flashing eyes. But that was in genial company. He has been seen to enter a fashionable " rout " " with a large moss-rose in his bosom," and after merely bowing to one or two stand near the fireplace " in an attitude of fixed abstraction," to the immense amusement of Jeffrey and some ladies watching him.

[1] D. Masson's *Edinburgh Sketches*, p. 236. After writing that book, Masson discovered A. Carlyle still had many of his uncle's class-tickets, and referred to him ; and A. C. found he had the 1812–13 mathematics ticket. As for Leslie, see also *Literary Recollections*, by F. Espinasse, p. 207, etc.

[2] J. G. Lockhart's *Peter's Letters to his Kinsfolk*, I, pp. 69 and 302–9.

Who knows what " might-have-beens " were before his " mind's eye." If he could not say with Confucius that " in eagerness to learn he forgot his food," he might truly have repeated the rest—that " in the joy of attaining knowledge he forgot his sorrows and did not even notice that old age was coming on."

He was one of the models of Teufelsdröckh.

VII

OTHER PROFESSORS AND TEACHERS

THE summer of 1812 was partly spent in Edinburgh. In the following session, his last in mathematics, Tom was easily first in the Natural Philosophy class as well, but the professor, Playfair, held him stiffly at a distance. " Many and many a time," Tom used to say, " when the class was called together, it was found to consist of one individual, to wit, of him now speaking. Still oftener, when others were present, the only person who had at all looked into the lesson was the same humble individual. I remember no instance in which these facts elicited any note or comment from that Instructor."

Playfair was about sixty-six years of age, and busied in wide scientific speculations. He would probably have been thankful if that solitary student had been absent with the others. He once asked him to translate a mathematical paper. Tom worked at it through the whole of a Sunday, and it was " received without remark or thanks." When Tom called to take leave, he received the usual formal certificate given to a good student. " Then he rang a bell, and ordered a servant to open the front door for me, without the slightest sign that I was a person whom he could have distinguished in any crowd."

Carlyle used afterwards to say he suffered from shyness. Perhaps this was an instance of that. When he found himself the only student at a lecture, he should have risen and politely begged the professor not to proceed for his sake only, and so on. Whereby he would have had a private talk and deserved some favour. Instead of which, " the exacting prig," Playfair would feel, produced his notebook and sat ready. In giving him the usual certificate, that he had " made good proficiency," Playfair paused and intercalated " I have reason to know," a " delicate distinction " Tom used to quote and laugh at, but not a laughing matter at the time to a fellow depending on teaching. Yet one can feel for the professor too. He was sincere. " I have reason to know "—haven't I, indeed—only too good reason ! [1]

The only other class in the session 1812-13 seems to have been chemistry, of which he used always to speak warmly as " the most brilliant and fascinating of the physical sciences." [2]

The summer following (1813) was the last he spent in the " auld house " in the garden at Ecclefechan, the original of the cottage in *Sartor*. It was dear to him and more than once revisited in later years, but like all who dwelt in it, vanished to-day.

He had now completed his course in " arts," and returned in November to " qualify for the pulpit," for which his father and mother intended him. But he saw the Divinity Hall was a " melancholy and unprofitable corporation " ; and used to mimic " very comically " the " extremely emphatic and dogmatic " professor there presiding, with " a face red like the setting sun on a misty day—such a man speaking of the ethereal and heavenly ! " The fellow was most in his element when describing Hell and embroidering the scriptures thus :—

" The Devil, after succeeding in his vile machinations, retires to his infernal den and grins with horrid satisfaction." [3]

Tom also grinned, but departed, and decided to take the slowest road to professional Christianity by doing six nominal sessions with trial discourses instead of four full sessions in that place. He took Jameson's Natural History this year, and used to tell how Jameson would run off the rails, quoting " Dante and other odd fellows," and then abruptly return to business with : " And now, gentlemen, we will proceed with the order Glires " (dormice). [4]

By this time he was making more use than ever of the libraries. [5] It cannot be said the University made reading easy. Its library was in an old building on one side of the quadrangle, not open all day, and lacking a catalogue. The clergyman who was " Librarian " took the pay as a

[1] David Masson's *Edinburgh Sketches*, p. 238. For what follows, *Ibid*, pp. 250-2.
[2] *Literary Recollections*, by F. Espinasse, p. 207.
[3] W. Allingham, *A Diary*, p. 232, confirming Masson as to Divinity lectures. For the professor, see W. H. Wylie's *Thomas Carlyle*, p. 346.
[4] Told David Masson, who told D. A. W.
[5] *Literary Recollections*, by F. Espinasse, p. 207. David Masson's doubts as to whether T. C. was in Edinburgh this winter (1813-14), *Edinburgh Sketches*, p. 252, were ended by the discovery of a class-ticket afterwards.

perquisite and did nothing. A fat Highlander with even less weakness for letters was in command, and considered students his natural enemies. In 1814 Tom was a six-footer and a good witness of what used to happen as he stood in queue at the door, and what he said he saw was as funny as a farce. At the appointed hour the students began battering the door and the Highlander opened it slowly, slowly. He could not use his feet or his fists to show his love for his foes, but he did what he could as they crowded in—he bent his body at the last moment to send sprawling as many of them as possible.[1]

Of all the books Carlyle got out, perhaps the Shakespeare volumes were the most important for him. He seems to have discovered him for himself. No teacher nor professor named him. Even David Hume did not mention Shakespeare among his " great poets," and dismissed him in his history as a barbarous genius, lacking learning, taste and elegance. In spite of which Carlyle luxuriated in the plays and recommended them to others. When by and by he discovered Goethe's admiration for his favourite, that would corroborate his convictions about Goethe—his faith in Shakespeare was already fixed and even Goethe could hardly make it more.

" From the chaos of that library," says Teufelsdröckh, " I succeeded in fishing up more books, perhaps, than had been known to the very keepers thereof. The foundation of a literary life was hereby laid : I learned, on my own strength, to read fluently in almost all cultivated languages, on almost all subjects and sciences ; farther, as man is ever the prime object to man, already it was my favourite employment to read character in speculation, and from the writing to construe the writer."

To Norton he once said :[2] " I remember reading Franklin's *Treatise on Electricity* when at college, a quarto volume which I found in the college library, and there was no book that I read at that time which made a deeper impression on me. I count him among the most sensible of the sons of men, a very large and open mind, with a gift of genius which could do its work with a sixpenny worth of string and an old key, while the French philosophers were building a tower to get at the clouds." The highest praise he could think of for Emerson's *English Traits* was : " I believe it

---

[1] David Masson's *Edinburgh Sketches*, p. 241.
[2] *Letters of C. E. Norton*, I, pp. 326–7.

to be worth all the books ever written by New England upon Old. Franklin might have written such a thing (in his own way) ; no other since ! "

From the free use of capitals [1] to reticence about religion there was much in the precepts and practice of Franklin that reappeared in Carlyle. For example, it was from the Preface to the 1750 *Almanack* that Carlyle seems to have copied a well-worn metaphor comparing money-profits to pudding ; and the Yankees can claim that Franklin did as much as the Quakers to start his " Gospel of Silence." Franklin preached it less ; but he practised it to perfection. Biographers say his longest speech took less than a quarter of an hour.

The Gospel of Silence, by the way, comes natural to mathematicians, for in no business so much as in theirs is the popular vote negligible as sure to be wrong. It goes naturally, too, with Franklin's opinion, that " the world is full of fools and fainthearts," but that great commonplace may be prehistoric, for it is a proverb in *Don Quixote*, and as palpably true as the Axioms of Euclid. It was familiar to Carlyle before he read Franklin. Esteem for libraries, too, he may not have needed to learn ; but disesteem for Latin and Greek was certainly a new idea to him, and it was only after many years that Carlyle assimilated that opinion of the Sage of Philadelphia.

[1] Many modern reprints of Franklin replace his capitals with small letters according to our present custom.

VIII

THE MORNING OF LIFE

(1814)

PRINCES STREET was then the fashionable afternoon promenade. From east to west and west to east went the lively crowd, many-coloured, many-voiced, and sprinkled with a ripple of laughter like the songs of the birds in the spring. The best men in the town were often there, and the young women always conspicuous, " elegant, polite." There was harmony in the hum of their voices, and a natural rhythm in the movement of the crowd, which made it pleasant to be among them, and convenient for a stranger who wanted to see easily the men who were talked about then or the women who were decorating the world ; but unless you were a passing stranger, you felt odd if not well-dressed ; and that was why there were never many students Carlyle said[1] :—

'I never could afford to promenade there ; and only a few times happened to float leisurely through, on my way elsewhither. Which perhaps makes it look all the brighter in far-off memory, being so *rare*. On an April Saturday of 1814 an elder comrade and I passing along Princes Street from the west beheld the promenade in all its beauty, in its sunny gaiety, growing ever denser as we proceeded. Not far from the Register Office' where, as usual, the swirl was thickest, the surplus of it escaping like spray into the side streets, he 'nudged me, and murmured— "Isle of Palms ; Wilson." I looked. A very tall, strong-built and impetuous-looking young man, age perhaps about twenty-eight, with a profusion of blond hair, with large flashing countenance of the statuesque sort, flashing pair of blue eyes, which were fixed as if on something far off, was impetuously striding along, regarding nobody to right

---

[1] MS. of T. C., edited by A. C., *Nineteenth Century Mag.*, 1920, January, pp. 103–17.

or left. We followed this figure looking over one's shoulder, and saw the head eminent above the general level for some considerable distance.'

Carlyle read the *Isle of Palms* with little admiration. Poetry was in fashion then, and he read a good deal of it. Among living writers, he liked Scott and Byron best of all. Mathematics and science had been his conscious work, but literature was his delight ; and Bossut's *History of Mathematics* was relieved by humaner histories and novels. He thought *Waverley*, when it came out this year, the best novel published these thirty years.

In debating societies or in private, the talk of " our Tom " was admired by many, who prophesied for him fame and fortune, calling him " the Dean " or " Jonathan," as if he were another Dean Swift. The Press was replacing the Pulpit as an " upward road " for genius. The fame of Burns and Byron and Scott was turning many heads, and making " Literature " seem a short cut to gain and glory. It was more so in Edinburgh than anywhere else, especially since the *Review*, which Jeffrey was editing there, began to awaken Britain and give a lead to those who believed in progress.

Nobody did more than Thomas Murray to foster in Carlyle by contagious example enthusiasm for literature, and Murray never repented it, declaring when old : " I would rather have been Homer than Alexander, rather Addison than Marlborough, and rather Burns than any man of his age."[1] At this time he tells us,[2] "My friend, Mr. Carlyle, had, like myself, got employment in town as a private teacher, and he and I spent our leisure hours together. He literally devoured books. He read through Chalmers' edition of the *British Essayists*, forty-five volumes, without interruption. His reading was miscellaneous ; but he preferred works of sentiment, such as the *British Essayists*, Shakespeare, the English poets, Burns, etc. He was not given to history or metaphysics. At college he excelled eminently in mathematics, and gained the friendship of Professor Leslie, and was like myself a frequent contributor to the *Dumfries Courier*."

About the time Carlyle saw Wilson, he and Davie Graham convoyed Bob Mitchell on his way to Linlithgow ; and after

[1] *Autobiographical Notes* (etc.), by Thomas Murray, edited by John A. Fairley, 1911, p. 30. [2] *Ibid*, p. 21.

parting from him went to Gogar,[1] where they found Andrew, "Son of Catgut," and after "considerable trouble," persuaded him to admit them to where he was living, content with no companion but his fiddle. "The most considerable of his movables," wrote Carlyle, describing his hut to Mitchell, "were a chair wanting a back, a joint-stool, eight potatoes, and a pot of brimstone: but to give you any idea of this den, its innocent inhabitant, and its villainous smells is impossible. And yet Andrew, good, easy man! shrugging up his shoulders, told us 'he was living like the ancients.' With all his oddity he is a good, honest lad."

It is easy to guess that the two students who forced their company upon the "Son of Catgut" had come with charitable intentions; and to anticipate a little, the ensuing winter was the last he lived in the manner of the ancients in Scotland. In spite of Tom's dissuasions he resolved to try life in the manner of the Americans, and went to see them; and our last sight of him is on the road to Greenock to embark, his box sent in advance with the fiddle in it, whatever else might be lacking. Tom wrote to Mitchell: "The Yankees are long-headed personages, and Andrew is a simple man. But he can fiddle, he can dig, and to beg he is not ashamed." So he went his way and is seen no more.

Here is another letter to the same :—

'30th April, 1814.

'Were I disposed to moralise, there is before me the finest field that ever opened to the eye of mortal man. *Nap the Mighty*, who, but a few months ago, made the sovereigns of Europe tremble at his nod; who has trampled on thrones and sceptres, and kings and priests, and principalities and powers, and carried ruin and havoc and blood and fire, from Gibraltar to Archangel. *Nap the Mighty is*— GONE TO POT ! ! !

'"I will plant my eagles on the towers of Lisbon. I will conquer Europe and crush Great Britain to the centre of the terraqueous globe." I will go to Elba *and be cooped up* in Limbo ! ! ! But yesterday, and Bony might have stood up against the world; now "none so poor to do him rev'-rence." "Strange," says Sancho Panza, "very strange things happen in the boiling of an egg."'

[1] Between Corstorphine and Ratho.

In the letter to which this was a reply, Mitchell described his endeavours to trisect an angle by simple geometry, and now he was told that was a " complete *wild-goose chase*," but even if accomplished nothing to an exploit Carlyle had projected. He had discovered how to bore a hole " right slap through the centre of the earth," and make an underground direct to the Antipodes. On such a switchback the saving of force would be worth much engineering !

In short, it is plain " our hero " may have been remembering himself when he wrote of Schiller that he was " conscious of the might that slumbered in his soul, and proud of it, as kings are of their sceptres."

A quarto volume in dark leather called *Collectanea Graeca*, a book of Greek prose, has been found with " Thomas Carlyle, student, 1814," written at the beginning, and these sentences at the end :—

' Oh, Fortune ! thou that parcellest out to man his lot of pleasure or of pain, that givest to one to feast upon fat things, and dash through life in a coach and six,—and to another to starve on his salted herring, and drive through life his Cutler's Wheel,—Bestow (if it please thee) crowns and kingdoms and principalities and purses and puddings and power, upon the great and the noble and the fat ones of the earth : Grant me that with a heart of independence, unseduced by the world's smiles, and unbending to its frowns, I may attain to literary fame.

' And though starvation be my lot I will smile that I have not been born a king ! ! ! ' [1]

" I am surprised at this," said David Masson, " but considering his letters it is plain he wrote it ; yet in later years I well remember that I have many a time heard him talk with scathing scorn of any desire for fame." [2] He was reminded of St. Augustine confessing he was prone to reprimand in others any fault he had corrected in himself ; and the parallel seemed perfect.

Fault-finding seems a virtue to Christian saints, and in 1814 Carlyle was looking forward to the pulpit as a profession. He attended the General Assembly this year as an apprentice actor might go to see a play, and studied the star performers, Dr. Chalmers and many more, with an

---

[1] *Thomas Carlyle*, by Rev. John Wilson, p. 8.
[2] To D. A. W. See also D. Masson's *Edinburgh Sketches*, pp. 247–8.

attentive ear to elocution, and particular heed to Jeffrey, because the whole of Dumfriesshire had been talking for a year of Jeffrey's success in humbugging a jury into acquitting a poisoner, who had plainly finished a farmer and his family, cats and all.

The General Assembly did not monopolise his mind. The curtain was rising in Vanity Fair. The young men still had about them the freshness of the morning of life, but they were scattering. Johnstone had been some years at Selkirk, reading theology for the secession pulpit under that amazing George Lawson, whose kind, shrewd features and Socratic pug-nose Tom sometimes saw in the pulpit at home. Lawson had the whole of the Bible by heart, English, Hebrew and Greek, "except one or two chapters" of genealogy, and yet was less of a man of one book than John Wesley, for he read his Gibbon and Aristotle, Epictetus and Marcus Aurelius, and many more. He was in his study one day when the maid came in screaming, " The house is on fire," and he answered, " Go and tell your mistress; you know I have no charge of household matters." He was a popular preacher, too, and a Bible-Christian of the highest type; but he could not shape James Johnstone into his likeness. James could not swallow his creed, and continued a teacher. Clint was settling at Lochmaben, with a wife. Poor Hill was less lucky; his woman had been in a " bad, shy humour," he confessed, but he repelled sympathy from Tom, remarking: " There are joys and sorrows, pleasures and pains, with which a stoic, platonic, humdrum, bookworm sort of fellow like you, sir, inter-meddleth not, and consequently can have no idea of."

Another offer of sympathy provokes Hill to give him advice (May, 1814) :—

'You seem to take a friendly interest in my *affaires de cœur* (love affairs). By the by, now, Jonathan, without telling you any particulars of my situation, can't I advise *you* to fall in love ? Granting as I do that it is attended with sorrows, still, Doctor, these are amply compensated by the tendency that this tender passion has to ameliorate the heart, " provided always and be it further enacted," that, chaste as Don Quixote or Don Quixote's horse, your heart never breathes a wish that angels may not register. Only have a care of this, Dean, and fall in love as soon as you can —you will be the better for it. Write immediately a very

long letter ; write an epic poem as soon as may be. Fall
in love as soon as you can.'

Which gave Tom something better to think about than
worship-shops, while watching the star performers at the
General Assembly.

IX

TO ANNAN

(1814)

BEFORE he could send the long letter requested, Carlyle was within speaking distance of Hill. He had applied for a vacancy on the Annan Academy staff—Teacher of Mathematics, £70—and was directed to appear at Dumfries for examination by Thomas White, Academy Rector there and renowned for mathematics.

Thomas Murray escorted him five miles on the road. It seems to have been about May.[1] They were discussing their futures rather dismally, in spite of the fine weather, little delighted to be dominies, echoing Burns in saying to each other—" Few know us, fewer heed us, we'll slip through the world inglorious and unknown." It is a great comfort when feeling like this to know the other fellows feel the same. At Moffat Carlyle took coach ; and as he wrote to Mitchell :—

' While my right worthy *compagnons de voyage* (or fellow-travellers) were sunk in politics, post-horses, farming, etc., I took out my friend's theorem, and leaving the base clod-hoppers to welter on among drains and dunghills and bullocks and balances of power, I entered Dumfries *wholly disengaged from sublunary things ;* and wellnigh persuaded that an angle *might* be trisected.'

White selected Carlyle and invited him to breakfast, presumably Saturday or Sunday, with time to spare. In the course of talk the trisection of an angle being mentioned Carlyle remarked—" I have in my pocket the result of an ingenious young friend and fellow-student's attempts on the subject. 'Tis here."

White no sooner saw it than he started up and uttering a wildly accented " Aye ! " he left the room and soon

---

[1] " April " wrote Murray afterwards, by mistake.

returned with an armful of dim and aged manuscripts. "Look!" he cried, and sure and surprising enough the recent "discovery" of Mitchell was written there. Vain was it to say—"coincidence." "Impossible!" he cried, and loudly complained that Leslie had shown it to Mitchell and never mentioned White. Even mathematicians are only men.

On Monday morning the new teacher was at work in Annan.

H

X

THE NEW TEACHER AT ANNAN

(1814)

ASIATICS say the celibate teachers of Europe are an abomination, and that only married people should be allowed to teach. Be that as it may, there never was a teacher less minded to continue a celibate than "our hero." Till October he was extra busy, as he was tutoring children in Mount Annan house as well as "teaching school," and so could not write to the like of Mitchell, who needed screeds on books or mathematics ; but a letter to Murray in August would have interested Hill.[1]—

'The more I know her and her species, the more heartily I despise them. It is strange, but it is true, that by a continued and unvarying exercise of affectation, those creatures in the end entirely lose any kind of real feeling which they might originally have possessed. Ignorant, formal, conceited, their whole life is that of an *automaton*, without sense, and almost without soul ! Once, for instance, I recollect that to fill up one of those awful *hiatus* in conversation that occur at times in spite of all one's efforts to the contrary, and to entertain Miss M——, I took up a *Tristram Shandy*, and read her one of the very best jokes within the boards of the book. "Ah-h-h-h ! " sighed Miss M——, and put on a look of right *tender melancholy* ! Now, did the smallest glimmering of reason appear here ? But I have already wasted too much time on her and those like her. Heaven be their comforter ! '

"Mr. Carlyle" was not nineteen, and little suspected Miss M—— might not be listening to what he read, but merely watching him as girls do, and mistaking the suitable reply.

"Alas, how easily things go wrong !—"
A sigh too much or an ah ! too long.

[1] *Thomas Carlyle*, by Moncure D. Conway, p. 160.

98

His cousin and predecessor, Waugh, the Bailie's son, now learning medicine at Edinburgh, had been socially successful. Annan was a " rising port," adopting the current gospel of cash-values for humanity. Young " Mr. Carlyle," the mason's son, was like a governess, on the social " border-line," and expected to affect the deference which Annan's " somebodies" were ever ready—Oh, how ready !—to show to those " above them." He discovered too late that he should have invited invitations. He fumed at the airs of the "greasy *sons of pudding*" passing us by, as he wrote to "My dear Mit." in October, " with all the *conscious dignity* of beings of a higher and a fatter order." He quoted Horace for their common comfort. Burns would have been more pat—" I hanker and canker to see their cursed pride."

The more he felt like this, the more he fumed at the conventions "light as air but strong as iron" which separated him from the choicest young women of the place. We have to remember that Burns influenced more than his Latin quotations.

It was mainly for the respectability of the thing that he continued a nominal " Divinity." He told Mitchell this October, discussing their " trial discourses" :—

' My sentiments on the clerical profession are like yours, mostly of the unfavourable kind. Where would be the harm, should we both stop ? " The best concerted schemes o' mice and men gang aft agley," ' a misquotation for "best-laid " schemes, which is curiously like him, spoiling the rhythm. The letter runs on.—' I intended to have said something of the bigoted scepticism of Hume—but as I am convinced you see through his specious sophisms and detect his blind *prejudice* in *favour* of infidelity, I shall defer it.'

He addressed to Linlithgow ; but Mitchell was now a neighbour, at Ruthwell, between Dumfries and Annan, tutor to the children and boarders of the Rev. Henry Duncan, who met Carlyle at Mount Annan house about 24.10.1814, and invited him to Ruthwell. James Johnstone, too, was at hand, having quitted the clerical career and come as a tutor to live in the family of Mr. Church, a farmer at Hitchill, on the way from Annan to Ruthwell and Dumfries. There also Carlyle was received for his friend's sake, and soon was welcome for his own. Ruthwell and Hitchill were to supply the lack of company at Annan. He needed it. He was working far too hard, and in addition reading mathematics for duty and literature for pleasure, and keeping such hours as may be guessed from seeing him in a letter to Mitchell (24.10.1814), "*scratching* and writing" on a "cold stormy midnight," "semi-frozen" and listless in consequence, with " a *nose* as cold as an icicle and I daresay as blue as indigo." He was always daring in description ; but even taking the words in a Carlylean sense, if he did not get liver disease he deserved it. Mitchell had it already, a tall fellow like himself ; and the sleeplessness which was making Carlyle repeatedly change his lodgings to escape from noises is ominous. As yet he was conscious only in a dim way of some connection between his bodily condition and the difficulty of controlling his temper.

His pupils saw no sign of it. As the son of his father he felt bound to earn his wages, and his employers were well satisfied with him as " a clear and correct expositor," while the boys and girls were still better pleased because he was not a thrasher, an eccentricity rather tolerated than approved by those above him. " I remember him as very strict," a girl in his class said [1] fifty years afterwards, " but we liked him."

He rather admired than imitated a senior colleague, old Adam Hope, whose " brown, quietly severe face " had been familiar in his youngest years in Ecclefechan Meetinghouse—" an inexorable logician; a Calvinist at all points, and Burgher Scotch Seceder to the backbone." The juveniles beheld him with awe. He was author of a good little English Grammar, and had taught many of their parents and teachers. " A bony, strong-built man," lean and brown, with sharp black eyes ; walking about in his schoolroom, a " stooping figure," hands commonly crossed behind his back, with the ever-ready strap hanging over his thumb, and on his mouth a " settled grin " which seemed to say—" Nothing *good* is to be expected from *you*, but we must get from you the *best* you have."

" He was contemptuous of the world and suffrages, an extremely proud man." In addition to the Bible, " he did not know very much—Euclid, Latin, Arithmetic, Syntax ; but what he did profess or imagine himself to know, he knew in every fibre and to the very bottom. More rigorously solid teacher " there could not be, " a praise and glory to

---

[1] Mrs. Jackson, Ecclefechan, to Thomas Graham, draper, who, in August, 1895, repeated it to D. A. W., Mrs. Jackson being dead.

well-doing boys ; a beneficent terror to the ill-doing or dishonest-blockhead sort," and he did his best to " separate the known from the unknown or misknown in those young heads. He had a Socratic way with him," which in short was disconcerting. James Carlyle once called on him during the midday interval, and saw " three or four bits of boys sitting prisoners in different parts of the room ; all perfectly miserable, each with a rim of black worked out round his eye-sockets " (effect of tears wiped by dirty knuckles), the dominie delighting in the sight. In spite of which Hope may have been a good teacher to many, so that even in Irving " you could always notice something of that old primeval basis of rigorous logic and clear articulation laid for him in boyhood by old Adam Hope. Old Adam, indeed, if you know the Annanites and him, will be curiously found visible there to this day."

Such was the man who gradually agreed to the common opinion in Annan, that the " new teacher " should have the conceit taken out of him.

There were several teachers and classes in the large room, known as the Rector's, near the end or beginning of some lesson. The attention of all was suddenly brought to a point by Hope turning and speaking loudly in the dry contemptuous tone familiar and terrible to the scholars, but highly agreeable to them when he was addressing a teacher, concluding—" Mr. Carlyle, can you favour me with *a definition* of virtue ? "

What preceded is variously told. It is certain Hope ended with these words, and equally certain that the expectant silence which fell upon all when he finished was broken by Carlyle replying :—

" Well, sir, if you have no notion of virtue within your own breast, I despair of ever communicating to you any adequate conception of it."

There was a kind of general gasp at this, and a silence " that was felt " and remembered. Then the work went on and Hope and Carlyle behaved to each other as if nothing had happened.[1] But everybody agreed the new teacher had been " far too sarcastic for so young a man."

[1] On 13.12.1895, John Carlyle of Langholm, nephew of T. C. and son of his youngest brother James, told D. A. W. he had heard this in the Annan Market about 1860, and took the first opportunity to repeat it to his uncle Tom and ask : " Is it true ? " He was told, " It is true," and what is here recorded is what was thus vouched for. T. C. was induced to retell it.

XI

HENRY DUNCAN
A SAINT IN THE CHURCH OF SCOTLAND

THE disconcerting reply to Hope implied a great deal more than was readily realised—the " right principle " of wise Asiatics, that right and wrong are everywhere but can nowhere be fully defined in advance. Behaviour, therefore, is more like an art than a science, though partly both. A man should cultivate his conscience and live in harmony with it, and not be like a slave who does the bidding of another ; for no bidding can excuse a man for doing wrong, and even law should be disregarded when contrary to common sense and conscience. To this day these are fundamental principles of all good systems of law, including English Common Law, though often overlooked. The defects of our " law " are due to the shortcomings of judges and legislators, not wise or honest enough to minimise mistakes. It is a curious coincidence that many years afterwards in the Model Prisons Latter-Day Pamphlet and verbally at the dinner-table several times Carlyle was able to closure " Law dignitaries," and once it is said a Lord Chief Justice, by the same sort of answer as now dumbfounded old Mr. Hope.

To Calvinist circles in Annan in 1814 such a doctrine seemed as dangerous as to Papists—sheer " anti-nomianism," like the Quakers' " Inner Light." The orthodox were like a horse with blinders, shut in between the Bible on the one side and the senses on the other, groping their way in a moral twilight more misleading than the dark. But that was not the main reason why the retort of the young teacher to the old one became the talk of the countryside for a lifetime. Nobody heeded young Carlyle for himself, but because he was answering Hope and may be revealing the inner mind of Henry Duncan, whose house he was seen frequenting, and who was conspicuous to the whole of

Scotland then, and particularly to his neighbours in Dumfriesshire.[1]

No wonder they looked at him. In the Middle Ages he would have been called a saint. In 1799 he was a young divine of twenty-five and had a choice of two parishes, and chose Ruthwell on Solway shore, the poorer of the two, because its hungry, rowdy smugglers with the wild habits of the Borderers seemed most in need of teaching. Though he had no " means " but his pay as parson, he gave his predecessor's widow the standing crops which were his " by law." It was a time of famine, and he had been a while in a merchant's office at Liverpool, and had brothers in business there. So on his own credit he bought and brought from there a cargo of Indian corn, which was sold to the hungry at cost price, according to their needs, with less than no profit to the faithful minister, who also imported seed potatoes and in many ways multiplied the means of useful employment. His example was widely followed, and many empty stomachs were filled with a minimum of profiteering.

Till 1804 he was the ideal minister of " moderate " type, tabooing doctrine and preaching " plain moral sermons " and lectures. His people thought him far too dogmatic about the earth going round the sun, and when he spoke of the sizes of the stars he seemed to them to exaggerate immensely. But these were trifling faults in a minister who was unwearied alike in visiting and catechising, and in fostering industry, and in making his own thirty or forty acres a model farm.

In 1804 he listened at Annan to Deborah Darby and two other English Quaker missionaries ; and infected by their simple, childlike faith, or maybe that of the young woman he married this year, Agnes Craig, his predecessor's daughter, perhaps moved by the need of inner harmony and hatred of hypocrisy, he declared himself " converted " by the Quakers. Nowhere were they less esteemed than on the Solway. An English Bishop or Roman Cardinal becoming a Salvation Army penitent in London to-day

---

[1] There have been two biographies of the Rev. Henry Duncan : one by his son, the Rev. G. J. C. Duncan, and one by his granddaughter, Lady (Sophy) Hall ; and many biographical notices, of which the only one quoted in this chapter is in Blackie & Sons' *Biographical Dictionary of Eminent Scotsmen*, VIII, pp. 201-11.

The article on Ruthwell in the *New Statistical Account of Scotland* is by Duncan himself.

would not seem more miraculous. He had been able to become really what the clergy all pretended to be, but few of the " Moderates " were, a Bible believer, like Cowper's old woman, who " knew her Bible and who knew it true, a truth the brilliant Frenchman never knew." The natives looking on saw no need for the conversion and no particular effect of it. He continued to be the realised ideal minister, and his new notions about doctrine and the resurrection and miracles not myth but history made him none the worse. The common evangelicals began to be proud of him as a pillar of their faith, but felt he was not altogether one of themselves. He could not grow backwards, and never was a " narrow-neb." Nor was he altogether a Quaker, though boldly avowing his obligations to them. When Napoleon threatened invasion, and the young men would not volunteer—for nobody in Scotland ever loved the London Government—then Duncan gave a lead which pleased his people better than the Quakers. He was the first of his trade to become a " fighting " Captain of volunteers, not a Chaplain. He did what nobody else could have done—he raised a company of local men who knew the coast minutely. Conventional critics compared him to the sky in Hudibras—

" When like a lobster boiled the morn
From black to red began to turn."

But he never minded. He changed from black to red and red to black again as often as needful, sometimes twice a week, till the danger was past, and then he laid aside his shooting-irons. This was one of the many items suggesting he was one of the models of Teufelsdröckh, who had a pistol handy when alone and in danger, and was physically, as well as morally, like Duncan.

In devouring activity, the sleep as of a spinning-top, the likeness was lively. " Work " was the gospel of Duncan, as the best way to uplift the poor—which brought him into collision with strong drink. It was the one thing always plentiful in that smuggling district. Thus he became a pioneer of the temperance movement. He abated by written pledges the free drinking of whisky at wakes and reduced the number of public-houses in his parish. Perhaps the best argument for calling him a kind of Teufelsdröckh was his belief in journalism. It was a great thing then to be a gentleman. In the scramble for gentility the Established Church clergy were just getting their heads up, and as the father of Burns expressed it, becoming the last of the gentry and ceasing to be the first of the people. But nobody supposed the editor of a newspaper could be a gentleman. Whoever was not " people," he was. Great, therefore, had been the sensation in the county when Henry Duncan started the *Dumfries Courier* and edited it himself, which he continued to do till 1817, with Thomas Carlyle for an occasional contributor.

The man had no scruples but conscience. What will he be doing next ? was a common question. When Scott began to ridicule the Covenanters, he also wrote a novel to rival the Great Unknown ; but Scott could laugh at that. It was the solid Dr. MacCrie, the biographer of Knox, who made Scott change his tune, by convincing everybody that the " Unknown " champion of Claverhouse was foolish and wrong.

Duncan is best remembered for founding a Savings Bank, which set a new fashion of thrift. In 1814 his bank had several years of success behind it, and he was receiving many letters of enquiry, so that he was writing an explanatory pamphlet on his parish bank when he made Carlyle's acquaintance. The new institution needed legal protection, the *Times* and Cobbett cat-calling against it in chorus with some benighted bankers ; but Duncan went to London and got the support of his county member, and the tide soon turned. The transparent sense and disinterestedness of the man were irresistible, and Canning, Wilberforce and others guiding, the Legislature did right for once. Biographers say Brougham had been an intimate of his at college and remained a " lifelong friend," so that " to his last days " he " could hardly mention the name of Henry Duncan without visible emotion "—which is the best thing told of Brougham—one hopes it is true.

" Your grandfather," wrote Carlyle half a century after now to a grandson of Duncan, " was the amiablest and kindliest of men ; to me pretty much a *unique* in those young years, the one cultivated man whom I could feel myself permitted to call *friend* as well. Never can I forget that Ruthwell Manse, and beautiful souls (your grandmother, grand-aunts and others) who then made it bright to me."

Antiquarians know of the Ruthwell Cross which Duncan discovered in broken pieces among the graveyard rubbish. Its runic inscription gave them amusement for half a century before they could agree. Geologists remember his discovery of fossil footprints on the sandstone. Like another Franklin, he had the kind of mind that *sees*. Like Dr. Chalmers, he delighted in astronomy. But nothing said in the " Manse " was more interesting to Carlyle than what Mrs. Duncan told him about Robert Burns. She was present when he visited her mother there a little before he died, and heard him saying—" I am a poor plucked pigeon." She rose to let down the blind to screen him from the glare of the evening sun ; but the poet beckoned to her to let it be and said : " Thank you, my dear, for your kind attention, but oh let him shine ! he will not shine long for me." [1]

[1] For this anecdote, compare Lockhart's *Burns*, Chap. IX, McDiarmid's *Report*, and *Personal Reminiscences and Biographical Sketches*, by the Rev. J. Dodds ; and see D. McKellar's picture, reproduced in Lady Hall's *Biography of H. Duncan*.

XII

APPRENTICE PREACHER

THE new teacher at Annan was not so unlike his neighbours as he supposed. If not so regular in church attendance as might have been expected of the son of his father, he was only the more like other young men. His very doubts were common. Both Johnstone and Mitchell preceded him in resolving not to make a trade of falsely pretending to believe the Bible the " inspired word of God." But as yet he did not think harshly of those who, like most Scotch parsons then, and Voltaire's favourite, Massillon, taught morality without dogma, or in simpler words, saw fit to preach the Christian Gospel to adults " to make them behave," exactly as they might teach children *Æsop's Fables*. Even Henry Duncan had done that for years. It was not only the pay that made the pulpit then attractive. A popular parish minister could say what he liked. One Sunday, Carlyle was sitting with the rest in Mr. Church's family pew at Cummertrees, a few miles west of Annan, when the Rev. David Gillespie was preaching upon " Youth and Beauty being laid in the grave." The preacher saw him smiling and frowned at him and rebuked him, saying : " Mistake me not, young man, it is *youth alone* that *you* possess."[1]

Which might have hurt more than it did if it had not been untrue, as anyone could see. Whatever qualification for the pulpit Carlyle lacked, it was not " good looks," which even Luther had said were needed ; and in the meantime all the Divinity Hall required of him was a " trial discourse," which he found pleasant to prepare, and the delivery of it gave him a holiday in Edinburgh. The occasion was his first of the kind, and Mitchell's last. They came to town together a few days before Christmas, 1814. As an apprentice preacher, Carlyle gave a sermon on the uses of affliction (text, Psalm cxix. 67), which he described fifty-two years

[1] *Præterita*, by John Ruskin, III, para. 64.

afterwards as " a very weak and flowery sentimental piece."
But at the time he was delighted with the approbation of
the Professors, who had an eye to the credit of the pulpit,
and he was made happy by the compliments of other
apprentice " Divinities."

He stayed several days longer than Mitchell, renewing
old acquaintanceships ; bought Campbell's *Poems* and
got a supply of other books from libraries ; and wrote to
Mitchell : " The tympanum of my ears " was " nearly torn
in pieces with the war-whoops of the Edinburgh Hogmanay-
night." Which seems Carlylean exaggeration. " Hog-
manay " was 31st December and 1st January—the merriest
night in Scotland long ago, when the " first-footers," or
visitors competing to be the first of the year, made sleep
unusual till long after midnight.

Next morning, Sunday (1.1.1815), he was in " the gayest
humour in the world " as he took a seat on the outside of
the coach, the crisp air bracing the nerves like fiddle-strings.
He saw nothing but fun in the contrast between the " woe-
worn visages, livid noses and rattling teeth " of two other
passengers and " the *dread-nought* appearance " of the fat
guard in broadbrim and stout cloth and leather, " dis-
placing as he stood not less than twelve solid feet of air."
But in spite of his young blood and " shaggy great coat,"
he was glad to go inside before six miles were passed, and
do his best to dose the rest of the way to Moffat. There he
had to await the Glasgow mail coach, which picked him
up at midnight and dropped him at Ecclefechan. On
Tuesday morning he was in his place at Annan Academy.

XIII

1815

MITCHELL confessed to "ennui, torpor and hepatitis" or liver disease, which was afflicting Carlyle also now, but he did not know it, and blamed the "winds and rains." Carlyle had to suffer for several years to come from the common medical mistake of attributing to "colds" a sore throat and other such "symptoms." The treatment thereupon prescribed made patients worse, and especially when the sufferers were no longer young, killed many who would have recovered if left alone, and after years of suffering cut off Mitchell by and by in his prime.

As yet Carlyle was thinking little of health. In March he began his "Exegesis," a Latin discourse for the Divinity professors in December, on "Natural Religion," which in Edinburgh then suggested David Hume, who had written on it famously and was a local hero. The street where he built his house is still called after him—"St. David's"— a joke, of course. In sneering at him last year, Carlyle was merely echoing the crowd; but when he had to deal directly with a subject Hume had treated, he felt bound to read him, and Mitchell lent the *Essays*, with the result expected. The new "St. David" was too reasonable to be reviled. Carlyle did not become a "follower" of his, for never any man went after another more reluctantly. But long before that Latin thesis was ready for the Divinity Hall, he was feeling he might not be at home in the pulpit.

He soon was telling Mitchell that he liked the *Essays* of the infidel "better than anything I have read these many days. I am delighted with the book," so that he would keep it a while to re-read it, and knowing of *Sartor* one wonders whether a thing he read there may not have lodged in his memory, like a seed borne by the wind: "Art may make a suit of clothes, but Nature must produce a man." Hume "has prejudices," he declared, "he does maintain errors— but he defends his positions with so much ingenuity that one would be almost sorry to see him dislodged. His essays

on ' Superstition and Enthusiasm,' on ' The Dignity and
Meanness of Human Nature,' and several others, are admirable both in matter and manner, *particularly the first*,
where his conclusions might be verified by instances with
which we are all acquainted." This cordial agreement with
Hume against "enthusiasm" or zeal without knowledge
is a stage in the evolution of Carlyle. Like most of his convictions, this one was rather overlaid then altered afterwards, sometimes latent, and at other times obtruding to
the surface like primeval granite, but always there, and
explaining many an utterance otherwise perplexing.

In deference to Mitchell, Carlyle had been reading Dugald
Stewart also, and declared he "has done me hurt. Perpetually talking about analysing perceptions, and retiring
within oneself, and mighty improvements that we are to
make—no one knows how—I believe he will generally leave
the mind of his reader crowded with disjointed notions and
nondescript ideas—which the sooner he gets rid of, the
better ! I know you think differently ; but probably the
fault is " in the subject. Carlyle went on to Paley and
Locke. Akenside sent him to Shaftesbury, and maybe it was
Cicero that sent him to the Stoics. Molière and Addison
were recreation.

He was twice at least in Dumfries. In May he and
Johnstone went to see the foundation stone laid of the
monument to Burns, and laughed at the Ettrick Yeomen
" cantering and parading " and at the genial Fee-Faw-Fum
of Freemasonry. Another visit was to " hear certain wise
and faithful counsellors display their eloquence at the
circuit trials."

The news of Waterloo left him cold. He was under no
delusion about the characters of the men in power, and needed
no effort to be fair to the French. His father found that
peace meant less work for masons, and that the new custom
of advertising for tenders in the newspapers diminished
prices. " Honest trade is done," said he ; and as both he
and his wife were the children of farmers and they had a
large family, James took a lease of Mainhill, a farm on the
main road about two miles north-west of Ecclefechan ;
and it became the family head-quarters for many years
to come.

His father had no misgivings as yet about Tom's future
in the pulpit. When at last he found quiet lodgings at
Annan, it was in the family of Mr. Glen, the minister of the

" Burgher " people who used to come to worship at Ecclefechan ; and in common politeness the lodger attended
public worship on special occasions when he might be missed.
He had ceased to hope he could ever believe as they did ;
but that would rather help than hinder a professional
Christian seeking a " settlement." Most of the " Moderate "
clergy and the " patrons " were on the side of Hume against
the " fanatics." His slight sicknesses had been like passing
showers. " We were so cheery then," he wrote by and by
to Johnstone, recalling this year, " so busy, so strong of
heart and full of hope ! "

What troubled him now was only Mitchell's downright
refusal to go to Edinburgh again for " theology." He did
his best to draw him in December. " The prevalence of
infidelity is on the decline," he had already urged, producing
an argument as absurd as it was sincere, and all the more
revealing his own feelings. The local weavers and shoemakers were taking to it, which would destroy the " glory "
which was its attraction, and so it would decline. That
these poor men, tied to their looms and stools, might be
right, and he with all his study wrong—

> " A bookful blockhead, ignorantly read,
> With loads of learned lumber in his head,"—

was a painful thought to a proud fellow, and he put it away
from him as many another has done, and wrote to Mitchell
now as if he saw no sin but poverty, and were already snugly
feeding on the tithes. " You may change your opinion
about becoming a clergyman," and a visit to Edinburgh
would be pleasant, and it is more respectable to keep up the
appearance of " a fixed prospect in life," and " I shall be
uncomfortable if you refuse."

In vain, in vain. Mitchell let him go alone, however
uncomfortable. The force of example is mysterious and
immeasurable, and the talks of the young men are not
recorded. None can ever know how far Mitchell helped
Carlyle to deliver himself from the sophistries in which he
was meshed, so that at last his soul escaped as a bird out
of the snare of the fowlers. We only know that when he
set out for Edinburgh with his " Exegesis " in his pocket
he was uncomfortable because Mitchell would not go with
him. But happily the bad weather soon distracted his
attention by discomforts more material. " The web of our
life is a mingled yarn " in many senses.

XIV

A MID-WINTER JOURNEY

December, 1815

THE first day was according to programme, Tuesday, 19.12.1815, Carlyle on the top of the Glasgow Mail as far as Moffat. In the hotel an English " Popinjay " was amusing, being over-earnest about details of feeding ; and when he had monopolised the newspaper and was asked the news—" The Aachdoocs have returned to England," said he, " and "—with three loyal nods of satisfaction— " the Prince Regent is gone to Brighton."

The snow was falling next day and the winds whirling it wildly as the Edinburgh coach was struggling up past Erickstane. Carlyle and two Irish doctors got out and walked, the Irishmen delighted to reinforce by " outlandish warwhoops " the distracted bellowing of the coachman. The end of the day found them less than half-way to Edinburgh. They stopped at Broughton Inn, already crowded. Carlyle went into the kitchen and found it full of shepherds and carriers, and standing in the midst of them, " like a breathing iceberg," stood the guard, describing the hardships of the day. The roads were blocked. There was small hope of Edinburgh on the morrow if one stayed by the coach ! And yet the Divinity Hall was expecting a Latin sermon on the day after (Friday).

The Irish doctors seemed both " vain and stupid." One wore a Kilmarnock bonnet. The other was meagre and small, with parchment skin and mahogany complexion, like an Egyptian mummy, but for his " little fiery eyes " and the sounds he uttered and the music he made on a flute. When he heard there was only one bed for the three of them, the mummy quickly " took possession of the middle " of it " to make the best of a bad bargain." Whereby he had a maximum of heat ; but the pressure of the Kilmarnock-bonnet man upon his sides was too overwhelming for sleep. After a desperate struggle he failed to release himself and whined bitterly aloud—" *Marciful* Heaven preserve my *sowl*—what will become of me now ? "

Luckily for his bedfellows, Carlyle had urgent business in town. At 4 a.m. they had the bed to themselves. The wind was hushed. The moon was shining on a snow-covered land as he started to walk what in ordinary weather he would have done by noon, as it was less than thirty miles. But it might have been the last walk he ever took. A " roadman " he consulted suggested the higher road might be clearer ; but when he took it he found it obliterated altogether and soon was floundering on a trackless waste, at one time literally up to his chin in snow. A single false step might have cost his life, and many a man has died in that way in old Scotland. By eight o'clock the sun rose on him in the wolds of Linton ; and a shepherd showed the way to Noblehouse, on the main road. He arrived about nine at night—seventeen hours after starting, in time for his appointment at the Divinity Hall next day, and declaring : " I never was more happy at seeing Edinburgh."

XV

ENCOUNTERING EDWARD IRVING

(1815)

THE philosophy and Ciceronian Latin of his "trial discourse" on "Natural Religion" were praised by the professors and his fellow-students. But a disappointment was awaiting him in the week of holidays left. His "college cronies" had departed, "nearly to a man." Many months ago the "Son of Catgut" had gone to America, and he was not looking for him any more at Gogar ; but to find the others vanished and be a stranger was a sad surprise ; and he did not at first suspect the value of a new acquaintance he made now.

He was sitting one evening in the room of his second cousin, Waugh, when in came Edward Irving with a friend, Nichol—teachers both—but Irving from Kirkcaldy on a holiday visit to Edinburgh. Carlyle was the youngest and there naturally was something of careless condescension in Irving's manner when he turned on him a volley of questions about Annan. Carlyle told what he could ; but his answers grew shorter and shorter.

" Has Mrs. X a baby ? Is it a son or daughter ? "

" I don't know."

Two or three " I don't knows " to such questions followed in succession, and Irving said rather gruffly, " You seem to know nothing ! "

" Sir," retorted Carlyle, " by what right do you try my knowledge in this way ? Are you grand inquisitor, or have you authority to question people, and cross-question, at discretion ? I have had no interest to inform myself about the births in Annan ; and care not if the process of birth and generation there should cease and determine altogether ! "

" A bad example that," cried Nichol, breaking into laughter, in which Waugh joined heartily. " That would never do for me " (a fellow needing pupils).

Irving was hurt but did not recriminate, and there never was another " passage of fence " between them ; nor did they ever speak of this again.

114

XVI

NEWTON AND METAPHYSICS

(1816)

ARCHIMEDES said he could move the world if he only had a place to stand on. Men often feel like that. Something to believe is what the growing mind is craving for, like the growing body for food. The right object of study is to "grasp right principles," or see general truths we can rely upon.

Carlyle was groping among the evidences of Christianity, feeling as if walking among quicksands worse than the Solway's. What doubled his desperation was that the "young ladies" at Annan were cold-shouldering him, and he needed something to distract his mind. The natural creed for a healthy young man of the right sort at the age of twenty is that of Romeo—" Hang up philosophy, unless philosophy can make a Juliet."

Many of his contemporaries had been taught at home what had now been the faith of all sensible people in Scotland for a century, and of the few superior men for several centuries, but Carlyle had to discover for himself : " Heaven and Hell are for knaves and fools to talk about and timid women to believe. With health and a clear conscience a man is all right, and should quietly look at the dark, and not be afraid to go into it when his time comes."

The topic, however, was dangerous. Such a judicial murder as that of Thomas Aikenhead, a medical student executed in Edinburgh for a proposition in divinity in 1697, was no longer possible,[1] but talking freely about religion might handicap a man in courtship or business. So tabooing it was like a Freemason's sign among men, and in general a readiness to " talk theology " showed a fool or a knave, or at best a simple person. Something said

[1] See Macaulay's *History*, Chap. XXII. M. misses the facts that the victim was guilty of nothing but trifling indiscretion, and that the loathsome Lord Advocate, Judge and Chancellor were coolly contriving the murder to discredit the clergy, and did so at the expense of discrediting the bench.

to that effect by one Galloway, apparently in the " back-shop " of the bookseller, David Brown, made Carlyle describe him as " a small dogmatical teacher of mathematics—a wrangler of the first order—of brutal manners." As Galloway was a bigger man than himself, if not taller, so that in this very letter he was likened to " the rugged Russian bear," the bias is palpable.[1] The pugnacity of a Scot and a borderer made Carlyle a partisan of the pious all his life ; and he never forgave Galloway, who was friendly and will appear by and by endeavouring to help him. A wound to vanity is the hardest to forgive.

Nevertheless, Carlyle himself was now turning his eyes more than ever to the only direction in which he saw much certainty as yet, mathematics or measuring, glorified then as if it were a means of moral truth. The clergy had discovered that Luther might be mistaken in supposing Scripture conclusive against Copernicus, and Galileo right as against the Pope and his inquisitors in saying the Earth moved.

So the only book in the heap he brought from Edinburgh in January, 1816, which he could not lend to Mitchell at once, was an edition by some Jesuits of Newton's *Principia ;* and for the rest of his life he remembered as " the happiest time of his earlier years " the evenings in his lodgings after his day's work was over, when he sat up reading it night after night, often till three o'clock. He hardly heeded, but could not fail to notice, the hypocritical notes of the holy fathers, affecting to contradict whatever was heretical.[2] Newton appeared to him then the grandest of mortals, and even in old age he once declared he never came across any scientific discovery equal to Newton's Gravitation, though he had met " thousands " of greater men.

Plodding through the book, he sent for Delambre's *Abrégé d'Astronomie* to help him, and read Wood's *Optics,* and so on, feeling his way as when among the winter snows on the wolds of Linton, until he saw with delight the *Principia* " at his feet." For a change he read Crabbe's poetry and some Waverley novels, Lucan's *Pharsalia* and Fénelon's *Dialogues des Morts,* and other light literature, and dipped again into Dugald Stewart. His comprehension of Newton maybe gave him more confidence in his own judgment.

---

[1] Galloway's sister was grandmother to D. A. W., and his brother spoke of Carlyle to D. A. W. to this effect, while T. C. was yet alive.
[2] *Literary Recollections,* by F. Espinasse, pp. 207-8.

At any rate it seems to have been in this year that he definitely desisted from thinking about thinking. He kept an open mind awhile, and read and listened; and soon admitted Adam Smith was "one of the very few writers" who do not become "delirious" on metaphysics; but he had now come to a conclusion which grew stronger on reflection and became a conviction often afterwards expressed, but never more plainly than to Mitchell now: "When *will* there arise a man who will do for the science of Mind what Newton did for that of Matter—establish its fundamental laws on the firm basis of induction—and discard for ever those absurd theories that so many dreamers have devised? I believe this is a foolish question, for its answer is—never."

In other words, a man should see the dark is dark, and not dawdle in dreams or guesses, but turn from what cannot to what can be known. Impatience of idle speculation was the best habit he had learned from his father.

XVII

A DEATH-BED LESSON

(1816)

HIS mother was nursing at Mainhill this summer his youngest uncle, Tom Carlyle, a man of forty, prematurely aged, and suffering " a general break-up, mostly from hard work " and exposure.

Sunday, 9th June. Home for the week-end from school, Tom was allowed to relieve his mother in the night-watching. It was only too easy for him already to be sure he could keep awake. Even if sleepy and well, he could have done it for this uncle, as he loved and admired him much, perceiving him to be both affectionate and a passionate concentrated soul of " true old-Roman " type, without fear and without guile. It used to be said of him that he never " told any lie." There was no restoring sleep for him to-night. His nephew the teacher beside him did what he could in vain, and after midnight saw a change for the worse, it was death that was coming ; there was nothing to be done.

His uncle fixed his " bright blue eyes " upon him with a wild stare and tried to lift his head from the pillow, but could not. " The eyes kept wide open till life went out of them about three in the morning." [1]

Addison is said to have sent for his profligate stepson to show him how a Christian could die. There was something better to be learned at the death-bed of a natural man of the right sort, who was not showing off but going into the darkness quietly, undismayed, His nephew never forgot the lesson. He was still talking of it after sixty years, and had often said in the interval that it suggested the " Everlasting No " of *Sartor*. His passionate grief at the time combined with the excessive study of preceding months produced his first serious illness.

When asked, sixty-two years afterwards—" Had you any kind of orthodox belief in your mind at that time ? " he answered—" No, I had given up all that some time before, but I said nothing about it one way or another." [2]

[1] William Allingham, *A Diary*, pp. 267-8. [2] *Ibid.*

XVIII

A CALL TO KIRKCALDY

(1816)

FOR more than a month after the death of Uncle Tom his nephew was "extremely melancholy," and "confined to the house" two weeks with a severe inflammation of the throat. Long afterwards he said his lifelong sufferings might have been prevented—he needed only a wise doctor. The best excuse that can be made for his advisers in 1816 is that his appearance and his family history suggested anything rather than indigestion. Yet the case was not at all uncommon in Scotland among young men from the country sent to breathe the city smoke. His friend Mitchell was down with liver at the same time, and none in the medical trade to-day could make a better suggestion to either than Carlyle made to Mitchell in the middle of July, an excursion across the Solway, implying long walks and sea-bathing.

Yet his remarks were right enough, say the wisest doctors who studied his case later. He needed more physical work and less hard reading, with diet and drugs for the liver. He was suffering from the unnatural delay of marriage which makes the right sort of young man ready to rush into extravagant exertions, which Nature punishes impartially. If as in China he had been brought up to feel the duty of becoming a husband and father soon after twenty, he would have found a woman willing, for he was more than passable, and with a wife " to make him uneasy," he would not have wanted to sit up night after night till three o'clock, not even for Newton.

Mitchell suggested a vacation visit together to France, but he could not afford the money for that, nor the time. Professors Christison and Leslie, when asked to advise the Town Council of Kirkcaldy, had recommended him for the Burgh school there, and it had been settled that he was to go to Kirkcaldy in the vacation to see and be seen and accept if possible.

It was there that Edward Irving had been teaching " triumphantly " for the last five years, in a private school. The Council was being moved to put a competent man in their school as an alternative to him by parents who thought that Irving flogged too much.

"About the end of July " the wife of old Adam Hope died suddenly, and on the second or third evening Carlyle went to condole with his colleague and was received in silence, with a " thankful pressure " of the hand. A number of people were already there, including Irving, home on holiday, and kindly taking a lead in the wake. He shook hands with Carlyle in a brotherly way, as if an old acquaintance, continued arranging things, and finally conducted worship, reading the Bible and leading off a psalm. That done he more than ever amazed Carlyle by coming up and saying—" You are coming to Kirkcaldy to look about you in a month or two. You know I am there. My house and all that I can do for you are yours. Two Annandale people must not be strangers in Fife ! "

This seemed too good to be true, but when the time came, the fine weather, autumn's best, was no brighter than the hospitable Irving, who not only took him into his house, but introduced him to his big collection of books, and flung out both his arms and cried in a country phrase of welcome— " Upon all these you have *will and waygate !* " And he went about with him, introducing him. From first to last there never was a shadow of rivalry between them, only friendship, the best Carlyle was ever to know in a long life rich in friends.

The mutual inspections were satisfactory. The Rev. J. Martin reported upon the young man to the Kirkcaldy " grandees " (16.9.1816).[1]—

'From the conversations I have had with him, I am of opinion there are few young men of his standing who have directed their studies to greater variety of objects, or have acquired a more extensive range of knowledge. In respect, therefore, of the science and learning necessary to qualify him for being a useful teacher, you need not doubt of his being amply furnished. In regard to other particulars I can be no judge as I have had no opportunity.'

[1] *Carlyle and Kirkcaldy*, by David S. Meldrum, *Scots Magazine*, November, 1891, pp. 437–8.

So according to the " Minutes " they " recommended
to the Town Council to make trial of Mr. Carlisle for one
year from the commencement of his engagement, it being
his own wish as well as that of the meeting, not to engage
for a longer space, emoluments warranted to amount for
one year to £80."

The Town Council agreed ; it only remained to give
notice to the Annan Council and return to Fife in November.
He visited Allonby for a few days, but mostly abode at
Mainhill till the day of his departure (13.11.1816).

XIX

A MORAL STEPPING-STONE

THE only joke in Tennyson was not intended—an Irish bull.

> " I hold it truth, with him who sings
> To one clear harp in divers tones,
> That men may rise on stepping-stones
> Of their dead selves to higher things."

As if a man could put off *himself* like a suit of clothes. The Irish saint who swam the Channel with his head between his teeth was nothing to this. " The poet alluded to is Goethe," says the Rev. Dr. Getty. " I know this from Tennyson "; but though he had it in writing, too, neither he nor the poet ever found the passage, which is not strange, for it is not in Goethe. Tennyson seems to have been misremembering what Longfellow quoted from St. Augustine [1]—" We make ladders for ourselves of our vices if we trample them underfoot."

Which is more witty than wise. The human soul is more like a tree or vegetable than a ladder or staircase ; but if the staircase metaphor be allowed, Carlyle's confessions might be condensed into saying he was now making a stepping-stone of the love of Fame paraded in 1814, which had replaced his hopes of Heaven. It had not lasted long nor led him far. The materials he gave printers in 1814–16 were mainly mathematical problems ; and now he was putting " Fame " underfoot and rising to the Stoicism of Epictetus and the best of the ancient sages. The clue to many a Carlylean " eccentricity " is there, and chapter and verse might be quoted for almost every one of them— which may be left as a pastime to posterity.

He felt lonely, and liked it ; for " every earnest man," they say, " should learn to walk alone like a rhinoceros." Which is so far true that the heart knows its own sorrow and no

---

[1] *Sermon No. 3, De Ascensione,* say commentators of Longfellow's " Ladder of St. Augustine."

stranger intermeddles with its joy.   Yet even in feeling the
need to go alone, a man is not odd—we have all to do it,
less or more, and many feel like that.   Carlyle as a young
man was first-rate commonplace and hardly peculiar at
all, and had the sense to congratulate himself on being
saved in that way from many of the poet's temptations.
Indeed, he was seldom like Burns or Goethe's minstrel :—

> " I sing but as the linnet,
>   That's singing on the tree,—
> The joy that we find in it
>   Suffices him and me."

His utterance was generally either conventional or conscious
work.   He was typically Teutonic or English, and matter-
of-fact to a fault, requiring heat to melt into rhythm—like
the common man who needs something to loosen his tongue
and then chatters for company.   His likeness to the crowd
is precisely what makes Carlyle's example precious.   A
Burns or a Shakespeare seems above us like the stars ;
but to feel the way upward as Carlyle had to do is what
anyone can see and imitate.   He continued growing wonder-
fully ; but as yet and for a long time to come he was
merely like the best of his neighbours.

There was many a man of Stoic temper in Scotland who
never heard of Stoics.   The Uncle Tom who died this year
was a type of them.   Such examples were more persuasive
than precepts.   Besides, the sentiments Carlyle expressed
in Greek and Latin quotations from Epictetus and Co.
were often first inspired by Burns, as when the gist of
oceans of philosophic platitudes, with names as many and
beautiful as the seaweeds, are distilled into the sentence :—

> " Tho' losses and crosses
>   Be lessons right severe,
> There's wit there you'll get there,
>   You'll find no other where."

' The subject for the good and wise man,' said Epictetus,
in tones that seem like the echoes of them still to be heard
in churches, ' is his own master faculty, as the body is the
subject for the physician, and the soil for the husbandman.
And the work of the good and wise man is to use appearances according to Nature.   There is but one road to Freedom—scorn of the things that are not in our own power,
the body, possessions, reputation, authority, and in brief,

all that is not of our own doing. Things that are in our own power are our opinions, impulses, pursuits, avoidances, and, in brief, all that is of our own doing.'

To be really above "fame" or reputation is rare. To be below it is not uncommon. It may have been the remains of religion in his mind that made John Bright honestly surprised when Disraeli suggested to him they were both living for fame. It certainly was faith in Calvinism combined with hopes of Heaven which made Dr. Chalmers despise the "hosannas of a drivelling and degenerate generation." But Carlyle was otherwise inspired. At present he was seeking truth wherever he could find it, getting rid of the blinders that shut the mind's eye off from seeing more than one set of "Scriptures."

'Remember,' said Epictetus, 'at anything that shall befall thee to turn to thyself and seek what faculty thou hast for making use of it. If toil is laid upon thee, thou wilt find the faculty of perseverance. If thou art reviled, thou wilt find patience. And making this thy wont, thou shalt not be carried away by appearances.
'If thou wouldst advance, be content to let people think thee senseless and foolish as regards external things. Wish not ever to seem wise, and if ever thou shalt find thyself accounted to be somebody, then mistrust thyself. For know that it is not easy to make a choice that shall agree both with outward things and with Nature, but it must be that he who is careful of the one shall neglect the other.'

With a feeling that this was the temper to cultivate, Carlyle departed for Kirkcaldy (13.11.1816).

AT EDINBURGH ON THE WAY TO KIRKCALDY

(1816)

HE stayed ten days in Edinburgh. One wet morning he was waiting with his cousin Waugh on the top of Calton Hill to see a predicted eclipse of the sun. They saw dainty ladies waiting and cavaliers attending with smoked glasses, but nothing else—the sky was clouded. Another disappointment was the opening meeting for the session of a debating society. He saw " many new members " but " no improvement," and was amazed to find himself before they finished departing " with little regret."

He confided to Johnstone that when he quitted Edinburgh in 1814 he felt he was " leaving the fountain-head of knowledge and good-humour," but now it seemed " uninteresting and unprofitable. Our views of the world are perpetually changing as we sail down the stream." [1] And we cannot cast the anchor in the stream of life.

He crossed to Kirkcaldy and opened his school on Monday, 25.11.1816. He had comfortable lodgings in a house near by in the " Kirkwynd," recognisable still by its outside stair. [2] Between his school and Irving's there was only a lane, and beside them both was the house where Adam Smith wrote *The Wealth of Nations*. It was eighty years since Adam Smith had been a boy attending the " Burgh Grammar School." One of the youngest of Carlyle's pupils was Patrick Swan, in his ninth year but tall for his age, the son of the Provost, and fated to become himself a Provost by and by, and preserve unaltered the schoolroom in memory of his teacher. [3]

[1] Much of this chapter is from an unpublished letter from T. C. to James Johnstone, dated Kirkcaldy, 10.12.1816.

[2] A letter was shown to D. A. W. examining it, which came from a Kirkcaldy man who made sure of it by direct enquiry of T. C. on his last visit to Kirkcaldy.

[3] " A tablet was put up a few months ago," reports the Town Clerk (7.3.1921). See also a *Life of Patrick Don Swan*, Provost of Kirkcaldy, published at Kirkcaldy, 1893 : p. 8, etc.

EDWARD IRVING

IRVING had come to Kirkcaldy under twenty to teach boys and girls little younger than himself, and soon became "engaged" to an ex-pupil, the eldest daughter of the minister, Mr. Martin. He "qualified" for the pulpit, but had early learned from Adam Hope and the "Burghers" to hate the patronage that dominated the Church. So he had taken boarders, and hired rooms and aimed at supporting a wife by teaching. But teachers were despised then as "stickit ministers," and his "Bella" had no mind to be a teacher's wife. So by 1816 he was looking mainly to the pulpit, and had drifted into a "long engagement."

He was drawn to Carlyle from the first. They were often seen together, a pretty pair of six-footers—Irving several inches the taller and much the bigger man—walking on the long sandy beach, to the mild surprise and not quite to the satisfaction of pupils who would gladly have taken the new teacher's place. Irving had always liked to walk there, and never lacked company in the five years past ; but his preference for Carlyle was palpable.

When the sea was over the sands in the afternoon, they would walk in the fields and woods, or through the town and along the shore, as far as Dysart or Wemyss. They tabooed theology, according to the custom of good company in Scotland, but otherwise their talk was unrestricted, ranging from Gilbert Burns in Haddington, and casual mention of some Welshes there, through all the far abysms of time and space. Irving also had been a friend of Henry Duncan [1] and a favourite pupil of Leslie ; [2] and nothing delighted him more than to hear from Carlyle reports of his reading. From Edinburgh they got books of travel and science, poetry and history, to say nothing of periodicals. On Pascal's *Provincial Letters* they could agree as cordially

---

[1] *Dr. Duncan of Ruthwell,* by Sophy Hall, pp. 90, 91.
[2] *Edward Irving,* by Mrs. Oliphant, Chap. II.

as on Adam Smith—there never was a young Divinity less
of a Jesuit than Irving, nor one more resolute for demonstra-
tion and critical of mere tradition, so that Dr. Welsh of
Haddington had been heard to say—" This youth will
scrape a hole in everything he is called on to believe."[1]
He had far more " practical knowledge on things around
him " than Carlyle, and " a most hearty sense of the
ludicrous " with infinite " good-humour," and was familiar
with the shibboleths of " society." Three years make a
great difference at twenty—he influenced Carlyle more
than Carlyle him. " Such colloquies and rich rovings about,
in bright scenes, in talk or in silence," neither the one nor
the other was ever to have again.

They thought nothing of walking thirty miles, and often
went far in the week-ends, occasionally including a sermon—
Irving in the pulpit and his crony in a pew. " His voice
was very fine," wrote Carlyle afterwards. " He affected
the Miltonic or Old-English Puritan style, and strove to
imitate it ; to his example also I owe something of my own
poor affectations in that matter. We were all taught by
Coleridge, etc., that the old English dramatists, divines,
philosophers, judicious Hooker, Milton, Sir Thomas Browne,
were the genuine exemplars ; which I also tried to believe,
but never rightly could *as a whole*. The young must learn
to speak by imitation of the Old who already have done
it : the ultimate rule is, Lear so far as possible to be
intelligible and transparent, no notice *taken* of your ' style,'
but solely of what you express by it.

" Irving's style was surprising," and that was nothing
to the novelty of his matter—" actual practice : ' If this
thing is true, why not do it ? ' " Imagine a sermon in such
a strain to a Scottish audience on the text about turning
the other cheek to the smiter ! Irving was not allowed to
suppose that people approved such stuff. Kirkcaldy in
particular felt that he had " ower muckle gran'ner " (too
much grandeur),[2] and let him know what it thought ; and
when his prospective father-in-law let him occupy the
pulpit, he was sometimes left to look at many a vacant
seat. Once, when the church " was well filled, and all
dead-silent under Irving's grand voice, the door of a pew
in front banged suddenly open, and there bolted out of it "
one Beveridge, a baker, " who, with long swift strides, and
face and big eyes all in wrath, came tramping and sounding

[1] *Ibid*, Chap. III.   [2] *Ibid*, Chap. IV.

along the flags, close past " Carlyle, " and vanished out of doors with a slam."[1]

The angry man may have felt like a contemporary old lady in Edinburgh who listened impatiently to a divine declaiming in a drawing-room where she could answer him, and closured him with—" Ye talk, sir, ye talk—as if the Bible had just come oot ! "

[1] *Edward Irving*, by Mrs. Oliphant, Chap. IV.

XXII

A "SCENE" IN THE SCHOOL AT KIRKCALDY

WHEN Carlyle was famous many tales which might have made a Plutarch happy were afloat about him in Kirkcaldy and occasionally emerged into print.[1] His work was teaching boys and girls about twelve, as it had been at Annan, but here he was alone in his school. With fewer pupils he had more subjects : English, Latin and French as well as Mathematics. Traditions agree vaguely that he made the children work well with a minimum of noise and violence ; but only one of the tales stood sifting, a trifle but true, and useful as a peg for the fancy, like a fossil bone from which a naturalist may figure out a beast.

It was described in an after-dinner talk thirty-five or thirty-six years afterwards by the Provost of Cupar, who had been one of the boys present, and told it to Hugh Miller, without suspecting he was speaking of a famous man.[2] He had only pleasant memories of an uncommon teacher, who was " a strict and gloomy disciplinarian " and " stormed and walloped learning into me." Yet unlike Irving, " he did not thrash us either very often or very severely, but we had fear." He did " not need " to wear " his lum-hat [3] to alarm us, never wore his hat in the school. His brow was so overhung and his large glowing eyes constantly shot forth wrath, while his protruding chin was laden with scorn. I have seen his mere scowl hush at once the whole school. The biggest and boldest boys especially dreaded his grins and his mocking words. How savagely his teeth

[1] See *Carlyle and Kirkcaldy*, by David S. Meldrum, *Scots Magazine*, November, 1891, pp. 435–42. Local enquiries by D. A. W. in 1895 confirmed Mr. Meldrum's sceptical conclusions in general.

[2] In 1853. He was a lawyer, and then Provost of Cupar, where Miller was lecturing and being entertained by the Provost. D. A. W. is indebted to Robert Cochrane, Edinburgh, for newspaper cuttings. See also *Thomas Carlyle*, by Miss Cochrane (Mrs. Cuthbertson) pubr. Chambers, pp. 25–8.

[3] Chimney-pot hat.

were wont to grind out 'dunce' or 'blockhead.' "   Other witnesses say " donkey " was a favourite word.

'He had a grim smile in reproving pupils, and a habit of tapping their foreheads with his knuckles, as he told them their heads would never be worth the price of hats.

'One morning a few minutes before the hour most had gone into the school as rain was falling. Bill Hood and I (met) a donkey broken loose from its tether entering the playground. Bill rushed to mount it and guide and force it into the school with desperate spurring over the threshold ; and what a reception both of them got ! Bags of books were at once fastened to the tail and around the neck ; and so busy were Bill and half a dozen others *urging the brute to ascend the short stair of the master's desk* that they did not notice time.

'Mr. Carlyle appeared. We expected a tremendous explosion of wrath, but he burst into a roar of laughter, a very extraordinary laugh, a train of queer chuckling, which exploded in a succession of loud and deep guffaws, that shook his whole body and displayed all his teeth like the keys of a piano. That roar produced a sudden and complete hush, and was renewed again and again when the ass, withdrawing its forefeet from the first step of the desk stair and turning round, took a pace or two slowly towards the master as if to salute him. "That," exclaimed Carlyle, "is the wisest and best scholar Kirkcaldy has yet sent me ; he is fit to be your teacher." He tapped the donkey's head as he was wont to do ours, and said, " There's something here, far more than in the skulls of any of his brethren before me, though these skulls are patted in fond admiration by papas and mammas, and though that far grander headpiece meets only with merciless blows." He then gave some hard taps on Bill Hood's head, and would not allow him to dismount, but for a penalty ordered him to ride up and down the school, whilst those who had been most active in helping had to march in pairs before and behind.'

Seated in his pulpit-like desk, Carlyle was watching the grotesque procession, the other scholars doing likewise, when in came an old and ragged Irishman, seeking, as he said, " My faithful Pat," surprised and angry at the sight of books tied to the tail. While these were being removed, Carlyle complimented him on the donkey's brain-power and wisdom. He did not seem to understand, but admitted,

" Pat has a very big head which all the shillelahs at Donny-brook Fair would not break." With a puzzled look of mingled simplicity and shrewdness he concluded : " If master has a fancy for Pat as a scholar, and wish to taitch him mathematics and the globes, I will let you have the brute for a single picture," meaning a one pound note.

XXIII

A GENTLE PARTING FROM THE CHURCH

(1817)

A T Kirkcaldy he was more comfortable than at Annan, but not more healthy. Before 1817 was a month old, a " sore throat " brought gargles and boluses and blisters upon him again, and confined him to his room for nearly a week. To excuse delay in writing he told this to Mitchell ; but soon afterwards, sending his mother a scarf and his father an offer of £20 towards the price of a threshing machine, he wrote : " My health through the winter has been uniformly good."

As this is the chief falsehood discoverable in his letters, it cannot be passed over. The excuse was his mother's illness. Her time of life was making her nerves unstable and she was sleeping very little. Nobody else would be deceived. His father would know the truth from his brother Alexander (Sandy), who was with him several months this winter, and " was getting fond of reading when he went away," as Tom wrote to their mother.

Another thing Sandy would see and whisper was that Tom did not attend the Divinity Hall this Christmas. In letters home Tom never said a word about that, and to the end of her life he never argued against his mother about religion, as some of her younger children did, in groping their own way. Tom always reassured her, adopting her dialect as far as possible, declaring there was no essential difference. How much of what she believed he considered essential, she could never quite make out—the topic was abstruse.

In the middle of March, 1817, he had called on the Divinity Professor, " old Dr. Ritchie," to enrol once more. But Ritchie was " Not at Home," and he never called again. The perfect gentleness of his parting from the Church, the reluctance on both sides to separate, is prettily shown by this, that either Ritchie himself or some other with his approval appears to have replaced Carlyle's name for one year more ; and so made sure the omission to enrol would not take effect unless intended and final.[1] But Mainhill was not waiting for quadrangle news, and long before the professors or fellow-students were sure of it, his father knew that he had given up his prospects of the pulpit.

Bitter was the disappointment to James Carlyle, but he was a man who lived by conscience without parading it, and was equal to the strain. His patience was beautiful.[2] Apparently he never asked a question, and excused his son from family worship when at home without a word. When the rest were singing psalms or praying, Tom might have been seen outside or doing something else indoors. Thus gently, with affectionate reluctance but conclusively, Carlyle put off his Christianity, " as when one layeth his worn-out robes away."

---

[1] David Masson's *Edinburgh Sketches and Memories*, p. 262 ; but *Early Letters*, I, p. 96, is conclusive for T. C.'s desisting in 1817. The hypothesis in the text, of the benevolent replacing of his name on the roll, has the approval of venerable divines skilled in local Church History, and of David Masson.

[2] *Literary Recollections*, by F. Espinasse, p. 207, and letters, etc.

XXIV

WALKING WITH IRVING

THE week-end walks with Irving often ended in
Edinburgh. They came home by the last ferry on
the Sunday night. This let them hear the best of the
preachers, including the fashionable Alison, who wrote on
" taste."

1817 was the year of the *Astronomical Discourses* of
Chalmers, which sold like Scott's novels, and made him
the first of his trade in Britain. Chalmers had been a class-
mate of Duncan, and like him, mathematical and scientific.
Like him, too, he had soon been comfortably started in life
as a " moderate " preacher in a country parish, and relapsed
into the common creed about Heaven and Hell and the
Holy Bible, which was what " everybody " was then wanting
to do. " If the fear of Hell can keep the crowd in order, they
cannot have too much of it." News of a man of sense who
really believed it was news indeed. The people stampeded
to hear the new Savonarola ; and found if not the light,
the heat of genius, appearing to weld into one new knowledge
and old creeds. So when he was to preach at Dunfermline
this year, Irving said to Carlyle : " Let us go and hear him
once more ! " It was a beautiful Saturday as they walked
along the coast to Inverkeithing, where they lodged with
a schoolmaster—happy in a wife who appeared to her
husband's visitors the model of what a wife should be—
an excellent housekeeper who worshipped her man. The
Sunday's sermon in Dunfermline seemed worth their walk.

Looking back after many years, Carlyle called Chalmers
" ill-*read*" and "ignorant in all that lay beyond the horizon,"
though naturally gifted with " dignity, sound intellect and
imagination. His tones in preaching would rise to the
piercingly pathetic ; no preacher ever went so into one's
heart. I suppose there will never again be such a preacher
in any Christian Church."

The horror of ignorance here was habitual with Carlyle.
As he wrote to Johnstone now about his own shortcomings :

" Without increasing in knowledge, what profits it to
live ? "

The *Astronomical Discourses* seemed to be sweeping off
their feet all sorts and conditions of men ; but the young
dominie stood steady and felt himself like a rock among
rushing waters, perhaps the more easily because he was then
specialising in that line himself, reading Bailly and so on.
" I wish I were an astronomer," he wrote ; and his letters
show him feeling as Ptolemy of Alexandria did.　There are
passages that read like a paraphrase of Ptolemy's song
about the stars, and all the more interesting because the
coincidence seems accidental :—

> " I know I am mortal and live but a day ;
> Yet in watching the myriads of stars on their way,
> I can feel Earth no more—I'm uplifted on high,
> As if dwelling for ever with God in the sky."

He wrote to Mitchell (5.7.1817) :—

' But Dr. Chalmers, it would seem, is fearful lest these
speculations lead us away from Christianity, and to prove
the truth of religion his best argument seems to be, that as
it is in the Scriptures, we have no business to think about
it at all—an argument well enough known before.　One
is a little surprised to see the Doctor so vehement in his
praise of Newton for rejecting all manner of probabilities,
and refusing to admit any hypothesis till it was supported
by direct and incontrovertible proof.　Without doubt this
answers in the present instance, but will lead to alarming
results.　Christianity itself is only supported by probabilities.　But here, we are to believe everything that is told
us ; which is a very comfortable way of reasoning.　It is
perhaps not surprising that the author should deal so largely
in denunciations against his adversaries.　It is very certain
that the unhappy sceptic cannot believe one jot the better,
tho he were brayed in a mortar.　Yet almost all the
writers on the evidences of Christianity that I have seen,
excepting Paley, have treated him in this manner.　When
a poor creature's sentiments, in such cases, happen to be
contrary to those of his neighbours, the less he says of them
the better.

' This same Doctor writes in the *Edinburgh Review* on
Mendicity.　After expatiating upon pauperism, he proposes,
as a remedy, to increase the number of clergymen.　They

who know the general habits of Scottish ministers will
easily see how sovereign a specific this is.'

Something to the same effect would pass between Carlyle
and Irving, bating the theology, which would never be
missed. At "this period" of Irving's life, his biographer
tells us,[1] "his personal religious sentiments are not very
apparent," nor is there any record of conversion, in short.
And she kindly attributes to his "great personal strength"
the best of her stories.—

' In one of his many walking excursions, for example, he
and his companion came to a little roadside inn, where there
was but one sitting-room, of a very homely description.
The young men left their coats and knapsacks in this room,
ordered dinner, and went out to investigate the neighbourhood while it was getting ready. On their return they
found the room occupied by a party of tourists, the only
table filled, their dinner forestalled, and their belongings
huddled into a corner. The intruders resisted their
entrance, and would neither share the table nor the apart-
ment, while the landlord could do nothing. So Irving
pushed forward to the window, and threw it wide open,
and facing the company, gravely addressed his comrade :
"Will you toss out or knock down?" Which made a
sudden peace.'

Once they saw tents on the eastern Lomond Hill, and
said to each other : "Trigonometrical survey : Let us go!"
And on Saturday they went. They saw the "theodolite"
inside a tent, and "a saucy looking, cold, official gentleman
diligently walking for exercise," and showing nothing, even
to the fine "County people" who came to look. But
Irving's polite remarks made him thaw. He invited them in
to inspect it, and showed them "the Signal Column," a great,
broad plank on the top of Ben Lomond, sixty miles off.
Then down they came to Leslie village for the night, past
the old town of Falkland and its Palace ruin, whose front
makes "one side of the public street,"[2] "like a black old
bit of coffin or protrusive shin bone, sticking through from
the soil of the dead past."

In August, Carlyle and Irving began their vacation by a
walking tour to the west. They were in the front of the fashion

[1] *Edward Irving*, by Mrs. Oliphant, Chap. IV.
[2] *The Picture of Scotland*, by Robert Chambers, II, p. 187.

set by Scott, and joined at Stirling by two other teachers, Pears and Brown, they slept on the second night at Doune, on the edge of the " Lady of the Lake's " country. They breakfasted at Callander and went on, rejoicing in the Trossachs with big " Bens " on either hand. Carlyle pronounced Loch Katrine " exquisite—my first taste of the beautiful in scenery."

On quitting their boat at the west end of it, they separated, to meet in Glasgow. Irving and Pears went south through the country of Rob Roy, while Brown guided Carlyle across the trackless heath to Loch Lomond. They slept at Tarbet, and walking down the shore of the " incomparable Loch " and along the river that links it to the Clyde, they read as they passed the Latin inscription on Smollett's pillar, and ferried over to Roseneath, where the minister, Story, was a friend of Brown and hospitably ready. They stayed there two or three days. He took them to the house of the local " factor " or land-agent, a Mr. Campbell, who unwittingly delighted Carlyle by letting him see for the first time the highest Highland polish of manners, politeness equal to the best in Asia, seldom matched in Europe. Both he and his two sisters, " excellent, lean old ladies, with genuine good manners and good principles," appeared to erudite but rustic eyes " of a superior, richly furnished stratum of society," and the admiration they showed on one or two evenings for the youngest of the party uplifted him. He departed with his head in the air, and feeling he might be somebody some day—more like a common, ambitious young fellow than a disciple of Epictetus.

From Roseneath they ferried to Greenock, " the first seaport of Scotland " [1] then, and saw the earliest steamers in business in Europe, plying to Glasgow—dumpy little boats, with a bit of red sail on the foremast to help the machinery, paddling in and out among the big ships like dogs among the cattle.

At Glasgow they were four again, and Irving took them by canal boat to Paisley. Then Pears went home direct to Dunse, and the rest went up the Clyde, admiring the Falls near Lanark, and visiting the " model school " of Robert Owen, the Socialist pioneer. Next day they were " joyfully " going down the lead mines ; then on to Annandale. Irving made direct for his father's in Annan. Carlyle

[1] Lawson's *Enlarged Gazetteer*, p. 606 (1841) ; and see also *The Picture of Scotland*, by R. Chambers, II, pp. 15-16 (1827).

had only Brown for company when he came to Mainhill,
and was upset by finding his mother delirious from want of
sleep.   Brown went away at once, of course ; but in later
letters did not hide his surprise at the violence of the distress
he had witnessed, which was certainly not like a Stoic, but
very like Carlyle.

XXV

PUBLIC OPINION IN PRACTICE

(1817)

MAYBE Brown did not know how ill his friend's mother was. In what the farm servants and neighbours used to say of this time the most curious detail is that they did not realise the serious nature of Mrs. Carlyle's sickness. They had seen her going about not long ago, and heard no mention of anything usually fatal, and did not know her reason was in danger from want of sleep. "Old James," as her husband was called, for he was approaching sixty and grey-haired, though still erect and strong, was overwhelmed and let himself go as none had ever seen him do before. "It was as if granite was thawing into water. He burst at last into a torrent of grief; cried piteously, and threw himself on the floor, and lay moaning." His children looking on were speechless with surprise; but they knew the only cause of his grief, which was not so clear to the servants.

It seems to have been about this time that a neighbouring farmer observed him in the Ecclefechan graveyard sitting sadly on some stone. His first wife was buried there. It was a habit of his to remember death and remind others of it; but the like of this had never been known before, and Ecclefechan's conclusion was that James must be heart-broken because his son had fallen from Grace and become an atheist.

So sure of this were they that they spoke about it to James Carlyle with a kindly intended sympathy which was strangely repelled. "Do you think my son is going to screech his guts out for a pack of blue-bellied weavers?" "Do you think our Tom is going to stand up to be criticised by a man like Mathie Latimer?"

"Feels it too much to hear a word about it," said Ecclefechan to itself, which went current the more readily because Mrs. Carlyle had been taken to Mr. Grierson's farm near Dumfries and was out of sight.

The medical problem was to get her to sleep and keep her from harm in the meantime. The first Mrs. Grierson, her sister, had been dead some years, but there were children of hers eager to help, and Mrs. Grierson the second was a kind and clever woman ready to nurse her husband's sister-in-law.

The patient herself said to Mrs. Grierson : " Watch me, my feet are like hind's feet." And so they found. In spite of all their precautions, she escaped them ; but merely walked to her brother's house, and was coaxed back.

The doctor prohibited whisky, which Mrs. Grierson suggested, as almost any farmer's wife would have done.

She continued to spend the nights awake in spite of drugs. She went out one day and mounted a horse and sitting astride it without a saddle galloped it about a field, and then dismounted quietly, unhurt. This made Mrs. Grierson take a bold resolution, as something must be done. She gave her whisky in spite of the doctor's " No, no, no ! " Mrs. Carlyle slept a long time like a baby, and wakened well—herself again, returning home in a week or so apparently in perfect health.

Which explains why Ecclefechan was more convinced than ever that what had broken the heart of James Carlyle was the atheism of his son.[1]

" And that'll be what's the matter with the mother, too," said one to another. " Poor woman !—No wonder ! —Who knows what he hasn't been doing away from home ? When a fellow's an atheist what can you expect ? " Many said : " It's a punishment on them for being too proud of him." But everyone was sorry for the mother. " Poor body, it's very hard on her " ; which made it seem all the stranger that she never noticed the sympathy in store for her ; perhaps because it was only after a year or two or more that she knew she might desist from hoping to see her son in a pulpit. That he had quite ceased to be a Bible-believer she never knew. His absence from Church did not put her on enquiry—it seemed natural. He was a man who should be teaching ministers, not sitting to learn from the like of them. Tom Carlyle at his proudest did not

[1] The notes of J. T. Wells left the matter a mystery till in July, 1903, John Grierson, Town Clerk of Dumfries, retired, and grandson of Mrs. C.'s sister explained it all. We rediscussed it, 13.9.1919, and decided it should be told. D. A. W.

A farmer quoted in *Thomas Carlyle*, by E. Paxton Hood, p. 2, *saw* J. C. in the graveyard.

esteem himself more highly than his mother did, and the
wary silence of his father helped him to save her nervous
spirit from misgivings. Thus when a neighbour-woman was
once pressing Tom into a theological controversy, " old
James " broke out : " Thou auld crack-brained enthusiastic,
dost thou think to argue with our Tom ? " [1]

[1] Notes of J. T. Wells and *Edinburgh Sketches and Memories*, by David
Masson, p. 282, footnote.

XXVI

THOMAS CUVALLO, A MODERN GREEK

(1817)

THE vacation ended happily, much of it spent in walks and talks with Mitchell and Johnstone; and on a bright September morning he sat in a cart with his brother Alick, driving as far as Moffat, where a kind Mrs. Johnston insisted on stuffing his pocket with bread and cheese for the long walk ahead. He overtook two travellers, one a " peasant of those parts," the other a square-built man of thirty in sailor's clothes, without a shirt or shoes, and an energetic simple face, well tanned by wind and weather. Carlyle presented to him the bread and cheese he had to carry, which made him " very communicative."

Thomas Cuvallo, born in Istambol (Constantinople), son of a man from Corinth, had served two years on the *Achilles*, English ship of war, and been discharged in 1814; sailed twice to India, and since his return to England in the spring had been travelling from port to port in search of a ship to take him home to Greece. Whereby he had spent all his money and was now on the way to Leith for either a passage to the Continent or work to keep him from starving. Though " thus forlorn upon the wolds of Tweeddale," he " seemed to view his condition with an indifference that Zeno himself might have envied," wrote Carlyle to Johnstone.

Cuvallo repeated the alphabet and named some things in Romaïc, which showed his companion how much the modern Greek was like the old. Byron's—" Zoë mou sas agapo " was quoted. " What does that mean? " Cuvallo, with a grin, replied—" My life, I love thee." Then he told of Mullahs and Imams and spinning Dervishes, and what he had had to endure as a " giaour," and his adventures in the Levant. He had much to reveal about magic and divination, miracles and spectres. " There are ten kinds of spectres," said he, and the Church of Saint Sophia (Holy Wisdom, or " The Word," not a " Saint ") was a standing

miracle. There are pictures there which the Turks have
never been able to efface, though scraping and whitewashing
for centuries ; and a pulpit they can never enter. Axes
and crowbars are useless. " Every Easter-Eve the figure
of a man appears in it reading in a book. When he shall
have finished the Muslim[1] Empire shall pass away for ever,"
according to Cuvallo. But that was nothing to the miracle
of the fish. " It happened to be frying in a pan in the
palace at the time the Turks were about to enter the city.
The sovereign declared to the General that he would as
soon believe that this fish would jump from his frying
pan and live as that the Turks were within many leagues of
him. Whereupon the fish sprang out with great agility,
and at this hour is living in its well—one side roasted and
the other raw—and intends to do so till Greece shall be
finally delivered from bondage. I never saw it, but my
mother did," declared Cuvallo.[2]

They were now at Bield, sixteen miles from Moffat ; and
the village was a likely place for a little begging, and safe
for shelter, at any rate, from the rain that seemed impending.
So Cuvallo decided to stop there, and Carlyle gave him a
draught of porter, a shilling and " half a foot of tobacco,"
and went on his way. He slept at Noblehouse and was in
Edinburgh before noon next day. He met Irving at Leith
in the evening, and they were in Kirkcaldy " in time for tea."

[1] " Mohammedan " in the letter ; but Muslim would be Cuvallo's
word.
[2] On 3.12.1919 an Armenian lady, born in Constantinople, told D. A. W
this identical story, saying she had seen the fish, etc.

XXVII

GIBBON AND OTHER BOOKS

(1817–18)

IN 1817, in the third edition of Leslie's *Elements of Geometry*, the professor said that the solution of a problem had been "suggested to me by Mr. Thomas Carlyle, an ingenious young mathematician, formerly my pupil." [1] As Leslie's opinion was much esteemed, these words ensured promotion if he stuck to mathematics and teaching ; and he still was meaning to do so when he returned to duty in September, intending to give all his leisure to it and science, except only the two hours he had to himself at noon. With happy self-indulgence he gave this, the best working-time of the day, " to the reading of history and other lighter matters," with the result that his " Fluxions " were suspended for ten days at a stretch in the first three weeks. Madam de Staël's *Germany* was what he was reading then ; and the Tory *Quarterly Review*, whose writers, he told Johnstone, were fond of parading " learning of that minute scholastic nature which is eminently distinguished from knowledge." Looking round for some external expedient to make concentration on his special subject easier, he wrote to Mitchell recalling the 1816 project of going to a French university.

" What wild-goose scheme is this of yours of going to France ? " wrote Mitchell in reply (4.10.1817). " Do you not know that the Polytechnic School is knocked on the head ? The rest are not worth the naming. I say, ' Laddie Dinwoodie o' the Gardenholm, compose yourself to your potatoes there.' "

He did compose himself in his own way, escaping from idleness by study. Fluxions and conics, astronomy and mechanics, Bossut and Lagrange required no greater effort than one makes for business. Laplace was even

---

[1] Book VI, p. 17, *Edinburgh Sketches and Memories*, by David Masson, pp. 260–1.

attractive, appearing in his *Exposition du Système du Monde* a " beautiful writer, and this is the smallest of his merits." [1] Such reading for duty was done " in intermittent spasms," while he read omnivorously for pleasure, with a frank and vulgar preference for the concrete and humane, impelled by the same instinct of Nature which makes the plants grow.

" My blessing," he said, " be upon the head of whoever invented books." He rarely bought them. He could not afford to buy more than the few he wanted to keep beside him, so it may be worth telling that this winter he bought a La Rochefoucauld (*Maxims*), and writing to Mitchell praised him more than Voltaire would have allowed, denying " that the basis of his system is the supposition of self-love being the motive of all our actions. It rather seems as if he had laid down no system at all. Regarding man as a wretched, mischievous thing, little better than a kind of vermin, he represents him as the sport of his passions, above all of vanity, and exposes the secret springs of his conduct." Which is like what Emerson once said of the author of *Frederick*.

Perhaps no other French book influenced Carlyle so much as the *Maxims*. It can be seen in his letters shaping his thoughts. Some of the Maxims give the gist of a great part of *Sartor*. " Il faut peu de choses pour rendre le sage heureux," and so on. " It takes little to make a wise man happy. Nothing can content a fool. Which is why most men are wretched." And this—" When a man has not peace inside himself, it is useless to seek it elsewhere."

He scoffed at phrenology, exposing the absurdity of its " vile show of induction " with a neatness like Euclid's, and derided Dugald Stewart, Playfair and Co., for magnifying Bacon, making a John-Bull-Aristotle out of him. Macaulay, Spedding and others by and by believed the bigwigs; but not so Carlyle, who now said—" It looks as if philosophers could not do without someone to worship." The horrors of Moore's *Lalla Rookh*, bepraised by Jeffrey, only made him laugh.

He read Hume's *England* and much else; but the event of the winter was the reading of Gibbon, who in the end appeared to him " the most strong-minded of all historians." But on 20.11.1817, when he had finished only the first of the twelve volumes, he told Johnstone—" I do not like him :

---

[1] Unpublished letter.

his style is flowery; his sarcasms wicked; his notes oppressive, often beastly." No Bishop could have abominated more the prejudices of Gibbon. But on he went. While following Nature he did so like a Stoic and not a slacker enslaved to inclination. In the words of *Sartor*— "'Truth!' I cried, 'though the Heavens crush me for following her : no falsehood! though a whole celestial Lubberland were the price of Apostasy.'" This is what Confucius calls making the thoughts sincere, and the first step to sense; and may be born in a man, or quickly learned, or the ripe fruit of study, looking till one sees the truth although it is disagreeable. It means a delight in reality as distinguished from dreams.

The history of Gibbon he seems to have read without skipping a note, and used to tell of the speed—in twelve days at a volume a day. This may have been a consecutive perusal in the Christmas vacation. He read it more than once, and had such a thirst for details that his wideawake way of reading for pleasure would seem to some hard work. Which helps to explain what is a credit to Gibbon as well as himself, that though he seldom after this winter looked into the work, he had a fair recollection of it for the rest of his life. He went with Gibbon in admiring Stilicho and Belisarius, Ætius and Boniface, and declared the history (16.2.1818) :—

'A work of immense research and splendid execution, embracing almost all the civilised world from Trajan to 1453. His style is exuberant, sonorous and epigrammatic. He yields to Hume in elegance and distinctness, to Robertson in general disquisition—but he excels them both in a species of brief and shrewd remark for which he seems to have taken Tacitus as a model. All three are abundantly destitute of virtuous feeling—or indeed of any feeling at all.

'I wonder what benefit is derived from reading all this stuff. What business of mine is it though Timur Beg erected a pyramid of eighty thousand skulls in the Valley of Bagdad, and made an iron cage for Bajazet ? And what have I to do with the desolating progress of either Zinghis or Napoleon ? It is in vain to tell us that our knowledge of human nature is increased by the operation. *Useful* knowledge of that sort is acquired not by reading, but experience. And with regard to political advantages— the less one knows of them, the greater will be his delight in the principles of my Lords Castlereagh and Sidmouth, with their circulars, suspensions, holy leagues, and salvation of Europe.

'Yet if not profit there is some *pleasure* in history at all events. I believe we must not apply the *cui bono* (or, what's the use ?) too rigorously. It may be enough to sanction any pursuit that it gratifies an innocent and still more an honourable propensity of the human mind.'

Thus did he think aloud at the time, confused, and wondering why he had read the book at all, like a wounded soldier asking himself—" What took me to the war ? " For months to come he was in the state of mind a man is in who knows a bullet has gone through him, but cannot guess whether he is to die at once or is only slightly hurt.

No wonder he remembered it all his life ! These " winged sarcasms, so quiet and yet so conclusively transpiercing, and killing dead," so " potent and illuminative," were " extirpating from his mind the last remnant that had been left in it of the orthodox belief in miracles." [1]

" I then first clearly saw," he said long afterwards, " that Christianity was not true." [2]

He looked about him, taking stock of what remained, like a shipwrecked sailor in a boat examining provisions. To Mitchell he expatiated (25.5.1818) on the use he made of study to divert the mind and master passions, and exalted the pleasures of astronomy like another Ptolemy, but he candidly concluded without self-deception—" I fear you are tired of these prosings—you must bear with them. Excepting the few friends whom Providence has given me, and whose kindness I wish never to forfeit, I have and am likely to have little else but these pursuits to derive enjoyment from ; and there is none but you to talk it over with. They are all preaching here, and care not a straw for Laplace and his calculus both. You will be preaching one of these days too, and perhaps—but it is needless to anticipate— you must not leave off mathematics."

But Mitchell did, though he continued a teacher ; and he had left off Christianity too. The loss of the old creed made Carlyle wretched ; but he was not alone. He was not even uncommon. It had been odd for a clever fellow to hesitate so long.

[1] *Edinburgh Sketches*, by David Masson, pp. 263–4.
[2] 1874. W. Allingham, *A Diary*, p. 232.

"Late in his life," Froude tells what would be otherwise incredible that, referring to what Froude called "the special miraculous occurrences of sacred history," Carlyle had to say to him—"it is as certain as mathematics that no such thing ever has been or can be." It is amazing evidence of the darkness of Oxford, stupefying worse than natural ignorance, that such a thing needed to be mentioned to a don. Carlyle had made sure of it in 1818. It is taken for granted in all he wrote. It was told or implied as often as needful—assuredly.

When allowance is made for reserve required by consideration for others, the letters of Carlyle from this date confirm the conclusion of David Masson that he was free from "ordinary 'doubts' and 'backward hesitations.' His clear intellect had cut down like a knife between him and the theology from which he had parted, leaving no ragged ends."[1]

[1] *Edinburgh Sketches and Memories*, by David Masson, p. 277.

XXVIII

THREE MEN IN A BOAT

ONE afternoon when the days were long Carlyle and Irving were walking on the sands and watching the Leith ships outward bound, becalmed or seeming so, and guessing that the one which was drifting near might be the same in which some friends of theirs were passengers, the Glens from Annan, bound for Astrakhan.

It was in the house of Glen that Carlyle had latterly boarded at Annan, and Irving and he had gone to Edinburgh last Saturday, and on the Sunday in " Peddie's Meeting-House " behind Bristo Street heard Glen preaching for the last time in Scotland. He was going abroad as a missionary with wife and children. At the door of Peddie's house, Mrs. Glen, a high-spirited woman, held out her hand to Carlyle to take leave, with " her old bright, saucily affectionate smile, fearless, superior to trouble."

" Farewell, then," said he ; and bethinking him it was adieu for ever he added, senselessly explicit—" good be ever with you." She shot all pale as paper, and they parted without another word. The sudden paleness went to his heart like an arrow, and all that night and for three or four days more a strange " bitterness of sorrow " haunted him, as he felt—" Parting *sadder* than by death. These good people are to live and we are never to behold each other more ! " The strange feeling left him as suddenly as it came, and it might be about the last day of it that he and Irving stood watching the ship which seemed as idle as a painted ship upon a painted ocean. Then said one to the other—" That one is Glen's, and it bends so much this way one might, by sharp rowing, cut into it, and have still a word with the poor Glens ! "

Irving's assistant was within hail and not to be left behind. The three young men together pushed off in a boat at their best speed ; but in half an hour saw the big ship was slipping farther from them, and since they were afloat

at any rate decided to treat themselves to a trip to the
island of Inchkeith, five miles away.

The lighthouse was a curiosity, the mechanism of its
revolving light a discovery to them all ; but the lighthouse-
keeper himself was the greatest surprise to Carlyle. He
appeared to have all a man could want, this prosperous
" Aberdeen native," with wife and children healthy and
handsome enough ; yet every feature of face and voice
confessed he was unspeakably bored. Surely he is " no lover
of the picturesque," thought Carlyle, looking round on the
most " glorious " scenery in Nature, and *not* recalling what
Cowper had written about such solitude as Crusoe's. Dr.
Johnson would not have needed Cowper to remind him
that a man who had no company but his family and seven
cows was bound to feel dull. " We left him almost sorrow-
fully, and never heard of him more," said Carlyle ; which
was the best thing could have happened. However it may
be with philosophers, a lighthouse-keeper can say without an
effort that he is most happy when he is not heard of. But
Carlyle's interest in the lonely man was of a piece with his
sorrow to part from the Glens.

They went and looked at the white wooden crosses on
the " Russian Graves " in the middle of the island. A
Russian squadron had wintered in the Forth about twenty
years ago, and buried its dead there. They reminded each
other of how the Russian sailors returning from sprees in
Edinburgh used to climb the lamp-posts and drink the
warm train oil and leave Leith Walk eclipsed.

As Irving took his place at the helm and they were
re-launching their little boat, the sun was setting in their
faces, behind Ben Lomond, and sending a " broad pillar
as of gold " to " under foot," like a " burning axle going
down to the centre of the world." Then one by one the
stars came out, " and Kirkcaldy crept under its coverlid,
showing not itself but its lights." Inchkeith was blinking
behind them. It was eleven o'clock when they leapt out
on the shore, in the clear grey dimness of a northern summer
night, and heard with surprise that their friends had been
anxious about them.

XXIX

THE CURRENT OF EVENTS

(1818)

ON week-ends in Edinburgh he did not enjoy the sight of " dandies " parading, but the " fair women " were so attractive that it seemed " madness to think of " them—which shows how wise the Chinese are in practising the early marriage which steadies a man. In politics one strident note was dominating the confusion of noises—" all singing to the tune of Burgh Reform," [1] while Tories were swearing that Hell might be reformed, but not the burghs. His coëvals were mostly " probationers," aspiring to the Church endowments, and dutifully attending the leading divines and all possible patrons, their pleasant conversation in such company meaning no more than the purring of pussy-cats craving for cream. Their private talk was gossip.

The cheeriest of his acquaintances was a schoolmate, now a tutor in Edinburgh, Donaldson, genial and good-natured, who died of malignant typhus in April, 1818. At the funeral Carlyle saw a pupil whose mother, Mrs. Inglis, had nursed Donaldson.[2] " I was standing by the open grave," said Henry Inglis afterwards to his wife and friends,[3] " and I was weeping quietly as the clods were rattling on his coffin, when someone laid a hand on my shoulder and said in a compassionate voice : ' My name is Carlyle. He was my friend, too. Come with me.' I did so, and that is how we became acquainted."

An obituary of Donaldson for the *Dumfries Courier* was written by Carlyle, who lay awake " in the stillness of the solitary night " and mourned—the more so because he felt the ancients were right, and death the natural end. He told Johnstone his reflections on Donaldson plunged him " into an ocean of fearful conjectures. . . . One thing let

[1] Unpublished letter.
[2] *Glasgow Herald* cuttings of 16.2.1882 may be consulted ; but D. A. W. has for many years been acquainted with Mrs. Inglis, widow of H. I., and was also told Inglis' stories by David Masson.   [3] *Ibid.*

us never cease to believe—an upright mind is the greatest
blessing we can obtain or imagine." He never ceased to
feel so ; but the sufferings had now begun which made
him say by and by that the pain of an evil conscience was
nothing to disease of the liver. He used to declare that till
this year (1818) he was " not conscious of a stomach," and
" had grown up healthy and hardy," [1] but now began his
" long curriculum of dyspepsia, which never ended," robbed
him of sleep and made him melancholy.

One midnight this summer he saw a moth dart into his
candle, " and—puff !—the moth is dead." He sat meditating on the miniature tragedy with the grim earnestness of
the Buddhists' Gautama. The very commonness of the
thing made it the more a type, and the better worth his
thought.

He was cheered by a visit from Mitchell, and soon after
midsummer the children in his school had a happy interlude
when a visitor came in unannounced, a grey-haired pensive
old man in tattered clothes, and stood up straight and silent
before the teacher. They had never seen him before ; but
their teacher had, and recognised and welcomed Stuart
Lewis, a man of taste and genius in spite of appearances.
Carlyle was " touched " to see the veteran " waging against
necessity the same unprosperous battle " which had lasted
forty years. He had been no man's enemy. His very
drunkenness was natural in one who had been born in Ruthwell about 1758 and learned the art of life among the
smugglers. For many years Lewis had been a shepherd
at the farm where the mother of Carlyle had served. Then
he crossed the borders and in England became a draper.
A partner swindled him, he used to explain, in telling how
he went to try his fortune in America and came back to
Scotland. At Ecclefechan he started a library which was
like a light in the darkness, but not so profitable as to keep
him there. He was himself a poet, and rather a man of
ideas than of trading habits. For years he was safe in
harbour in a lodging-house his wife kept for poor students
in Edinburgh. As long as she lived he had some kind of
home. But though she was the younger she died before

[1] See the Rev. W. H. Milburn's report in W. H. Wylie's *Thomas Carlyle*,
p. 57. Date fixed from letters, reminiscences, and many other sources,
such as *Some Personal Reminiscences of Carlyle*, by A. J. Symington,
p. 93 ; T. C.'s talk to Mrs. Anstruthers of Ballikinrain, recorded in her
Notebook, 17.6.1876 ; and the talk of Alexander Carlyle, Edinburgh, to
D. A. W., October, 1919.

him when he was approaching seventy; and then he had nothing to do but die. He lingered many months, wandering " all over the five border counties, selling his poems," with a young son at his heels.

A little success was easily too much. Whatever cash he had to spare went into whisky. When kindly received by Carlyle, he said to him : " I have been protracting a miserable, useless existence ever since my wife died," and gratefully told of a young lady in Wigton who, for the sake of Thomas Murray, to whom Carlyle reported it, " sought out his lodgings and replenished his purse." He sold enough of his ware at Kirkcaldy to be able to carouse there before stepping onward, like the wandering Jew, to die soon on his way to Ruthwell,[1] to which some strange instinct made the old man turn, like a child running home to its mother, as the lights were going out and darkness closing round him. Mitchell was at his funeral, and in a letter to Carlyle described his last days and the " stone with a suitable inscription" that was to be put in the churchyard. " Fair Helen of Kirkconnell Lea" and other verses procured him a place in the *Dictionary of National Biography* for awhile.

Writing about Lewis, etc., on 28.7.1818 to the aforesaid Thomas Murray, now the *Rev.* Thomas, his " first and oldest correspondent," Carlyle moralised :—

' With most young men, I have had dreams of intellectual greatness, and of making me a name upon the earth. They were little else but dreams. To gain renown is what I do not hope, and hardly care for. I now perceive that any man's opinions depend not on himself so much as on the age he lives in, or even the persons with whom he associates. If his mind at all surpass their habits, his aspirings are quickly quenched in the narcotic atmosphere that surrounds him. He forfeits sympathy, and procures hatred if he excel but a little the dull standard of his neighbours. Upon this principle, I could tell you why Socrates sacrificed at his death to Esculapius—why Kepler wrote his *Cosmographic Harmony*, and why Sir Thomas More believed the Pope to be infallible. Nevertheless one should do what he can.

' I have quitted all thoughts of the Church, for many reasons, which it would be tedious, perhaps displeasing, to enumerate.'

[1] Notes of J. T. Wells, who begged for mention here of Stuart Lewis, who had done a great deal of good to others if not to himself by his enthusiasm for libraries. The likeliest date of birth is 1748.

Then, after contrasting Byron to his disadvantage with the Stoic Epictetus, he continued :—

' I heard with pleasure that you had got licence. May you soon obtain a settlement. A Scottish clergyman, when faithful, is both a useful and honourable member of society. When he neglects his office, and has subscribed his creed " with a sigh or a smile " (as Gibbon spitefully remarks), the less one says of him the better. But I hope other things of you.'

Thus had Carlyle added to the faith of all sensible people a horror and open reprobation of humbug that made his seniors smile, and his kind and wise teacher, Leslie, say to him this year, when he saw the young man determined not to continue teaching : " Upon the whole I see nothing so eligible for you as to learn the engineer business ; and then go to *America*. Great business there—Swiss gentleman went lately—making a large fortune—many bridges and canals— I must have you introduced to Jardine."

It was Irving's example which was leading Carlyle to quit the trade they had. The day after writing to Murray he departed with Irving on their summer vacation.

XXX

BY PASTURES NEW

(1818)

IRVING could not recall Carlyle to Christianity, but his self-confidence was catching. His decision to quit his school in 1818 helped to make Carlyle do likewise, and in many little things his lead was followed. Thus it was he who took Carlyle across to the west last summer ; and when vacation time came again and they were walking home together, instead of sticking to the coach road up the Tweed, Irving guided him across the stream and through the road-less, grassy sheep-hills by Manor and Meggat Waters to St. Mary's Loch, from which Yarrow flows ; and thence, after a night in a cottage, past Loch Skene and the " very beautiful " waterfall of the Grey Mare's Tail to Moffat, and on to Mainhill in time for tea.

When " old James " heard their route, he described what he had seen in coming that way forty years before, and the genial Irving delighted Carlyle by praising his father to him. Next day (1.8.1818), Carlyle set out with Johnstone and Mitchell to walk at large, geologising and exploring. They crossed the border and roved among the lakes and climbed Helvellyn and Skiddaw. In an Inn near Skiddaw Mitchell discovered that the pious Carlyle disbelieved the Bible miracles, and Mitchell said that he himself had done so long ago.

The holidays went by like a breeze. In returning to Kirkcaldy alone, Carlyle walked by Eskdale Moor and Ettrick Pen to Ettrick and Yarrow Waters, and wrote a description of his tour and sent it to an Edinburgh magazine editor, who did not print it. He sent his mother a black bonnet from town, and had a two-hours' talk with Leslie. From Kirkcaldy his first letter home to his father (2.9.1818) enclosed £15 and said he had £70 in reserve, and intended to hand in his resignation " against the beginning of

December." He asked advice, but did not wait for it, and left his father guessing. " Irving is going away, and I shall have no associate. I have thought of trying the law, and several other things, but I have not yet got correct information about any of them."

To Mitchell he admitted an intention to " write for booksellers," but that was merely like private teaching to eke out his savings while qualifying for another profession. " To live by authorship was never my intention."

Mitchell was puzzled by his discontent—it was so commonplace and unworthy of him. Why should he not do as bidden, " compose himself to his potatoes " ? They both were better off in wages and prospects than most of the students and teachers of their age. He was supposing himself a Stoic too, and quoting Cleanthes and Epictetus, yet he could find no better foundation for content than that we would soon be all dead, while his avowed excuse for quitting his school was one that a Stoic should be ashamed to mention— that dominies were not sufficiently respected. Mitchell did not make the mistake of imagining he had " not succeeded." In fact he might have remained and prospered more and more, if he could have been content with what Kirkcaldy could pay him for teaching, and Provost Swan and other friends were sure to do their best for him. No wonder Mitchell was puzzled.

Carlyle said his long letter to Mitchell was an " auricular confession," and it was certainly franker than Erasmus advised one to be in the Confessional, but except by vague reference to " the undefined station I have hitherto occupied in society," it did not let out what appeared by and by, that he was hurt by the girls in general sniffing at him as merely a poor teacher. He never pretended that young women were unattractive. Still less did he sympathise with the holy men who blamed their God for making sexes. True, he held in from the dissipations which make the common man too like a monkey or a jelly-fish ; but that only made him the more susceptible ; and at the latest soon after the vacation of 1818, and before he wrote to Mitchell, he had been introduced by Irving to Margaret Gordon ; and was almost immediately dominated by the wish to please her and win the goodwill of Mrs. Usher, the aunt who managed her. From the first his trade seemed " paltry " because it seemed so to the girls who value work by wages ;

and now that it seemed to stand between him and Margaret Gordon, he lost all patience with it. He weighed his words to others, but what he said to himself he remembered vividly as long as he lived—" It were better to perish than to continue schoolmastering."

XXXI

THE ETERNAL FEMININE

(1818)

ASTRONOMERS have sometimes made discoveries by observing in stars they were watching movements which could not be explained except by the influence of something yet unseen. It is the same with men. Neither Irving nor Carlyle are now intelligible unless we remember both were needing partners.

To please the women generally, and Bella Martin in particular, Irving was seeking " a career " in the pulpit, held in by the spiritual spider-webs that have enmeshed so many, while in school and elsewhere observing another pupil, a blue-eyed yellow-haired Margaret Gordon, a child when he came, but swiftly expanding into a stately and beautiful woman. She was witty and merry, yet soft-speaking, gentle, as kind as she was " bonny," one of the living flowers that decorate the earth and inspire men's dreams of heaven. He cursed his luck and groaned when he thought of his " engagement." His Bella was jealous. He had to be wary. " It is not lost, what a friend gets." So he introduced Carlyle to this heavenly apparition, which satisfied Bella and everybody else, at first. The " lean, proud, elderly dame " she lived with, her aunt Mrs. Usher, was delighted to entertain the new acquaintance, singing Scotch songs beautifully, enjoying his appreciation, and maybe not immediately apprehending what brought him to the house. It seems " there was another man in the case," [1] to say nothing of an older sister. Mrs. Usher never faltered in her single-minded aim at a " good match " for Margaret, but she was off her guard.

She had been an old maid herself before she married a parish minister, which is the last resort of a " county lady " ; and for her fine nieces she entertained more elevated expectations. She must have had many good qualities. Her brother had been an Army " Hospital Mate " or

[1] *Carlyle's First Love, Margaret Gordon*, by R. C. Archibald, p. 79.

surgeon ; and when she adopted his two girls, Margaret
was " rising " five and the other not much older ; and Mrs.
Usher brought them up in cheap Kirkcaldy till they were
finely developed women on a total income of about a pound
a week.[1] Their Irish mother eked out a pittance smaller
still at American Halifax by dressmaking, it is said ; but
soon became the wife of another medico from Scotland
in the army, Guthrie, and came home with him. And now,
after distinguished service on Peninsular battlefields, he
was a prosperous London physician, a friend of Wellington,
and on the road to fortune, and a good husband too, who
left his wife and Mrs. Usher to scheme as they liked for her
girls. Besides, their own father and Mrs. Usher had " connections " in Aberdeen of high cash value, county folk and
investors, wholesalers and wine merchants ; and both of
them, and Margaret in particular, seemed as sure to draw
the men as honey to draw bees. So it did not occur
to Mrs. Usher to suspect that the mere dominie would
aspire to her Margaret. But he did ; and Margaret recognised he was a handsome and superior fellow, and wished
the other man was like him. She did not say so to him,
of course. He heard nothing about the other man for a long
time. They had plenty of other things to talk about, for
Margaret had read much, and had abundance of candid
curiosity about the beautiful old world she had lighted
upon. There is nothing equal to oral instruction, occasion
ally. They drew together as naturally as the flowers grow
in the spring—as long as Mrs. Usher was off her guard.

He had a fine innings and was envied by several. Mr.
Martin found it growing easier than usual to get probationers
to come over to Kirkcaldy to preach, and there were other
young men who came without even a pretence of business.
Galloway, for example, might brutally bully down with his
" Bosh ! " the speculative theologians in the " backshop "
of David Brown the bookseller ; but he would have gone
to church with Mrs. Usher—and her nieces—if allowed, and
so would Esbie, who came over with him, described by
Carlyle as " a double-refined travelling tutor " and dandy,
" a beauteous vision," though with no better prospects than
" some devil of a curacy," as he candidly said himself, but
not to Mrs. Usher. She was on the qui vive, and did not
need to be warned against the like of them.

[1] *Ibid*, pp. 41–5. Other details here which are not in Carlyle *Letters*,
etc., are taken without further reference from Mr. Archibald's book.

In November, Carlyle went to Edinburgh. On 27.11.1818, he was sending Mitchell thanks for letters of introduction from Henry Duncan :—

'Conceive to yourself a person of my stamp seated in a small room, revolving in his altered soul the various turns of fate below—whilst every time the remembrance of his forlorn condition comes across his brain, he silently exclaims, "Why, then the world's mine oyster ; which I will open "—as best I may : and you will have some idea of my situation. I am not unhappy—for why ? I have got Saussure's *Voyages dans les Alpes ;* and it is my intention to accompany him to the summit of the Dôle.'

Whereat it is easy now to smile. The sympathetic Mitchell would suppose the happiness a make-believe and conclude he was drowning misery in study as often before, whereas his studies were never so slack, nor his happiness more genuine. It escaped in spite of himself when he was writing to Johnstone (8.1.1819) :—

'About the end of 1816, I remember informing you, that, in the space of two years, my views of human life had considerably altered. A similar period has again elapsed and brought with it a change less marked indeed, but not less real. Till not very long ago, I imagined my whole duty to consist in thinking and endeavouring. It now appears that I ought not only to suffer but to act. Connected with mankind by sympathies and wants which experience never ceases to reveal, I now begin to perceive that it is impossible to attain the solitary happiness of the Stoic—and hurtful if it were possible. How far the creed of Epictetus may require to be modified, it is not easy to determine ; that it is defective seems pretty evident. I quit the stubborn dogma, with a regret heightened almost to remorse ; and feel it to be a desire rather than a duty to mingle in the busy current which is flowing past me, and to act my part before the not-distant day arrive, when they who seek me shall not find me.'

The melancholy is as laughable as melancholy can be, a kind of involuntary make-believe melancholy. We have to remember the shibboleths of his childhood and Johnstone's. The saints supposed it a duty to be wretched, and even these emancipated young men would by sheer habit feel good when avowing misery and rather enjoy doing it.

Margaret Gordon or Bannerman

Margaret Gordon, Mrs. Bannerman, from a water-colour miniature painted about 1824. George Walker, Bailie of Aberdeen, told Prof. Archibald, the biographer of the lady, that he could "recollect" seeing her and her husband walking along Union Street in Aberdeen, where they lived. Both were tall and fine-looking. She was leaning on her husband's arm, and was "stylishly dressed in dashing costume with a showy hat and ostrich feathers, in Gainsborough style, while he actually kept his hands in his pockets, seemingly unaware of the interest and attention directed towards his beautiful wife; he was a hero to all the boys of the time."

[face p. 160

Looking round for a text to quote on this occasion, Carlyle could only think of La Rochefoucauld : " Nothing should so much lessen our self-complacency as the discovery that we now think wrong what we used to think right."[1]

Then he talks of engineering plans and concludes, but adds a P.S.—" I forgot to say (what was indeed of no consequence) that I spent, along with Irving, the Christmas holidays in Fife. They were the happiest, for many reasons which I cannot at this time explain, that for a long space have marked the tenor of my life."

The vagueness here is delicious. " Fife," says he, not even Kirkcaldy. None need forbear to laugh at him. Many a time he laughed loud enough himself with less excuse. To-day this P.S. is more intelligible than it was to the addressee a hundred years ago, which does not often happen with old letters.

A few weeks later he seems to have been in Kirkcaldy again, and carrying an umbrella, which was then and there an approximation to dandyism. He had a curious prejudice all his life against umbrellas. Was Mrs. Usher partial to them ? We are left guessing, but know that one of the least absent-minded young men left his umbrella behind him in Kirkcaldy. The Provost recognised it, retrieved it and sent it to its owner, who wrote home with self-revealing frankness—" Last week I received an umbrella which I had left in Fife, and a kind letter from Mr. Swan. If ever I come to anything, that is one person whom I shall remember."

Historians have wrongly said he went back to Kirkcaldy only once after he left it in 1818, and that no love-letters passed between him and Margaret Gordon ! Which shows how prone they are to blunder like the scientists when they forget what Darwin used to insist upon—the imperfections of the record. The custom of keeping secret and returning or destroying love-letters was better observed in Scotland than in England, and sacred to Carlyle. It was in spite of all he could do that people have been enabled to read what afterwards passed between him and Miss Welsh, and the abundance of these later love-letters, to say nothing of their skill, suggests there were plenty now.

In Mrs. Usher's presence they would behave without an effort as perfectly as if in church ; but she was not always present ; and the restraint required before her was a reason

[1] This part of his letter is omitted in the printed version.

M

the more for letters. In short, the probabilities are all in the same direction. Margaret Gordon had a ready pen, and so had he ; and it was the golden age of letter-writing. The danger of alarming Mrs. Usher was easy to minimise when the Post Office collected fees on delivery and nearly every traveller was ready to oblige by carrying letters for nothing. Contemporary anecdotes of love-letters written in secret and smuggled might be multiplied to make this argument swell like another Golden Bough and blossom into endless octavos.

Take a sample. A venerable dame described her own doings in those days.[1] Parents on both sides being hostile her lover had enlisted and after many adventures was " bought out " and they were happily married. The mystery no senior ever solved was how they had corresponded unsuspected. The problem of Margaret Gordon in Kirkcaldy was simple compared to hers, for she was in a lonely country house, and watched by many. A candle in her bedroom would have betrayed her. She went down in her nightdress to the empty kitchen after midnight, and stepping on the cold hearth stood inside the big old chimney, and lighting her candle there she stuck it on a brick, and so she could write as much as she liked. A smuggling shop-keeper did the rest.

The like of David Masson could only smile at the supposition that no letters passed between Margaret Gordon in Kirkcaldy and him in Edinburgh because none were kept. It would have been strange to see them. Such reticence as kept Mrs. Usher more than a year in the dark was easy to modest people of the right sort and commoner then than now. They felt without saying it that to keep their secret was to keep their freedom. So he said nothing of their courtship even to Irving, and Irving said nothing to him of the revival of his interest in an ex-pupil, Jane Baillie Welsh, whom he had left a child at Haddington and found more noticeable now at " sweet seventeen." A story Masson was fond of shows the general feeling at this time. An old lady in Edinburgh, who was the pattern of propriety in that formal age, was startled once by a credible report of the loose babbling of George Guelph, the " fat and flabby " German Adonis who was " Prince Regent." She sprang to the middle of the room and shook her fist at the ceiling as she cried—" The daumned villain, wad he kiss and tell ? "

---

[1] To D. A. W.'s mother. He knew the old lady.

BOOK III

APPRENTICESHIP
1818–22

I

AMONG THE ROCKS

(1818–19)

CARLYLE had reckoned on tutoring and writing for booksellers to eke out his savings while preparing for more profitable occupation ; but he never got beyond what was intended to be only a makeshift. The steps by which he was led to live by writing appeared almost providential, and he often said it was against his will. Yet he showed this winter a surprising lack of appetite for money, and what seems an untimely eagerness for knowledge. He hardly gave a thought to the engineering which Leslie pointed out to him as the way to wealth ; and he attended Prof. Jameson's class on mineralogy in the hope of learning more about geology than he had been able to get from books.

Tho careless of introductions to engineers, he had lost no time in using those to Bailie Waugh, who was planning a new review, and to Dr. Brewster, who was editing the *Edinburgh Encyclopedia* and invited him to a Royal Society meeting in George Street. He sat out their dull debate on fossils, but once was enough. Carlyle was never less like a fossil than this winter, a time of change.

There was no translation of " the illustrious Werner " who had told best the secrets of the rocks ; but Carlyle would not let the German language stand between him and any knowledge Werner had to give. Besides, Madame de Staël's *Germany* had made him curious.[1] He was going to learn Italian at any rate, as Irving was doing, and he undertook German too, which was even easier because German had been in fashion in Edinburgh for thirty years.[2] The Scotch appreciation of modern languages was what then distinguished their culture from the English. He discovered easily a Dumfriesshire man who had been at Göttingen, and agreed to give him now in Edinburgh and at home in

---

[1] *Letters of C. E. Norton*, I, p. 480.
[2] Lockhart's *Life of Scott*, I, Chap. V, pp. 276–80.

summer a weekly lesson in German in exchange for one in French. He probably had several advisers, for somebody also said to him—" You'll find in German what you want." [1]

Even among the rocks, however, Carlyle was in little danger of forgetting humanity in science. He was reading Madame de Staël's *Considerations* on the Revolution, and questioned a " small Genevese " attending Jameson's class, who said, " she was very ugly and very immoral—yet had fine eyes, and was very kind to the poor." Perhaps Carlyle replied what he said to Mitchell in reporting him—" With all her faults she possessed the loftiest soul of any female of her time."

One day he met Leslie, who requested him to attempt " a most difficult problem " which he was going to put into a book he was publishing and had not time to do himself. Carlyle worked at it for a week without success, in his lodgings in a flat near Nicolson Street. A schoolmaster " right over his head " had a glee party in his house every week, where they sang together so " clamorously " that the lonely young man downstairs, distracted from his problem, "almost wished the throats of these sweet singers full of molten lead, or any other substance which might stop their braying, for the time." When Leslie heard he had failed, he advised him to—" let it alone awhile." Carlyle agreed. " And then try it again." To which also he agreed. " A queer fellow," Leslie could not help thinking him, and in their frequent talks there must have been on Leslie's part a kind anxiety to see how to help him.

For his stomach's sake Carlyle did a great deal of walking, often in company, perhaps the best esteemed of his companions being John Fergusson,[2] a " sensible, pleasant man " between two and three years his senior, and situated like himself. He had been an assistant of Irving, but disliked school teaching, and—what else shall we do ?—was the theme that beguiled the tedium of their winter walks. Each thought the other should take to writing ; but there seemed to be no wages for that obtainable there. Thomas Murray was preaching in Galloway, in hopes as yet of a church he never got.[3] Fergusson was to prosper as a teacher.[2]

---

[1] Quoted to Emerson, 1832 : *English Traits*, Chap. I.

[2] See the *Fortnightly Review*, April, 1914, pp. 628–39, for an article on J. F., and the full text of letters from him to T. C.

[3] *Autobiographical Notes* (etc.), by Thomas Murray, pp. 22–3.

James Johnstone had announced he was going to try America ; and tho Carlyle said—" I look upon emigration as a fearful destiny," in a few weeks more he was mentioning it to Mitchell for themselves to think of, as an alternative to some " Academy." This was 15.2.1819. The letter excuses his good spirits in spite of bad prospects by vague generalities which mystified Mitchell, concluding— " Thus while I seek a rule of life—life itself is fast flying away. At the last, perhaps, my creed may be found to resemble too nearly the memorable Tristrapedia of Walter Shandy, of which the minute and indubitable directions for Tristram's baby-clothes were finished when Tristram was in breeches."

The restlessness might be unworthy of a Stoic ; but the cheeriness was undeniable. Not even biliousness could make him gloomy this year. Margaret Gordon was filling his life, unseen by others, as the sun lights all the world although the clouds may cover the sky.

II

REFUSAL TO BLACKLEG

(1819)

ABOUT the middle of February he went by appointment to see a man who wanted to arrange for private teaching in mathematics. "A stout, impudent-looking man in red whiskers " met him, and " just perceptibly " returned the bow of Carlyle coming in.

" I am here by the request of Mr. Nichol to speak with you, sir, about a mathematical teacher whom he tells me you want."

" Aye. What are your terms ? "

" Two guineas a month for each hour."

" *Two guineas !* For private *teaching*—that is perfectly extravagant ! "

" I *believe* it to be the rate at which every teacher of respectability in Edinburgh officiates ; and I *know* it to be the rate below which *I* never officiate."

" *That* won't *do* for *my* friend."

" I am sorry that nothing less will do for *me*. Good morning."

He retired with " considerable deliberation," repressing his wrath by reflecting that the man naturally wanted the work done cheap, and that his ill-breeding might be his misfortune as much as his fault.

It may have been next day, at any rate it was on Tuesday, 16.2.1819, that he was coming back to town from a walk in the country, in the company of Fergusson, and met Dr. Brewster and two companions. Brewster stopped to ask him—" Can you translate for me a French paper on Chemistry, by Berzelius, a Stockholm Professor ? It is to be published in April." Carlyle said " Yes," and went and received it next day, six long sheets in a cramp hand— more than a week's work and frugally paid, but welcome as a start. The last bit of its proof was corrected before the end of March.

It was for the *Edinburgh Philosophical Journal*, to which he also contributed before long " Remarks on Professor Hausteen's Enquiries concerning the Magnetism of the Earth," and a translation of " Professor Mohs' New System of Crystallography and Mineralogy." [1]

[1] The credit of discovering these belongs to John Muir, who in 1897 kindly lent to D. A. W. his pamphlet, *Thomas Carlyle's Apprenticeship*.

III

JANE BAILLIE WELSH

(1818–19)

IN contrast to himself, Carlyle observed this winter that
Irving was gloomy, as if under a cloud. He never knew
why, though he remembered hearing him call Dr. Welsh of
Haddington " one of the wisest, truest and most dignified
of men " and his daughter " a paragon of gifted young
girls," as well as an only child and kind of heiress.

Irving's biographer explains [1] he had " met once more
the little pupil " Jane Baillie Welsh, whom he had once
" superintended." She was seventeen now, and for a year
or more she had been " finishing " at an Edinburgh boarding
school,[2] and by and by she confessed she had " an affectionate recollection of her old master ; and the young man
found a natural charm in her society."

It was so " natural " that if Bella Martin had been in
sight she would have intervened, as she did when she saw
him slipping towards Margaret Gordon. Miss Welsh had
the field to herself, and her " old master " was a very handsome young man, in spite of his squint, and soon they were
discussing the eternal question—to be or not to be.

He was frank about his previous engagement ; and so,
she said, she held him at arm's-length. She used to tell that
Irving once heard her praising " too warmly " another man
and let his " pique and mortification " escape in spite of
himself. She left the room, but he recalled her, and she
found " the simple-hearted giant standing penitent " and
saying to her, like the hero of a novel—" The truth is, I
was piqued. I have always been accustomed to fancy that
I stood highest in your good opinion, and I was jealous to
hear you praise another man. I am sorry for what I said
just now—that is the truth of it."

What made Irving gloomy was the memory of Miss Martin.

[1] *Edward Irving*, by Mrs. Oliphant, Chap. V.
[2] *Life of J. W. Carlyle*, by Mrs. Ireland, p. 19.

The chance of a wife with money—" a lass with a tocher "—was one of the standing attractions of the Church, and to miss an opportunity like this was unprofessional; but he was trustworthy, and as soon as he made sure in some way that his Bella held him to his word, he agreed to abide by it and broke off with Jane. The dates are vague. The only scrap of contemporary paper not destroyed was a sonnet he sent her—" To a Lock of my Lady's Hair." [1] Miss Welsh cut it out of the letter it was in, and we can read on the back of the paper—

" . . . I have resolved neither to see Isabella nor her father before I . . . cannot brook the sight of either until this be explained. . . ." The rest of the letter is wanting. The sonnet began—

> " Thou raven lock ! On which mine eyes do rest
> Unwearied. Thou dear emblem of my Jane
> Whose hand did crop thee from her head, fit test
> Of her affection ever to remain. . . ."

And so for fourteen lines ; but here 'tis best to stop, lest laughing much might give us pain.

After the thing had blown over, he wrote to Jane Welsh referring to it thus—" When I think of you my mind is overspread with the most affectionate and tender regard which I neither know how to name nor how to describe. One thing I know, it would long ago have taken the form of the most devoted attachment, *but for one intervening* circumstance." Which shows that Jane may have been flattering herself when she said she " persuaded " Irving to wed Miss Martin and so " preserve his honour from reproach." A glimpse of reality is always pleasant for spectators. It is plain that Irving's tender of love to Jane was never more than a might-have-been ; and she " loved passionately " as was then the fashion ; but at different times before she met Carlyle in 1821, and for some time after then, she loved several as passionately as Irving, and George Rennie more. [2]

She needed less effort than usual to turn her back on Irving ; for her father died soon after (in September, 1819), and sorrow filled her mind. There is no evidence that after then she ever thought of Irving as a possibility, nor he of her ; but he continued a friend of her mother and herself,

[1] *The Love Letters of T. Carlyle and Miss Welsh*, II, pp. 49 and 404-5.
[2] See *Early Letters of J. W. Carlyle*, by D. G. Ritchie.

and tried to influence her as an ex-teacher and pastor, and
in letters posed as a brother and even as a father, till she
lost patience with him and " discharged " him from preaching to her. But he continued a favourite of her mother.

How many other preachers cast eyes upon her does not
appear; perhaps as many as came within sight. But she
did not incline that way. Besides, the clergy were expected
to take the leavings, as the first pick in the marriage market
was for men of money, and Jane appeared attractive to
several such,[1] tho she never had her mother's looks.
" Her face was too angular for beauty," according to a good
observer, who was young enough to be impartial.[2]

[1] See *Early Letters of J. W. Carlyle*, by D. G. Ritchie.
[2] Samuel Smiles, *Autobiography*, pp. 5 and 34.

IV

HOME TO MAINHILL, WITH ROUSSEAU'S "CONFESSIONS" AND OTHER BOOKS

(1819)

IRVING and Carlyle were much together this winter, though as silent to each other about sweethearts as decent Chinese or Muslims. The talk at Irving's table was up to the best level in the town, and privately Irving pressed upon him more and more advice to give his life to letters. He was to leave free for business or pleasure the time required, but " set apart some portion of each day or week " for a " continuous effort not for getting knowledge, but for communicating it, that you may gain favour, or money, or opinion " (that is, reputation). " You have not the pulpit as I have. The *Edinburgh Review* you are perfectly fit for. . . . *Blackwood's* presents bad company, but a good field for fugitive writing. Writers in the encyclopedias do not get out from the crowd ; but writers in the *Review* come out at once and obtain the very opinion (or reputation) you want among intelligent and active men, not among the sluggish savants alone. You will open up ultimate prospects which I trust no man shall be able to close." In short, " Find vent for your notions. Get them tongue upon every subject."

Some months later Irving wrote to explain the exasperating indifference of Carlyle's hearers at table :—

' Your information they will bear the display of for the value of it, but not your feelings and affections, which, being of finer tone than theirs, and consequently seeking a keener expression, they are apt to mistake for a rebuke of their own tameness, or for intolerance of ordinary things, and asperity of mind.

' Your utterance is not the most favourable. It convinces, but does not persuade ; and fascinates very few. Your audience lay (lie) in wait to catch you in your words, and give

history or geography, science or politics or letters, humanity
for choice as a rule, but never theology.

In the mornings his mother waited for Tom with a cup of
tea when he came in from his walks ; and he told Masson
by and by that " no cups of tea ever seemed so fragrant
and so delicious as those his mother had ready for him
those mornings." [1] He said what he could to quiet her
misgivings about faith ; and though as a Christian she might
try to grieve to see him " too much at ease in Zion," as a
mother she was glad that his bilious attacks were growing few
and faint, and his spirits high in spite of them. She wondered
who the girl was, but did not venture to enquire, and told
her daughters : " There is no use trying to get anything out
of Tom by questions unless he wants to tell you. Besides,
one never asks about such things." [2]

With John Fergusson, who had gone to his father's farm
in Perthshire, he continued to discuss on paper the topics
of their winter talks. [3] The humour of exaggeration like
Mark Twain's appears in his coolly comparing their condition, when in danger of needing to continue teaching,
to that of Milton's Satan and Co., when suddenly pitched
from Heaven into Hell. The fun was made palpable by
a candid confession that he cannot compel himself to care.
" I have been happy—perhaps too happy, because too little
disturbed about my future destiny." This left leisure for
a spiritual bird's-eye view of humanity ; and he sent
Fergusson a description of the Annandalers so free from local
prejudice that even the Celt Maclaren might have called it
candid—" senselessly candid."

' The people are mostly peasants, and display the usual
sentiments and habits. Those in other stations are scarcely
more refined. Their want of commerce tends to keep them
ignorant and unenterprising ; while smuggling and moss-
trooping have left but too deep traces in their minds. With
regard to our gentry—a stranger only would call it petulance
to say that their principles and pursuits are often little different from those vouchsafed to cattle and each beast.

' Small sorrow is excited in me at hearing of the indifference
with which you view the squabbles of the General Assembly.

[1] *Edinburgh Sketches and Memories*, by David Masson, p. 268, footnote.
[2] Conversations of Mrs. C. with her daughters afterwards, corroborated
by letters in various passages.
[3] Besides the correspondence published by Messrs. Froude, Norton
and A. Carlyle, see the *Fortnightly Review*, April, 1914, pp. 628-39.

The familiar miniature published by Mr. Froude was never recognised as a likeness by those who knew Jane Baillie Welsh in her youth.
It was merely a standard type of beauty. The original of the picture
published here was a portrait in oils done in Haddington by a travelling
artist, nameless now, and it was hanging in Carlyle's house when he
died. His niece gave it to Mrs. Chrystal, the nearest living relative of
Mrs. Carlyle, a cousin on her mother's side. It is still in Glasgow, in
the house of Miss Chrystal, the cousin's daughter, who kindly allowed
Susan Crawford, a Glasgow artist, to make an etching of it for use in
this book.

When the Carlyles were at Craigenputtock it was at Mrs. Welsh's
house, Templand, and she lent or gave it to Jeffrey. Mrs. Carlyle insisted
on the return of it, which remains mysterious only till one looks at it.
It was far too good a likeness to please her. In a letter from London,
(4/7/1831), Jeffrey chaffed her about it, saying: " My very dear child, I
have that precious picture. I lent it for a week to Mrs. Montagu, and I
believe they have been copying it. You do not grudge that? She says
she had fancied you would look nearly so. I do not believe it—nobody
ever anticipated that peculiar countenance. Those very lovely, but *too
thoughtful* eyes, and that half-*obstinate*, half-capricious lip, which does
not agree very well either with them or with itself. I have studied the
enigma carefully, and think I half understand it."

[*face p.* 176

The worship of idols belonging to the *tribe* or the *den* is, doubtless, a pleasant exercise : it is also a debasing one, and may continue, for some ages, to provoke "a sigh or a smile." The condition of the State is scarcely more exhilarating.'

He went on to curse the taxes on tobacco and the Prince Regent ; and some weeks later, to " punish any aristocratic prejudice which you may have contracted among those Celtic clans," he quoted to Fergusson the Abbé Raynal's fervid invective against kings in general.

To him and to Mitchell also, his " Father Confessor," he had to admit (14.7.1819) he was enjoying himself and lazily reading at random, and he promised no amendment, though vaguely suggesting to Fergusson a joint good-resolution to spend an early hour, seven to eight, " throughout winter " to " read together Italian one day, Greek the other." He had only read six pages of Tasso, and the German was " dubious." The German authors had disappointed him as yet, and Frederick's wars were dull ; but Lessing had " some spirit," and before September was out he had started Goethe.

In that month he had spent three or four days at Annan with Irving, and heard his joyful news. Dr. Chalmers had offered to appoint him his assistant at Glasgow. On Monday (20.9.1819) Irving set out for Glasgow, walking thirty miles to Moffat, escorted by Carlyle and another friend as far as a hill-top overlooking the neighbourhood of Moffat. There they paused to part. " The blue sky was beautifully spotted with white clouds, which the wind was chasing." They watched the shadows of the passing clouds on the landscape. " Like life ! " said Carlyle. Irving squeezed his arm— " Good-bye ! " " Good-bye ! "—and strode swiftly away to catch the Glasgow coach.

Writing to Fergusson a few days later (25.9.1819), he admitted anxiety lest Irving's " fervid genius prompt him into extravagances, from which more stupid and less honest preachers are exempted." Which seems prophetic after a hundred years.

About himself he added : " What to do is not so certain. I think at times of law and advocates." On Wednesday (10.11.1819) he was arriving at Edinburgh, and that day week (17.11.1819) was enrolled in the Scots Law class. Dr. Duncan had introduced him again to Bailie Waugh, who

N

might employ him in a Review, and there were advocates
to see, to say nothing of the Advocates' Library, enough to
keep him in Edinburgh, when the weather was wet and the
roads at their muddiest. Yet he had to tell Mitchell that
" most " of the first week had been " consumed " in " travelling to Fife, etc." How much can be put into an etc. !
Tacitus himself never put more in any word. A later letter
shows that Margaret Gordon approved his design, and this
remark to Mitchell shows he went over to see her before
he 'enrolled—" Etc. ! "

VI

A STUDENT OF LAW

(1819–20)

FROM a man who had been a fellow-lodger last winter he received " four very ponderous quartos of notes " of law-lectures " in short-hand," which were of " much use." Avoiding company as waste of time, and taking a walk before breakfast and again before entering his law-class at half-past one and listening to pleadings in the Law Courts for recreation, he plunged into law books in his hours of study, though he had to tell his brother of the best—" you would think the very Goddess of dullness had inspired every sentence." Nevertheless, to his mother and Mitchell he prophesied, " I shall not dislike the science."

The winter was very cold. Peterloo in August had shown how easy it was to slaughter heaps of unarmed people, and now when thousands were starving, the gentry of Scotland prepared for Peterloos, and disgusted Carlyle by their funk and their gloating over the sorrows of the hungry workmen in Glasgow. Early in December that city was surrounded by soldiers, and the Edinburgh barracks were emptied and refilled by volunteers. In Princes Street, Carlyle used to watch " courier hussars come in from the Glasgow region covered with mud, breathless, for head-quarters," and overhear the " old powdered gentlemen in silver spectacles " who passed him " talking with low-toned, but exultant voice, about ' cordon of troops, sir.' "

He saw the " Lothian Yeomanry " going to " do their bit " in the " cordon " on a " bleared Sunday morning " (12.12.1819), between seven and eight. He had left his lodgings in Bristo Street for his walk before breakfast, and seeing a crowd of stragglers " with redcoats interspersed " at the Riding-house at Nicolson Street, he went and saw the troop take the road. They were " ill-ranked," and not formidable fighting men, though maybe equal to killing weavers without weapons, which was all they intended.

They had a "send-off" he never forgot—"a farewell cheer," he declared. "The strangest shout I have heard, not loud but it said with emphasis : 'May the Devil go with you, ye peculiarly contemptible and dead to the distresses of your fellow-creatures ! ' "

At Irving's instigation, Carlyle was casting around for a topic to write on, while feeling as if groping his way from the bottom of a cave. A life of Horrox the astronomer was one of many plans abandoned. He wrote an essay on Pictet's *Theory of Gravitation* for Jeffrey's *Edinburgh Review*, and handed it in himself to the editor's house in George Street, on Monday, 24.1.1820, with a letter ; and heard no more of it at all and never enquired.

Dr. Brewster was now losing the services of Thomas Campbell, who did biographies for the *Edinburgh Encyclopedia*, which had begun in 1810 and was still only at the letter M. Becoming an editor himself, Campbell had no more time,[1] and so Brewster tried Carlyle " on frugal terms " for biographies. " I do not get on very readily," wrote Carlyle to his brother, " but this is like my apprenticeship, in time I shall do it far more readily." *Montesquieu* was handed in on Saturday, 19.2.1820, and *Lady M. W. Montagu* finished on Wednesday, 1.3.1820, by which time several more had been done or commissioned, including *Montaigne, Dr. Moore, Sir John Moore* and *Nelson*. Thus the winter went busily by.

The " gentlemen volunteers " were much in evidence, and one fine, spring morning he met one of them, an advocate he knew, with a musket in his hand, going to be drilled.

" You should have the like of this," said the gentleman volunteer, cherrily patting his musket.

" Hm, yes ; but I haven't yet quite settled on which side ! " said Carlyle. Which sounded liker quiz than it was. He had to make an effort not to smile in the faces of these fellows, and apropos the Cato Street conspiracy he cursed both King and ministers for meeting " well-founded complaints of poverty, almost starvation, with indifference or cold-blooded ridicule."

Till after the end of February he worked hard at law ; and seeing quickly the hocus-pocus of it, was enquiring among practical people how business was got. The lecturer, Professor Hume, had none of his uncle's genius, but seemed

---

[1] See *Edinburgh Sketches and Memories*, by David Masson, p. 292 ; and *Lives* of *T. Campbell*.

to Carlyle " most perspicuous " and better than the books, at his worst.

Something happened in March. Hume became suddenly " disgusting " beyond endurance. " Our hero " went to the courts no more and enquired no more of " practical people." He returned the voluminous notes he had thank-fully borrowed and heeded the lecturer no more. He attended the class because he had begun it and the end of the session was near ; but he was like a steamer whose engines have stopped and which continues to move from mere momentum. When he started afresh it was in a different direction. His pursuit of law was ended. Why ?

In middle life he said once that he might have gone on if he had had the two hundred pounds required for admission fees. In old age and at the time, he dwelt on the difficulty of finding employment and the meanness and dullness of the trade, with " nothing but money as wages. Details about points not of the slightest importance, the formalities of customs which ought to be instantly and for ever abolished ; uncounted cases, with what Stair thought, what Bankton, what the poor doubting Dirleton ; and then the nature of actions of—O infandum ! " (Un-speakable !) It ceased to seem worth the pains, in short. As every effect has many causes, the reasons he gave were true so far as they went, and yet not all the truth.

VII

MARGARET GORDON OBEYS HER AUNT

(1820)

"THEY say" it was only a coincidence. But Margaret Gordon thought differently at the time,[1] and must have known better than anyone to-day. What is certain is only that about the beginning of March, 1820,[2] Carlyle was in Kirkcaldy and she told him he must cease to be a lover, and be only a friend, to which he strongly objected. Mrs. Usher was to go with her nieces to London and live there with their mother, Mrs. Guthrie,[3] who was a fashionable doctor's wife and could easily start them husband-hunting to the best advantage. It was not with Mrs. Usher's approval but by way of compromise that Margaret was allowed to invite Carlyle to call again ; and when he came, Mrs. Usher remained in the room beside them. The scene can be imagined. Forty-five years later he wrote in the *Reminiscences* : " Speak to her, since the ' Good-bye, then,' at Kirkcaldy, I never did or could."

The unfinished romance of Wotton Reinfred was used in the second part of *Sartor*, and the publication of it in 1892 left no room for doubt that Margaret Gordon was the original of *Sartor's* Blumine. The heroine of Wotton is called Jane, but is recognisably Margaret Gordon in all the essentials and many external circumstances, such as the strong-minded aunt so proud and poor who has adopted the orphan and " shared her all " with her, and now had " high hopes from her niece," and so on.

The parting described would correspond not to the one superintended by her aunt, but to the one before it.[4]

' One morning he found his fair Jane constrained and sad ; she was silent, absent ; she seemed to have been weeping.

---

[1] Unpublished letter.

[2] 1819 is given in the *Reminiscences* as the date of parting, but A. Carlyle's edition of the *Love Letters*, II, p. 391, and M. G.'s letters here following, corroborated fully, prove the later date.

[3] *Carlyle's First Love, Margaret Gordon*, by R. C. Archibald, p. 51, etc.

[4] *Last Words of Thomas Carlyle*, pp. 36-39.

The aunt left the room. He pressed for explanation with increasing apprehension; but none was to be had, save only broken hints that she was grieved for herself, for him, that she had much to suffer, that he must cease to visit her. It was vain that the thunder-struck Wotton demanded, " Why ? why ? " " One whom she entirely depended on had so ordered it, and for herself she had nothing to do but to obey." She resisted all entreaty; she refused all explanation : her words were firm and cold ; only by a thrill of anguish that once or twice quivered over her face could a calmer man have divined that she was suffering within. Wotton's pride was stung ; he rose and held out his hand : " Farewell, then, madam! " said he in a low, steady voice; " I will not——" She put her hand in his ; she looked in his face, tears started to her eyes ; but she turned away her head, hastily pressed his hand, and, sobbing, whispered, scarcely audibly, " Farewell ! " He approached in frenzy ; his arms were half raised to encircle her ; but starting back she turned on him a weeping face—a face of anger, love and agony. She sternly motioned to him to withdraw. ' This look of hers he had long time to meditate, for it was the last. How many burning thoughts he had to front ; how many wild theories he formed of his misfortune ; how many wild projects to repair it ! But all in vain : his letters were unanswered, or answered in cold, brief commonplaces. At last he received a pressing entreaty, or rather, a peremptory injunction, to " write no more." '

Which rather anticipates this history, correctly enough ; and there is a " Bernard," who corresponds to Irving, and soothed him with " human sympathy " in the months that followed.

What Carlyle wrote to Irving at once may be inferred from his reply (14.3.1820) :—

' You talk of renouncing the law. I would not have you renounce the law. Law has within it scope ample enough for any mind. The reformation which it needs, and which with so much humour and feeling you describe, is the very evidence of what I say. Did Adam Smith find the commercial system less encumbered ? And see what order the mind of one man has made there.'

Which was flattering, but irrelevant. Still more so was what Irving wrote about " the example of the Saviour of men." It was becoming needful to be more candid with Irving if their intimacy was to last. So he accepted his invitation to visit him in April; and he occupied himself till then in arranging for hack work to keep him busy at Mainhill. He felt he must not be idle this summer. The first use he made of the leisure given by rest from love and the law was to write a letter overdue to Mitchell—a hasty scribble, but all the better evidence of his feelings. It shows how his disappointment was clearing the mind's eyes and making him look down the " Gulf of Time." He had not yet reached the sunlit summits of thought where his life was passed, but he can here be seen on the upward way.

VIII

A LETTER TO MITCHELL

(1820)

IT is easy now to guess what was in mind when he wrote (18.3.1820) of " privations and calamities " in this letter, though maybe Mitchell never knew.

'MY DEAR MITCHELL,—
    'Ever since January a train of ill-health, with its usual depression, aggravated by other privations and calamities too tedious to particularise, has pressed heavily upon me. I could not resolve to afflict you with my sorrows or my dullness. Three months have passed before answering your letter.
    'You would suspect me of closeness if I did not attempt to trace you a sketch of the life which I have led for some time past. It must be brief for many reasons. Zimmermann has written a book which he calls *The Pleasures of Solitude ;* I would not have you to believe him : solitude in truth has few pleasures, uninterrupted solitude is full of pain. But solitude, or company more distressing, is not the worst. The thought that one's best days are hurrying darkly and uselessly away is yet more grievous. It is vain to deny it, my friend, I am an altogether unprofitable creature. Timid, yet not humble, weak, yet enthusiastic ; nature and educaion have rendered me entirely unfit to force my way among the thick-skinned inhabitants of this planet. Law, I fear, must be renounced ; it is a shapeless mass of absurdity and chicane.'

Which is not Carlylean exaggeration, but the simple truth, as true to-day as then, and likely to continue true as long as the gullible public allows " professionals " to exploit for private profit the administration of justice. The letter continues :—

'The ten years, which a barrister commonly spends in painful idleness, before arriving at employment, is more than my physical or moral frame could endure. Teaching a school is but another word for sure and not very slow destruction : and as to compiling the wretched lives of Montesquieu, Montagu, Montaigne, etc., for Dr. Brewster —the remuneration will hardly sustain life. What then is to be done ? This situation—but I touch a string which generally yields a tedious sound to any but the operator. I know you are not indifferent to the matter, but I would not tire you with it. The fate of one man is a mighty small concern in the grand whole of this best of all possible worlds ; let us quit the subject, with just one observation more for your benefit. It is to keep the profession you have adopted, if it be at all tolerable. A young man who goes forth into the world to seek his fortune with those lofty ideas of honour and uprightness which a studious secluded life naturally begets (will generally come to grief, in short). Dissipation is infinitely worse : I thank Heaven I am not a poet ; I shall avoid that sad alternative.

'I was glad to learn that you had finished the perusal of Homer. Certainly the blind bard is little obliged by your opinion of him : I believe, however, Candour is, and that is better. . . . (Homer) has had his day—at least the better part of it ; the noon was five-and-twenty centuries ago ; the twilight (for he set in 1453) may last for another five-and-twenty centuries—but it too must terminate. Nothing that we know of can last for ever. The very mountains are silently wasting away, and long before eternity is done, Mont Blanc might cease to be the pinnacle of Europe, and Chimborazo lie under the Pacific. Philosophy and literature have a far shorter date. Error, in the first, succeeds to error, as wave to wave. Poetry, they tell us, escapes the general doom : but cannot escape. . . .

'Tho some of the affections which Homer delineates are coexistent with the race, yet in the progress of refinement or change his mode of delineating them will appear trivial or disgusting—and the very twilight of his fame will have an end. Thus all things are dying, my friend— only ourselves die faster. Man ! if I had £200 a year, a beautiful little house in some laughing valley, three or four pure-spirited mortals who would love me and be loved again, together with a handsome library, and—a great genius, I would investigate the hallucinations that connect themselves with such ideas. At present I must revisit this nether sphere.

' I know not whether I shall see you in summer; most probably I shall leave this town—if for ever I need not greatly care.

' Yours ever,

' THOMAS CARLYLE.'

The conclusion had a latent meaning in his mind, like the beginning. He was really thinking of going to London, whither Margaret Gordon was bound, if—well, if she wanted him to do so. To the right sort of man, the " authentic will " of the woman is the voice of nature.

IX

DR. CHALMERS TRIES TO CONVERT CARLYLE

(1820)

NATURE has many voices. A winter like that of Iceland and careless feeding, overwork and excitement, made him relapse into biliousness worse than ever. The gentle Brewster saw he was ill, and was a little sorry for him, and said to cheer him—" I was at death's door for fifteen years, and now in my forty-second year am perfectly well." Approving his plan of going to work in the country, Brewster gave him articles to write, two screeds to translate, and a book to review. Thus provided he set out for Glasgow in April to visit Irving.

He went by steamer to Bo'ness and thence by canal, and coming on deck when approaching Glasgow he saw nothing but smoke and yellow vapour, through which " pulsated an extraordinary light—a red glare that flashed up and across the skies, as if the whole world was in conflagration."

He turned to the man at the wheel and asked—" What does that mean ? " " Dixon's Blazes—Ironworks," was the answer.[1]

Irving welcomed him. For over a week it was like old days back again. In taking him about the first evening, Irving left him half an hour at " The Tontine," the first sight of which was " a treat to my rustic eyes," he confessed. " Several hundreds of such fine, clean, opulent, and enviable or amiable-looking good Scotch gentlemen, sauntering about in trustful gossip, or reading their newspapers—I remember the shining bald crowns and serene white heads of " some, and thought them happier than they knew. The gentry of Glasgow were cordial and hospitable, especially the old men buzz-buzzing at sight of Irving about their

---

[1] Told to William Black. See the last volume of Black's *Works* (1903). The man was sure to begin by saying, Dixon's Blazes, and then add— Ironworks.

souls, and the "exuberant" young ladies, agog about
what Chalmers was doing. He was "the continual topic,"
reviving interest in the half-forgotten gospel of redemption,
salvation and so on. The shrewd old men did not need
Pascal to teach them to insure against the slightest risk of
fire in Hell or anywhere, and many of them had been so
busy making money that they knew little about anything
else. Two Annandalers among the merchants became
Carlyle's friends—David Hope, a nephew of Adam Hope,
the Academy teacher,[1] and William Graham, described by
Irving [2] as the "best-hearted of men and most intelligent
of merchants." Graham had lived in Philadelphia and
could tell about life in the West.

Both Hope and Graham preserved with pious care the
letters received from Carlyle, whose shrewdness was
remarked in Glasgow.[2] The letters give us a bit of talk.
The money-men wanting to "enjoy" their money itched
for "power," and envied the lairds, who seemed to be
dominating Scotland, under the providence of the Devils
(in the shape of London politicians). So the Glasgow
merchants talked the cant of the Tories, as if they were all
Dukes or, better still, the likely founders of families of
Dukes. Such had been the identical mean ambition which
ruined Sir Walter Scott. So Graham and others defended
"entails," which Carlyle declared to be in every country
"fatal things and worthy of all condemnation." [2]

The reverence for Chalmers in Glasgow would be more
difficult to match to-day. The great man invited Carlyle
to breakfast, but the morning was cold and foggy, the light
was dim, and little was said. The young man was wideawake, but noticed that Chalmers was not. He felt glad
to escape unnoticed ; but he was rejoicing too soon. Another
day, in the rather "fine drawing-room" of a Mr. Parker
at a "rather solemn evening party," Chalmers put his chair
beside Carlyle's in some clear space of floor, and talked long
and earnestly about a new plan he had for demonstrating
Christianity, the same he afterwards diluted into college
lectures and books. It is proved to be true by its "visible
fitness for human nature"—"it is all written in us already
as in *sympathetic ink*. The Bible awakens it and you can
read ! "

The young man "listened respectfully with a clear sense

[1] *Thomas Carlyle*, by W. H. Wylie, p. 398.
[2] Unpublished letters.

of the geniality and goodness of the man," but was plainly no longer interested in " evidences," as Chalmers had the sense to see, for he declared " that laddie " [1] was " a lover of earnestness, more than a lover of truth." [2] This was a good shot, but Chalmers was like the rest, who take their creed as an axiom, and think they are in love with truth when they are only looking for a way to make their creed seem plausible.

Some instinct of genius made him uneasy at the sight of Carlyle's indifference ; and Irving by and by wrote—" He never ceases to be enquiring after you." Perhaps he was told a little of what had passed between the young men. The visit ended on the first of May, a Monday, the preacher's day of rest, when Carlyle and Irving went to Paisley. Next day they walked together as far as Drumclog, the scene of the fight between Claverhouse and the Covenanters. Loath to part they sat a long time in the sunshine there on the brow of one of the peat-hags, and talked " of many things, perhaps more confidentially than ever before." Away to the south-west they saw Ailsa Craig, which carried their thoughts to the seas and foreign places, and somehow Irving discovered that Carlyle would like to correspond with Margaret Gordon.

At last the declining sun made them saunter slowly into the highway between Muirkirk, about ten miles off, and Glasgow, twenty. Some masons building a cottage were packing up on ceasing for the day. The young men leant their backs against a dry stone wall and looking into the west continued to talk. " It was here," wrote Carlyle, " just as the sun was sinking," that Irving " drew from me by degrees, in the softest manner, the confession that I did *not* think as he of Christian Religion, and that it was vain for me to expect I ever could or should. This, if it were so, he had pre-engaged to take *well* of me—like an elder brother, if I would be frank with him ; and right loyally he did so, and to the end of his life we needed no concealments on that head ; which was really a step gained."

The sun had set as they turned away—" Good-bye ! " " Good-bye ! "—Irving for Glasgow, Carlyle for Muirkirk.

[1] Heard by David Masson, Chalmers' way of alluding to T. C. Told by Masson to D. A. W.
[2] *Thomas Carlyle*, by Professor John Nichol, p. 29. This is likely to be accurate though the authority is not mentioned. D. A. W. was a pupil of Nichol and knew him well.

X

MARGARET GORDON AND OTHERS

(1820)

FROM Muirkirk to Dumfries was fifty-four miles, the
longest walk he ever did in a day, taking sixteen
hours to do it. The pillar of smoke at Muirkirk Ironworks
reminded him of a story his father used to tell. A poor
old crazy woman came and stood beside the lonely stoker
there, who was used to her and did not heed her till a
puff! made him look round, and behold! she was floating
on the molten metal, the red-hot, semi-transparent figure
of her like a ghost above it for some moments before crumb-
ling into ashes.

As he crossed the moors between Muirkirk and Nithsdale
he was so filled by " the deep matters " he had been discussing with Irving that he did not weary.[1] In a shepherd's
cottage on the edge of the waste he was receiving refresh-
ment and wondering how life could be worth living in such
a " hovel " with a dirty wife and " squealing " children,
when three women arrived with three more children—a
widow, whose man had just died, being taken home by her
mother and sister. Whereon the dirty " shepherdess "
seemed suddenly beautiful to the young cynic who had
been wondering how any man could endure to live with
her ; for now he saw her " genuine heartfelt sympathy and
benevolence " to the weeping women and orphans ; and
he departed wishing he were an angel and able to relieve
them, and wondering at the woman's sensibility.

When his road came near the Nith, he had other company
than his own thoughts. The roads were not so lonely then
as now, so that a wayfarer might be like Bunyan's Pilgrim,
and his fatigue be diminished by talk on the way. Thus
an " old peasant " he now overtook was plain-spoken in
his politics, declaring that " unless these times alter, folks

---

[1] Unpublished Letters of Carlyle (1820, etc.), *Scribner's Mag.*, April,
1893, pp. 416–25.

will all be Radicals together." He passed several parties
going to Dumfriesshire in search of work and food, " like
the Israelites of old to Goshen in the dearth." Henry
Duncan himself had lately published a story to persuade
the people to die content in hopes of Heaven, but even the
peasantry were beginning to suspect that was a dream.

Carlyle confessed to Johnstone—" I have no great reason
to complain," but the contrary ; and yet, he said—" I am
altering very fast. Hope will not always stay with one ;
and despair is not an eligible neighbour. I do not think
I am ever to have any settled way of doing, too old for
beginning any new profession."

He was sick and dreary, like one without hope ; but
Irving was not only stimulating him to preach on paper,
declaring—" I have no more fear of your final success than
Noah had of the Deluge ceasing " ; he was also dropping
a hint in the proper quarter. Margaret Gordon was as far
on her way to her mother as Palace Craig, near Airdrie,
and it was like sunshine breaking through the clouds when
a letter came from there.

'PALACE CRAIG,
'June 4th, 1820.

'MR. THOMAS CARLYLE, MAINHILL, ECCLEFECHAN.

'DEAR SIR,—

'Having understood from our friend, Mr. Irving, that
you had returned to Dumfriesshire, I take the opportunity
this information affords me, of thanking you for the very
friendly visit you paid us some time ago at Kirkcaldy.
Perhaps you may be inclined to think, when I had last the
pleasure of seeing you, I might have expressed my sense of
the favour, without now writing a formal epistle on the
subject. *This*, had our short interview permitted, I would
have gladly done. *You* know the cause that prevented me.
If your call had been merely one of ceremony such as I am
accustomed to receive from the ordinary *herd* of men, I
should neither have seen nor declared any obligation ;
originating, as it did, from a true greatness of soul, the result
of feelings little akin to those that occupy common minds,
I should be wanting in duty to myself as well as to you, did
I not show by my gratitude that the kindness was bestowed
on one who is at least sensible of its extent. To *possess*
your *friendship*, I have often said, was a constant source

of delight to me ; to *lose* it, you may believe, was propor-
tionably painful. Your coming to see me in Fife, appeared
not only a proof of the noble triumph you had obtained over
your weakness (forgive the expression), but seemed to be
an intimation that I still was thought worthy of that esteem
with which you formerly honoured me. If ever I may have
an opportunity of hearing from yourself that in this my last
conjecture I am not mistaken, time alone can determine.
In a few weeks I bid adieu, for a season, to Caledonia's
rugged shores where I leave, still blessed to gaze on her
ever-varying charms, a few, and but a few, friends whose
partial regard has soothed many a sorrowing moment of my
past existence. When I may again behold the scene which
so many circumstances endear to my recollection is very
uncertain. I mentioned to you I intended to remain a
twelvemonth in London : my Mother will not consent to
my being so much a stranger in my family as so long a
separation endangers. Yet why entertain you with so much
egotism ? If it offends you, blame my vanity ; for I will
confess *that* alone urges me on ; it is only the assurance that
such a relation of my proposed wanderings will not be
troublesome to a *friend*—a name by which I hope I shall
always call *you*.

'I was very sorry to hear your health had been impaired
by the severity of your winter's study. Your "native
breezes," I trust, have already produced the desired effect
of removing the consequences of your stay in Edinburgh.
You must not wear out your constitution by such continual
application ; still, permit me to entreat you not to desert
the path Nature has so evidently marked you should walk
in. It is true it is full of rugged obstacles, interspersed with
little to charm the sense ; yet these present a struggle which
is fitted only for minds such as *yours* to overcome. The
difficulties of the ascent are great, but how glorious the
summit ! Keep your eyes fixed on the end of your journey,
and you will begin to forget the weariness of the way. You
see I have taken the liberty of a friend, I had almost said
of a *Sister*, who is probably addressing you for the last time,
and who would regret to learn hereafter that Nature, in
spite of her unusual bounty, had been cruelly opposed.

'May Fortune prove propitious to you, in every part of
your voyage through life ! Or if this is indeed too much
happiness for any one mortal in this changing scene, may
the storms of adversity ever find you prepared to resist

o

their overwhelming violence, and ever be followed by that peaceful calm the virtuous alone are capable of enjoying. Whatever be the situation allotted you, be assured I shall ever

'Remain your sincere friend,
'M. GORDON.'

The last part of the letter recalls the custom of toasts prevailing then. Mrs. Usher had not neglected to train her beautiful niece to be able to honour the wine with suitable " sentiments." The young man she was writing to snatched the chance of correspondence, like a drowning man clutching at a straw. We are left guessing what he wrote from the reply.—

'PALACE CRAIG,
'*June 28th*, 1820.

'MR. THOMAS CARLYLE, MAINHILL, ECCLEFECHAN.

'What a risk did you run in sending your Letter! I was from home when it arrived, and was much astonished to find it waiting me. I was much pleased to hear your health was improving. *Remove those " troubles of the soul,"* and you *must* be well. Why indulge those miserable racking thoughts ? . . . You ask me to write you often ; this, I must repeat, would not be doing justice to you—think me not vain. I have adopted the title of Sister, and you must permit me to usurp the privileges of one You promise never to indulge those " vain imaginations " which have made us both so unhappy. Yet tell me, do they not still require steady restraint ? And would not I, by acceding to your request, encourage that "*weakness*" it has been my object to remove ? Oblige me not to refuse, by asking me to do what is not in my power. Willingly

would I advance your happiness, anxious will I be to hear
of that happiness, but (think me not severe), from another
source my information must come. . . .

I have only a few moments to devote to this; by the
time you receive it I shall have commenced my wanderings.
You are too generous to *wish* me to act against my sense of
duty. If you have no cause to speak gently of this friend
(meaning her aunt, which is suggestive of much), remember
'twas a regard for what was considered the interest of her
charge that tempted her to look unkindly on you. She
really esteems you. For my sake return the kindness. I
am to be under a Mother's care, it is true, for a time ; but
to the guardianship of this worthy relation I again return.
And while in London I shall equally be under the eye of
both, as she determines to accompany me.

' And now, my dear friend, a long, long adieu. One advice,
and as a parting one, consider—value it—*Cultivate the
milder dispositions of your heart, subdue the more extravagant
visions of the brain.* In time your abilities must be known ;
among your acquaintances they are already beheld with
wonder and delight ; by those whose opinion will be valuable,
they hereafter will be appreciated. *Genius* will render you
great. May *virtue* render you *beloved !* Remove the awful
distance between you and ordinary men, by kind and gentle
manners ; deal mildly with their inferiority, and be convinced they will respect you as much and like you more.
Why conceal the real goodness that flows in your heart ?
I have ventured this counsel from an anxiety for your
future welfare ; and I would enforce it with all the earnestness of the most sincere friendship. " Let your light shine
before men," and think them not unworthy this trouble.
This exercise will prove its own reward. It must be a pleasing
thing to live in the affections of others. Again Adieu—
Pardon the freedom I have used : and when you think of
me, be it as of a kind Sister to whom your happiness will
always yield delight, and your griefs sorrow.

'   Yours with esteem and regard,
'   M. GORDON.

' I give you not my address, because I dare not promise
to see you.'

" There was another man in the case," is all that even
Margaret Gordon's biographer can tell us now; [1] but Irving
and Carlyle knew more about him in the summer of 1820.
Neither she nor Carlyle let Irving know of the June correspondence. He was not even told there was any ; but
though left in the dark he acted like a brother and played
the game most gallantly. He squired the fair lady to the
top of Ben Lomond, and appears to have there presented
to her an agate cross as from Carlyle; [2] and he saw her off
in the boat for London, and in letters to her there as in
words when beside her did everything possible to help his
friend. He went so far as to " get over the fingers sorely "
from her for intimating that perhaps she was not so deeply
in love with the other man as she supposed. So he warned
Carlyle to hint no doubts of that, while quoting what she
wrote about himself : " What a noble character is Mr.
Carlyle ! Nature has endowed him with many a rare and
valuable gift. I have no hesitation in saying the corre-
pondence of one with a mind so richly gifted would be
spleasant and improving to me ; but it would be unfair.
I may write (to) Mr. Irving, because no evil can result from
the interchange of friendship, he being under an engagement,
and I in no danger of falling in love with anyone, least of all
with my quondam Teacher."

The gist of the advice these words suggested was : " Begin
platonically and be wary, but begin to write " ; but the
letter of June 28th had let Carlyle know better. Nothing
happened. She remained a romantic figure in his fancy
till he met Jane Welsh.

When after half a century Margaret Gordon was selling
her jewels to give the money to the poor, she kept the little
trinket received on Ben Lomond ; but except by a word
about it to her sister, she had never been known to allude
to the courtship of Carlyle, though many of her intimates
were eager to hear. [3] Whereas he liked to speak of her after
many years, and to hear of her from Aberdonians with
news to tell. [4] Which is a score for Margaret—in a contest
of sentiment the woman generally wins. But nobody can

[1] *Carlyle's First Love, Margaret Gordon*, by R. C. Archibald, pp. 79–81.
[2] *Ibid*, pp. 70 and 160. The hypothesis in the text is the only one
that explains all the facts.
[3] *Ibid*, pp. 128–9 and 168, qualified by p. 70. The lady quoted,
pp. 128–9, was Mrs. Stark of Glasgow, of whom by the kindness of a
Glasgow friend, D. A. W. was able to make more enquiries.
[4] David Masson to D. A. W. ; and see his *Edinburgh Sketches*, p. 259.

blame him. There are sorrows that grow sweet in memory. The poetess was as far wrong in fancy as in physics who said that the " old wound when stricken is the sorest." Nature is kinder than that. It is when it is fresh that it hurts. In 1820 the only hope was that she might change her mind, and as that hope was fading, the light of common day appeared to fail. The universe grew dark and seemed like a machine that was black with the hues of death.

Easy for the like of Voltaire or David Hume to grin at such a sight ; but for a fellow who has lost a Margaret Gordon—— The strong man felt his sickness and the proud man was humbled. It was lucky for him he had a lot to do and little leisure. His biliousness was both cause and effect of his low spirits, and sleepless nights prevented the country air and quiet from steadying his nerves. " He should have been married before now," say Chinese admirers. As the diseases of children are sore on adults, so is love-making, —the business of youth. They would agree with Brigham Young, who was not the only saint to scoff at making a fuss about any one woman.

XI

" GEY ILL TO DEAL WI' "

(1820)

H IS mother did not speculate about the cause of his
sickness. The sight of it was enough to make her
see little else. The only flesh he could digest was that of
chickens, and she often provided it, " almost daily " this
summer, as his young sisters remarked. They were in charge
of the poultry, and observant of this elder brother, an
interesting and petted invalid. The custom thereabouts
was for the children to chase and catch and kill whatever
bird the farmer's wife had indicated for execution ; and
they thought nothing of the screeching that invaded every
room and disturbed their brother at his books indoors.
It seemed queer to the young barbarians that he objected
to the *suffering* of the birds which he was about to *eat* !
So they never heeded his remonstrances, and made the
fowls screech more than ever, and mother never bothered,
till one day he said :

" If you cannot stop the screeching, mother, I can stop
the eating. I won't eat another chicken if it's killed in
that way."

" Eh ! " cried his mother amazed, " what'll thou eat
then ? " And presently she added in mockery : " Thou's
gey[1] ill to deal wi'," to the huge delight of the listening
youngsters who thought she petted him too much, and never
let it be forgotten. It became a family joke, misleading
to a simple stranger.[2]

[1] Very.
[2] Told D. A. W. in Canada by Carlyle's sister, Mrs. Hanning.

XII

PULLING THROUGH

(1820)

H E had begun his work at once, and the essence of the next period of his life is in the " Sorrows of Teufelsdröckh " in *Sartor*. External details can no more show the soul than the ashes after cremation show the shape of the body. " Who endureth, overcomes." He " pulled through." The sickness which made his mother sad and nobody else took seriously made him fast, which delivered him from sexual temptations. " I had a presentiment that it would stay," he wrote of his dyspepsia in old age, " as it has done. Woe on it, yet perhaps a benefit has been in it, priceless though hideously painful ! "

He shared his savings with his father and brothers, which was a common thing then. Several acquaintances were doing the same.[1] Neither was his biliousness so very uncommon. It has led to many a suicide.[2] A man who had failed for years to comprehend his sufferings was suddenly enlightened by an accidental overdose of liver medicine. In lieu of which, here is from a letter to the incredulous Irving referring to this summer and the next.[3]—

' I have had no leisure for many days to think of anything, the pain has so distracted me. . . . The state of my health you do not believe. My earnest prayer is that you may never believe. I was once as sceptical as yourself. Such disorders are the heaviest calamity life has in store for mortals. The bodily pain is nothing or next to nothing ; but alas for the dignity of man ! The evil does not stop here. No strength of soul can avail you ; this malady will turn that very strength against yourself ; it banishes

[1] Such as his contemporary, Galloway, and many others known to D. A. W.   [2] D. A. W. could name several, one a friend of T. C.
[3] Unpublished Letters of Carlyle, *Scribner's Mag.*, April, 1893, p. 418.

all thought from your head, all love from your heart—and doubles your wretchedness by making you discern it. Oh ! the long, solitary, sleepless nights that I have passed —with no employment but to count the pulses of my own sick heart—till the gloom of external things seemed to extend itself to the very centre of the mind, till I could remember nothing, observe nothing ! All this magnificent nature appeared as if blotted out, and a grey, dirty, dismal vapour filled the immensity of space ; I stood alone in the universe—alone, and as it were a circle of burning iron enveloped the soul—excluding from it every feeling but a stony-hearted dead obduracy, more befitting a demon in its place of woe than a man in the land of the living ! I tell you, my friend, nothing makes me shudder to the inmost core—*nothing* but this. One's spirit may be bruised and broken by moral afflictions ; but at least it will break like the spirit of a *man ;* moral affections will irradiate its painful strugglings, and the last gleam of feeling will be pure if it is feeble. But here—I declare I will not speak another word on the subject. I can hardly excuse myself for saying so much.'

Which shows why he was soon exhorting his brother John, whose medical studies he was about to finance, not to " play the same miserable game that I have played, sacrificing both health and peace of mind to the vain shadows of ambition. Continuous study will waste away the very best constitution." And once when sick he said— " I would consent to become as ignorant as a Choctaw— so I were as sound of body."

In the same way he comforted his brother Alick, who was to stick to farming—" The husbandman keeps hold of Health, and I tell you the possession of that blessing is better than the empire of the world. When strong outwardly, I seldom feel depressed within."

About the same time he was quoting to Mitchell with gusto the proverb of the French, that the greatest pleasure is to forget oneself and let oneself go (*l'abandon de sôi-même*), and he always acted in that spirit, a man of action rather than of meditation, to the end of his life. This is a key to his character, and enough to show the silliness of supposing he can be better understood from casual letters and papers than from the scriptures he spent his life in making as true as he could. One cannot understand a hero by dint of meditation upon his exclamations in moments of sickness or fatigue. Any sparrow can spy upon a great man ; but it cannot see what makes him great, or tell us more than a twitter.

His presentiment was fulfilled. The dyspepsia stuck to him all his life, and often depressed him by bile and lack of nourishment. The sorrow of it was the background of all he said and did, like the drone of a bagpipe, or like the roar of traffic to a Londoner. It killed him by starvation in the end ; but not till after he had lived for more than eighty-five years ; and as Bismarck said—" The first eighty years of a man's life are always the happiest."

He forgot himself in work to some purpose in the sixty years in front of him now ; and even this summer, the most dismal of his life, was able to forget himself much of the time. His " work " was hack-work, and not engrossing ; but also not exhausting. The best days were when Irving was on a holiday visit to his father's family in Annan, where Carlyle was ever a welcome guest for a night or two. Irving used to meet him on the way, and the birds and running waters floated in music the sound of their voices as they walked along " the bonny river's bank."

Annan was then a port for travellers between Edinburgh or Glasgow and Liverpool, and between England or Scotland and Ireland. And there was often time to talk with one or another of them and " measure minds " and " be on your best behaviour as to matter and manner." Thus in the reading-room Irving and Carlyle had once a chat with the " musical Thomson " who got songs from Burns, and saw him to be " a clean-brushed, commonplace old gentleman in scratch-wig " ; but it was the friendship with Irving that made these visits seem to Carlyle in old age the pleasantest of his life. Their dialogues wandered " wide over the world." It was mainly for a " point of union " with Irving that Carlyle had taken up Italian, which served him little otherwise, though he read a good deal of it. For the same reason he was eagerly urging Irving to " persist in German," [1] offering to lend him " the very best of Schiller's plays." Though Irving's " brows would suddenly contract " on mention of Goethe's *Faust*, he had to listen to a great deal about it, for Carlyle was now full of it. As he wrote to Fergusson [2] he was " living riotously with Schiller,

---

[1] Unpublished Letters of Carlyle, *Scribner's Mag.*, April, 1893, p. 417.   [2] *Thomas Carlyle*, by Moncure D. Conway, p. 202.

Goethe and the rest. They are the greatest men at present with me." So he could not spare Irving, and wrote to him in June, 1820,[1] an estimate of *Faust* wherewith he was ready to fill " many hours " as soon as they met.

'It is not for his masterly conception of human nature—from the heroes of classical story, down to the blackguards of a Leipzig alehouse—that I admire him above all others ; his profound sentiment of beauty, his most brilliant delineations of all its varieties—his gaiety of head and melancholy of heart, open all the floodgates of my sympathy. *Faust* is a wonderful tragedy. I doubt if even Shakespeare with all his powers had sadness enough in his nature to understand the arid and withered feelings of a passionate spirit worn out by excessive studies and the want of all enjoyment.'

Apparently the likeness of *Faust* to himself, now overfed with knowledge and asking—what's the use of it ?—went to his heart. Of course he discriminated among German authors, warning Irving that Kotzebue and Co. were trash. Failing with Goethe, he tried to interest his friend in Schiller ; but the best of their talk was on personal plans and prospects. Irving revived his confidence in himself when it was needed most.

There are few young people never tempted to suicide. Many refrain as Hamlet did from doubts about what may follow ; and Teufelsdröckh said—" From Suicide a certain aftershine of Christianity withheld me." But Teufelsdröckh was not altogether Carlyle. His early diaries show him thinking on paper, unreserved. No twilight of departed creeds was in his eyes. No thought of what might follow death puzzled his will at all. To that extent the diaries confirm what he said in old age to young men in despair, that but for Goethe he might himself have " pistolled his way through " his difficulties. Yet there is none of Goethe's toying with the topic. When in physical agony he felt he might be tempted to "hang himself like Judas," he faced the suggestion and thought it out. He said to himself there was hope of recovery, and that, even " when hope had utterly fled," it would be wrong to " break " the hearts of " my *friends*, my mother, father, brothers and sisters." To him, as to Confucius, what was wrong was not to be touched, like boiling water. So the temptation faded

[1] Unpublished Letters of Carlyle, *Scribner's Mag.*, April, 1893, p. 417.

quickly from his mind, like the shadow of a passing cloud that leaves no trace.

The agony itself was occasional, and the mere cessation of it was delightful ; and perhaps the friendship of Irving did as much for him as the teaching of Goethe. Irving would not hear of his gloomy " prognostications " and " impossibilities," declaring " the real impossibility " to be " that such a talent should not cut itself clear one day." More than once, in a laughing way, with self-mockery enough to save it from being vain, he roundly declared— " You will see now. One day we two will shake hands across the brook, you as first in Literature, I as first in Divinity ; and people will say—' Both these fellows are from Annandale : where is Annandale ? ' "

" He was very sanguine," said Carlyle in old age, " I much the reverse ; and had his consciousness of powers, and his generous ambitions and forecastings ; never ungenerous, never ignoble : only an enemy could have called him ' vain,' and occasionally did. His pleasure in being *loved* by others was very great ; and this was manifest ; never more or *worse* than this ; and this too he had well in check at all times : if this was vanity, then he might by some be called a little vain ; if not, not. To trample on the smallest mortal or be tyrannous even towards the basest of caitiffs, was never at any moment Irving's turn ; no man that I have known had a sunnier type of character, or *so* little of hatred towards any man or thing. On the whole, *less* of rage in him than I ever saw combined with such a fund of courage and conviction. Noble Irving, he was the faithful elder brother of my life in those years ; generous, wise, beneficent, all his dealings and discoursings with me were. Beyond all other men he was helpful to me when I most needed help."

By the middle of September (15.9.1820) Carlyle was able to mention Margaret Gordon with composure in a letter to William Graham,[1] who had noticed with surprise that Irving, however attentive, was " not in love with that exalted creature." [2]

" I hear not of Margaret, and know not if I ever shall. Such beings are shadows, radiant shadows, that cross our path in this dark voyage ; we gaze on them with rapture for a moment ; and pass away—borne onward by the tide of Fate, never to behold them, never more."

[1] Unpublished letters.   [2] *Ibid.*

XIII

FIRST VISIT TO ENGLAND

(1820)

A DOCTOR now employed in York Asylum, Matthew Allen, had lectured on phrenology in Kirkcaldy in 1817, and become a friend of Carlyle who denounced such nonsense. This summer's letters show him receiving from Carlyle advice about some " Christian Lectures " he had been publishing, and suggesting to Carlyle to fall back upon regular teaching himself.[1] He mentioned a vacancy at eighty pounds a year for teaching mathematics. Carlyle might have taken it if teaching some hours a day had been all the work, but " to give all my time, see the boys to bed, etc., would never suit me." " Come and visit me," said Allen, but Carlyle had no " money to spend on travelling," till in September Allen offered him at his own figure (£150) a " travelling tutorship " of a young man advised to travel " on account of bodily and mental weakness." [2]

It seems likely that all Carlyle received in the course of two years for eighteen Encyclopedia articles, enough to fill a volume, was not more than fifty pounds ; [3] and he could not make money by tutoring in Scotland unless he lived among the noises and stinks of Edinburgh. Nevertheless, he enquired of Allen—" What kind of weakness ? If it were of a kind needing constant attendance and sympathy, etc., no money would be enough ! And would the head of the family forget the distinctions of rank, which I wish to forget and not to trespass ? Would he speak to me as man to man ? Solitude is always painful, whether it be profitable or not ; and a populous solitude is worst of all." The replies were satisfactory. Graham also, the Glasgow merchant, assured him there was " no snobbery among the Yorkshire-

---

[1] Letters read in MSS. by D. A. W. in Edinburgh in 1896. He consulted David Masson, who agreed they were genuine.

[2] Letter from T. C. to John Fergusson, in *Thomas Carlyle*, by Moncure Conway, pp. 199–202.

[3] *Edinburgh Sketches*, etc., by David Masson, p. 293.

men." [1] So he accepted Allen's invitation to " come and examine before engaging," and in October, 1820, paid what he used to call his " first visit to England." [2]   He was as much at home in Cumberland as in Annandale, and did not feel away from home till he crossed into Yorkshire.

He enjoyed the sight of a " most rich and picturesque country," and besides free talks with Allen on " all imaginable isms,"[3] " conversed with all kinds of men from graziers up to knights of the shire." But the pupil offered him was " a dotard, a semi-vegetable," and he at once excused himself, writing to Fergusson [4] that nothing would have hired him to take such a job. He added :—

' York is the Bœotia of Britain ; its inhabitants enjoy all sensual pleasures in perfection ; they have not even the idea of any other. . . . York is but a heap of bricks ; Jonathan Dryasdust (see *Ivanhoe*) is justly named. It was edifying to hear the Principal of the University College lament the prevalence of mysticism in religion ; and their newspaper editor is made of lead.'

Indeed, it cannot be denied that Yorkshiremen do not appear at their best to anyone whose stomach is out of order. There was humour that smacked of the soil in a trifle Carlyle recalled with pleasure. He used to meet at the dinner-table of York Asylum " a small shrivelled, elderly man," a harmless patient. " He ate pretty fairly, but every minute or two inconsolably flung down his knife and fork, stretched out his palms, and twisting his poor countenance into utter woe, gave a low pathetic howl—' I've la-ast mi happetayte ! ' "

[1] Unpublished letter.
[2] See *L. and M. of J. W. Carlyle*, I, p. 282, footnote, where by a slip of memory the year is erroneously given as 1819.
[3] Letters read in MSS. by D. A. W. in Edinburgh in 1896. He consulted David Masson who agreed they were genuine.
[4] Letter from T. C. to John Fergusson, in *Thomas Carlyle*, by Moncure Conway, pp. 199–202.

XIV

THE CROWNING KINDNESS OF IRVING

(1820–1)

HE returned to Edinburgh as sick as when he left it, but with Kant and Fichte and Co. to fling at those who thought about thinking, and with his head full of *Faust*. Job had long been his favourite book in the Bible, and *Faust* was Job up to date.

He had many plans " in the way of authorship," and as fast as one withered another sprouted. Of translation on commission he could not get enough. Having no pupils to keep him in Edinburgh, he spent the Christmas week with Irving in Glasgow, where he watched the fat merchants " shovelling their beef over by the pound, and swilling their wine without measure, declaiming on politics and religion, joking and jeering and flowing and swaggering along with all their heart." On New Year's Day he was " listening to music and the voice of song amid dandy clerks and sparkling females ; laughing " till he was " sore." The next day he returned to his own work ; and a few days later at Brewster's dinner-table was taking stock of contemporary engineers, including Jardine and Telford. " My friend the Duke of " this, " My friend the Marquis of " that was Telford's way of talking. Carlyle escaped from them as soon as convenient " without regret," and salved the rest of the evening—dinners were early then—by supper in the company of a journalist, Ritchie, and the Rev. Thomas Murray, whom he always liked to see.

Murray was giving up hope of ever getting a church, and taking a house in town to live by private teaching and providing board for students, a plan that prospered.[1] For himself as yet Carlyle could see no outlet. " Literature is like money," he now wrote to Allen (22.1.1821).[2] " The

[1] *Autobiographical Notes*, (etc.), by Thomas Murray, p. 23.
[2] Unpublished letters.

appetite increases by gratification. The mines of literature, too, are unwholesome and dreary as the mines of Potosi, yet from either there is no return, and though little confident of finding contentment, happiness is too proud a term, I must work, I believe, in those damp caverns, till once the whole mind is recast or the lamp of life has ceased to burn within it."

It was only because his work was in Edinburgh that he stayed there. He wrote to Graham that he liked Glasgow better (28.1.1821)[1] :—

'The jolly west is full before me. Every one will praise the fair, of course, as his own market has gone in it : and so in spite of all that small dapper jurists and other " waiting gentlewomen " can say to the contrary, I shall still continue to assert the worth of your city, and the superiority of her solid house-wife qualities to those of her lean, prim, mincing, more ambitious neighbour.'

Gladly would Irving have kept him in the west for months, and passing through Edinburgh in February, on the way to Kirkcaldy, he called and persuaded Carlyle to go with him and be the welcome guest of Provost Swan.

The sea breezes made him feel well in a week ; and when he returned into the smoke, he took to climbing Arthur's Seat as often as possible. Some private teaching kept him moving, and in March he was commissioned to write on Joanna Baillie's Metrical Legends for the *New Edinburgh Review*.[2]

What he wrote was sincerely commonplace. He exhorted the authoress not to stick to the chronicles but invent.—

'The facts of a hero's life are worth nothing to us except as they represent the powers of his mind. The real occurrences of the world are too circumscribed and prosaic to give scope to our full energies. The faint traces they (great characters) have left are to the poet's eye like the fragments of an antediluvian animal (to) a Cuvier.' The authoress had failed with Wallace, but so had Metastasio, whose opera hero resembles 'our own rugged, massy, stern, indomitable Wallace wight, just about as much as a Vauxhall tin cascade resembles the falls of Niagara.' So he recommends Wallace to Scott.

[1] *Ibid.*   [2] *N.E.R.*, I, pp. 393–414 ; October, 1821.

He was writing at the same time to Mitchell :—

'About twenty plans have failed ; I have about twenty more to try ; and if it does but please the Director of all things to continue the moderate share of health now restored to me, I will make the doors of human society fly open before me yet, nothwithstanding my petards will not burst, or make only *noise* when they do : I must mix them better, plant them more judiciously ; they shall burst and do execution too.'

One of his many failures was an early draft of the romantic autobiography in *Sartor*.[1] " Stephen Corry " was born in the south of Scotland, in a village called " Duckdubs," and was the son of a mason who built so badly that he had to leave the trade. " My whole life," said he, " has been a continued fever dream, and my awakening will be in Hell." That is like what the author felt in a fit of the bile. In which condition Irving found him in the latter end of May, unable to sleep or eat. Irving had come to attend the General Assembly ; but as he was going to Haddington to fill the pulpit there one Sunday, he remembered the February cure and prescribed fresh air again. " Come out with me and see the world for a day or two ! "

They walked to Haddington (over seventeen miles), and went to see Gilbert Burns, the brother of the poet, first of all ; but did not stay long. Familiarity with females was the best perquisite of the pulpit, and here as in Glasgow, Irving lost no time in showing his companion the best the ground yielded. Soon after arrival, they were being entertained at the minister's house by a shapely, tall young lady of the airy, giggling kind, a Miss Augusta, pronounced " Disgusta " by Jane Welsh, who was the next on their list. To Irving's great amusement, Carlyle was so content with her that he troubled him no further.

It was nearly two years since his own flirtation with her had ended in composure ; and he could not have brought his friend at a more propitious hour. " Jeannie Welsh " was within seven weeks of twenty, and writing to her friend Bess Stodart in Edinburgh, " I'll die a virgin if I reach twenty in vain." [2] Not long ago (8.3.1821) she had written

[1] The MSS. was last seen by D. A. W. in the Carlyle House, Chelsea. " Illudo Chartis," item 135, of the loan collection of 1895 ; lent by Alexander Carlyle, who has kindly assured D. A. W. there are no external means of dating it.
[2] *Early Letters of J. W. Carlyle*, edited by D. G. Ritchie, pp. 25 and 31.

to Bess : " A visit from any man with brains in his head would be an act of mercy to us here."[1] So while Carlyle was doing his best to be agreeable to the beautiful widow Mrs. Welsh, who dominated the drawing-room, he noticed for a moment the daughter also listening and "that bright pair of eyes enquiringly fixed" on him. James Brown, who had succeeded Irving as teacher at Haddington, had lately been speaking to her about Carlyle, and so had his friend Story of Roseneath, who said : " Talent plenty, fine vein of satire in him." She remembered this, and thought he was talking like her father, whom she idolised.

He never noticed what every one else saw, that her features were plain compared to her beautiful mother's, and she had little to say as yet ; but then, that little was good, and as a listener she was miraculous, so that her big black eyes seemed to be flashing with comprehension and sympathy, and men felt impelled to talk to her without reserve.[2]

Such sympathy is both cause and effect of affection. It is the best of female charms, and keeps marriage popular in spite of bad laws and meddling clerks, and must have been what inspired a description of a woman of the best kind by a Chinese poet many centuries ago :—

> " Her eyes have the brightness
>   Of water that's clear ;
> She moves with such lightness
>   As swallows appear ;
> In figure a woman ;—
>   In heart and in mind,
> She's a gem that is human,
>   Both polished and kind."

No wonder the fair ghost of Margaret Gordon ceased to haunt the daydreams of Carlyle. As he and Irving were retiring to rest in their double-bedded room at the Inn, Irving asked jocosely : " What would you take to marry Miss Augusta, now ? " He answered hotly : " Not for an entire and perfect chrysolite the size of this terraqueous globe." After hearty laughter, Irving tried again : " And what would you take to marry Miss Jeannie, think you ? " " Ha, I should not be so hard to deal with there, I should imagine."

---

[1] *Ibid.*

[2] This is the gist of what was said to D. A. W. by Sir C. Gavan Duffy. David Masson and others who knew her well, abundantly corroborated.

P

XV

CARLYLE AND IRVING

(1821)

THEY stayed till Thursday. Carlyle was "as happy as a lark" and so reverential to Mrs. Welsh that she made the same mistake as Mrs. Usher—she never supposed there was any attraction but herself and showered invitations upon him. Thereby he had many a talk with her daughter. The time was short, but they made the most of it, "several hours, almost every evening"; and he fell in love like a boy, as frankly as if he had never done it before. Forty-five years afterwards he recorded: "I was supremely dyspeptic and out of health during those three or four days; but they were the beginning of a new life to me." His letters at the time show the same.

When conversing like Ferdinand and Miranda in *The Tempest*, Miss Welsh had settled he was to teach her and begin by sending her a *list* of books for study, and some from the libraries to read. This was peg enough for a love letter on the 4th of June, which fills three pages of print, and gives six months' guidance in advance, and more. "It seems as if we had known each other from infancy upwards," he remarks. She had started German before they met, and after mentioning he had sent to London for a good *German Grammar* for her, he said that if only her "present German master would shift his quarters," he would fetch it, "and deliver such a lesson on those Saxon Roots as you never heard. Positively, I must see you soon, or I shall get into a very absurd state. And then if I should come to visit Jane herself *professedly*, *what* would Jane say to it? what would Jane's friends say? Would to Heaven some authorised person would 'force me to go voluntarily.'"

The last phrase was Napoleon's, and was pat, as Jane was a great admirer of Napoleon. But altogether it was too much for a start. So she wrote no reply, and after about three weeks sent back the books—" to Mr. Carlisle, with Miss Welsh's compliments and very best thanks."

He confessed this upset him. " I had a hundred thousand things to tell you ; but *now* I may not mention one of them. Those *compliments* have put the whole to flight " ; but he sent her the rest of De Staël, and to show how far he was from coming to Haddington unasked, he said he was going down to Annandale with Irving about the first of August.

In eight days she sent back the volumes with a common-looking letter of thanks, for which he was extremely grateful, saying, " The very seal has beauty in it." No wonder ! " I have dismissed my German master," said she. He proposed to come to Haddington " to inspect and accelerate your progress in German." But she knew her mother too well to let him do so. She came to town herself instead, and stayed with her dear Bess Stodart in George Square, where Bess was housekeeper to her uncle, Mr. Bradfute, and a deeply interested observer of such a tutor. Mr. Bradfute was a bookseller and had many pleasant talks with him, and did not need to be told that the German was an extra. Jane enjoyed his company for five or six weeks, though Carlyle had tosit up late over his work in order to have leisure to be with her by day. Here is a fragment of their talk as they walked together along Princes Street. " How many things are here which I do not want," said he. She answered, " How many things are here which I cannot get." He admired her smartness, declaring it " the honest language of nature " and concluding, " Both these sentiments are correct in their proper season, both erroneous out of it."

A surer sign of intimacy is his knowledge of her ill-health. While adoring her " genius," and everything else that was hers, he counselled her to restrict her reading and give most of her time to common duties and pleasures. Thus even in the presence of the " fat, contented " Mr. Bradfute he deprecated her studies and advised her to abandon them, for which he had to apologize ; but still he insisted on moderation. " Nourishment of any kind may by injudicious application be converted into poison ; and mental nourishment forms no exception. Observe the *Golden Mean*, so easy to talk of, so difficult to find. . . . My subject is scarce begun." In short, give me an excuse to write more. The letter fills three and a half pages of print. " I still entertain a *firm trust* that you are to read Schiller and Goethe with me in October. I never yet met any to relish their beauties ; and sympathy is the very soul of life."

However, she was not to be in town in October, and he could stay in the country till November, as usual.

Meanwhile Irving prayed her " not to put religion away from you. Study it with half the intensity you have studied literature," while he remonstrated with Carlyle, saying he did not want her to read Schiller and Goethe, she had read too much already. Of course there was nothing of the lover in any of Irving's letters to her. He was merely an anxious friend ; and Carlyle reassured him, saying : " I saw the fair pupil in Edinburgh. She is certainly the most —fit to read German of any creature I have met with. Take no fear of those people, I tell you. They are good men— some are even excellent. Schiller, for example, you most certainly would like. He has all the innocence and purity of a child, with the high talents and strong volitions of a man : a rare union, of which I never but in one instance saw anything like a *living* example," which meant Irving, of course.[1]

Such lofty praise could hardly be more delicately put ; and still it seems sincere and well-deserved. No wonder Irving stood aside ; and while never missing a chance of putting in a word for Jesus with Jane, said nothing against the Germans to whom Carlyle was introducing her. He had the sense to realise he could no more shape the relations between these two than a man who had fired a mine can control the explosion. Before the year was out he saw Margaret Gordon again and minutely described her appearance to Carlyle, concluding : " She has not Jane Welsh's heart."

[1] Unpublished Letters of Carlyle, *Scribner's Mag.*, April, 1893, p. 419.

XVI

THOUGHTS OF OTHERS

(1821)

IRVING had seen little of Jane Welsh since their flirtation in 1819, and did not hide from Carlyle his distress
to see her adoring Byron and Rousseau's *Nouvelle Héloïse*.
Carlyle had as little patience as Irving with sentimental
fictioneering. The books he sent and recommended to
Jane were from the first designed to bring her into touch
with "great minds or exalted thoughts" and "real knowledge." He failed to practise the Golden Mean he preached
to her. Thus his summer programme was "Robertson and
Hume, to be studied with maps and chronologies; Watson's *Philip II and Philip III;* Russell's *Modern Europe;*
Voltaire's pretty little histories; with Tasso and De Staël"!
The *German Grammar* itself was light work in comparison,
as if intended for relaxation. His letter reveals how
great a glamour had fallen upon his eyes—so that a
county town coquette with natural gifts not hard to match
in any town in Scotland appeared a re-incarnation of all the
muses. His talking and writing to her as an intellectual
equal has the simplicity of a child at play with a kitten
or a puppy, expecting them to talk. He prescribed to her
the same course of reading as to William Graham of Glasgow,
who was older than himself, and answered (18.5.1821) :—

'I always feel some inches taller when I get a letter from
you, yet I find it exceedingly difficult to compose my mind,
under existing circumstances, to anything like a regular
course of reading.' (He was in difficulties in business.)
'Now it is not easy for you to understand this, because you
owe no man anything ; your reading and study is not only
a relief—a pleasure—to you, but in fact is constantly adding
to your mental mine of wealth. You can read without
distraction of mind ; but my reading can never pay my
creditors ! A *rap* at my door at any time may be the signal

213

note of a Bank-Bailiff—ye ken naething about that! Nor I hope ever will. Our friend Mr. Irving often whirls me out of myself; he is really a most warm-hearted, worthy man. I see him often, and always with new pleasure. One in every ten thousand such as he would reform the world.' He ended with news and an invitation to Glasgow, and a notable question : 'Are you writing *the Book* ?'

In answering (12.6.1821), Carlyle said Graham would have heard from Irving of what had happened at Haddington.—

'Since my return, I have been busily engaged in that important thing, doing nothing. It is so fine to wrap yourself up in the bright bespangled webs of the Imagination. . . . It is very friendly in you to keep so sharp an eye on *the book*. But alas ! my dear sir, do but consider. How am I, poor grasshopper as I am, to make my small chick be heard among the many Bulls of Bashan that on every side fill the valleys with their lowing ? The thing is barely possible, if I had health and friends and capital—all of which I want. I believe I am destined to get better. I am far happier for the last three months (to say nothing of the last ten days) ; so I abide in hope. I am to see you about August.'

Like William Graham, Jane Welsh was too much pre-occupied for such study and found his list of little use. " No profit grows where is no pleasure ta'en." She made him keep his distance till she could take his measure.

Carlyle was doing like St. David (Hume) in thrusting history upon his sweetheart. As the great man has explained :—

' My female readers may learn from history. I am sorry to see them have such an aversion to matter of fact, and such an appetite for falsehood. I remember I was once desired by a young beauty, for whom I had some passion, to send her some novels and romances for her amusement in the country ; but sent her Plutarch's *Lives*, assuring her that there was not a word of truth in them from beginning to end. She perused them very attentively till she came to the lives of Alexander and Cæsar, whose names she had heard of by accident, and then returned me the book, with many reproaches for deceiving her.'

So there never was any Mrs. David Hume. At the time
Carlyle was trying to beguile Jane Welsh into history, she
was writing to Bess Stodart what would have been an eye-
opener to both him and Irving.[1]—

'MY DEAR BESS,—

'The most proper way of testifying my gratitude
to the amiable Jean Jacques for the pleasure he has
afforded me is to extend the circle of his admirers. I
shall begin with you. Do read this book. You will find
some of its scenes culpably indelicate; but for eloquence,
sensibility and passion it has no match in French. Fear
not that by reading *Héloïse* you will be ruined, or undone,
or whatever adjective best suits that fallen state into
which women and angels *will* stumble *at a time*. I promise
you that you will rise from the *Héloïse* with a deeper impression of whatever is most beautiful and most exalted
in virtue than is left upon your mind by Blair's *Sermons*,
Paley's *Theology*, or the voluminous Jeremy Taylor himself. I never felt my mind more prepared to brave temptation of every sort than when I closed the second volume of
this strange book. I believe if the Devil himself had waited
upon me in the shape of Lord Byron, I would have desired
Betty to show him out. Sages say that every work which
presents vice in the colours of virtue has a tendency to
corrupt the morals.' (This sounds like Irving. She goes
on.—) 'They are without doubt in the right; but when they
say that Julia Étange is vicious, they are in a most egregious
mistake. Read the book, and ask your heart. *I do not
wish to countenance such irregularities among my female
acquaintances;* but I must confess, were any individual
of them to meet with *such a man*, to struggle as she struggled,
to endure as she endured, to *yield* as she yielded, and to
repent as she repented, I would love that woman better
than the chastest, coldest prude between John o' Groat's
House and Land's End. One serious bad consequence will
result to you from reading *Héloïse*—at least, if your soul-
strings are screwed up to the same key as mine. You will
never marry! Alas! I told you I should die a virgin, if
I reached twenty *in vain*. Even so will it prove. This book,

[1] *Early Letters of J. W. Carlyle*, by D. G. Ritchie, pp. 29–36. The guess
of the editor that T. C. may have " first induced her to read Rousseau " he
would probably now admit to be a mistake, as Alexander Carlyle has
shown : *Love Letters*, II, p. 413–14 and note, etc.

this fatal book, has given me an idea of a love so *pure* (yes, you may laugh ! but I repeat it), so pure, so constant, so disinterested, so exalted, that no love the men of this world can offer me will ever fill up the picture my imagination has drawn with the help of Rousseau. No lover will Jane Welsh ever find like St. Preux, no husband like Wolmar (I don't mean to insinuate that *I should like both*) ; and to no man will she ever give her heart and pretty hand who bears to these no resemblance. George Rennie ! James Aitken ! Robert MacTurk ! James Baird ! ! ! Robby Angus !—O Lord, O Lord ! where is the St. Preux ? Where is the Wolmar ? Bess, I am in earnest—I shall never marry. I will, in short, do penance for laughing at old maids by writing a novel with one for heroine in an elegant little garret.

'What did you think of my aunt ? Poor thing ! she does not understand love. She never read *Héloïse ;* but she has got a husband—such as he is.

'Mr. Craig Buchanan has put me to the expense of postage twice within the last fortnight. He is improving in his style, and . . . It will . . . come to a crisis : what do you think ? He is about the age of Wolmar ; but Wolmar had not a bald head, nor a lame leg, neither did Wolmar make puns or pay compliments. I have just had a letter from Thomas Carlyle : he too speaks of coming. He is something liker to St. Preux than George Craig is to Wolmar. He has *his* talents, *his* vast and cultivated mind, *his* vivid imagination, *his* independence of soul, and *his* high-souled principles of honour. But then—Ah, these *buts !* St. Preux never kicked the fire-irons, nor made puddings in his teacup. Want of Elegance ! Want of Elegance, Rousseau says, is a defect which no woman can overlook. It is the decree of fate ! dear Eliza, it is the decree of fate ! So look about for a nice, pleasant, little garret and we will take up house together.

'I have never seen him since I came home.' (She meant George Rennie, as Bess did not need to be told.) 'His mother and Janet called one day, and I saw John at the foxhounds. Oh, wretch ! I wish I could hate him, but I cannot ; I despise him, but I do not hate him ; and when Friday comes I always think how neatly I used to be dressed, and sometimes I give my hair an additional brush and put on a clean frill, just from habit. Oh ! the Devil take him ! He has wasted all the affections of my poor heart, and now there is not a vestige of a flirt about me : but I will vex that renegade heart of his yet.'

This letter shows Jane Welsh like other young women. Admiration of Byron was in fashion, and the vogue of Rousseau had lasted half a century. She had been schooled " like a boy " ; which was also common enough in Scotland. " It makes a girl equal to any match she can get and fits her to get a good job as governess," said parents. The only thing odd about her was her comparative freedom from housework, and that was partly affected, partly accidental. She had always been her father's pet, and had just finished her schooling when he died in his prime. Her mother was able to go on doing all the housework, which was now much less. They had a maid equal to the help required, and as mother and daughter were never long together without quarrelling they agreed that she was to do nothing but read and take exercise and spin her spider webs in maiden meditation with undivided attention.

She had many suitors, as she was reputed an heiress, and was pleased with one of them, George Rennie, the younger son of a rich engineer in the neighbourhood ; but he was shying off, as Bess would learn from this letter.

Her father had invested his savings in buying from his own father an ancestral farm, Craigenputtock, on the moors, fourteen miles west of Dumfries. The rent of it, about two hundred pounds, was all the widow and daughter had to live upon ; and tho the law courts made most of it belong to Jane, any man of sense would suspect it might not all become his when he married her.

It might not, but then it might, as Mrs. Welsh could never forget. If Jane needed the rent because she married a man who had nothing, her mother would have to choose between living as second-in-command in her daughter's house or going back to her father's farm almost as poor as she left it. She had warmly invited Carlyle—" Come to Haddington often, as if you were going *home* " ; but when she heard Jane wanted to write to him, she forbade her to do so, and began to repent these invitations.

XVII

"YOU BULL-BACKËD SCOUN'REL"

IT was a bad time for farmers. Their only topic when
they met was what abatement of rack-rents might be
expected—twenty per cent ? or more ? or less ? And if
a man were broken altogether, as many were, would he have
enough to take him to America ? James Carlyle was a
" sociable body " and sympathised with his neighbours.
An anecdote told to show his sympathy [1] needs this explanation.

James was in the kitchen of a neighbour when a joiner
from the village, Robert Jardine, sat down to breakfast and
put the neighbour to shame by loud complaints against the
food. He, maybe, hoped for support from the visitor, who
was said to feed workmen well ; and James did survey the
table critically ; but what he said was—" The porridge is
good, and the milk is good. What more do you want, you
bull-backëd scoun'rel ? "

" Bob ceased to be Jardine," it is said, " and was *the
bull-backëd scoun'rel* for the rest of his life, perhaps forty
years. He had conspicuously the hump which carpenters
get from carrying tools and planks on one shoulder, so that
it was a picture of him. He was as proud of it as of a title.
A young fellow does not object to be compared to a bull—
he published it in the village himself."

[1] To D. A. W. in August, 1895, by Thomas Graham, draper, Ecclefechan,
who had the details from John Jardine, who had them from his brother
Robert Jardine, named in the text.

XVIII

TAKING HEART AGAIN

(1821)

NOT even sickness could depress Carlyle this summer. Just as after a good dinner " the soul subsides and wickedly inclines to seem but mortal e'en in sound divines," so when the right sort of young fellow sees he is likely to get the girl he wants, he does not really worry about anything else and drops back into the worship of things as they are, like those Hindus who pray for nothing but " to live all our days as our forefathers lived, and have children a-doing the same."

He had always a partiality for Scotland ; but its immense superiority to every other part of the world was now first palpable. He dissuaded a brother from emigrating, and implored Johnstone, who had come home, never to leave it again. To his brother John and to Mitchell, about to go to a school in Kirkcudbright, he recanted his own devotion to study, exhorting them to take warning from his errors and remember—" there is no real happiness out of the common routines of life." At the same time he was confessing— " My confidence in Fortune seems to increase as her offers to me diminish. I must forward now. When you launch a boat upon the falls of Niagara, it must go *down* the roaring cataract, though rocks and ruin lie within the profound abyss below : and just so if a man taste the magic cup of literature, he must drink of it for ever, though bitter ingredients enough be mixed with the liquor." Which is like Byron, whom he admired.

What was making him repent of overstudy was mainly the rapidity with which his health grew worse when overworking in Edinburgh this summer. As soon as he was in the country he went " gadding " about Galloway, " riding and running in all directions without measure," in the company of his oldest crony, Thomas Murray, whose only fault was that he praised too freely other men and Carlyle in particular, insisting he was a "genius." Carlyle tried not to believe him, imputing it to Murray's warmth of heart ; but he much enjoyed his company. He was not fond of flattery, but pleased by praise.

James Johnstone came to Edinburgh with him in November and stayed some days. His praise was as strong as Murray's and more convincing because he was more discriminating and "meeker than Moses," declared Mitchell, and a man "in whom there is no guile." Brewster also was encouraging, received him kindly, "spread out his bank draft for fifteen guineas like a man," and promised him the well-paid and easy job of translating Legendre's *Elements of Geometry*, in addition to Encyclopedia work. The *New Edinburgh Review* editors had found his article a kind of hit and commissioned another, while pupils presented themselves in plenty. He had become known for an uncommonly good tutor. So he promised his brother John to pay the cost of his medical studies, sent his mother a new bonnet and his father a pair of silver spectacles, which were welcomed with joy, and went in search of a quieter locality than the University and Nicolson Street neighbourhood, where as yet he had always lodged.

His first choice was Jamaica Street, near Royal Circus, a mile to the north-west ; but Provost Swan persuaded him back from there, to tutor his son at night. The boy was living with his aunt, a widow, and she undertook to find quiet lodgings in her own suburb, the north-east, and did so before the end of the year.

He went to work lustily. Rising between seven and eight, he began the day with Legendre translation till the breakfast was ready. Then came a mile's walk to Great King Street, where two young women and one young man had an hour's teaching in mathematics together ; and after them a sea-captain in George Street was ready to "gasp and burr and repeat Euclid" till eleven. Then back to his lodgings in College Street to finish his daily four hours' stint of Legendre, by which he made three guineas a week, which was followed by an hour's walk and dinner at three. After which he dozed or walked, wrote letters or read for pleasure till five, when he was expected by young Patrick Swan. It was after six when he came home again, and the evening was his own. "It is a laborious life," he wrote to a brother, "but suits me. Nothing gives such scope to discontent as idleness, whether forced or voluntary : a man had better be darning stockings than doing nothing. The evenings I design to devote to original composition, if I could but gather myself."

" I design to," said he, which was true ; but Jane Welsh was with her dear " Bess " in Mr. Bradfute's in George Square, and as long as she was there, the evening was the flower of the day, the time for giving her lessons in German and—Natural Philosophy. Posterity is left guessing whether it was Schiller they read, or Goethe. Most of their talk was about something else. When she returned to Haddington, she had to promise to write to him in spite of her mother— in common pity she could do no less.

The closing months of 1821 seem to be the likeliest date possible for what he told in 1875 to one of the best of his Boswells.[1] He told her he had been " plunged into miserable doubts and speculations " on finding the creeds incredible, and was delivered by " German writings " and in particular Goethe's *Wilhelm Meister.* " I remember taking a long walk one evening from my lodgings near the College to Coates Crescent—there were no houses there then— when the full meaning of it burst upon me."

It was " a windless, Scotch-misty Sunday night," as he walked through the vacant streets, thinking of the book he had just finished as perhaps the best he had ever read. " Grand, surely, harmoniously built together, far-seeing, wise and true ! " To another Boswell in 1877 he spoke of it, saying [2]—" Goethe taught me that the true things in Christianity survived and were eternally true ; pointed out to me the real nature of life and things—not that he did this directly, but incidentally ; and let me see it rather than told me. This gave me peace and great satisfaction."

The shorthand report of the last of the 1838 Lectures completes the story.[3]—

' To explain them (the German writers) best, I can only think of the revelation, for I call it no other, that these men made to me. It was to me like the rising of a light in the darkness which lay around and threatened to swallow me up. I was then in the very midst of Wertherism—the blackness

[1] Mrs. Anstruther of Ballikinrain. See Preface. Coates Crescent is beyond the west end of Princes St.
[2] William Allingham, *A Diary,* p. 253.
[3] *Lectures on the History of Literature,* etc., 1838, by Thomas Carlyle, reported by T. C. Anstey, edited by R. P. Karkaria, Bombay. Curwen, Kane & Co., 1892, pp. 186-8.

and darkness of death. There was one thing in particular which struck me in Goethe. It is in his *Wilhelm Meister*. He had been describing an association to receive propositions and give responses. A number of applications for advice were daily made (and) answered. *But many people wrote in particular for recipes for happiness.* All that was laid on the shelf and not answered at all. This gave me great surprise. " What ! " I said, " is it not the *recipe* of happiness that I have been seeking all my life ? And is it not precisely because I have failed in finding it that I am now miserable and discontented ? " I could not think it (a paradox). After turning it over [1] a great while in my own mind, I got to see that it was *very true*. It was the thing all the world was in error in. No man has the right to ask for a *recipe* of happiness : he can do without happiness. There is something better than that. All kinds of men who have done great things—priests, prophets, sages—have had in them something higher than the love of happiness. Spiritual clearness (is) a far better thing than happiness. Love of happiness is but a kind of hunger at the best : a craving because I have not enough of sweet provision in this world. If I am asked what that higher thing is, I cannot at once make answer ; I am afraid of causing mistake. . . . There is no name for it, but pity for that heart that does not feel it. There is no good volition in that heart. This higher thing was once named " the Cross of Christ "—not a happy thing *that* surely,—" the Worship of Sorrow," (and it appears in) all the heroic sufferings, all the heroic acts of men. It would be absurd to say that the whole creed of German literature can be reduced to this one thing. But that was the commencement of it.'

And that was what it revealed to Carlyle—pity he had to go so far to learn so little ! But as the Papists say of Purgatory—" You may go farther and fare worse." For a long time to come he was as lavish in prescribing German for spirits in distress as the doctors were with calomel for his stomach ; and as the *New Edinburgh Review* editors had left him to choose his subject, he decided now to give their readers a dose of Goethe's *Faust*.

----

[1] " Up " in the report—a clerical error.

XIX

CROSS-PURPOSES

(1821-2)

ON a dim winter night near Christmas, Carlyle was sitting in the coffee-room of a hotel with Irving, reading his testimonials, and saw him depart for London by the early coach to preach to the congregation of the Caledonian Church there, which wanted to hear him. By this time the aunt of Patrick Swan had done what she undertook—Carlyle was in quiet lodgings at 3 Moray Street, now Spey Street, behind Leith Walk. His windows looked on trees and fields with the Fife and Ochil hills as a background.[1] The intervening Forth he did not see from the house, but on stormy nights he heard it, hoarse and harmonious, helping to sleep. He was safe outside of Edinburgh, and still " within a mile " of it, and little farther from the bathing places on the shores on both sides of Leith. During the holiday week which ends the year, he spent two happy days in Kirkcaldy, where the Rev. Mr. Martin had the pleasure of offering him the editorship of a Dundee newspaper at one hundred pounds a year and a percentage on the profits. He said " No " to that, and on the last day of the year he started to write his *Faust* for the *New Edinburgh Review*, and finished it in a fortnight.

He had a motive for haste which nobody could guess but a young woman in Haddington, " Your sincere friend, Jane Baillie Welsh," as she described herself in a letter—her first attempt at a love-letter to a Scottish St. Preux. It was in the style of Rousseau.—

'Chance seems leagued with conscience in preventing me writing to you. My Mother has been beside me this whole day ; and to sit down to deceive her before her very face

---

[1] The windows looked west and north. The obstructions to the view have all been built since then. The flat upstairs wherein the rooms of Carlyle were has been subdivided ; but the flat on the ground floor shows (1920) how they all were in 1821.

required more audacity than I possess. Even now she is gone for a few minutes only, and should she return and ask me who I am writing to ! You say there is no harm in our correspondence ; and I believe it. But assuredly there is harm in disobedience and deceit. And is it for you to teach me these ? Is it for you who talk of generosity so well to require the sacrifice of my own esteem to your selfish gratification ? What have you done for me ? What greater than I can command from any fool who comes in my way ? My Friend, do something for my sake. Render your friendship as honourable in the eyes of the world, to my Father's child, as it is already honourable in her own eyes to Jane Welsh, and then you may *exact* as your *due* favours you have yet no *claim* to *ask*. Oh, Mr. Carlyle . . . do not laugh at fame. It is indeed a name, perhaps an empty name ' (which pleasantly suggests what their private talk may have been). ' But yet it is the object of no low ambition, and ambition is the crime of no low soul.

' I will not write again. Do not urge me, lest you wear out my patience and with it my esteem. You may think it unlikely *that* should ever happen ; as you have sometimes found me weak and thoughtless, you may expect to find me always so.' (Which is also " significant of much." She goes on.) ' But there are moments when the weak are strong, when the thoughtless think, and such moments are more frequent with me than you suppose.' (Which means what he little suspects, that a girl who is yet uncertain whom to take, and who feels she has time to choose and time to lose, can keep any fellow at a distance when she likes. She concludes.)

' When you have finished your review of *Faustus*, send it to me with such a letter as my Mother may read without anger. And when you have written four-and-twenty pages of your Book, bring them.'

The incitement to begin a " Book " at once shows Carlyle had been confiding his plans to her ; but though he was not aware of it, he was only one of several to her. The great engineer, Rennie, had produced many fine bridges and other things, but in the eyes of Jane Welsh nothing to equal his son George, who was still easily the first favourite ; yet a live St. Preux all to oneself was too good a catch to let go before she was sure of better.

Her letter was perhaps inspired by Byron as well as

Rousseau. If the pleasure of fame is a lover's esteem, as Byron said, it was heresy in love to belittle it as Carlyle had been doing. He had to recant as much as he could, and seems to have seen the sense in the young woman's point of view. The road to glory was the road to gain, and money meant marriage. There were plenty of young women then pointing to such examples as Scott and baiting young men with a turn for writing—" Go and do likewise ! "

The limit to his complaisance was any disguise of his feelings, such as she was trying to force upon him by bidding him write what her mother could see. He tried to meet her wishes, but the thing was impossible. He never ceased to strive instinctively with a force like expanding steam to emerge from the affectations of youth and be straightforward, which handicapped him in sentimental scribbling. As soon as he had finished with *Faust*, he sent his essay to her as allowed (Monday, 14.1.1822), and the diplomatic young woman read with horror in what was supposed to be suitable for her mother such stuff as this :—

' Nothing but the pleasure (of writing to you) could have induced me to submit so very insufficient a performance to your perusal. What motive have I *not*, which man can have ? *Nil desperandum, te duce et auspice te !*' (I need never despair with you for a leader and augur.) ' I have a motive and a rallying-word in the fight for life. *Alles für Ruhm und Ihr !* ' (All for glory and her !).

On reading this, the judicious Jane kept the letter to herself, calculating that the sight of it " would not improve " her mother's temper. There was worse to follow. To please her he sent Byron's latest (" Sardanapalus "), and entreated leave to come and see her as soon as he had done some pending Encyclopedia work, although she had bidden him wait till he had " written four-and-twenty pages of your Book." He told her : " If one page of it were written, nine-tenths of the difficulty would be over. It shall be forthcoming : have I not said it ? " But what did that matter to the young woman ? Her real problem was to keep him from coming at that time because George Rennie was in his father's house near by ; and if her quick-sighted St. Preux happened to see her in Rennie's company—she shuddered to think of what might happen. Love is only blind in some directions.

Q

He was painfully plausible. Irving had recommended him as a tutor to the Bullers, a rich Anglo-Indian couple in perplexity about two of their boys. By Irving's advice they were to be sent to Edinburgh University for a year or two, and Buller, senior, was offering Carlyle, if he would be their tutor, £200 a year and board, with leisure for reading and perhaps travel and other advantages. He sent a provisional acceptance on the day he received the offer, but hastened to urge upon the young woman at Haddington : " Let me see you before I decide : it may not be so easy afterwards."

Her mother had only repented, not cancelled, her invitation. Jane had to veto the visit and scold him, in her most commanding style. His Latin quotation had been tactful —that was a kind of Freemason sign, " the parole of educated men "—and in her desperate need to stop him she took the hint and wrote :—

' I beg you to understand that I dislike as much as my mother your somewhat too ardent expressions, and that if you cannot write to me as to a man who feels a deep interest in your welfare, who admires your talents, respects your virtues, and has often overlooked your faults ; if you cannot write to me as if—as if you were married, you need never waste ink or paper on me more.

' " *Alles für Ruhm und Ihr !* " On my word, most gay and gallantly said ! One would almost believe the man fancies I have fallen in love with him. If you render yourself an honoured member of society, I will be to you a true, a constant, and devoted *Friend*—but not a Mistress, a Sister but not a Wife. Falling in love and marrying like other Misses, is quite out of the question. *I have too little romance in my disposition ever to be in love with you or any other man.*[1] . . . You propose coming here. If you come you will repent it. I trust your *Good Genius* will lead you to make an effort of self-denial. In that case, I shall be glad to hear from you some weeks hence.'

By which time the coast will be clear ; but as she could not possibly be explicit as to the obstruction, he was rash enough to act on the rustic rule—a man should do what he sees fit and let the woman say what she likes. " I am coming out to see you shortly," he replied. " I daresay I am very selfish "

[1] Italics by D. A. W.

About 23.1.1822, Charles and Arthur Buller arrived at
the house of Mr. Fleming in George Square, where they were
to board till their parents came north ; and they instantly
set out for a walk with Carlyle, who was waiting for them,
and led them round the foot of Salisbury Crags, and then
home by Holyrood and the Castle and the Law Courts.
" And really," said he, " I recollect few more pleasant
walks in my life." The boys took to him " with unhesitat-
ing liking " and the " teaching " was a pleasure. Charles
in particular, the elder, soon became " the best company
I could find in Edinburgh," being " one of the cleverest
boys I have seen : he delights to enquire—and argue, and
—be demolished ; he follows me nigh home almost every
night."

Here was something to talk about ; but Jane Welsh had
bidden him accept the tutorship at once and be thankful.
Above all, he was not to come out. He came to Haddington
one Friday (1 or 8.2.1822), nevertheless, and spent most of
his time with the Welshes. The mother did her best to
make sure he would never return, and Jane held him tight
to the German and snubbed him so that on the Monday
morning he went back to town " a perfect wreck," not
knowing " what to do or think."

He wrote a long letter to her, and burned it. He wrote
another, and burned it too ; while she wrote to Bess Stodart
what flings more light on the facts than ever she vouchsafed
to any man.

XX

WHAT SHE TOLD BESS STODART

(1822)

SHE began with enthusiastic praise of the " divine Julia," Rousseau's heroine.[1]

' Alas! like everything *perfectly* glorious and beautiful, she is a vision!

' But back to beings of this world! George Rennie—read, wonder, but be silent—George Rennie is on the sea! And will soon be in Italy! What does he seek there? you will ask. His friends answer " Improvement in the art of sculpture." I answer " ruin." Yes! the die is cast—his fate is decided! This liberty, this fatal liberty, that his too-indulgent father allows him can lead only to ruin. False, heartless as he is, I tremble to think on all the dangers, the allurements to which he is about to be exposed—and in such a frame of mind! How little fit to offer any resistance! It is some weeks ago since Nancy Wilkie told my mother that he meditated going abroad for this stucco business. Chantry and Joseph have cruelly told him he has a genius for it. Dr. Thomson told us he was to leave on the Saturday following. Can you believe it? This intelligence afflicted me. We had not seen each other for months, and yet it seemed that we were now for the first time to be quite parted. I had not heard his voice for many a day; but then I had heard those who had conversed with him, I had seen objects he had looked on, I had breathed the air he had breathed. But now seas and countries were to lie betwixt us. The sun and the moon were to be the only objects we could behold in common. *This* looked like *separation!* Yet do not blame me or think me weak : it was the recollection of the past which made me weep at his departure, and not the pain of the present. I supped at the Davidsons' that night; James Wilkie told me he

---

[1] *Early Letters of J. W. Carlyle*, by D. G. Ritchie, pp. 37–42 and 55.

had called with George at our house some days before !
but found us out. I had not heard of this. My mother
had concealed it from me. What did she fear ? Absurd !
Next day was the day preceding his departure. I resolved
to return him his letters, lest I might *never* have another
opportunity, and I seemed to keep them like a sword over
his head. I sealed them, and scarcely had finished when I
heard a rap. I knew it at once ; long, long I had not heard
it, and yet I recognised it in an instant to be his. I ran out
of the room. On the stairs I met Janet Ewart, who was
staying here. She is very nervous, and thought proper
to utter a loud scream.'

"You look so pale, I took you for a ghost!" said she.
But Jane Welsh said she behaved as resolutely as a Roman
and answered only : " The hurrying out of the room to
change my shoes has made me sick, but as I hear it is *only*
George Rennie, we may go down."

'Down we accordingly went. He half advanced to shake
hands with me ; I made him a cold bow. He placed a chair
for me, and went on conversing with my mother. He looked
well—handsome—quite in high health and seemingly in
high spirits. I scarcely heard a word he said, my own heart
beat so loud.

'Thinking that Janet Ewart might *remark my silence*, I
summoned forth my fortitude, and enquired for Margaret.
"She is very unwell," said he, "and wearying exceedingly
to see you. *We* have been expecting you at Phantassie [1]
for a long time. *I* wish you would go to-day. The carriage
is up. I brought it for a Miss Wilson who has come from
Edinburgh ; so you had best just go with *us*." Oh, the
Devil incarnate ! I have been once at Phantassie since he
left it. It was *trying*, but I went through it *bravely*. Poor
Margaret is now confined to bed—to all appearances dying.
How could he leave her at such a time ?—his favourite she
was too. And yet perhaps it was to save his feelings from
the melancholy——But he has no feelings—none.

'At length he rose. He took leave of my mother ; then
looked at me as if uncertain what to do. I held out my
hand ; he took it, and said " Good-bye ! " I answered him,
" Farewell ! " He left the house ! Such was the concluding
scene of our *Romance !* Great God ! He left the house—
the *very room* where—no matter—as if he had never been
in it in his life before—unfeeling wretch ! It was a dreadful

[1] Place where the Rennies lived.

trial to me to be obliged to save appearance even for some minutes *after* he was gone ; but I went through it bravely ! I returned his letters that night, and now I am done with him *for ever*.

'Mr. Buchanan has not yet been here. I forgot to answer his letters. No wonder he has not come, when I never said he would be welcome. Mr. Carlyle was with us two days, during the greater part of which I read German with him. It is a noble language ! I am getting on famously. He scratched the fender dreadfully. I must have a pair of carpet-shoes and handcuffs prepared for him the next time. His tongue only should be left at liberty : his other members are most fantastically awkward.'

Steel-mounted drawing-room grates were then in fashion in " genteel " houses in Scotch county-towns ; and men who put their feet upon the fender on a winter night had to submit to be scolded, especially when under a cloud at any rate for such disobedience as coming to call when bidden stay at home. That he might not go away altogether as one without hope, she condescended to indicate some books he might send her, including one whose title was apropos : Madame de Staël's *Influence des Passions sur le bonheur des individus et des Nations* (The Influence of the Passions on the happiness of Men and Nations) ; and it was about such a commission he started to write the letters that went into the fire. At last he received a letter Irving had written to her (9.2.1822),[1] with news of his London doings, and addressed to " care of T. Carlyle " in Edinburgh. This had to go on without delay.

[1] Printed in full in Mrs. Oliphant's *Life of E. Irving*, Chap. VI.

XXI

"BLESSED ARE THE MEEK"

(1822)

THE Buller boys had been with him three weeks, and a six months' engagement had been made when he wrote (13.2.1822) :—

'I have a volume of things to express to you, yet I scarce can find one word to say. After that unfortunate visit, it seems as if our connection depended on a single hair ; and I tremble lest some unguarded word may dissolve it for ever. I appeal to the tribunal of my own conscience, and plead *not guilty* of any intention ever to displease you. Why then am I so unfortunate ?

'You bid me write as a *friend*. Vain injunction ! I must exhibit the true state of my feelings when I write, or else write like a shallow fool ; and I never felt *friendship* of this sort towards any one. Be not displeased however, I am as far from pretending to be a lover at this period of my history. I have had too much experience ever to find much enjoyment in the languishings and delusions of boys and girls.' (Which seems foolish ; but the unfortunate philosopher was feeling after her affectations in order to conform to her wishes.) 'I am a perfect wreck. Forget the roughness of my exterior, if you think me sound within. Let me write to you with frankness and from the heart, if you would not have me altogether despicable. The Graces cannot live under a sky so gloomy and tempestuous as mine. I lament their absence, since you lament it ; but there is no remedy. I pass Mr. Bradfute's door every day, and seldom without thinking of the *last* time I saw you there. Would I had never seen you since ! I should then still think what perhaps I must never think any more.'

She replied in a letter of "elegant mockery" and sent him for correction her rendering of some difficult bits of

Schiller's *Don Carlos*, the first present he had given her. She was letting him suppose she was planning a complete translation of it. He hastened to do all she wanted and sent books with the papers returned and entreated her to write to him (26.2.1822).—

' The three grains of knowledge mixed up in three bushels of error, which people make such a din about, are taught in colleges and schools, and set forth in the thousand times ten thousand heavy tomes ; why should our poor scanty pages be employed in adding to the heap ? Man's noblest part is not his poor glimmering taper of an understanding ; Lucifer *knows* far more than ever Bacon knew : it is the heart that makes us great or little ; and who would not rather be the meanest creature that can *love*, than the highest that could but *perceive ?* '

And so on to nearly three pages of print, begging " a letter," and ending with a postscript dated the next day (27.2.1822), to say that Irving and Graham were coming from Glasgow that night to stay a week with him. In short, he was making love to her from the start, preferring word of mouth and face to face dealing, but ready to use every and any means to please her.

To this particular letter she felt moved to answer nothing. Which was safe. Her feelings were so mixed at the time that it would have been rash to utter them " without reserve," as anyone can see now from a long letter she wrote within a week (3.3.1822) to Bess Stodart, describing a funny interview with a young George Cunningham, and recurring to George Rennie.—

' One night when it was very stormy, I lay awake till four o'clock in the morning, thinking on the perils of such a night at sea. What dreadful weather this is ! The very elements seem to have leagued with *that wretch* against me ; for it is impossible to hear such winds and not to *think* of him. God grant he may not be drowned ! and that he may return to Scotland alive ! Were he dead, you know I should forget his faults ; and that—that would be dreadful. Could I ever forget *his faults ?* He might then indeed have the *glory* of having made the proudest heart in Britain *break*. But do not—for mercy sake do not *pity* me. And shall I not be revenged ? My revenge shall be great as his fault is great, and noble as his fault is base.' (So much for George

Rennie, in the most approved style. Then followed shopping
commissions and sundries, including :) ' Mr. Irving is making
a horrible noise in London, where he has got a church. He
tells me, in his last, that his head is quite turned with the
admiration he has received ; and really I believe him. The
boys Mr. Carlyle is attending are Bullers, with Dr. Fleming,'
(your neighbour in George Square.) 'They are *great boys,
singularly great*. But I will tell you all about my two learned
friends in my next.'[1]

Her " learned friend " was often seen by Bess attending
his pupils ; but he left her alone, and feeling " called " to
write a book, he thought of the Civil Wars and Commonwealth of England, and began to read it up with more than
Teutonic thoroughness. His letters and notebooks reveal
he was meditating to write unlike a German, in the manner
of De Staël's *Allemagne*, or the histories of Voltaire, with
better regard for the truth. He intended to display " the
national character " and " intersperse all the ideas which I
can gather," and give " mental portraits of Cromwell, Laud,
George Fox, Milton, Hyde, etc., the most distinguished
of the actors in that great scene." The mention of George
Fox, the first of the Quakers, in such company is an early
sign of an original way of thinking, which slowly emerges
from his notes. His private feeling about critics too would
have been more pleasing to Fox and his " Friends " than
to the French : " If it once please my own mighty *self*, I do
not value them or their opinion a single rush."

The boys took about five hours of every working day, and
Legendre much of the leisure left. He looked in vain for
some one to relieve him of it. Printing began about April
and was not done till July. But the boys were bright and
the teaching pleasant ; and even Legendre gave him a happy
Sunday forenoon, when he flung off at a sitting the Doctrine
of Proportion—as good a substitute for the fifth book of
Euclid as could be given in speech,[2] and still admired by
mathematicians, who looked on him as on Pascal—a great
man lost to their science ! A " Life of Pascal " was one of
his last articles for Brewster, and likely to have been written
not later than this spring, and the French biographers are
justified in claiming that it and his other early " Lives "

[1] *Early Letters of J. W. Carlyle*, by D. G. Ritchie, pp. 53–8.
[2] Prof. de Morgan's *Paradoxes*, quoted in D. Masson's *Edinburgh
Sketches*, p. 309.

for the *Encyclopedia* show him already at home in their literature. He was now declining the offers booksellers were making him for editions and translations and ceasing to write for the *Encyclopedia*, and telling Graham in Glasgow : [1] " ' In spite of Nature and my stars,' I am going to *write a book*." He admitted he had not found a subject, yet prophesied it would be out " before this time twelvemonth." He was like a preacher full of utterabilities, uncertain only about his text.

A week or two after Jane Welsh received the letter from Carlyle which she did not answer (26, 27.2.1822), there came to her (6 or 13.3.1822) a significant letter from Irving. He had been staying with Carlyle, and his letter shows he had gone out to Haddington, and been entrusted with some volumes of Rousseau to return, with advice to look into them himself, which he did ; and at the same time he must have been confidentially commissioned to observe and report how Carlyle was taking his dose of silence ; and so he told her—" Carlyle is not so aggrieved as I could have figured. Such a parting from you would have gone far to kill me."

Satisfactory or not, the report was true, as appears from a letter of condolence Carlyle was writing a few days later (23.3.1822) to another Glasgow friend, David Hope, who had appealed to him for sympathy in affliction.

[1] Unpublished letter.

XXII

COMFORTING DAVID HOPE
JILTED BY "A PERSON OF GENIUS"

(1822)

IT is likely that Hope knew something of Carlyle's first disappointment in love. At any rate, he now sent him news of his own, and here is part of the answer (23.3.1822).—

'Some account of your projected marriage had reached me, but I received your authentic detail with fresh interest. Various thoughts strike me. You have acted with perfect integrity and honour throughout. As for the loss itself I am not sure that you have much cause for regret, when all is reckoned up. The young lady's conduct I can find an explanation if not an excuse for, and her general demeanour displayed many graceful qualities. But she was a person of genius, if I mistake not ; and much as I admire, not to say idolize, that characteristic in a mistress (or *sweetheart*, as we call it), I confess I should pause before recommending it to any honest man in a wife. These women of genius, sir, are the very devil when you take them on a wrong tack. I know very well that I myself—if ever I marry, which seems possible at best—am to have one of them for my helpmate ; and I expect nothing but that our life will be the most turbulent, incongruous thing on earth—a mixture of honey and wormwood, the sweetest and the bitterest —or, as it were, at one time the clearest sunshiny weather in nature, then whirlwinds and sleet and frost ; the thunder and lightning and furious storms—all mingled together into the same season—and the sunshine always in the *smallest* quantity ! Judge how you would have relished this : and sing with a cheerful heart, *E'en let the bonnie lass gang !*
'Before long I trust to see you more happily mated. There is no happiness without a good wife. You know the old story of the scissors : a single blade is good for nothing,

235

together they clip everything.' (And so on to current news.) [1]

Irving was in Glasgow when Hope received this and he would see it, as he and Hope were in the habit of showing each other the letters from Carlyle. The genial man would "grin intelligence from ear to ear," and maybe tell about Miss Welsh. In private he was perhaps by this time counting his own escape from that "person of genius" among his special mercies, and could corroborate the comfort given, which was truly a "word in season." Graham was soon reporting that Hope was "in prime health and spirits."

[1] Unpublished Letters of Carlyle, *Scribner's Mag.*, April, 1893, pp. 419–20.

XXIII

ON "FAUST"

(1822)

CARLYLE was correcting the proofs of his essay on
Faust [1] at the same time (March, 1822); and replying
to a letter sending for consideration the remarks of a Mr.
Hodgkin, he thanked him for information about German
metres, and explained :—

'I do not say that Byron took the idea (of the wicked
and clever remarks in "Don Juan") from Mephistopheles;
it is unhappily easy for many a one to find such ideas
nearer home if he is blackguard enough to indulge in them.
I only meant to say that Byron might have found his fundamental conception realised already in Goethe's play. The
Diable Boiteux (of Le Sage) is a very pretty little fellow but
no devil, rather a smirking little French Abbé.'

In the article Byron is styled " a generous imitator, who
rivals what he imitates," though Mephistopheles is a " much
shrewder fellow than the biographer of Don Juan."

This essay was not reprinted. The best of it is in that on
Helena, the second part of *Faust*, which appeared in 1828;
but in the interval there had been a great change. By
1828 Carlyle was able to show *Faust* revealing reality;
but in 1822 he wrote what explains why he never reprinted
the article.—

'When we see Mephistopheles ruin a being so greatly his
superior, it seems as if the spirit of evil were made victorious
over that of good. But Rashness must be punished.
(Faust's) criminality began . . . *when he allowed his mind
to wander—even in the search of truth*—till it doubted the
existence of a Providence, and the foundation of moral distinctions. All his subsequent miseries and crimes originated
in this—at first view *so pardonable—a transgression.*'

[1] *New Edinburgh Review*, April, 1822; and the letter quoted readers
owe to Miss E. Reid, Wishaw, who showed it to D. A. W.

He had a long way to travel yet before the " pardonable transgression " appeared to him the first of duties. "Truth!" cried Teufelsdröckh, " though the Heavens crush me for following her : no Falsehood ! though a whole celestial Lubberland were the price of Apostasy ! " A nimble spirit may feel like that soon ; but Carlyle was like other pedestrians—" cabined, cribbed, confined " by conventions that seemed to cover the life of man as the buildings of a town cover its soil. He had a long way to travel, and was as heavy laden with learning as Faust himself ; and moralises over the erring brother somewhat in the style of Bunyan's Mr. Worldly Wiseman of the town of Carnal Policy, directing afflicted Christian to go with his bundle to the town of Morality (where he always goes himself when he goes to church), and seek guidance from Mr. Legality and the respectable people there. Edinburgh was Carnal Policy and Morality combined ; and Carlyle had only escaped as yet from its material, not from its spiritual, smoke and noise and smells.

It is an amusing guess that when Goethe was praising in 1828 the essay of that year, the " Edinburgh Reviewers " he contrasted with Carlyle may have included the Carlyle of 1822. " It is pleasant," said he to Eckermann, " to see how the earlier pedantry of the Scotch has changed into earnestness and profundity. When I recollect how the ' Edinburgh Reviewers ' treated my works not many years since, and now consider Carlyle's merits, I am astonished at the important step for the better. The temper in which he works is always admirable. What an earnest man he is." [1]

The pioneer is seldom popular ; and the bookseller who had commissioned the essay of 1822 was pleased with it. True, he paid only fifteen pounds instead of twenty-five pounds as promised, but his excuse was—" The *Review* has so limited a sale," etc. Carlyle gave " him no rude words," partly because he might have more business with him, and explained to a younger brother—" rude words generally degrade the person who employs them as much as the person who endures them." This is as close perhaps as Europeans have yet come to the Eastern sages who think the speaker of rude words is the only party degraded.

[1] *Conversations of Goethe with Eckermann*, translated by John Oxenford, p. 337.

XXIV

PRIVATE AND PUBLIC RESEARCH

(1822)

HIS explanation of Faust being a " criminal " because
he rashly doubted Providence was hardly in type
before he was wondering whether Milton was sincere in
affirming " some views of Particular Providence." He was
reading Milton for the Civil Wars and Commonwealth.
The subject had gripped him ; and he was at it " day and
night, when I have any leisure," as he told James Johnstone.[1] It was to see all round that he was reading Milton,
Ludlow, Fox and other contemporaries. He began with
no doubt about Cromwell's " dissimulations and crocodile
tears " and no suspicion of Clarendon's carelessness about
the truth, which after many years he had to reveal, regret-
fully ; and he always shared his esteem for Falkland, while
Macaulay never honoured Hampden more than he did now,
and even continued to do tho in time he discovered
better men.

Even in 1822, when almost on the same level as Clarendon
and Macaulay, he could understand a Ludlow, and began
to suspect that Cromwell was beyond the reach of conventional analyses. Thus he was noting :—

' I admire Ludlow's patient unaffected character very
highly. Neither Russell nor Sidney were better men. Did he
blanch before the Royalists at Oxford ? before Cromwell at
London ? before Monk and the new " Convention " ? And
when he fled to Vevey—though banished from his friends,
his country, his wife, his property, and cheated of his just
fame, and daily beset with barbarous assassins in a far
land—does he whine or make lament ? Compare him with
Rousseau or Ovid or Necker—he is like a pillar of marble
compared with a weeping willow. How was it such noble
minds were generated in those times ? I know not, but think
it well worth enquiring into.

[1] Unpublished letter.

'Cromwell is a *very* curious person. Has his character been rightly seized yet ? I must peruse the late documents about him. His first Parliament was in September, 1654, and fairly elected—though by a rule different from the common. " Strange man—don't know him—don't." '

Instead of being a recreation, the reading of history was putting a strain upon him. He was seeking the wherewithal to make a book, not reading purely to see what was what ; and poor Rousseau, with whom he felt he had too much in common, has explained how any such secondary motive takes the pleasure out of research in even simple botany.

As the days grew longer he took to bathing. On Thursday, 18.4.1822, he had a lesson in the pursuit of knowledge for its own sake. As he was emerging from the sea at Newhaven, he saw appearing among the fishing-boats on the shore the " broad fat face " of a cousin, Dr. Waugh, the son and heir of the just shoemaker in whose house he had been boarded when a boy at Annan. Waugh had called at Carlyle's lodging, and hearing he had gone a-bathing, followed to the shore. It was approaching one o'clock, and they were to go home directly ; but Waugh had of course to wait while the other dressed, and he discovered the flayed carcase of a porpoise, and eagerly began to dissect it. Soon, as Carlyle wrote to his brother John, he was " up to his elbows almost in gore and filth, descrying with a rapturous shout the various midriffs and puddings and cat-collops of its bestial belly—stretching its guts along the gravel and measuring their length with a measuring-reed (made of sea-tangle—one of the small guts of the beast was like a short day's journey in length—somewhere about sixty feet, if I recollect)—the whole of this amid a crowd of brown fishermen, idle serving-maids, and scrubby boys, who eyed Waugh with astonishment and awe, and stood waiting *till* he would extract the oil or ambergris or balm or precious stone, for which they felt sure he must be digging so painfully."

The disinterested man of science noticed next a shark which also tempted him ; but he let himself be pulled away to a wash-up and lunch. " Waugh is the placidest man on earth for certain," concluded Carlyle. " At the instant when he was gutting this, I believe he could not have commanded sixpence anywhere in Nature," which lets us guess what his errand may have been.

He was short of cash ; but too lazy to relieve Carlyle of the well-paid Legendre work, or do some teaching he passed on to him. He was the elder of the two. His mother was Carlyle's mother's aunt. When Carlyle had been going as a teacher to Annan, Waugh was quitting it and going to Edinburgh to study medicine. The war had made the doctor's trade appear the road to fortune ; and the money his father left him made him despise too long the pay of common practice. He wrote medical books which were never published, and at last he subsided out of sight into some corner in Annan, saved by his cousins from lack of oatmeal. But as yet he was full of hopes and vague plans, too much preoccupied for common drudgery, and his placid presence kindled hopes of health in Carlyle. " Ey, mon," he would say, and smile incredulously now when the wiry, restless Tom Carlyle said—" I would give all the world sometimes to have no nerves." Waugh had suffered from the stomach, too, the other remembered, in their student days, " and now never knows the name of distemper." But his disinterested carelessness could not be copied.

R

XXⅴ

"AS YOU WERE"

(1822)

AS if indigestion and overwork were not worry enough, Carlyle sent a note to Haddington next day (Friday, 19.4.22), forwarding to "My dear Madam" Cowper and some other books which " I happened to fall in with lately," he explained, as if by accident, remarking—

' I have got no German queries from you for a long while. One or two things have occurred to me which I thought might perhaps be useful to you as subjects of literary composition : if you care, they are at your service. Present my kind respects to your Mother. Yours with sincere and affectionate esteem,

' THOMAS CARLYLE.'

Her answer was not long delayed (27.4.1822).—

' From a sheet of paper pretending to be a Letter, that came to me some days ago, I learned to my great surprise and satisfaction, that the wrecked Mr. Carlyle has been restored in mind and body to his lamenting friends. Truly, Sir, to my mind you have made a far more wonderful escape than Jonah did. I will thank you to transmit to me the papers which you mention before you set out on your next voyage. Cowper is charming, but draws so largely on my pity that I cannot spare him much of my admiration. I am in a *terrible* hurry. My mother has called on me half a dozen times. I will be at home on Wednesday to receive your expected communications, if it is convenient for you to write on that day. Yours with humility,

' JANE BAILLIE *Penelope* WELSH.'

Assuming the name of the faithful wife of Ulysses was meant as a hint, of course. " If," she wrote, " it is convenient for you to write." If ! If ! On Tuesday, 30.4.1822, he sat up till he heard the watchman singing " One o'clock," while he completed a letter to her which fills six pages of print, about a great poem she was to write. She seemed to him to have " a dramatic genius " equal to a tragedy on Boadicea. He had sent her Cowper's ode. He told her all that was known, and suggested more in the way of romance, and wished her " to commence writing " immediately and " make something fine of it." She replied that she could not write a tragedy " at present," and added, in returning De Staël's *Delphine*—" I am not at all the sort of person you and I took me for. I begin to think that I was actually meant by nature to be a fine-lady. For the last month I have spent all my time in riding, dressing, singing, and playing at shuttlecock ! " (With Dr. Fyffe every day, she might have added. The letter went on.) " Dear Sir, what will cure me ? Even my ambition is expiring. I will never excel the hundreds of female Novelists who infest the Kingdom."

He tried to revive what he supposed to have been her own " idea of translating *Don Carlos*," and multiplied the inducements to a visit to Edinburgh, such as—" Your Mother will hear Chalmers if she come to town." As for their own writing—" One half hour's conversation would enable us to settle all those things better than a whole day's scribbling."

Mrs. Welsh brought Jane to town ; but did not give her notice till a few hours before they left home, and succeeded in preventing her from seeing the tutor fellow at all. But Jane wrote to him that she had done her best to see him, underlining, " *I really wished it.*" Irving had told her Carlyle had been speaking to him about writing the lives of literary great men. " Have you that project still in view?" she enquired. " I liked it much. It is a pity you should allow year after year to glide away without making any vigorous effort to become known. You may suppose my wish to see my friends famous is one of the effects of my ruling foible ; but surely there is nothing weak in longing to see those I love happy and filling the station in life Nature designed them for. Shandy sends you his love." Shandy was the sheep-dog which ornamented Mrs. Welsh's drawing-room.

She enclosed her translation of a poem by Goethe which he had given her long ago, a ballad about a fisher who was beguiled under water by a mermaid ; and now (in May, 1822) they began writing poetry at each other.

XXVI

A NEIGHBOUR'S DOG

(1822)

THE quiet of Carlyle's present lodgings seemed suddenly in danger when a neighbour chained a dog in a grass-plot twenty yards from his window. The dog spent the whole night lamenting aloud, and by five o'clock in the morning Carlyle confessed to his mother that he " would have given a guinea for its hind legs firm in my right hand by the side of a stone wall." The street at large had been kept awake and threatened prosecution. So there was quiet the next night, but then the nuisance began again ; and after lying awake for half an hour, about one o'clock Carlyle reflected the thing was legally preventible and arose and dressed, went out and found the watchman and begged him to stop it. But he was an Irishman and courteous, saying—" I cannot for the world interfere with a gentleman's rest at this hour, but in the morning I will certainly——"

" Show me the door."

Carlyle pulled the bell ; and again, and again, and again and again, the other standing by ; and about the sixth peal a servant came to the door and tremulously asked—" What is it ? "

" I have come for the instant, total and everlasting removal of the dog, or to-morrow I will see whether justice is in Edinburgh or the shadow of British law in force."

" Do you hear that ? " chimed in the watchman, perhaps explaining to the woman, half-asleep, that she would need to keep the beast quiet somehow, even if she had to take it into the kitchen as usual, which of course was done. Then all within hearing would " swear a prayer or two " and fall to sleep again.

Though want of sleep had made him feel willing to kill the dog, it is curious that dogs and children were always drawn to him as if by instinct. Thus in answering Miss

Welsh's letter which sent him Shandy's " love," he wrote
(27.5.1822) :—

'If Shandy understood articulate speech, I would gladly
return his compliments ; for he is a dog of worth undoubtedly.
He would give me welcome wherever he met me, which is
all he can do, poor fellow—and more than every one of our
human friends can do.'

If Mrs. Welsh had always welcomed him as blithely as
Shandy did, the course of true love would have run smooth—
unless something else had happened to prevent it.

XXVII

INSPIRED POETRY

(1822)

HE was unequal to the comprehension of Cromwell at present—the young woman at Haddington distracted him too much. He got farther than any other as yet. He discovered that he did not see, and that none of the writing men yet had seen the secret of Cromwell. So he quitted the topic when he finished Legendre, the very time when he had planned to begin to make a " book " about it, as if feeling with Goethe that a man should only write of what he knows for sure. He continued silent for many years upon the Commonwealth, in a state of tentative doubt.

His mind was handcuffed at present by tentative doubt about Jane Welsh. She could not or would not see him, and the poetry he began to produce was like that of the gentlemen in *Love's Labour Lost*, inspired by the very instinct which makes the larks sing, and the tom-cats too. " We are not all equally gifted," said the gander to the lark, " but we have the same feelings." Once started, he went on awhile like Shakespeare's Holofernes, following fashion and tradition. He wished that the time he had given to mathematics had been spent in learning to rhyme. It took him several years to discover what he confessed at last in this connection,[1] the futility of will against Nature.

It was a sign of the times that the lady took to poetry too ; and as any other man would have done he fooled her to the top of her bent in all sincerity ; but she soon knew better. She was emotionally the older of the two, though in years the younger. Whatever fictioneering biographers may say, she seems to have desisted from rhyming in 1822,[2] and what she wrote to him in May, " I shall never hold

[1] To David Masson who told D. A. W. and in his Journal.
[2] *The Love Letters of T. C. and J. W.*, edited by A. Carlyle, Appendix, II, p. 360.

a respectable place among literary ladies," was as sincere as anything she ever wrote. Except as a possible makeshift if she could not get a man to her mind, she had no literary ambition. However, literature was the link with Carlyle, and though he seemed less elegant than St. Preux, he came nearer than any other suitor for her favour and her farm to Rousseau ideals. George Rennie himself was below that level, or began to seem so now at any rate.

Carlyle was sure she was a genius. All the literary ladies put together were of no significance compared to her. It seems to have been in June, replying to his letter mentioning Shandy, that she sent him some lines beginning " I love," which he liked " the best of all." No wonder ! They ended—

> " I love the soul no danger fearing,
>   Still onward rushing to its goal,
> All that impedes its course down-bearing,
>   Proud, fiery, brooking no control."

' In these,' he assured her gravely, and the fun of reality is beyond any farce, ' the ideas are brilliant, the language emphatic and sonorous, the rhythm very musical and appropriate. Proceed as you have begun ; and I shall yet see the day, when I may ask with pride : Did I not predict this ? And look to the reward. Kings and Potentates are a gaudy folk that flaunt about with plumes and ribbons to decorate them, and catch the coarse admiration of the many-headed monster, for a brief season—then sink into forgetfulness or often to a remembrance even worse : but the Miltons, the de Staëls—these *are* the very salt of the Earth : they derive their " Patents of nobility direct from Almighty God," and live in the bosoms of all true men to all ages.'

Which shows how ready he was to fall in with her way of thinking. He suggested to her an essay on Madame de Staël and offered books. She enquired what he thought of the siege of Carcassonne in Sismondi for a tragedy. He replied it would hardly do.

' The persecution of the Albigenses has little to distinguish it from other persecutions. Yet much depends on the natural bent of your own inclination. But why not pure invention ? '

Why not? She was following her "own inclination" then in a way he little suspected, and his tentative doubt about her was more reasonable than he ever knew. To the satisfaction of her mother, it seems likely, she had taken a fancy to a "frank-hearted, tasteful, promising young man,"[1] whose name is hidden from us by the editor of her *Early Letters*—"Benjamin B——." This enabled her with little effort to meet the maternal wishes and neither go to Edinburgh nor let Carlyle come to Haddington. She tactfully sent him a detailed account of a proposal of marriage she had received from a lawyer she did not like, and mentioned Dr. Fyffe as if accidentally, indifferently; discussed Byron and Washington Irving, and professed herself "quite delighted" with the poetry he was sending her, declaring, to keep him busy: "Oh, if I had your *genius*, your learning, and my own ambition, what a brilliant figure I should make!"

In reply he sent her (13.7.1822) a long epistle, declaring her "charming Letter dashed every cloud from the mind, and left me cheerful as Summer." With much crowing over the lawyer—"his presumption exceeds all measure"—and no suspicion of his own danger of sharing the same fate, he sent advice as to reading and urged her to seek for literary fame.

'I see a niche in the Temple of Fame—still vacant or but poorly filled—which I imagine your powers will yet enable you, if so cultivated, to occupy with glory to yourself and profit to others—and that as a proper *woman*; which is more than our favourite De Staël ever did. "We are both *disguised* as women," was one of Talleyrand's jokes at her expense. Above all, tell me *when* I shall see you: consider, I have been a "reasonable person" for a very long period now—about half a year as I reckon; and a few more such periods will put us both—God only knows where! God bless you, my dearest friend, whether I see you or not! I am ever yours,

'THOMAS CARLYLE.'

Next day, maybe the day she read this, she was taking a tender leave of "my own gallant artist," Benjamin B——, who was about to go to Germany to "inhale the

[1] *Early Letters of J. W. Carlyle*, by D. G. Ritchie, pp. 63-4.

atmosphere of Goethe " [1] as a gentleman should, not by deciphering books, but by the grand tour, apparently.

Which explains why she would not see Carlyle, and answered further importunities by nothing but a " sharp note." " I am not happy at present," he pleaded to her, " I only beg for a little respite. Will you not write to me soon ? It were a kind act. I am always, Your affectionate friend,

THOMAS CARLYLE."

Worry and work combined to damage his digestion. Tobacco soothed his stomach and the rest, but spoiled his sleep. He once said of this time that he did not sleep a wink for three weeks. This was in spite of the quiet lodging and the daily bathe in the sea, and the deduction due for Carlylean exaggeration was maybe less than one might suppose. Distracted by want of sleep, he was approaching the crisis of his life

[1] *Ibid.*

XXVIII

THE EVERLASTING NO

(1822)

HE was well aware he had been overworking, and in desperation thought of laudanum ; but read De Quincey's *Opium Eater* first, and said to himself on finishing it : " Better, a thousand times better, *die* than have anything to do with such a Devil's own drug ! " [1]

As he lay awake his thoughts reverted to the sleepless summer night he had spent six years ago, sitting by the death-bed of his uncle Tom, the natural Stoic, who had lived without guile and died without fear. One afternoon about the end of July or beginning of August he was going down Leith Walk to the sea, when something happened ; and half a century afterwards he confessed he could still show the place. There was nothing for anyone else to see but a lanky fellow with a towel in his pocket. He was looking at nothing particular himself ; but before his mind's eye, like an everlasting nightmare, lay the material or sensual view of the Universe natural to animals, and which was all that the best of his contemporaries saw, even the like of David Hume beholding in the world but a " great machine, subdivided into an infinite number of lesser machines, ravishing into admiration all men ! " But not Carlyle. " Void of life," he called it, a " huge, dead, immeasurable steam-engine." He could not believe that Nature was blind, indifferent to right and wrong, as Hume and Voltaire supposed. He would not and could not adore any such object. The Puritans he had been reading about were as fresh in his mind as his brave dying uncle ; and he thought what a comfort it would be to face the Devil in his darkest den and " tell him a little of my mind." As he faced the horror of reality worse than any Devil, feeling himself as if paralysed and pushed down, the instinct of self-preservation suddenly asserted itself like a spiritual earthquake.

[1] " Recollections of Carlyle," by C. E. Norton, *New Princeton Review*, July, 1886, p. 9,

'I lived in a continual, indefinite, pining fear; tremulous, pusillanimous, apprehensive of I knew not what : it seemed as if all things in the Heavens above and the Earth beneath would hurt me; as if the Heavens and the Earth were but boundless jaws of a devouring monster, wherein I, palpitating, waited to be devoured.

'Full of such humour, and perhaps the miserablest man in the Capital or Suburbs, was I, toiling along over pavements hot as Nebuchadnezzar's Furnace; whereby doubtless my spirits were little cheered; when, all at once, there rose a Thought in me, and I asked myself : "What *art* thou afraid of? Wherefore, like a coward, dost thou for ever pip and whimper, and go cowering and trembling? Despicable biped! What is the sum-total of the worst that lies before thee? Death? Well, Death; and say all that man may, will or can do against thee! Hast thou not a heart; canst thou not suffer whatsoever it be; and, as a child of Freedom, though outcast, trample Death itself under thy feet, while it consumes thee? Let it come, then; I will meet it and defy it!" And as I so thought, there rushed like a stream of fire over my whole soul; and I shook base Fear away from me for ever. I was strong, of unknown strength; a spirit, almost a god. Ever from that time, the temper of my misery was changed : not Fear or whining Sorrow was it, but Indignation and grim, fire-eyed Defiance.

'The Everlasting No had said : "Behold, thou art fatherless, outcast, and the Universe is mine (the Devil's)"; to which my whole Me now made answer : "I am not thine, but free, and for ever hate thee!"

'From this hour I began to be a Man.'[1]

Besides omitting irrelevant details, the only change made here in turning the poetry or fiction of *Sartor* into history is writing *Death* instead of "Tophet," meaning Hell, which the real Carlyle had long ago perceived to be a superstitious nightmare.

He returned from the sea refreshed as usual, and able to look around him with a strange composure and new interest. He was feeling his freedom, as if moving aloft in the air and looking down upon the world—he had found his spiritual wings.

[1] *Sartor*, II and VII., *The Love Letters of T. C. and J. W.*, II, pp. 380–2 correct the common misdating of the Everlasting No in 1821.

The Everlasting No is the denial of Righteousness. Denying the Everlasting No is therefore affirming Righteousness as a fact of Nature, seen by the mind as the light of the sun is seen by the eyes. No words can describe it, as no paint can picture the sunlight. The Chinese sages said it consisted in behaviour in harmony with the conscience, and Carlyle would have agreed with them.

The "Everlasting No" has as many shapes as there are shams or lies or sinners ; and a few days after his defiance of it in general, an easy thing, Carlyle beheld a particular incarnation of it in a placard about the impending visit of the fourth George Guelph, announcing that the magistrates devoutly hoped that in honour of the Advent of His Royal Majesty everybody would be carefully well-dressed—"black coat and white duck trousers," if at all convenient. "Scandalous flunkeys !" said Carlyle. "If I were changing my dress at all, I should incline rather to be in white coat and black trousers." As leave of absence could be had for the asking at such a season, he gladly gave up his rooms to Graham and Hope from Glasgow, and departed for a holiday in the country. He had several weeks at Mainhill and many days of riding in Galloway, returning to town when the hurly-burly had rolled away.

BOOK IV

WANDERING YEARS
1822–24

I

WHAT NEXT?

(1822)

MRS. WELSH had of course brought Jane to town to see the royal George and the other shows, and after two weeks there they went to Fort Augustus in the highlands to stay with a cousin and enjoy the vacant sublime in scenery and garrison society. At Mainhill Carlyle was meditating poetics. A " fat bookseller," Boyd, who was compiling a profitable book on the Visit of George IV, had offered to " go half " in a poetical translation of Schiller's *William Tell*. Carlyle said " No," reluctantly. He " made the younkers sing " to him ; and as Burns had said a sight of the " Glenkens of Galloway might make a poet of a block-head," he pilgrimed to the place on horseback and looked at these hills, and even made a prose description of them for Jane Welsh, but never a rhyme would come. He commenced an Address to an Old Church, and stuck ; but finished a poem on the Battle of Morgarten, which Froude has cruelly printed in the spirit of the son of Noah who exposed his father drunk. Another scrap in print was done now, a translation of Faust's curse, and maybe also an Adieu (to Margaret Gordon) which he never put any name to and did not send to Jane at present. Its music was the best he ever made, but merely an echo of Burns,[1] and its sentiment— " Adieu for ever now, my dear "—is prehistoric.

Returning to Edinburgh (7.9.1822) he settled into a pleasant routine which lasted eight or nine months. He was at home in his quiet lodgings all morning, free for any masterpiece he might be moved to write. Charles Buller and his brother were agreeable pupils and needed him only four hours a day. They lived with their parents in India Street. Their father and Carlyle drew together, recognising each other's sense, while both had livers out of order. Mrs. Buller was well pleased with the tutor and had him as much

---

[1] " It was a' for oor rightfu' king."

in the drawing-room as he seemed to want. She avowed to him her admiration of Napoleon, from whose grave at St. Helena she had taken sprigs of willow. She had " called him the greatest of men in the presence of Mr. Croker himself." Carlyle acquiesced in this ; but they differed about Byron, whom he defended and Mrs. Buller called a charlatan, because his warmest admirers were boarding-school girls and young men under twenty.

Soon after his return, Carlyle sent a long letter to Jane Welsh, declaring : " I am dying to hear from you." She was delighted, as she was beginning to be tired of adapting herself to garrison society by playing the part of " a lively, dashing, good-humoured, thoughtless blockhead of a girl," whereby she told him she had " turned the heads of all the men in the place." And in reality perhaps some speculative officers might have been overheard discussing her—" how much do you think she's worth ? " She tried to think them more " frank, natural and true-hearted " than " the cold, selfish, well-bred beings " of Haddington, but there was no denying they were dull, dull. So she gladly sent Carlyle the long letter he wanted—humorous history—and in October, as soon as she was home, begged a plan for winter study. She did not want to " die and be forgotten," she said : " Send me all your verses ; and tell me, are those on the Night-moth a translation ? "

He proudly replied the Night-moth was original, and was told : " Your last verses are very like Campbell's. Pray send me some more : you cannot think what pleasure they afford me." And she confessed to having put some of his verses in an " Album," and so sent them circulating in good society. She was more sincere than Polonius fooling Hamlet, but equally absurd.

In pleasant contrast to the piffle about poetry was the advice he gave her as spaciously as she wanted upon reading history, " the easiest, the most entertaining and the most instructive of all " studies. Had she maps and books of reference ? " Geography and Chronology," space and time, are " *the two windows* of history."

' You should try to fix in your mind the few great events which influenced all the rest, and understand them. They stand like beacons, each commanding a large space around it : the lesser occurrences naturally group themselves about them, and are held in memory by cause and effect. Taking

notes' may be 'a good practice if used in moderation.
Keep looking at your maps : Remember the *two windows*—
just in proportion to the vividness and distinctness of your
original conception of anything, will be the length of time
you remember it.'

And so on, with the iteration easy to a teacher ; but as
the months slipped by without a sight of her, a single sentiment pervaded his letters, like the drone in a bagpipe's
melody, a craving to see her again. It creeps out quaintly
in his history teaching, which had to be too vague, he explained, because of " the impossibility of writing all that
might be said. If I saw you for two hours—to question and
suggest—to consult and discuss by word of mouth, it might
be different. If you let me see your face, I promise to make
everything clear and precise."
She could not take the hint ; but said as much as she
could think of to make him content.

'If ever I succeed in distinguishing myself, thine will
be the honour. When you saw me first I was wretched.
Without plan, hope, or aim, I had lived two years when
my good Angel sent you hither. I had never heard the
language of talent or genius but from my father's lips ;
I had thought that I should never hear it more. You spoke
like him ; your eloquence awoke in my soul the ambitions
His first kindled there. I wept to think the mind he had
cultivated with such anxious, unremitting pains was
running to desolation ; and I returned to the life that he
had destined me to lead. But I am *alone*, and no one loves
me better for my industry. Your friendship restored me
to myself.'
(She concludes a long letter tactfully.) 'Is your history
of *Faust* printed yet ? Procure me a reading of it. Tell
me what you have decided on with respect to the proposal of the fat bookseller. Write soon. Your very
sincere friend,

'JANE WELSH.'

Boyd had offered him £150 for a Life of Milton, with
notes, etc. He declined it ; and also another offer received
from Mr. Galloway, a Professorship of Mathematics at Sand-
hurst, £200 a year, plus house and garden, coals and gas,
and two vacations of seven weeks. Not long ago he would

s

have thought this a prize, and there was a time coming again when he would have been glad of it. Not so now, when he was averse to mathematics and wishing he had learned to make poetry instead. He consulted Jane Welsh. She was not charmed, and in a long letter barely alluded to it. " What more of the Professorship ? " In answering he asked her—" You would not have me go ? " This lets us guess why he said " No " to it better than Galloway could, who told him he was whimsical.[1]

In truth he was feeling and trying to make Jane Welsh feel that except in the pursuit of literature there was no peace for him in this world. " It is the ' radiant orb ' as Nelson expressed it," he wrote to her (18.11.1822) alluding to Nelson's account of his early despondency and the " sudden glow of patriotism " which made him exclaim to himself— " Well then ! I will be a hero ! And confiding in Providence, I will brave every danger ! " " From that time a radiant orb, as Nelson expressed it, was suspended in his mind's eye which urged him onwards to renown."[2] Carlyle continued in this letter :—

' None but a very young or a very stupid person can exist at all without some determinate purpose to fill up the mind ; and of all I know none so praiseworthy as this. How much more noble than to toil and jostle for wealth or worldly precedence, which even when they are gained are but the *symbols* of dignity and are often worn by the basest of mankind ! Here, on the other hand, is a free and independent scene of effort, where no low artifice, no pitiful humiliation of the mind can be of any use, where all that is worthiest in our nature finds ample scope, where success is in our own hands, and each addition to our knowledge, each improvement in our sentiments *is* a genuine treasure which the world can neither give nor take away.'

In coaxing her to feel as he did, he dealt with her love of fame as gently as with his mother's religion. When *they* were concerned it was easy to recall the dreams of his youth and sympathise. But it was too late to dissemble with Jane—she knew his opinion and did not object in the least to the like of this.—

---

[1] Unpublished letter.
[2] *Montaigne and Other Essays*, by T. C. (reprinted from the *Edinburgh Encyclopedia*), 1897, pp. 70-1.

' I am far from insensible to the pleasures of fame : at the
same time, it is to *be*, not to *seem*, that one should labour ;
and if the former is attained the latter will inevitably
follow—or may stay if it likes. What matters it indeed
whether another pays you reverence, provided you are sure
that at any given moment you *have* force of mind enough
to lay him prostrate whenever you think proper ? There is
even a kind of pleasure in being despised by some block-
heads.'

The pugnacity of this is unpleasant. The warmth of it
shows how far he was from genuine indifference. Indeed
he never was a man to defy the public opinion—until he
was sure he was right. To that extent the hostile indict-
ment, that he was in spirit a dweller in a little town, seems
true. Which may be why there is nothing about him to
hide. But public opinion is an outside thing, to be heeded
like other things outside us. Force comes from within ;
and both he himself and the young woman in Haddington
were now expecting him to start a masterpiece, and he
could not think of anything to write about except their own
private affairs ! Would she collaborate with him in writing
a novel ? She said she was " willing to attempt anything,"
but wanted him to begin. " Proceed then ! "

II

COMFORTING JAMES JOHNSTONE AND HIMSELF

(1822)

HE seldom went into town. His brother John was a " medical " student now and staying with him. Occasionally some student or preacher came to chat an hour away with them ; but such visits were seldom repaid. When a man feels called to write a masterpiece and cannot make up his mind what it is about, he wants to be left alone.

Robert Mitchell was now Rector of a school at Kirkcudbright, and to him Carlyle now wrote to beg him to " console and encourage " James Johnstone, also now a " Scottish Teacher " for life, but being victimised at Broughty Ferry (Dundee).

' He has got planted among a very melancholy race of people—Psalm-singing captains, devout old women, Tabernacle shoemakers, etc., etc., who wish him to engage in exposition of the Scripture, and various other plans, for the *spread* not of grammar and accounts, but of the doctrines of Theosophy and Thaumaturgy (miracle-working).'

" You must write," he concluded, and of course he did so himself (24.11.1822), and exhorted Johnstone to be patient, "rather struggling with the most ungainly obstacles than again committing yourself to the guidance of fickle chance, and flying, as you and I have been too much of late, a prey to every turn in the eddies of this world's fitful current, as powerless over your own destiny as a wreck without sails, oar or rudder." Habit, " the great smoothener of existence," will make things easy. Then followed details of his own more prosperous life, so worded as to predispose James Johnstone to patience, and concluding :—

' For a man of ordinary penetration after five-and-twenty there is nothing new under the sun. Happy the dunce who forms no general propositions, who institutes no comparisons, to whom in consequence all things to the end of time will wear the charms of novelty, and supply a fund of interesting contemplation ! Happy too the man who seeks successfully to gild the inanity of this world's movements by interest for the friends whose comfort is involved in them. The eye is sated with seeing, the head with thinking ; but not the heart with feeling those honest sentiments of mutual kindness which form at least the only balm of life. Adieu, my dear Johnstone ! I am very bilious, but ever yours sincerely,

'TH. CARLYLE.'[1]

This shows him cherishing the feelings of simple Nature —" the heart's aye the part aye that makes us right or wrong," while awake to the light of general truths, the sight of which is the best reward of study. General truths, " right principles " or " ideas,"—the most erudite who lacks them is like an ass whose back is bending with ingots he cannot use, while the wisest wishing nothing else, content with light alone, encounters soon the chill that made Byron shudder, when " tho the eye may sparkle still, 'tis where the ice appears." Happy are they who follow Nature simply, and, rejoicing in whatever combination of heat and light may be vouchsafed them do the best they can. Nothing could be better than the advice Carlyle was now receiving from Graham who wrote from Glasgow.[2] " I see you have not begun the Book. Have patience, I pray you ; the fault is not yours. When the *subject* comes, the Book will in its train."

[1] Unpublished letter.   [2] *Ibid.*

III

HIS FIRST AND LAST SHORT STORY
"CRUTHERS AND JONSON"

(1822)

EARLY in December he sent Jane Byron's "Werner," and told her she should not give him up.

'Byron,' he said, 'is a person of many high and splendid qualities.' (Then, as if to show how far he could share her ideas :—) 'If I had his genius and health and liberty, I would make the next three centuries recollect me.

'I have spent a stupid day in reading the Abbé de Sade's *Memoirs of Petrarch*. What a feeble whipster was this Petrarch with all his talents! To go dangling about, for the space of twenty years, puffing and sighing after a little coquette, whose charms lay chiefly in the fervour of his own imagination, and the art she had to keep him wavering between hope and despondency—at once ridiculous and deplorable—that he might write sonnets in her praise!— a very worthless employment for a mind like Petrarch's— he might have built a palace, and he has made some dozen snuff-boxes with invisible hinges—very pretty certainly but very small and altogether useless. If you reckon this impertinent, impute it to headaches' (which means, take the hint if you like, but please don't take it too seriously. He goes on.)—'One thing is certain : I have no genius, not a whit : yet I have planted myself at my desk and almost sworn that there I will sit during my three free hours every morning, with no book before me, nor other instrument but pen and paper, that whether bright or stupid, sick or sicker, I may write *something*, or undergo the pain of total idleness, whichever I prefer. When will you write to me ? Whether seeing you or not seeing you, I am always yours,

'THOMAS CARLYLE.'

" Poor Petrarca ! " she answered at once (6.12.1822).
" As long as I live I shall not see a snuff-box without
thinking of him ! I am glad you do not like his ' puffing
and sighing ' : I never could endure it."

This was encouraging. He now sketched the outline of
a novel, a romantic version of their own courtship, ending
in both the lovers dying of love ; but after writing two
letters he stuck and decided to try instead a series of short
stories.

Though unable to get on with fictitious love-letters, he had
abundant practice in the real thing. She now agreed with
him that the day they met was an epoch in their lives ; and
began her letter mentioning Petrarch—" My dear friend,"
and ended—" Write to me soon, and never apologize for
the length of your letters. Oh ! I had a great deal more to
say. Yours affectionately." Her letter covers three and
a half pages of print, and shows she was studying eagerly
as he had advised. She let herself go so gaily and frankly
that it feels impertinent to mention that her sincerity is
proved by what she wrote to Bess Stodart. " Often at the
end of the week my spirits and my industry begin to flag ;
but then comes one of Mr. Carlyle's brilliant letters that
inspires me with new resolution, and brightens all my hopes
and prospects with the golden hues of his own imagination.
He is a very Phœnix of a Friend ! "

He found her letters equally delightful. There was about
her and them an infinite variety like Cleopatra's. This one
(6.12.1822) came with a " beautiful little jewel " she was
sending him, and it ranged from a new way of cutting her
hair, and the time of day she played with Shandy, to her
latest ideas about Socrates, and how the loss of an amethyst
brooch upset her and made her feel and act like other women.
Apropos a stock excuse for refusing invitations—" Letters
to write," she put in a parenthesis, " God knows *you* are my
only correspondent."

He was fairly uplifted and read her letter till he could
almost say it by heart ; and then sat brooding in a delicious
idleness and went wandering in solitary places, " dreaming
over things," he wrote to her, in a reply which fills nine
pages of print, " which never can be more than dreams.
My dear Friend, if you do not grow more cross with me
soon, I shall become an entire fool. Write to me without
reserve, not minding what or how. Related as we are
dullness is often best of all, for it shows that we are friends

and put confidence in one another. How many men, the latchet of whose shoes I am not worthy to unbind, have travelled through the world and found no noble soul to care for them! While I—God bless you, my dear Jane—if I could deserve to be so treated by you I should be happy. Now you *must* not grow angry at me. Write, write!—I am ' hungering and thirsting ' to hear of you and all connected with you. I am ever yours,

"THOMAS CARLYLE."

He made use of the fact that he had stuck in the novel— " I found that we should require to see one another, and consult together every day." He enclosed what was meant to be the first of his series of short stories, *Cruthers and Jonson*, wherein the heroine was after her own image.

This was a sketch of the lives of two friends in Annandale, who had been boys together at Hoddam School. It lay unpublished for eight years (*Fraser's Magazine*, 1831) and is plainly what he called it, a " true story," told as he had heard it. It adheres to tradition so closely that when " Barry Cornwall " (Procter) read the tale in *Fraser* by and by, he remembered how well he had heard Irving telling it,[1] and noticed no difference. In describing a young woman who married one of the friends, the writer filled in the blank left by tradition and made her after the image of his own, a fancy picture of a type—" formed in the very mould of beauty," wrote Carlyle. This may explain what the real Jane Welsh wrote to him as soon as she read it :—

' Would you continue to enjoy the sunshine of my smiles, you must also abstain from flattery—at least of the *common sort*. I have been stuffed with adulation ever since I left the boarding school—at that time I was as ugly a little bundle of a thing as ever you set eyes on; and adulation, like sweetmeats, palls the appetite when presented at all hours of the day. I value one compliment to my judgement above twenty to my person—for the latter, my glass declares to me every morning, is totally unmerited, whereas I may be tempted to believe the former has some foundation.'

The sense this shows is remarkable. There is more in what follows.—" You cannot but know that were I to rack

[1] *Bryan Waller Procter* (Barry Cornwall), p. 159. Pub. Bell & Son, 1877.

my heart and soul, I should never be able to extort anything
worthy of being mentioned in the same century with the
Story you have sent me." This was modest and partial,
like her appreciation of his verses. A fictioneer would say
the story has no plot. Two schoolboys fought, and one
went home and reappeared in the playground with a pistol
in hand, for which he was being expelled from the school,
when the other interceded and he was pardoned and they
became friends for the rest of their lives.

The whole thing is barely readable commonplace—like
the gossip of country folks, who counted time by generations
and could hardly speak of a man without telling you of his
father, not forgetting anything they had heard about his
grandfather and the rest, and his children and grandchildren.
It feels like what the hills might tell if they could speak. It
might interest the like of Carlyle's father and mother,
whom he was vainly inviting to visit Edinburgh this winter,
and to whom he was sending sermons and offering other
books. What the old man was curious about was Paley's
Horæ Paulinæ, and John returning home took it to him,
and wrote to Tom that he seemed to be " much pleased "
with it.

Another article in *Fraser* for 1831 may have been written
now[1]—a " Rhapsody " in rhyme on Peter Nimmo, a student
loafer who haunted the quadrangle for many years and
became a laughing-stock. It is an awful warning of the
danger of sitting down at a desk resolved to poetize in spite
of Nature and to write with nothing to say. The more is
the pity that it cannot be denied that Carlyle wrote it.

A letter to William Graham [2] (22.12.1822) congratulating
him on taking to reading runs on with the fervour of an
Apostle of Wisdom.—

'After all, there *is* no pleasure like those of the mind.
Kings may surround themselves with a manufactured splendour to please the eye, and often vainly meant to hide
the squalid nakedness of the " Man within." Our mental
faculties, if we would cultivate them, can do better. The
peasant Burns " that walked in glory on the mountain side,
behind his plough " could wrap himself in grandeur more
than royal when he pleased, could raise around him a world
as beautiful as Eden and be alive to all its beauty. If it be

[1] *Edinburgh Sketches and Memories*, by David Masson, pp. 285–91, and
footnote, pp. 290–1.   [2] Unpublished letter.

happiness to have the mind continually solaced by the presence of noble thoughts and lovely images and inspiring scenery, then make me a poor man that can think and study and imagine, and be a king yourself without these gifts.'

When not making himself write, Carlyle luxuriated in reading. Massinger, Beaumont and Fletcher and others such as they disappointed him by lack of " real insight," he said. " Rich and royal Shakespeare ! We should read his contemporaries in order rightly to prize him." There was compensation in some new books. Two days before Christmas he was claiming Mitchell's admiration for Byron's "Vision of Judgment," of "the wickedest and cleverest turn you could imagine,"—the identical masterpiece which curdled the soul of Edward Irving and moved him to write his *Argument for Judgment to Come*, and be a champion of old beliefs, a spiritual Don Quixote.[1]

[1] *Edward Irving*, by Mrs. Oliphant, Chap. VIII.

IV

MRS. WELSH RAISES THE BLOCKADE
BUT WILL NOT LET JANE COME TO TOWN

(1822–3)

ON Christmas night he sat up late on a long letter to Jane in reply to hers of the day before. How am I to see you again? had just inspired a paragraph, when there was a sound of revelry by night, some neighbours singing "Auld Lang Syne" and "calling back my thoughts," he wrote, "from those Elysian heights to the vulgar prose of this poor world." A more melodious spirit would have enjoyed the music, as Edward Irving did in London at the same time, when he heard the fiddlers under his window playing that very air and others like it. He wrote to Mrs. Welsh, who showed his letter to Jane, who sent a scoffing summary of it to Carlyle. They crowed in chorus over his bad "taste"; but nevertheless Carlyle declared his friend—"One of the best men breathing—he loves us both as if he were our brother." Before long he was writing to her that Irving said in a letter to him: "I pray you to give my dearest affection to my beloved pupil Jane Welsh, if you are in correspondence with her."

The "fat bookseller," Boyd, proposed a translation of *Wilhelm Meister*, on hearing it was "very clever." Carlyle agreed to consider this; but in the meantime nearly started a tragedy of his own, supposing he saw an opening in that direction. "Is it not strange," he wrote to Jane, "that they cannot get up a decent play in this country? All try it and fail," even Byron. As for the joint novel they were planning, he compared it to some alchemist's job, with infinite discussion and no result. She was as eager as he could be to begin. "If you have one spark of humanity within your breast," she wrote, "send me an outline of some tale to work on. How can I enjoy a moment's peace? Were I sure that Fame is within reach, I would not care how I loitered. But I am not sure. I *cannot* turn back *now*, and I *would* not if I *could*."

Impatient of visitors staying with them, she began to think she might like to " decamp and turn Hermitress in some wild Highland Glen." Whereupon he asked : " And would you not let me be of the party ? " She was suffering from bile,[1] and he was uneasy. His conscience smote him lest he had led her into over-exertion, and as the best way of soothing her down, he discounted " Fame," revealing more frankly than before his own convictions. A " glorious name " was an external reward. " If I had cultivated my soul to the very highest pitch that Nature meant it to reach, I think I could be happy though no suffrages at all were given me ; my conscience would be at rest, I should actually *be* a worthy man, whatever I might *seem*. There is nothing satisfying in applauses of others : the only gratification, worth calling by that name, arises from the approval of the *man within*. Then study to keep down this strong desire of notoriety," and so on—more than she could stand.

' My dear friend,' she answered, (23.1.1823), ' How could you find in your heart to inflict on me five whole pages of admonition, for scarce as many words of complaint ? " Tell you all that lies upon my heart ! " Truly you give me fine encouragement to be so very communicative ! Were I to tell you all, or half, I should expect your next lecture by the carrier's waggon.

' As to my *love of fame*, you will scarcely understand what I would be at ; I scarce do myself ; but I feel clearly that I wish to be loved as well as admired. To be loved as I love Schiller and De Staël ! ! ! All women love admiration, and *I* do not pretend to be an exception. No, it is to the hope of being loved as it were, in spite of *fate*, that I sacrifice ' (everything in short. Then comes what lets us guess how they used to talk in private.)—' You will say that it is my own fault that I am not loved, *alive* and seen. It is not ! Indeed it is not ! All the hearts mine is cast among—all but one—are intrenched within self-love. I might indeed attach many to me by benefits ; but of these I make no account. These love me for their own sake, not mine.

' I have news for you that will I hope please you as much as it did me : my mother wonders you do not think of coming out ! Now do you see the fruit of my restrictions ? Had you come sooner on your *own* invitation or mine, you would have found nothing but cold looks, and I should have

---

[1] *Early Letters of J. W. C.*, by D. G. Ritchie, p. 112.

been kept on thorns until you left me : and now I am
formally desired to invite you here, " in case it may be
that you are standing on ceremony." And come when you
like, Dear, you are sure of a hearty welcome. You cannot
think how glad I am.'

So Friday evening (14.2.1823) saw him at tea at Haddington, and Saturday and Sunday went by like a breeze. It
seemed to him that her mind had almost doubled in power
and real wealth in the past year, and his admiration for
everything about her was undisguised—which may have
been why the treatment he received from others did not
seem to her to be " as agreeable as it might have been."
But he noticed nothing amiss.

He might have been seen looking with tell-tale tenderness
at the " small arm-chair " in a corner beside the hearth.
It set him fancying what Jane was like when she was sitting
in it ; and Jane lent him the manuscript of a tragedy she
wrote at fourteen to the admiration of her impartial father.
He wondered when at home on the Monday what had made
the Sunday night so nice—" We said nothing worth remembering," he reminded her, in a long letter on the Tuesday (18.2.1823), " the scene was simple, our employments
still simpler : what then made me happy ? The French
say truly : ' Le plus grand des plaisirs, c'est l'abandon de
soi-même.' " (The greatest pleasure is to let yourself go.)

He begged her to come to Edinburgh in March to " read
German or do something " that would let them be together.
Another thing in his letter is like him. His affection for
her tragedy, which he read with " real enjoyment," was
classed by him with his love for her baby chair, and the
most he could say of it was that " for a girl of fourteen,
it seems a very curious affair." Which was disconcerting,
and so was his avowed reluctance to send her a Boccaccio
she wanted, because of its " impurities." Of course when
she returned it she said she had only read three of the stories
and " will never open the book again " ; and he believed
her and said he " liked her the better " for that.

In spite of such unskilful courting, she shared his eagerness
to be in town together in March, when it had been arranged
her mother was to leave her at Bess Stodart's and go alone
to Dumfriesshire. But Mrs. Welsh was not so simple as
they supposed. She made preparations for the visit and
spoke of it, but never would name a day for departure,

and put off till Jane was so much " out of humour " about it that she would ask no more.

Carlyle was about to write another " tale " when he learned that Irving had persuaded Taylor of the *London Magazine* to accept from him an article on Schiller, as a start for his intended " picture-gallery of literary great men." It was begun on the evening of a memorable Monday (24.3.1823). That afternoon he had been walking in Princes Street with a small divine who had so much to say that maybe he did not notice his companion's monosyllables were less to the point than usual. An increase in the pace was less likely to be ignored, but it did not last. Carlyle had thought he recognised from behind Jane Welsh, by dress and form and gait ; and he could not listen until he had overtaken her and seen a long, long nose, not Jane's ; whereupon the divine could get a hearing.

A letter was overdue, to say nothing of the visit ; and as he was sitting down to write *Schiller* that evening, chagrined and sour, his landlady, Mrs. Wilkie, came gliding in with : " A parcel, sir." Inside it was a letter from Jane that cheered him like a light in the darkness, and started him working like a happy boy, with nothing to wish for except that he might be always as well. He began to hope to finish *Schiller* before she came in April, as she promised now, and that would let him have all the more time in her company.

Meanwhile it was something to know she was being held in Haddington against her will. She made a pleasanter report to Bess Stodart than to him, and told her : " I battle away with Time pretty successfully ; my lessons employ the greater part of the day, and a little trifling with the ' professional callers,' or a game at chess or battledore with our *constant* man of physic, Dr. Fyffe, consumes the rest. I have got a fine head of hair lately ; altogether I am looking rather more captivating than usual. I pray Venus it may last till I get to town."

Something said to that effect would be too much for the patience of the " constant " man so handy for chess or battledore. Dr. Fyffe exploded.

V

DR. FYFFE

(1823)

BEFORE the end of March (1823), Carlyle had made a good start with *Schiller*; but his sweetheart's literary schemes that month were shattered. Instead of writing a romance, she had to act one. Love is a cruel thing when it pulls you in different directions at the same time.

Dr. Fyffe was a prosperous, " strutting " young doctor of high spirit and genteel pretensions—with an uncle who had a fine house near Moffat, and another a Baron at Vienna. He deserved to prosper if he was as described—" a jewel of a creature, made of the kindliest clay," with " goodwill towards many, illwill towards none," brisk as a squirrel and as brave as a bull-dog—a tough little rival in love or in war. He rented the surgery on the ground floor of Dr. Welsh's house, and pleased many of his patients, and for years he had been doing his best to please the daughter too, by the kind of long-drawn courtship only too common in Scotland. He seemed to be succeeding. If there had been no Carlyle, she could without an effort have pleased her mother and become Mrs. Fyffe. She never denied she liked " my dear wee doctor," as she called him, and could always kill time comfortably in his company. In 1822 he asked her to marry him and received what is considered the answer next to Yes, a hint to " wait a bit," in some such words as : " Oh, you're joking." In the twelve months following they met daily or nearly so " as cordially as ever," and played chess or battledore and shuttlecock. The sight of his steady progress in favour may have made Mrs. Welsh think it safe to raise the blockade against Carlyle in February (1823). She had been kept a little in the dark. The natural reserve of lovers is prescribed by modesty rather than fraud, but the effect is the same. The eager welcome Jane gave Carlyle, his undisguised devotion to her, and her wish to be in Edinburgh beside him as soon and as long as possible opened Mrs. Welsh's eyes.

As soon as she saw the tutor fellow was still the leading favourite, she set her face like a flint against Edinburgh in March. She did not say so. She merely would not name a day for going and took care not to go or let Jane go without her. She must have dropped a hint to Fyffe. He announced there was no remaining in Scotland for him—he must leave the country, and among other preparations for going abroad, he called to say adieu. It cannot have been an accident that Mrs. Welsh was out of the way and Jane had to face him alone. He was excessively agitated, pale and red by turns, speaking " loud and fast one moment, and the next scarcely able to articulate."

She talked of everything she could think of to divert him, she said,[1] but his only answer was " such a look of suffering and reproach " that she became ashamed of seeming cheerful. His departure being mentioned, he said in tones of agony : " You do not care whether I go or stay."

She assured him he was mistaken, and said : " You have not an acquaintance in East Lothian who will regret your going more than I do."

" An acquaintance ! " he cried. " And is that all ? Jane, Jane ! " He sprang from his seat beside her and threw himself on a couch at the other end of the room and sobbed as though his heart would burst. She was sorely tempted to " one word, one look of kindness," which she felt " would be enough to make him happy for the time " ; but held back awhile. His head seemed " ready to turn." To excuse what followed, she said : " He swore I made him weaker than any child ; stormed through the room, talking with violence on the most trivial matters," and finished with a frightful fit of laughter that seemed to make " every drop of blood in me stand still." She threw her arms about his neck and begged him to be himself, and before there was time for another word, they were interrupted.

They were alone again next day for a minute or two, long enough for him to say he would not go abroad. Something had happened to change his plans ! As she and her mother were to be away for a long time, he begged her to write to him ; and thinking that way of explaining would suit

[1] Letter of Jane Welsh (6.6.1823), published by A. Carlyle, *Nineteenth Century and After* Mag., January, 1914, pp. 93–6 : see also *Reminiscences*, etc.

her well, she said at once : " Yes, I will write." Hurriedly,
for there was no time to lose, and with " a terrible effort
at composure," he said to her, fixing his eyes on her face
as he spoke : " Take care, Miss Welsh, take care, Jane,
what you do ; write to me as to one who loves you more
than his own being, who has no hope, no wish that is not
bound up in your single self, or do not write at all. My
God ! The hour that brings me another such Letter as your
last will be the last of my existence." They gazed at each
other. He lingered as he left the room. " God bless you ! "
he said, and departed without a word from her. At least,
that is how she told the story soon after.

Mrs. Welsh had sense enough to feel that Fyffe had little
chance against Carlyle if the contest was to be by correspondence, and so she wanted the matter to be settled before
they went away. Fyffe was willing for anything. He shaved
his whiskers, and looked like one in woe.[1]

The young woman seemed as serene as Werther's Char-
lotte, who when she saw " his body Borne before her on a
shutter, Like a well-conducted person, Went on cutting bread
and butter." What she wrote to the other man in the letter
that made him happy as he was starting *Schiller* (24.3.1823)
was only this :—

' These nonsensical people with their Heirathsgedanken
(thoughts of marriage) and Heirathsvorschlagen (proposals
of marriage) will assuredly drive me mad : like Carlos,
ich fürchte die wie die Pest (I fear them like the plague).
To cause unhappiness to others, above all to those I esteem,
and would do anything within reach of my duties and
abilities to serve, is the cruellest pain I know ; but positively
I cannot fall in love ; and to sacrifice myself out of pity, is a
degree of generosity of which I am not capable. Besides,
matrimony under any circumstances would interfere shock-
ingly with my plans.'

Carlyle replied at once on an assumption, not corrected,
that she had refused an offer of a rich husband, and bade
her wait for him with an amplitude of phrase and praise
which neither Italy nor Spain could have surpassed :—

' In the common world the great object of a young woman's
existence is to get a rich Husband, and a fine house, and give

[1] *Early Letters of J. W. C.*, by D. G. Ritchie, p. 88, read with *Reminiscences*, etc.

T

dinners ; just as it is the great object of ravens to find carrion, or of pawn-brokers to amass. But if each ought to follow the good its nature aims at, then *you* are right to take another path—to press forward towards mental eminence ' (and so on—the letter overflows six pages of print and ends :) ' Yours, Mia Cara, per sempre ' (meaning, my beloved for ever).

It has to be confessed that both Italian and German were used to mystify Mrs. Welsh, but whether she read this or not, her eyes were open now. And though the gowns for the summer were made and the weather was fine, and Jane could see no reason why they did not depart, Mrs. Welsh would not even fix a day. Jane wondered how much Carlyle might hear of Haddington gossip and sent him a hurried note to make sure he " was not angry " with her, and saying : " We shall never quarrel more." He neither knew nor cared what Haddington was saying, and answered with a warmth that made her happy : " This *coming* is a weary business : but I were a Goth to accuse *you*, for I see you have my contentment well at heart." Which helped her to go through an ordeal for him in these weeks.[1]

She used to tell the story to Geraldine Jewsbury, and was thus reported. Corrections intercalated are made possible by the publication of letters that passed at the time :—

' There was a young man who was very much in love, and he had had reason to hope she cared for him : and she only liked him. She refused him *decidedly* when he proposed ' (1822, and *jocularly*, to be exact) ; ' but he tried to turn her from her decision ' (by a year's courtship, at chess or field games almost every day). ' She refused him peremptorily this time ' (1823, and " peremptorily " is not in harmony with her own report in June. By 1824 he was becoming desperate, and by 1825 he was more so ; but he kept on hoping till she was married.)

She did not take example from Margaret Gordon, held up to her by Carlyle, without names mentioned at the moment. Maybe she resented being told—" to spare him

[1] Many pages would be needed to set out all the pros and cons for dating, etc., what follows. See *Early Letters of J. W. C.*, by D. G. Ritchie, p. 87, and the letter of 6.6.1823, already quoted,

all needless pain. Admire him, praise him, be his Sister,
anything but his Mistress or Sweetheart. . . . In six weeks
he will look upon the whole transaction with composure ;
in twelve months it will be faded into distance. God help
him ! poor fellow, he will be very miserable for a week or
two, but that will be the worst of it."

She must have approved this as the better way, for she
afterwards tried to believe she took it ; but she certainly
did not take it at the time. Her later story runs on :—

'When refused he fell ill, and took to his bed, and his
mother was very miserable about her son. She was a widow,
and had but the one.' (This must be a romantic touch of
Geraldine's. Jane knew of at least one brother, a brewer
at Dumfries.)

'At last he wrote her another letter, in which he declared
that unless she would marry him, he would kill himself.
He was in such distraction that it was a very likely thing
for him to do. Her mother (Mrs. Welsh) was very angry
indeed, and reproached her bitterly. She was very sorry
for the mischief she had done, and took to her bed, and made
herself ill with crying. The old servant' (Betty, only a year
or two older than Jane, but like one of the family) 'kept
imploring her to say just one word to save the young man's
mother from her misery. But though she felt horribly
guilty and miserable, she was not going to be forced or
frightened into anything.

'She took up the letter once more, which she said was very
moving, but a slight point struck her ; and she put down
the letter, saying to her mother: "You need not be frightened, he won't kill himself at all ; look here, he has scratched
out one word to substitute another." Nevertheless, the
poor young man was very ill, and the doctor' (apparently
Howden, Dr. Welsh's partner) 'brought a bad report of him
to the house. She suddenly said, "We must go away, go
away for some time ; he will get well when we are gone."
It was as she said it would be ; her going away set his mind
at rest, and he began to recover.'

This shows how Mrs. Welsh became at last content to fix
a day for Edinburgh, and was only a week or so late in
keeping it ; but the sequence of events is not stated exactly.
Assuredly Fyffe rose from his bed of sickness this April
like a fellow refreshed, with victory in view.

Young Howden, a son of Dr. Howden and in the same trade, had been at school with Jane. He must have been one of the best informed of the onlookers, and one of the soonest to suspect that Fyffe was fooling himself again. He said Jane Welsh was " an impudent baggage," and continued to say it all his life.[1]

[1] He succeeded his father in Haddington, and survived Mrs. Carlyle. He was often heard to say this by Dr. Wallace James, who told D. A. W. on 6.5.1920.

VI

"LIFE OF SCHILLER"

(1823)

TO Carlyle, resolved on a career in letters, an article in the *London Magazine* was like a maiden speech in the Commons to a politician starting his life-stump. Familiar with Schiller's works and all that had been published about him, he could not but feel there was no excuse if he failed to distinguish himself now. Writing and rewriting, he did his utmost. His early Christian training to "crucify vanity" survived the dogmas, and started his lifelong habit of cultivating modesty. This has escaped notice because of a dogmatism which had nothing personal about it, but was like that of a teacher of mathematics handling propositions as sure as daylight to himself and to any who can understand. In Schiller, however, there was little dogmatism. He was still uncertain on many matters about which he was soon to be sure.

He soliloquised in his Note-book, March, 1823 :—

'What *should* I think of Goethe ? His *Wilhelm Meister* instructed, delighted, moved and charmed me. The man seems to understand many of my own aberrations still mysterious to myself. He is wise and great.

'These German critics, Grüber, Wieland, Doering, Schiller, are curious beside our *Edinburgh* and *Quarterly Reviews.* *How much* better are they ? More learned, at any rate, more *culture* than usual this side the water. I rather fear, however, there is more cry than wool. I must read some of them anyway. Herder I have good hopes of.

'A playhouse as an arena for the moralist is even inferior to the synod of the theologian. One is tired to death with Schiller's and Goethe's *palabra* (or jargon) about the nature of the fine arts. Did Shakespeare know aught of the æsthetic ? Did Homer ?

'What is Schlegel's great solution of the mystery of life—

" The strife of necessity against freewill "? Nothing
earthly but the old, old story that all men find it difficult
to get on in the world ; and that one never can get all his
humour out. They pretend nature gives people intimations,
but the *bildende Künstler* (constructive artist) and the
richtende (critic) ought to set these obscure intimations
fast on the basis of reason. Stuff and nonsense ? I fear it
is. The people made finer pieces of workmanship when
there was not a critic among them. Just as people do finer
actions when there was (or is) no theory of the moral sentiments among them. Nature is the sure guide in all cases ;
and perhaps the only requisite is that we have judgment
enough to apply the sentiment implanted in us without
our effort to the more complex circumstances that will meet
us more frequently as we advance in culture, or move in a
society more artificial. Poor silly sons of Adam ! you have
been prating on these things for two or three thousand years,
and you have not advanced a single hair's breadth towards
the conclusion. Poor fellows ! and poorer me ! that take
the trouble to repeat such insipidities and truisms.'

(Then came a drawing of a burning candle, and the legend
over it—TERAR DUM PROSIM, meaning, let me wear while
I am of use. The Note proceeds.) ' But what if I do not
prodesse (be of use) ? Why then *terar* (let me wear) still—
dum (while) I cannot help it ! This is the end and beginning
of all philosophy—known even to Singleton the Blacksmith
—" we *must* just do the best we can, boy ! " Herder hated
the new philosophy (preferring) French *rationality*. Goethe
was wiser than either ; he was clear for " letting it have its
day as everything has." This was right, old Goethe, and
I respect thee for the solid judgment of this saying. The
distinction of Coleridge's, which he may have borrowed
from Woltmann, about *talent* and *genius* is completely
blarney—futile, very futile.'

With thoughts like these fermenting in his mind, he
started to write *Schiller* on Monday night (24.3.1823), and
on Wednesday (26.3.1823) he was confiding to his sweetheart :—

' Oh ! I could beat my brains out when I think what a
miserable pithless ninny I am ! Would it were in my power
either to write like a man or honestly to give up the attempt
for ever. Chained to the earth by native gravitation and a

thousand wretched fetters, I am miserable unless I be soaring in the empyrean ; and thus between the lofty will and the powerless deed, I have no peace, no peace. Sometimes I could almost run distracted ; my wearied soul seems as if it were hunted round within its narrow enclosure by a whole legion of the dogs of Tartarus, which sleep not, night or day. In fact, I am never happy except when *full* of business, and *nothing more.* The secret of all is " I have no genius," and " a dibbil of a temper." We must just submit.'

In the second week (6.4.1823) he was writing :—' That miserable farrago of mine goes on as ill as anything can go. I have been thrice on the point of burning it, and giving up the task in despair. Did you never hear of Rousseau lying in his bed and painfully wrenching every syllable of his *Nouvelle Heloïse* from the obscure complexities of his imagination, writing every sentence *five times over*? He is my only comfort when I sit down to write. I feel the greatest dunce. I think Goethe the only living model of a great writer. You make a right distinction, he is a great genius and *does not make you cry*. He does not yield himself to his emotions, but uses them. It is one of my finest daydreams to see him.'

By the end of the third week, in writing to press her to come or write immediately (14.4.1823), he told her that *Schiller* was " swelling on his hands " and would run to three parts instead of a single essay. The first would be finished in two days more so that he might be free when she arrived. " Worse and worse " he called his writing, comparing it with what he thought it ought to be ; yet comparing it with other people's stuff, which he hardly paused to do, he had an amazing self-confidence. What he was sending to the London editor was not what had been expected, a lively screed affecting to tell everything worth knowing about Schiller in short. It was the first instalment of a *Life*, the first twenty-five years. The hero was left like his biographer, " conscious of the might that slumbered in his soul, and proud of it, as kings are of their sceptres," looking forward to " an undisturbed life of intellectual labour," obeying " without reluctance the bias of his nature." Devotion to Literature is boldly justified as implying all that is great and noble—" a life consecrated to the discovery of truth and the creation of intellectual beauty. The writer of a work, which interests and excites the spiritual feelings of men, has as little need to justify himself by showing how it exemplifies some wise saw or modern instance, as the doer of a generous action has to demonstrate its merit, by deducing it from the system of Shaftesbury, or Smith, or Paley. The instructiveness of the one, and the virtue of the other, exist independently of all systems or saws, and in spite of all."

There is a sparkle of the humour which was to make much of his writing like fireworks :—

'The Grand Duke expressed his disapprobation of Schiller's poetical labours in the most unequivocal terms. Schiller was at length summoned to appear before him ; and it then turned out that his Highness was not only dissatisfied with the moral or political errors of the work, but scandalised moreover at its want of literary merit. In this latter respect he was kind enough to proffer his own services. But Schiller received the proposal with no sufficient gratitude.'

When sending off his manuscript in April, Carlyle wrote to Graham that he designed to finish the *Life* in his spare time by August, and that "if the Cockneys boggled in the least about it," Oliver and Boyd would publish it as a book ; which is a handsome score for the "fat bookseller" of Edinburgh, Boyd. Indeed, it is worth notice that if the public business of the country had not been engrossed by do-nothing Downing Street and Scotland had had as much of a capital of its own as every canton in Switzerland has, Carlyle would never have needed to go to London for employment.

In the meantime he desisted from writing, as he was thinking of more important matters. On Wednesday (16.4.1823) Dr. Fyffe was ushered into his room, beaming with pleasure, happy and bringing happiness. Carlyle knew nothing yet of what Jane called "his pretensions," and in writing to her declared this messenger of Venus and her mother to be "one of the prettiest dapper little gentlemen I had ever set eyes on—the Letter was so large" (six pages of print) "and he handed it in with such a grace."

The news was that Mrs. Welsh was coming to town with Jane on Friday or Saturday (18 or 19.4.1823). No wonder the civil little man was treated with more than civility ! One begins to guess at what young Dr. Howden meant in calling Jane Welsh "an impudent baggage." Here was she using

Dr. Fyffe himself to carry and deliver a long letter to the other man ! Maybe this was her mother's doing. If it was Jane's, she was punished as she deserved. Fyffe was not a fool. He departed in a mixed and chastened mood. What he reported to Mrs. Welsh remains a mystery. Only —she changed her plans and did not come to town that week ; and the tutor fellow was left squirming with hope deferred.

VII

A CHAPTER OF CHANCES

(1823)

ON the last day of April he received the long-expected
message from Jane, that she and her mother were
in town and staying with Bess Stodart at Mr. Bradfute's,
where he might call the next day. " Be very reasonable
for a little while," she admonished him ; " when my mother
goes to Dumfriesshire, I will see you as often as you please.
Yours affectionately."

He obeyed. In the next ten days they saw each other
only four times and counted only one hour together. He
told her he felt like growing *demented*, while she was saying :
" We might as well be at the Antipodes as here under such
restraint." [1] Bess Stodart was unsympathetic. Mrs.
Welsh was alarmed, and uneasy at the thought of leaving
her behind while Carlyle was in Edinburgh.

To please Jane, Carlyle was arranging for a bookseller
to pay for and print a novel she was to translate from the
German. Her mother vetoed it, and he persuaded her
to drop it obediently—" we should respect your Mother's
will because it is hers."

On the very Saturday to which they had both been looking
forward for deliverance (10.5.1823), Mrs. Welsh left Edinburgh as she had planned, but took her daughter with her.
There was only time for a hurried note to him :—

' Here is a fine consummation to all our schemes ! You
will come here to-day and find me gone. Muster all your
philosophy, for I can spare you none of mine. They are
driving me distracted among them : my Mother all at once
got it into her head that I must accompany her. My
Dumfriesshire relations have treated me with little kindness. I opposed the proposal manfully for two days ; at
last my Mother's extreme displeasure forced me to yield.
It was determined finally only yesterday.'

[1] Letter of 2.5.1823; *Nineteenth Century Mag.* January, 1914, p. 90.

The details of their debates are interesting only for what is not in them—Carlyle was apparently never mentioned, only understood. The letter continues :—

'I meant to meet you this morning, but my Mother invited a gentleman' (probably Fyffe—there are signs of him in town) 'here to an early breakfast, and desired me to get all my packing over before he came, which kept me busy. And so I must go without a word. We set out in a few minutes. It is impossible to say how much I am vexed. A thousand things are harassing my mind. My Mother's unkindness is not the least of it. She is resenting my disinclination to go with her as much as she could have done my refusal. I am very unhappy. I wish to God I could fall asleep for a twelvemonth. I dread how this year may end. But "I am full of devices"—you have told me that so often that I begin to believe it. Well, I shall need all my ingenuity to bring me safe to port.
'Do write to me immediately—with hurry and vexation together, I can scarcely hold my pen. Your affectionate friend at all times and everywhere.'

He answered at once (Sunday morning, 11.5.1823), and copiously, as may be read in the *Love Letters* by the young ; but men and women who " have made their market " may be content with this :—

'There is nothing that can frighten us ; no might or dominion upon Earth or below it (those above are *with* us) that can take from ourselves the direction of our destiny. We will both of us *do as we please*, in spite of all that can be said or sung to the contrary ; and both of us, if it so please God, be happy and dignified in our day and genera-tion. Fear nothing, my best and dearest Jane ; this year will pass as others have done and everything will be as we would have it in the end. What have we to dread, seit wir uns rund umschlungen, fest und ewig ' ! (since we have clasped each other firmly and for ever). [These bits of German provoked Mrs. Welsh.]
'I purpose finishing *Schiller* and translating *Meister* in spite of all its drawbacks. *Meister* will introduce us to its author ; for you must know that you and I are to go and live six months at Weimar, and learn from Goethe himself : I settled it all the other night. I intend *to oblige you to go*

voluntarily! Forget me not, my dearest! Farewell and love me! I am yours for ever and ever.'

His letter found her and her mother at Corstorphine, near Edinburgh, where they were staying some days on the way to Templand Farm—Walter Welsh's, by Thornhill, Mrs. Welsh's father. Her maiden name had been Welsh. Another letter next day (12.5.1823), same to same, shows Carlyle making one more futile effort to see her at Corstorphine. Which failing, he went home to Mainhill, as the second best way of employing a few days' leave. The Bullers were going now to a country house (Kinnaird) on the Tay, above Dunkeld, where he was to join them.

He spent a week at Mainhill; and climbing Burnswark in the afternoons, beheld the western sun shining red on where Jane was dwelling, and "thought prayers for her welfare," but of course said nothing of such things to anybody else. She had written him: "If my Grandfather has anything like a decent horse, I shall try and scamper over to Mainhill. My head is quite topsy-turvy at present. The vexation I have endured for the last week or two is doing me a deal of harm; I cannot fix my mind a single moment—my Mother is stuffing me with physic by way of improving my appetite. It is not that that will do me any good. I will write you a long legible letter next time." So till the last day he continued hoping, but nothing happened. On Thursday (22.5.1823) he rode to Moffat, and took a seat on the top of the coach. Then he heard a glad voice name him from below, and saw the merry little Dr. Fyffe take a seat beside him. The uncle in Moffat being sick, Fyffe was "travelling like a weaver's shuttle from Edinburgh and back to it." But as if he knew what would interest his fellow-traveller, Fyffe said to him, with an air of complacent "knowingness" which was "very little relished": "Miss Welsh, sir, arrived at her grandfather's the night before last."

With the "cast-iron" face imaginable, Carlyle was studious to taboo the topic for the rest of the day, and they talked of politics or trade or crops or—anything but Miss Welsh.

VIII

IN THE HIGHLANDS—HIS HEART ELSEWHERE

(1823)

AT Edinburgh, Fyffe and he did not protract their parting, but were friendly. Carlyle said: Fyffe "is of the *genus* cricket, and I like all crickets," while confessing that compared to Fyffe he felt like a lion to a squirrel. Nature is kind, and Fyffe was equally self-satisfied. His clothes were in Edinburgh's best professional cut, and as he looked at the loose-fitting village suit the other man wore, he could not but remember how Jane disliked it and his country accent. Fyffe hoped she would soon lose patience with him, and wondered how much he knew of the recent events in Haddington.

In going north, Carlyle remembered *Macbeth*, and did not fail to look for "Dunsinane's high hill" and Birnam in approaching what he called the "pretty village" of Dunkeld—"the ancient capital of Caledonia standing in the lap of the mountains, with its quick broad river rushing by, its old gray cathedral, and its peak-roofed white houses and stately trees, all gilded from the glowing west as if it had been a city of fairy-land." He wandered round it before going on. Kinnaird House, which he reached on Saturday (24.5.1823), was half a dozen miles farther up the Tay, near the mouth of the famous Killiecrankie Pass and the foot of the Grampian Mountains.

His rooms were in the "*old* mansion," a hundred yards or two from the new big "House" and used for overflow guests and servants. To get a room there suited him best, as it left him master of his own time. He breakfasted with Charles and his brother before nine, and they worked from half-past nine till one. Then a two hours' interval allowed a walk and a dinner for Carlyle, who found the family dinner at a late hour every day but Sunday did not agree with him. So except on Sundays or some special occasion he did not dine with the family. "Twice or thrice in the daytime," and always in the interval, he went to the "*old* house" to smoke. From three to nearly five completed the teaching and left him free for the day. He had settled to translate *Wilhelm Meister*, and hoped to finish it before the second instalment of *Schiller* would be wanted. In a voluntary way, as the spirit moved him, he used to go to the " House " for a chat in the evening and was always welcome.

The boys were fond of him. He used to say afterwards that he found Charles had been fed at Harrow " on Latin and Greek *husks*, unsatisfying to a young fellow of the keenest sense for everything from the sublime to the ridiculous, and full of airy ingenuity and fun. I tried to guide him into reading, into solid enquiry and reflection ; he got some mathematics from me, and might have had more. He got what expansion into wider fields of intellect, and more manful modes of thinking and working my poor possibilities could yield him ; and was ' generously grateful ' to his teacher." Arthur Buller had similar sentiments, and their father and mother were always well content. They did everything copious cash and goodwill could do to make Carlyle happy in the highlands.

About noon one Tuesday (10.6.1823), he was standing at the parlour window. The boys perhaps were bending over some work ; and he was looking at the mountains. He noticed the grey-haired postman approaching on his Shetland pony, and two minutes later entering, smirking and scraping, with a large letter for Carlyle in the handwriting of Jane. The tutor was in such a hurry to go to his room that he nearly overset the postman. He returned to work as if nothing had happened, but writing to her next night confessed he had been able to think of nothing else since he received it. He read it repeatedly, he told her : " No part of it escaped me. Such a letter was worth waiting through a twelvemonth for." [1]

This explains what he told Murray, though the reverend gentleman did not hear of Jane Welsh :—

' My time passes in the most jocund and unprofitable manner you can figure. I have no professional labour that deserves being named ; I am excellently lodged. There are plenty of books too. I read, or write and burn, at rare intervals ; I go scampering about on horseback, or lie down by the grassy slopes of the Tay, and (in short) live as idly as if I were a considerable proprietor of land.'

[1] *Nineteenth Century Mag.*, January, 1914, pp. 93–6.

Any man would forget a little trouble in the stomach on receiving from a woman he was courting a very long letter like this:—

'MY DEAR FRIEND,—The pleasantest moment I have enjoyed for the last two weeks was when the Postmistress handed me your Letter. (In short, I could not) imagine you could forget me for a single day. If ever you do you will be very ungrateful; for every day and every hour of the day I think of you. "Forget you by August!" What an idea! My best Friend, be assured you can never be forgotten while I recollect *myself*. Your idea is so identified with all my projects and pursuits, that it can only be effaced when I have ceased to feel, or when my being has undergone a change even worse than annihilation.' (This was not referring to Hell, but only to the possibility of shrivelling into what she called "a stick.") 'Oh, no! we shall never forget each other; *our* friendship is no paltry intimacy contrived by interest or idleness. I am persuaded it was planned by Mother Nature before we saw the light, and founded on a surer basis than fortune or caprice. There is no doubt of it: "We shall be friends *for ever.*" This assurance often comforts me when I have need of consolation.'

What made her need it then she did not conceal—the chaff of her grandfather, who was very fond of fun, and having been a bit of a dandy in his own youth may have had a fellow-feeling for the afflicted Fyffe. He had said in Jane's hearing to her mother—was "eternally" saying it, Jane complained to Carlyle—that he wondered "how you came to have a daughter so very short, so very sallow, and altogether so very unlike yourself."

Her father's father, John Welsh, at Penfillan Farm across the Nith, was apparently co-operating by ironical deference to her as a "lady." They may have imputed the refusal of Fyffe to vanity. So she wept on paper; but prudently told her lover about him, omitting to mention his name and the encouragement she had given him. She went so far as to allow her vague replies had "given a sort of tacit consent to this man's pretensions," concluding: "Write soon, soon; your letters always give me a new being. Befall me what may I cannot be utterly wretched while I have such a friend. Ever yours."

She added in a P.S. : " Would to God we were at home.
I can have no peace till then." This made him suppose
some well-endowed one in Dumfriesshire was his rival,
and he adjured her to put the man out of pain by a definite
refusal, saying : " I shall be on thorns till I hear what has
become of it." This was on 11.6.1823, when he was " beginning *Meister*." But at such a soul-shaking time he did not
finish three pages a week.

Three weeks passed. No letter came to reassure him.
He could hardly sleep for thinking of her ; and told Buller
his health was growing worse. It was no mere excuse.
He was sick. He said he would make one more effort to
endure Kinnaird, if he might have short leave of absence
to fetch a riding horse from Annandale. This was instantly
and kindly agreed to. Mr. Buller had an Anglo-Indian's
liver, and could feel for him. More visitors were coming in
a week or two. It would be convenient to have his rooms.

He sent the news to Jane at once, that she might be ready
to expect him soon. He was to go by Edinburgh, convenient
for Haddington, to Mainhill, convenient for Thornhill and
Walter Welsh's house. So he reckoned on seeing her somewhere and clearing up things, and wrote to her on the day
the leave was promised him (1.7.1823).

IX

LOVE LETTERS BY DON QUIXOTE

(1823)

HIS letter (1.7.1823) overflows eight pages of print—
" an hour or two's conversation with you," he calls
it—and lets one guess that their private talk was what might
have been expected. The proposition he wanted to prove
was that her only hope of happiness was a life of literature
in his company. He proposed to translate together German
tales, and suggested to her the *Libussa* of *Musaeus*. It
tells how a fairy dwelling in an oak wins happiness and longer
life by taking a plebeian husband, and the best of her
daughters, Libussa, elected a queen, does likewise with the
best of consequences. " If you want to be a happy and
worshipped wife, do like them and marry Carlyle "—is the
lesson of the story.

Like Don Quixote, he could not realise that his Dulcinea
did not appear to others as adorable as to himself, and he
supposed she was now refusing riches for his sake. He
afterwards heard of Fyffe, but heeded not the gossips of
Haddington, and never knew what favour Fyffe had
earned.

David Masson, who heard far less, was able to guess
correctly that if she had missed Carlyle, she would have
married " some professional man in Haddington " ; [1] but
that never occurred to Carlyle himself, and assuredly it
would have seemed blasphemy in 1823, when he was writing
to her as if he had to dissuade her from marrying a peer :—

'As a fashionable fine-lady I do not see how you could get
through the world on even moderate terms : a few years at
most would quite sicken you of such a life ; you would begin
by becoming wretched, and end by ceasing to be amiable.
I see something of fashionable people here ; and truly to

---

[1] David Masson to D. A. W. verbally, 1896, describing friendly chaff
between Mrs. C. and her husband.

my plebeian conception there is not a more futile class of persons on the face of God's earth.' (This refers to the visitors of the Bullers.) ' If I were doomed to exist as a man of fashion I do honestly believe I should swallow rats-bane or apply to hemp or steel before three months were over. There is something so *very* unsubstantial in their whole proceedings, such toiling and wrestling and so very little realized, that really I know not well how even stupid people can endure it. From day to day and year to year the problem is not how to use time, but how to waste it least painfully ; they have their dinners and their routs, they move heaven and earth to get everything arranged and enacted properly, and when the whole is done, what is it ? The uneasy destruction of half a dozen hours. Think of this lasting through forty years—insipidity around you, before you and behind ! It is no wonder that poor women take to opium and scandal. There is something in the life of a sturdy peasant toiling from sun to sun for a plump wife and six *eating* children : but as to the Lady Jerseys and the Lord Petershams—peace be with them. For *you*, my heroic Jane, there is nothing here, though in its utmost perfection, that could give one hour's true satisfaction ; and wisely have you judged it better to choose a path of your own, leading to glory and true nobleness.

' " Oh ! but I have no genius ! " I tell you on the con-trary that you *have* a genius, you unthankful creature ; every day I am growing surer of this.

' I expect to be with you probably in three weeks. I do trust you will let me see you. . . . . I figure out myself and you sitting unmolested for hours in your drawing-room talking with each other of high matters—matters high to *us*, and taking counsel in concert about the affairs of the *commonwealth*.

' My life here is the most unprofitable and totally inane I ever found it. I think of little or nothing else but you ; and that not like a man of sense, but like a foolish boy. I read none, I do not translate three pages a week. Good Heavens ! am I growing mad ? I form ten thousand plans, each rejected in turn. I am also fast losing health : some days I suffer as much pain as would drive about three Lake poets down to Tartarus. Why do I talk to you of it ? Because you have a kind heart. Never mind me, my good Jane : *allow me to fight with the paltry evils of my lot* [1] as

[1] Italics by D. A. W.

best I may ; and if I cannot beat them down, let me go
to the Devil, as in right I should.   Too much of this !
   ' How full of sunshine ' (and so on) ' all things appear when
I turn to *you !*   Something of an ethereal nature ' (and so on).
'Write to me whenever you have *any* time.   I have no pleasure
like what I get from listening to you.   Tell me *all* that you
feel or care for, all that is on your heart—as I do.   *What is
become of that poor Youth?*[1]   What are you doing ?   Are
you well and happy ?   Write, write !   I am ever yours.'

   " Allow me to fight," wrote he.   A sage of Asia might
say this shows his limitations ; but the word fighting in
Scotland meant struggling.   A farmer ploughing soil that
was stiff would say he had to fight it, and in the same sense
a fellow sick with bile and other worries would feel he had
to " fight " them, that is, to master them and not be mastered
by them, the very behaviour that sages most admire.   They
should not haggle over words, but grip the idea.
   Three days later, Friday (4.7.1823), he wrote to tell his
dates and amplify his argument :—

   ' Now, what is to be done, my Dear ?   Must I turn home
without seeing you, and begin a month, intended for enjoyment, in a humour soured by such a disappointment,
instead of sweetened by all the inspirations I looked forward
to ? '   (Whether at Haddington or Templand, she had only
to let him know, and, he said) :   ' I shall linger no moment.'
(Nevertheless, if she could not contrive it, he assured her) :
' I have resolved to obey you.   Let me see or not see you,
your orders shall be executed :   the only decision that I
totally and with all my soul protest against, is one which
nothing but a wicked demon could inspire you with, the
decision *that we are to part !*   To this I will never consent.
Never !   You may do what you please to make me ; may
force me to hold my peace about it, but not to acquiesce
in it :   I will say that it was a wrong decision with my
dying breath.   But in all other points, I am " as clay in
the hands of the potter " ;   direct me according to your
own sovereign will and pleasure. . . .
   ' The glorious fact that you are my friend is dear to me
as his creed is to the bigot ;   I will hold fast my conviction
of it till I *can* hold it no longer.   Yet you will write me long
letters often, often ?   Will you not ?   Yes, you will.

[1] *Ibid.*

'Some great revolution must take place in my poor history ere long. There are things tossing up and down this wretched soul of mine that *must* finally drive me mad, or kill me, or come out of me in some shape. There are times when I feel it sinful not to let go your hand for ever '—(especially when I suppose I am keeping you from being a fashionable fine lady.) . . . 'It would be a pang more bitter than any that ever struck through my heart, if I had to think that your happiness had been marred by *me*.' (And so on.)

'Are you laughing at me ? Perhaps it is best : for the picture has a bright as well as a dark side. Suppose this genius that is in us—for there *is* a kind of genius in us both— were developed fully and set before the world !—Fame, and wealth enough, and peace, and everlasting love to crown the whole !—O my Jane, what a life were ours ! There is no Emperor that ever swayed the world whom I would change with. *But we are both foolish persons, both far too ambitious* [1]—can we ever be happy ? One thing alone is certain : I *will* love you to the last breath of my life, come of it what may. So God be with you, my best Jane ! There is nothing that I fear but *for you*. Adieu ! '

This shows how easily these young people would have been satisfied ! And let us guess how they used to talk to each other when alone together. No wonder Fyffe was cut out. The Pharmacopœia could not help him here. The sample may suffice ; for love which made Hercules ridiculous made Carlyle monotonous. " We are foolish . . . far too ambitious " is noticeable as a sign of maturity, but what is best worth remembrance is his obvious belief that she was refusing grandeur ; and many later sayings about the sacrifices she had made were inspired by the same delusion. Reality is more entertaining than any fiction.

On Friday (11.7.1823), he rode to Dundee with £300 in his pocket, his salary for eighteen months, nearly " all he had in the world."

[1] Italics by D. A. W.

X

DULCINEA RESPONDS

(1823)

H E found nothing waiting him at Edinburgh on "the
Monday" (14.7.1823). He was at Mainhill before
she knew that he had left the north, and it was only on
Thursday (17.7.1823) that he received a letter explaining
the delay from "Yours Ever Affectionately." She magnified
the pains she had taken to write, as he wanted, to the other
man—in spite of which Fyffe continued curiously hopeful.
However, Carlyle was delivered from doubt and what he
called "a load of perplexities." "Thankful that all is
right," he wrote to her (18.7.1823) :—

'I have only to add my humble prayer that Mademoiselle
would never again keep me as long ignorant of her proceedings, never while we both continue in this world. *This
you call rather an impudent prayer ; but the most part of
prayers are so :* [1] you will do your best to grant it. I am
not Job more than you are, tho both of us are of kindred
to Job's wife. You have need to be called away at times
from dead books and studies into the living world. There
is a world that is not of types and printers. I rejoice that
you are with sensible persons that love you and are of
habits so foreign to your own.'

"Who told you the people I am with are *sensible ?* " she
retorted. "They are no such thing ; neither do they love
me. My mother does," she admitted as if reluctantly ;
for indeed the hitch in their correspondence had been
her mother's doing, sending her away on a visit to an
uncle on a farm south-west of Criffell, with a weekly post ;
no amusement within, not even books, and nothing but
rain without. She posted at Dumfries on the way home
(16.7.1823) the letter that made Carlyle content ; but in
the weeks that follo~ed they were as in May unable to see

[1] Italics by D. A. W.

each other, and even letters were not easy. One morning (21.7.1823) she was up at six on purpose to write to him, and then back to bed till breakfast. The size of her letter—five pages of print—may explain the firmness of her mother, who was not allowed to read it, and if she had read it would have been angrier than ever.

'To-morrow I am off again on another visit to be tormented. Alas! my beloved German! my precious, precious time! Well, you are an inimitable correspondent! But you must not come here!

'You must send me *Bridekirk's Hunting*, in all haste. My Mother was expressing her surprise the other day that you had never thought of transcribing *her* song in any one of the many letters I had received from you since you mentioned it. Write nothing on the same page that may not meet the inspection of a dozen people.' (Thanking him for a "beautiful little Tacitus," she added :) 'It is a pity there is no other language of gratitude but what is in everybody's mouth. I am sure the gratitude I feel towards *you* is not in everybody's *heart*. I have a good deal more to say . . . but . . . Kiss little Jane for me.' (She had just sent a present to his sister Jane, and concluded :) 'Yours always affectionately.'

He consoled her strangely for delay on the road to glory by the examples of Johnson and Cowper, Milton and Hooker, but he fumed and fretted at not seeing herself : " Heaven give me patience ! I am weary of this wayfaring existence I have led so long : but *what* to do to alter it ? "

While thinking and writing thus, he " was looking out in the Valley of Milk " (between Ecclefechan and Lockerbie, in Mainhill neighbourhood), " for some cottage among trees, with a stable, a garden and a rood of green, where," he wrote to her soon, " I might fairly commence housekeeping, and the writing of books ! They laughed at me, and said it was a joke. Well ! I swear it is a lovely world this, after all. What a pity we had not *five* score years and ten of it ! " He sent the song Mrs Welsh was wanting ; but she would not say he might call.

Delivered from worry by Jane in spite of her mother, he found his holiday at Mainhill made him almost well. He had the sense to be idle and go " galloping about." At Annan one day he was told by Irving's mother that his

friend was coming north to be married, and passing on
the news to Jane excused him to her (10.8.1823) for not
replying to their letters.—

'The reason is, not that he has ceased to love his friends,
but that his mind is full of tangible interests continually
before his face. I could wager any money that he longs
above all to know what we do think of this monstrous
flourishing of drums and trumpets in which he lives and
moves. I have meant to write to him, but know not how.
He will be talking about "The Lord," and twenty other
things, which he himself only wishes to believe, and which
to one that knows him and loves him are truly painful to
hear. See that you do not think unkindly of him. . . .
'Happy Irving that is fitted with a task that he loves and
is equal to ! He entertains no doubt that he is battering to
its base the fortress of the Alien, and lies down every night
to dream of planting the old true blue Presbyterian flag
upon the ruins. When shall you and I make an onslaught
upon the empire of Dullness and bring back *spolia opima*'
(plunder of such as a conquered king) 'to dedicate to one
another ? Some day yet, I swear it ! Let us fear nothing :
but believe that diligence will conquer every difficulty, and
act on that belief. Heaven grant I may get a letter from
you ere I go. My solitary ride will otherwise be full of
speculations. You will not keep me waiting at Kinnaird.'

She did not. When he returned to duty (21.8.1823) he
found a letter from her awaiting him.—

[POSTMARK, THORNHILL, 1823].
'HELL, 19*th August.*

'MY DEAR FRIEND,—
'Your last Letter was especially welcome : it came
in a lucky moment. I just was ready to hang or drown
myself'—(the worst affliction being that her mother would
not fix a day for going home)—'but the sight of your handwriting can cheat me out of ill-humour at any time ; it
always presents so many delightful images, and excites
so many delightful expectations ! Oh, you have no notion
how great a blessing our correspondence is to me ! When
I am vexed, I write my grievances to you ; and the assurance
I have that your next Letter will bring me consolation,
already consoles me. And then, when your Letter comes—

when it repeats to me that *One* in the world loves me—will love me ever, ever,—and tells me more boldly than Hope, that my future *may* yet be glorious and happy, there is no obstacle I do not feel prepared to meet and conquer. I owe you much! feelings and sentiments that ennoble my character, that give dignity, interest and enjoyment to my life. In return, I can only love you, and *that* I do, from the bottom of my heart. . . .

'When shall a world know your worth as I do? You laugh at the stir I make about fame; but my sentiments are not very dissimilar to your own. *You* are *not satisfied* living thus, bowing a haughty genius to daily wants' (and so on). 'When will your genius burst through all obstructions and find its proper place? It *will*,—" as the bolt bursts on high from the black cloud that bound it!" Of *that* I have no fear; but when? Oh! that I heard a nation repeat your name! You may call it a mistaken ambition, a weak dependence on the opinion of others—you may call it what you will, but I *will* wish you *famous* as long as there is room for such a wish.

'I heard your *Life of Pascal* criticised. My face was crimson. Write soon. Yours ever.'

The verse she quoted was from Byron, one of the authors they loved in common.

XI

ALL RIGHT, BUT BILIOUS

(1823)

H E read and re-read her letter, to make sure it was not
a dream ; and buckled to work so briskly that by
the end of the month (31.8.1823) he was reporting to her
that his daily stint of *Meister* was ten pages, although he
was seldom started till six at night. He admitted he was
"not satisfied" and, in short, was bilious; but even that
"difficulty," which he called the hardest of all, "I will
overcome," said he. "I have brought a horse—I am trying
every precaution."

Diagnosis is sometimes easy too late. What made him
ill at Kinnaird was the cold. He was living in a draughty
house built long ago. His room was small, yet had three
windows, none of them air-tight. The door was shrunk,
and the walls were pierced with many crevices. He wore
a gown and had roaring fires of wood "that would melt a
stithy"; but the weather was wet and cold, and the
draughts that whistled through had the nip of the ice on
the western mountains over which they came. Whatever
the "airt," there was admittance free; and as the days
grew shorter the bitterest blasts in Scotland rushed from
the north through Killiecrankie Pass like a funnel and
laughed at the sheltering skeletons of trees. Carlyle confessed to Johnstone that he felt as "cheerful, warm and
inspiriting" as the moon in Greenland. For his biliousness
not to come back in such conditions would have been the
kind of miracle that does not happen.

Poets may say what they like. Even a Don Quixote may
despair about Dulcinea when he is bilious. So Jane was
shocked by signs of diffidence, and did not realise she had
made the poor man imagine she was making a mighty
sacrifice for him.—

'MY DEAR JANE,—

'I often ask myself: "Is not all this a dream?
No! it is not. Jane loves me! she loves me! and I

swear that she shall yet be mine, as I am hers." In more reasonable moments, I perceive that I am very selfish and almost mad. Alas! my fate is dreary and obscure and perilous: is it fit that you, whom I honour (and) love, should partake in it? No, my own best of Maidens, I will not deceive you. Think of me as one that will live and die to do you service; *but whom it is dangerous and useless to love.*[1] You are the most delightful, enthusiastic, contemptuous, affectionate, sarcastic, capricious, warm-hearted, lofty-minded, half-devil, half-angel of a woman that ever ruled over the heart of a man. I will love you till the last moment of my existence; and if we both act rightly our lot *may* be the happiest of a thousand. So let us cling to one another (if you dare when thus forewarned) for ever and ever! If your happiness be shipwrecked by my means, then woe to me. All these incoherent inconsistent things you have often heard already; but you will bear with me in uttering them yet again.'

This was too much to expect. "Half-devil" indeed! The letter followed her home to Haddington, and was answered on the day it was received (16.9.1823) :—

'MY DEAR FRIEND,—

'Your Letter has troubled me. It is so hard to explain oneself. But I must. Any reserve might be fatal. You misunderstand me. You regard me no longer as a Friend, a Sister, but as one who may be more. I have been to blame. I might have foreseen (I) might mislead you.

'My Friend, I love you. I repeat it, tho I find the expression a rash one. But were you my Brother I would love you the same; were I married to another I would love you the same. And is this sentiment so calm, so delightful, but so unimpassioned, enough to recompense the freedom of my heart, enough to reconcile me to the existence of a married woman, the hopes and wishes and ambitions of which are all so different from mine, the cares and occupations of which are my disgust! Oh, no! Your Friend I will be, your truest, most devoted Friend, while I breathe the breath of life; but your Wife! Never, never! not though you were as rich as Crœsus, as honoured and renowned as you yet shall be.

Italics by D. A. W.

' You may think I am much too serious ; there is nothing to fear. It is well if it be so ! But *suffering as I am at this moment from the horrid pain of seeing a true and affectionate heart near breaking for my sake,*[1] it is not to be wondered at tho I be overanxious for your peace. Write to me and reassure me, for God's sake, if you can. Your friendship at this time is almost necessary to my existence. Yet I will resign it, cost what it may—will, will resign it, if it can only be enjoyed at the risk of your future peace.

' I had many things to say to you, but I must wait. At present I scarcely know what I am about.

' Ever affectionately yours.'

" Espérance, ma chère " (Hope, my dear), she had written to Bess Stodart a while ago,[2] sending her news. " David S. is to be speedily married to Miss R.'s thousand pounds. When such women as Miss R. get Lieutenants, *we* shall have generalissimos at least."

Poor little Fyffe had an exciting time ; for chess and battledore and shuttlecock can stir when they are the weapons of rivals in love. But he was hopelessly outclassed at long range. He should have consoled himself with another woman sooner than he did. Carlyle replied to Jane instantly (18.9.1823) :—

' MY DEAR JANE,—

' If I were not a fool, I should not have vexed you. I honour your wisdom and decision : you have put our concerns *on the very footing where I wished them to stand.* So be of good cheer, for no harm is done.

' I know very well you will never be my wife. Never ! Never ! I never believed it above five minutes at a time all my days. " 'Tis all one as I should love a bright particular star, and think to wed it." My fancy can form scenes, indeed, with you to share them, worthy of Heaven. Such illusions do in truth haunt me, nor am I very sedulous to banish them.

' Thus then it stands : you love me as a sister, and will not wed ; *I love you in all possible senses of the word,*[1] and will not wed, any more than you. Does this reassure you ?
. . . So long as you have charity to hear me talk about affections aud plans, I will speak and listen;

---

[1] Italics by D. A. W.
[2] *Early Letters of J. W. C.,* by D. G. Ritchie, p. 72.

when you tire of this, *when you marry*,[1] or cast me off, I
shall of course cease to correspond with you, I shall cease
to love Mrs. ——, but not Jane Welsh.'

(He told her how in the summer he had been looking for
a cottage in the valley of Milk, and the long letter ended
with a P.S.)

'Have you arranged any hours for your studies ? Do the
gossips interfere with you ? Are you happy ? *Are you ?*
Tell me *everything*. I am your Brother, and more than
fifty brothers, to the end of time. Farewell ! Be good and
diligent and fear not.'

This was a bit fatherly but not " senselessly civil," as
young women in Scotland have been known to describe the
conduct of a lover too prudent. Before he got an answer,
in about three weeks, he had many misgivings and " unpleasant speculations " for which there was more cause
than he ever knew. Fyffe took to his bed and threatened
to die ; but could not. Jane did not expect him to. She
knew her Byron well, and Byron had written of an " Irish
peer, who killed himself for love, with drink, last year."
But the servant Betty and her mother and his were not so
clear on that point, and unanimous in blaming her ; and
she liked her " dear wee doctor " ; and if Carlyle had not
been so warm and flattering, and the hope of a livelier life
with him so alluring, she might have come down from the
fence on the doctor's side. Some recollection of such
hesitation may have made her say in old age, " I married
for ambition," or something to that effect, as sundry persons
have declared she did.[2] What she certainly did when Fyffe
lay down on his bed to die was to take to hers, and plead
a " headache." In a week or so the death of her grandfather at Penfillan, her father's father, relieved the strain
of sentiment by a timely diversion.

While these events were interesting Haddington, where
everybody knew more than the parties themselves, Carlyle
was going through *Meister* " like steam machinery." One
Friday (26.9.1823) he saw a sorry entertainment. Among
the visitors at Kinnaird were two young men, Richard

[1] Italics by D. A. W.
[2] Alexander Carlyle declines to believe the reports that Mrs. Carlyle
said this.

Buller from Oxford, a cousin of Charles and Arthur, and a companion of his, Reginald de la Pole, who had been preparing for a successful career in the " Church " by a serious study of horses. Both were eager to taste the sweets of slaughtering venison veal. Carlyle led about the pony Mrs. Buller sat upon, and entertained her with talk as they sat for hours in open spaces among the heather beholding the English style of deer-stalking. The noble youths with their guns stood ready at fixed points. The wretched natives jabbering Gaelic went about hallooing and beating bushes till they chased out a little fawn, whose flesh might be worth sixpence. It was killed by Pole ; and Richard Buller cried : " I would have given a sovereign for that shot "—the correct thing for him to say. If a man can barely afford to tip the servants, he should cry, " a thousand pounds," or " ten thousand." Another little beast followed its companion, and Pole had the pleasure of butchering it too, which was too much for Richard Buller's etiquette. He was struck dumb, " chop-fallen for four and twenty hours," with admiration, envy, disappointment, wrath at the unfairness of Providence, or some other feeling equally fine.

October brought the *London Magazine* with the first part of *Schiller* in it, and a flattering letter from the editor, desiring the remainder without delay. So *Meister* was stopped ; and at the same time came a letter from Jane, dated Monday (6.10.1823). Irving, on his way to Kirkcaldy to be married, was preaching at Haddington and causing a sensation by his presence.[1] The very wind of his coming would help Carlyle, who read with joy a long letter like a fantasia on the simple theme, I love you :—

' MY DEAREST FRIEND ' (not only dear as hitherto),—

    ' Just a furious pain in my head that laid me up for a week' (and so on) 'kept me from writing. I beseech you never suspect me of being unmindful of you ; never, unless you know for certain that I am either deranged or dead. . . . Oh, I do love you, my own Brother! I even wish that Fate had designed me for your Wife, a destiny happier than mine is like to be. And so you will cease to correspond with me when I marry ! Do you think I will ever marry at such a cost ? Where is the Lover on the face of this earth that could console me for the loss of my Friend ?

[1] *Life of Edward Irving,* by Mrs. Oliphant, Chap. VIII, and *Love Letters of Thomas Carlyle to Jane Baillie Welsh,* I, p. 289.

We *shall not* cease to correspond ! Never, never as far as it depends on me. If " Mrs. —— " is to be estranged from your affections, I am Jane Welsh for life.

'Are you better ? . . . Tell me particularly. . . . What can Providence mean . . .? . . . Oh, be careful of yourself ! for the world's sake, and for mine. Were I again to lose the friend of my soul '—(meaning Carlyle, in succession to her father)—' how ruined I should be ! But you shall live to be my Guardian-angel—it cannot be the will of a merciful God that I should return to the dreary existence which I endured before we met—it cannot be His will that a soul born to enlighten the earth' (meaning Carlyle), 'to be the Daystar of ages ' (still Carlyle), ' should be obscured by the shadows of death ere a world has perceived its splendour. You shall live to love me while I live, and to mourn for me when I die. . . . I wish you were settled in your Hermitage and I with you ; you would be well in a month's time ; and then such books should we write ! ' (And so on.) ' God Bless you, my Beloved Friend.' [1]

She wrote again (14.10.1823), "almost out of my wits with joy," she said, "to tell that Irving and her mother had agreed she was to spend three months next summer in his house in London, when Carlyle would also be there. A letter from Carlyle (12.10.1823) arrived as she was writing. In celebrating her perfections,—" Blame not Nature for making you ambitious,"—and so on, he adored her very defects of character, even as he thought her plain face beautiful.

His own restlessness was more like vital force than ambition, the impulse of Nature which makes the buds open and all that lives " move on " continually. He was like other people, but more so. Electricity is always the same in kind, but varies in voltage. He was as fit as Faust to wager with the Devil—

> " If e'er you make me feel content
> And bidding time stand still,
> To death you then can have me sent
> And bind me as you will."

In a torrent of warm words, his nearest approach to the music of the skylark, he not only told his love, but showed it when he was not thinking of it by his anxiety about her

[1] *Nineteenth Century Mag.*, January, 1914, pp. 97-9.

illness, adjuring her to beware of excessive study, and putting questions. She had heard from Irving they would be some days together, and prudently revealed enough to remove any risk of his displeasure in case the eloquent divine gave him too much news (14.10.1823) :—

'I shall have idle business enough to keep me from too hard study. My sickness was caused by bile : and my bile was caused by that unfortunate Youth who persuaded me he was going to die in good earnest. But I expect he will live after all ; and I do not intend to be bilious again— unless I am prevented from going to London. I have a great deal of business, three pairs of silk stockings to darn ' (and so on).

'Tell me how Mr. Irving gets on with a Wife. Yours for ever and ever.'

Mrs. Welsh's consent to the London visit showed she might desist from pressing Jane to take Fyffe. She had only intended kindness. Fyffe had been a favourite before Carlyle appeared, and remained a favourite still. Before this month was out (October), he was attending Jane for a feverish cold, and she noticed his hand shaking as he felt her pulse. She had herself been delivered from love for him by what Dr. Chalmers called " the expulsive power of a new affection." Perhaps she should have told him so sooner ; but she was not going to delay very much longer.

XII

THE TRANSIT OF IRVING

(1823)

MRS. BULLER had bought Irving's new *Argument for Judgment to Come*, and laughed at it along with her husband and Carlyle, who dealt faithfully with Irving by letter. This cleared the air when they met at Dunkeld (Friday, 17.10.1823). Irving had married Bella Martin at Kirkcaldy on the Monday, and was using his holiday for a tour in Scotland to see old acquaintances.

Carlyle spent two days with them, and was not blamed for his scepticism, but told jocosely: "Well, Carlyle, I am glad to hear you say all that; it gives me the opinion of another mind on the thing."

Saturday saw Irving and his wife and Carlyle together, looking as fashion required at the river among the "Birks of Aberfeldy."

"Doesn't this subdue you, Carlyle?" said Irving solemnly, "something of falsetto noticeable" in the question, but none of it in the answer which set him laughing: "Subdue me? I should hope not! I have quite other things to front with defiance, in this world, than a gush of bog-water tumbling over crags as here!"

Carlyle reported to Jane that Mrs. Irving had "no enthusiasm, and few ideas, but many household virtues, and loved her husband and would love his friends," so that Jane should be ready to accept in due course an invitation she expected to stay with them in London. Carlyle himself was invited there and then, but excused himself, pleading other engagements.

The tact that made Irving talk weaving to weavers had led him to talk of London's literary stars to Jane Welsh, so that she now scoffed at Carlyle's thought of agreeing to Buller's proposal to spend next winter with them. London was the place for him. "Barry Cornwall (Procter) made a thousand pounds the first year he was there, and you have ten times the genius of Barry Cornwall," she wrote, as if that settled the matter. Carlyle heard out the simple-syren strains of Irving, and wrote to his young woman :—

'We could come to no conclusion. He figured out purposes of unspeakable profit to me, which when strictly examined melted into empty air. He seemed to think that if set down on London streets some strange development of genius would take place in me. There is but a very small degree of truth in all this. Of genius (bless the mark !) I never imagined that I possessed beyond the smallest perceptible fraction ; and this can only be turned to account by rigid and stern perseverance through long years of labour, in London or any other spot. Stubborn effort is the remedy : help cometh not from the hills or valleys ; my own poor arm must work out my deliverance, or I am for ever captive and in bonds.'

Which shows his feeling when he had such an infinite itching for " success " that he felt a prisoner without it. " You have none to love or reverence in Scotland," said Irving. This was like what Carlyle had said to Jane about herself and Haddington, and she may have repeated it, so that the preacher might feel he was saying now what was sure to suit the hearer. But Carlyle was ever meditating contradiction, and wrote to Jane first what he thought, and then what he said :—

'Kind, simple Irving! I did not tell him of the hearts in Scotland that I will love till my own has ceased to feel ; of *her*, whose warm and pure and generous affection I would not exchange for the maudlin sympathy of all the peers and peeresses and prim saints and hypochondriacal old women of either sex in the creation.

'I told him that love concentered on a few objects or a single one was like a river flowing within its appointed banks, clear, calm, rejoicing in its course; diffused over many it was like that river spread abroad upon a province, stagnant, shallow, cold and profitless. He puckered up his face into various furrowy peaks at this remark, and talked about the Devil and universal benevolence, reproving me withal because I ventured to laugh at the pretensions of the Devil.

x

'Our friend's mind seems to have improved but little. It does me ill' (a French idiom, revealing him thinking in French) 'to see a strong and generous spirit putting wilfully on the fetters of a thousand prejudices, very weak though very sanctified; dwindling into something like a canting preacher. However there is affection and wholesome feeling. I love the man with all his nonsense; I was *wae* (woeful) to part from him.'

The parting was at Taymouth, on the Sunday afternoon (19.10.1823). They were returning all three from the "kirk," and coming down the wide short street or village Forum. Irving had pulled off his big hat and was looking mostly at the sky, his fleece of copious coal-black hair a-flowing in the wind. Some drops of rain were falling. A man in livery ran up, and asked: "Please sir, aren't you the Rev. Edward Irving?"

"Yes."

"Then my Lord Breadalbane begs you to stop for him one moment."

Exit flunkey. Up comes old Breadalbane and civilly invites Irving and party to dinner: but Carlyle's horse was ready, and he rode home to Kinnaird.

XIII

DOCTOR'S FAILURES

(1823)

NEXT Tuesday (21.10.1823), retiring to his rooms in
the "old mansion" directly after tea, as usual, he
was about to spend an hour in writing to Jane when his
conscience smote him that he would have to say the second
part of *Schiller* had not yet been started. Already he had
pleaded guilty of idling for a week, "as is my custom, when
changing employments." So he now put letter paper aside
and began the best bit of writing he had yet done—the
ideals of men of letters, contrasted with reality around
them, and their temptations and sufferings when trying
to live by writing. As nobody can be sure of another's
feelings, the ideals he imputed to Schiller and to Milton,
"the moral king of authors," remain a theory of his and
doubtful as biography, but as autobiography all the better
because he was not aware he was describing himself. The
remark of Schiller that "genius is always a secret to itself"
is duly quoted in its place, and by and by became one of his
predominant maxims. He was deliciously absurd in quoting
it to Jane to prove that she had a genius for literature ;
but he applied it to Schiller judiciously, and exalted men
of letters as "the vanguard in the march of mind," and when
"hallowed not less for their conduct than their writings,
the flower of this lower world."

For the next five weeks he was writing and rewriting every
night. He had the "old mansion" to himself, and after forty
years recalled how he sat there night after night : "good
candles, good wood fire, and such silence and total absence
of company, good or bad, as I never experienced before or
since. I remember still the grand sough of those *woods*, or
perhaps in the stillest times the distant ripple of Tay."

He explained to Jane that he could do translation like
clockwork. His method was to read and re-read a passage
till the whole of the meaning was clear, and then, but not

till then, putting pen to paper, the words flowed out "as smooth as oil." Original composition was "ten times as laborious. It is an agitating, fiery, consuming business when your heart is in it : I can easily conceive a man writing the soul out of him ; writing till it evaporates ' like the snuff of a farthing candle,' when the matter interests him properly."

He began at six, and evening work of such a sort not only made the liver worse, it interfered with sleep. He wrote so slowly that he seldom finished in a night of many hours as much as one might read aloud in five minutes. But nothing stopped him till the end of the fifth week, Monday (24.11.1823), when he was able to send the waiting editor the second instalment. By that time he had not had one good night's sleep for a week. Before he began, he had told Jane not to worry about him—"no one ever dies of such disorders" ; but he had not been at *Schiller* long before he felt "half dead" as he sat down to write, and was sure he was "dying by inches." He said he decided to give up his situation and retire into Annandale to try to recover his health, and if he could not do so in six months, "to go distracted and take arsenic and so be done with it." His way of talking may mislead a reader who has not heard of Goldsmith's dog in Islington, which "to gain its private ends *went mad* and bit the man." Buller said it would be better to consult a doctor. They were anxious to keep him, said they would winter in Cornwall next year, and gave him a letter of introduction to George Bell, a medico famous then in Edinburgh.

On his way to town the postman handed him an angelic letter from Jane. He arrived on Friday (28.11.1823), and reported to her next day :—

' The business now in hand is *when* I am to see you? I have a horse, and no engagement that I will not give to the winds for the sake of *ours*.

' It will be the cruellest thing your mother ever did if she make objections to our meeting. Nevertheless if she act *perversely*, it is ours to submit. Do not quarrel about this, my own best Jane ! I will love you through all eternity. But . . . *Lovely Damsel of the many Devices*, see to put your skill in force on this occasion.'

She did so by telling her mother at once what was in the letter and asking, "awkwardly": "May he come?"

" With a portentous smile," Mrs. Welsh repeated the question, " May he come ! " and added : " If *you* can answer that question, I suppose it is quite unnecessary that *I* should be consulted." So he was bidden come on the Friday and " stay till Sunday, at all events, and longer if you can, and if my mother *will*." As he had said he had only " about a week " altogether, Mrs. Welsh was minimising her concession by fixing Friday.

Before going to Haddington he saw Bell. After enquiry about the past, Bell put a question bearing on the future : " *Can* you give up tobacco ? " [1]

The reply was startling. " Give it up, sir ? I can cut off my left hand with an axe, if *that* should be necessary."

This cleared the air. " Your trouble is all tobacco— give it up."

The doctor had made a common mistake. Discovering in tobacco a possible cause, he jumped to the conclusion it was the main cause. There was worse to follow. He was a leader of the professional flock, and plentiful purging was in fashion. So he "threw mercury into the system," which was what the patient had said he anticipated— mercury washed down by " hogsheads " of castor oil, enough to kill or cure.

The patient suffered, but he might have fared worse. " My dear wee Doctor," wrote Jane to him, referring to Fyffe, " has been on another ' weaver-shuttle ' expedition to Moffat ; and fallen in with you. He tells me you are very unwell. Why did you hide this from me ? I shall have him to prescribe for you when you are here. I wish to God you were better." Fyffe would perhaps have felt it might be dangerous for him to prescribe. He was a fiery little fellow, and at this very time was giving a " rascal " rival practitioner the " lie direct " to his face twice over in hope of a challenge, for duelling was still in fashion, like purging and bleeding.

Carlyle came to Haddington on the Friday and made the most of his time. Mrs. Welsh may have been influenced by the recent visit of Irving. She was afraid of making her daughter ill, and willing to say she might marry Carlyle " when he had made a position for himself " ; but she still had hopes of Fyffe and may have given him a hint. He was watching Carlyle at the George Inn on the day of departure, counter-ordering a horse. The stable-men doubtless

---

[1] *Edinburgh Sketches and Memories*, by David Masson, p. 320.

swearing there was no pleasing some people, a superior
smile mantled the face of the doctor, who was not aware
Carlyle had noticed the beast was spavined. So he tried
to ridicule the performance in some such style as the stable-
men, and had a flare-up with Jane who reported to the
other man :—

'I had observed the workings of his little mind during
your visit, with some feelings of contempt and displeasure ;
and his subsequent conduct completely ruined him in my
esteem. Only think, the creature had the intolerable presumption to attempt to ridicule you to my very face ! He
had heard me express high admiration for decision of mind
and proportionate contempt for the opposite quality ; and
so in the enviousness of his heart, he set about giving me
a detail of your proceedings at the George Inn, which was
meant to show you off as most irresolute, fickle-minded.
. . . I kept my temper and heard him to an end (and then),
asked him : "Now, sir, if *my Friend*, knowing you to be
possessed of my good opinion, had turned *his* talent of
satire—which I assure you does not come short of yours,
however much it may exceed it—to render you absurd and
contemptible in my eyes, what would you have thought
of him ? " The creature ruffled up like a bantam about
to fight, and chattered with an astounding command of
absurdity, about your impertinence in presuming to suppose
him *drunk*. To which volley of nonsense I replied with a
volley of female eloquence which—I have a notion—is
tingling in his ears up to this hour. I am pretty certain
I have not spoken so long or so warmly since the day' (when
you and I had a tiff). 'Mercy! what a delicious walk that
was ! I have laughed at the recollection of it many a time.
But the M.D. had not the policy to give me the last word,
like you ; and we parted mutually incensed.'

Doctors' failures in general afflict their patients, not
themselves ; but in personal matters they are only human.
Fyffe deserves all the sympathy can be spared him. Our
modern Don Quixote was easily capable of the magnanimity which gives the loser leave to chide, and purred
to his Dulcinea with the pen :—

'You are a dear, warm-hearted, fiery-tempered, faithful,
affectionate creature : and though you should not have
done the doctor so much honour as to get enraged at him,

it was kind and like yourself to despise and disbelieve his little calumnies. Small as the man's feelings may be, ridiculous as we may think his fancied injuries, to him they are not ridiculous : the least and weakest of living creatures is a universe for itself : the hopes and wishes of a grass-hopper are to that grasshopper all in all.

'For the rest, though I regret that you should have taken the trouble to *quarrel* with little Fyffe, I rather rejoice that your intimacy is concluded. Blind chance never in its most capricious mood brought two more uncongenial souls into contact than yours and his : friendship it was impossible that *you* should ever feel for him ; and what *he* was presuming to feel the most careless might discover. I declare it did astonish me : the impudence of the human heart seemed to me to pass all calculation ; I should as soon have thought of perching myself upon the horns of the moon.

'How delightful it is that we have no secrets ; but love each other, and trust each other, and are of one heart and mind even now.'

He meant it all ; and she began to make good resolutions for the future. They had to agree that her mother might see his letters, which accordingly have for some time to come to be read on the lookout for a double meaning, with a great deal to be understood between the lines.

About this time, maybe when idle in Edinburgh, Carlyle seems to have written a fiery article on the College Library which appeared in the current academic paper,[1] and vexed the Doctor of Divinity who was head librarian. He was said to hold a very snug sinecure and never appear among the books. The sting of this was the truth of it. Messrs. Baine and Small, the sub-librarians, were the only active men the students had to look to, and they did their best, but could not do " what the students had a right to expect, not from them, but from the college." The students had no means of knowing the books, no catalogue but a medical one which was " a most valuable relic of antiquity " ; and were often kept waiting an hour to know the result of an application, in rooms without a fire or a chair. It was a practical article, comparing the college to its dis advantage with Oxford and Cambridge, Aberdeen and Glasgow, and it had some effect.

[1] *Lapsus Linguae* or *The College Tatler*, No. V, Friday, 16.1.1824. Professor David Masson told D. A. W. of this.

XIV

A NEW IDEA ABOUT HISTORY

(1823-4)

THE drugs delivered him from pain but left him very weak. He gave up tobacco and spent his evenings reading till about eight, when he joined the others and chatted an hour away. The weather was bad. Frost, snow, and sleety vapour in cycles was the December report. The moors were white. The roads were slush. The slaves of the liver, Mr. Buller and Carlyle, went walking about together below a canopy of dismal fog, wading to the ankles in half-melted snow, and buffeted by bitter northern winds. More than once they met an " ancient weather-beaten smuggler " astride his pony, two kegs of whisky and a truss of straw for saddle, " his face of a mahogany colour, and whiskers jingling with a load of frozen sleet." He seemed in his element ; but the other " Celts " went about " with livid noses, and a drop at the end—the picture of cold and destitution."

Copying into his notebook one evening (14.12.1823) a list he had made three years before of French books, " to be read if ever I have leisure and fall in with them," he concluded :—

'Alas! alas! Oh! Schiller, what secret hadst thou for creating such things as Max and Thekla' (in *Wallenstein*) 'when thy body was wasting with disease? I am wellnigh *done* I think. To die is hard enough at this age ; to die by inches is very hard. But I *will* not, though all things human and divine are against me, I will not.'

It is a commonplace in medical science that consumptives continue cheerful and absurdly hopeful ; and the biographer blundered in supposing Schiller was like himself and other bilious subjects, and had to rise by force of will above despondency. Mercury made even a cheery Walter Scott feel vile. But Schiller was never so tempted. The description of Schiller's conquest of feelings he never felt is unwittingly a document of Carlyle's sensations. He rose, as he imagined Schiller did, above his affliction, which never was seen in his public speeches, and could hardly be suspected from his published writings. That he had much to suffer appears only in confidential letters and papers which he gave his niece when in old age he was too feeble to sift them, and which she unfortunately, but innocently, trusted to Mr. Froude. On this occasion (14.12.1823), he went on :—

'*Schiller*, Part II, is off to London three weeks ago : it was very bad. Part III I am *swithering* to begin : would it were finished. I am to write letters and then *begin Schiller*.'

He shied at it two weeks more ; had not " the heart." He read Boswell's *Johnson*, finding the hero commonplace —" he only does well what every one can do in some way." The overpowering feeling, " it *must* be done ere long," made him force himself to start on 28.12.1823, but then he felt, as he noted on the last day of the year looking back upon 1823 : " I am scribbling, not writing *Schiller* : my mind *will* not catch hold of it ; I skim it, do as I will, and I am (as) anxious as possible to get it off my hands." With mercury inside him and " a gnawing pain," he moralised on his agonies :—

' They talk of the benefits of ill-health in a moral point of view. I declare solemnly without exaggeration that I impute nine-tenths of my present wretchedness, and rather more than nine-tenths of all my faults, to this infernal disorder in the stomach. If it were once away I think I could snap my fingers in the face of all the world. The *only* good of it is the *friends* it tries for us and endears to us. Oh ! there is a charm in the true affection that suffering cannot weary, that abides by us in the day of fretfulness and dark calamity—a charm which almost makes amends for misery. Love to my friends—Alas ! I may almost say relations !— is now almost the sole religion of my mind.'

Carlyle's love-letters show a harmony with his journal which few would have ventured. " It appears to me," he told Jane, " that rest were well exchanged for fame. I maintain that you and I are far too ambitious : one of the first steps in our improvement will surely be the diminution of that feeling. If we are ever to be happy it must be so." She did not agree, declaring : " When I cease to be ambitious I am a ruined woman," with nothing to live for, in short. She was losing hope, and had to confess she had been ill herself, but she was sure that *he* would struggle through, and nothing but death could prevent him becoming " one of the brightest ornaments of the age we live in." At any rate, she would not desist, not she ! Her mother had melted into tenderness on sight of her illness, and all was nice between them again.

On Sunday (4.1.1824) he was surprised and pleased to see the Introduction to Part II of *Schiller* about Men of Letters quoted at length in *The Times.* This raised him in the esteem of the Bullers and seemed to confirm the anticipations of his Jane. He called it " almost the *first* testimony to merit on my part which *could* not be warped by partiality," and confessed it made him " cheerful for a whole afternoon." He made a fresh effort to finish Part III. It started with Schiller a Professor of History at Jena. His *Thirty Years' War* appeared to Carlyle the best history in German, and the *Revolt of the Netherlands* a noble fragment. Nevertheless he thought Schiller had missed many opportunities of picturesqueness and bored the reader. Meditating on the matter like a mathematical problem, remembering Voltaire and others, for history had long been his favourite reading, he suddenly saw daylight, and wrote in his notebook on Wednesday (7.1.1824) :—

' I have got half a new idea to-day about history : it is more than I can say for any day the last six months.'

Next day he scrapped all he had written and made a fresh start. We are left guessing the new idea.

Discussing the latest and best plays of Schiller, he puts *Wallenstein* above Corneille and every play in our own literature since Shakespeare. He reprobates Voltaire's *Pucelle*— " a poem, the wittiest and most profligate for which literature has to blush," contrasting with it Schiller's splendid *Maid of Orleans* while intimating that the real Joan of Arc was finer still. He insisted on the greatness as well as the goodness of the woman—" Quicquid vult, valde vult (whatever he wills he wills strongly), is ever the first and surest test of mental capability "—and " this peasant girl could subdue the minds of kings and captains to her will." The genius of Michelet has shown this in detail.[1] To have divined before Michelet wrote that the sorceress of Shakespeare, the half-crazy fanatic of Voltaire and Hume, was a well-inspired heroine, whose very delusions were beautiful, the deliverer of France and the fairest figure in its history, this was the best sign as yet of Carlyle's genius for sympathy.

In praising *Wilhelm Tell* he said that even Wordsworth's peasants were "whining drivellers" beside Schiller's, which made Wordsworth an enemy in a mild way, and explains one of his sonnets perhaps.

By and by Carlyle said he thought Madame de Staël had Schiller's *Revolt of the Netherlands* "in her eye," when writing on the French Revolution, and the same might be said of himself. His description of its method, proceeding "from eminence to eminence, combining the details of events briefly and impressively" needs little alteration to fit his own history. Yet it is unlikely that this was the new idea he saw on 7.1.1824, which is more likely to have been the revelation of "Nature at first hand" as Schiller said, so that he became instinctively as scrupulously accurate in History as he had learned from Leslie and Newton to be in Mathematics and Astronomy. That there is no chance in Nature, no more in morals than in materials, is another way of saying the same thing. At any rate, quitting conjecture, here is what in old age he said to Norton, when scouting the suggestion that he had ever believed that might made right:—

' This is the very precise and absolute contrary to the truth I hold and have endeavoured to set forth, namely and simply, that *Right makes Might*. Well do I remember when in my younger days the force of this truth dawned on me. It was a sort of Theodicy to me, a clue [2] to many facts to which I have held on from that day to this. But it's little matter to me at this hour. I'll not undertake to set myself right now. If the truth is in my books it will be found out in due time, and if it's not there, why then the sooner they utterly perish the better.' [3]

[1] Michelet's *Histoire de France*, Book X, Chaps. III and IV; Vol. VI, pp. 176–307.
[2] Pronounced with a liquid "u," i.e. u=yu, —clyu, according to Norton, talking to D. A. W.
[3] "Recollections of Carlyle," by C. E. Norton, *The New Princeton Review*, July, 1886. Abundantly corroborated.

Goethe was the first to detect the new kind of historian who had appeared. Soon after discussing his *Schiller*, he remarked to Eckermann : " It is admirable in Carlyle that, in his judgment of our German authors, he has especially in view the mental and moral core as that which is really influential. Carlyle is a moral force of great importance. There is in him much for the future, and we cannot foresee what he will produce and effect." [1]

What " Right makes Might " implies Carlyle put quaintly in many ways with many a mistake in detail. To err is human. Only his phrases were new. His merit was his grip upon right principles and his earnestness, seeking always sincerity. He meant the same thing as Confucius and was equally genuine. As against contemporary scribes he was generally right—they were almost as foolish if not as false as the kings and politicians misleading the absent-minded peoples, setting up the false idols of Empire and Mammon in place of the "Everlasting and Almighty God," which is Nature. We left undone the things which we ought to have done, and we did the things which we ought not to have done, and there was little good in us. Humanity humbugs itself, but not Nature. The living Universe makes no mistake. Events take charge. Our diseases and disasters, losses and distresses are the effect of our sins—it is our folly that lets them be so badly shared—

> " And, spite of pride, in erring reason's spite,
> One truth is clear, *whatever is, is right.*"

[1] *Conversations of Goethe with Eckermann*, translated by John Oxenford, pp. 276-7.

XV

ON LIVING BY WRITING

(1824)

IN the midst of his haste in starting Part III of the *Life of Schiller*, who shoved aside his surgical tools and gave his strength to the drama, history and poetry, Carlyle had to explain at length to his brother John, whom he was supporting as a medical student in Edinburgh, the reasons why he should not follow any such example and try to live by writing (1.1.1824) :—

'I am glad your repugnance to medicine is wearing away. Persist, and you will like it. It is a noble thing to have a profession : it makes a man richer than a lord, for no *external* change can destroy the possession. Nor is there any weight in the fears you labour under about failing in more interesting acquisitions by your diligence in following after this. It appears to me that a man who is not born to some independency, if he means to devote himself to literature properly so called, even ought to study some profession which as a first preliminary will enable him to live. It is galling and heartburning to live on the precarious windfalls of literature ; and the idea that one has not time for practising an honest calling is stark delusion. I could practise the most laborious doctor's occupation at this moment in less time than I am constrained to devote to toiling in that which cannot permanently profit, and serves only to make a scanty provision for the day that is passing over me ; but I will preach no more, for you are a reasonable youth, Jack, and are already bent on persevering.'

From this it is plain Carlyle was not opposed on principle to living on the proceeds of books and not compromising with his conscience in so doing. Like Confucius, he stood on common sense and expediency. As Confucius would not serve unworthy kings and had to support himself and family, he was a teacher, and his ideal was to be ever ready to teach, refusing no fee, however small, and tolerating no stupid pupil, however rich. In the same spirit the modern sage was aiming to write the best he could and take what came as payment. Aware of the temptations of the trade, he was sorry for himself, and dissuaded from it his brother and everybody else who consulted him ; and by degrees he climbed himself to where the gifted rose without an effort, and saw the true idea—that it is spiritual prostitution to need payment for words. Such was the belief of Buddha and Socrates, of Paul and many another saint, of the Quakers and many another sect, of Burns and Byron and Tolstoy and many another writer. So when Lockhart was perplexed and censorious over Burns in poverty refusing money for his songs, Carlyle could understand the poet and admire him, and bid us all admire.

XVI

FINISHING "WILHELM MEISTER"

(1824)

IN Kinnaird House Carlyle and his pupils were busy, but their elders were bored. What was there to talk about when a sensational murderer, Thurtell, was securely hanged and the newspapers as tedious as usual ? The squires around and " the numerous baronets of the age," as Arthur Buller called them, were discovering old Buller was respectable and gave good dinners ; but they themselves were duller than the deer. A witness in Thurtell's trial had defined respectability as keeping a gig, and Carlyle made a word " Gig-man," intelligible there and then, which amused the family ; but though he stuck to it long, it has been cut out by Thackeray extending the old word—snob.

Though the tutor felt safe against suicide himself, he wondered how his fellow-sufferer and employer could resist the temptation of it :—

'Mrs. Buller has the secret,' (he wrote to Jane), 'of spending seven or eight thousand a year with a *minimum* of comfort. If I were in Buller's place, I would swallow ratsbane ! To roast out thirty years of his best beneath the burning sky of India, and come home to this ! He is the most honest, patient good soul I ever saw.'

What makes life bearable is hope, and none of the family expected to see such horrors continue. They were planning to winter next in Cornwall, and going to Edinburgh on the way to London, Buller and his wife on 20.1.1824, and Carlyle with the boys about the end of the month. He was able to send off the last of *Schiller* before coming to Edinburgh, " not in my right vein," he told Jane, " though nearer it than anything I have yet done " ; but before he started to rewrite Part III, on 8.1.1824, he had provided his " Lovely Damsel of the many Devices " with such a letter as her mother might see, in comical contrast with what had been written for Jane's eye alone. A Hercules twirling a distaff could not be funnier than Carlyle attempting humbug. On 18.9.1823 she had been plainly told that his love and letters ended together if she married another man ; but now (8.1.1824) he was as meek as a tailor's dummy :—

' Lost my affection ? O Jane ! that you were equally secure against all other losses ! My affection for you is not grounded on vague and transient delusions, but on congruity of disposition, on respect for your qualities, and tender concern for your fate : it is calm and steadfast, and will not change, till you are tired of it. I will correspond with you to the end —if your future Sovereign will permit so pleasant an arrangement ; and if he will not, he must be a churl undeserving the happiness of such a wife. As for the amiable Mrs. C. that shall be, it is not likely that *she* will disturb us for several years yet.'

In his last letter for herself alone (22.12.1823) he had written :

' My late visit has convinced me too well that you are not happy ; indeed how could you be so ? What communion has light with darkness ; or you with the inane people your lot is cast among ? You are encircled with drivelling and folly ; nothing that your mind can relish or care for ; companionless though your heart is full of warm affections : you have sacrificed all for the sake of your improvement, yet you are obstructed, almost stopped, in your progress towards it. My dearest Jane ! . . .'

On 8.1.1824 enquiries about her health led on to this :

' The misfortune of people such as we are, is that we can find no proper dissipation, we rather dwell in the solitude of our own chagrin than in the midst of follies. This I believe is altogether wrong. One *should* have company— communion and fellowship with our kind—even if it were but with drivellers. My dearest Jane ! if you would avoid being wretched, never estrange yourself from the beaten ways of men : mix in their concerns, participate in their interests, imitate their common habits, and with health and competence you will be happy.'

Mrs. Welsh purred like an old tabby stroked the right way, continued to use her daughter kindly, and allowed her to go to Edinburgh on a long visit to Bess Stodart for the improvement of her health ; and on Tuesday (10.2.1824)

in the drawing-room of the " frigid " Bess, Jane saw Carlyle
by appointment between eleven and noon. By that time
the young Bullers had followed their parents to London, and
he was free of them for three months, and hoped he might
escort Jane to make her visit to the Irvings when he rejoined
them in town. Wintering in Cornwall had been left un-
settled. Mrs. Buller could not make up her mind.

His immediate business was to finish *Wilhelm Meister*.
Jane stayed in Edinburgh all February. They had to be
what she called reasonable, lest Bess might become suspicious and report to Haddington. Perhaps she did. Mrs.
Welsh decided to come to town on Monday (1.3.1824) and
take Jane home next day, and on the Saturday before then
the lovers had their least agreeable meeting. The next
day, Sunday, she would be unobserved while the rest were
at church, and sent a letter to his brother's lodgings in
Bristo Street, beside George Square, to be conveyed to him
quickly. It gives a peep at them :—

'MY DEAREST FRIEND,—

'You predicted sensibly enough that my conscience
would punish me for behaving to you in such a nonsensical manner. You had no sooner taken yourself off,
pulling the door to with a vengeance behind you, than
I was ready to hang myself for having occasioned you pain,
and wasted such a fine opportunity for conversing with one
another freely, as may not occur to us again for God knows
how long.

'I do not know how it was. I believe the Devil tempted
me to be absurd and ill-humoured at the outset ; and your
imperturbable patience provoked me to continue so until
the end. And now that I am come to myself, I appear far
more despicable in my own sight than I can possibly do
in yours. Unkind to *you* who are always so kind to me, so
. . . so . . .' (and so on). 'Can you forgive me ? Indeed,
indeed I do love you and respect you for all my nonsense,
as well as I may. Say that you forgive me, that you love
me not a whit the less for my yesterday's *tirevee*' (Scotch for
a preposterous passion with wild gestures) ; 'and I will give
you a whole dozen of voluntary kisses at the earliest opportunity. Think of this : I assure you I never offered such
liberal terms of reconciliation to mortal man before.

'And now, when am I to see you and hear your mind ? '
(On Tuesday) 'we return to Haddington ; but I shall pack

Y

my duds the night before, and endeavour to be at leisure from eleven to twelve, if you will call then. Idiot that I was to kick to the Devil the two good hours that fortune offered me to talk with you !—I do not think you can forgive me in your heart. Can you ? You will call on Tuesday, however. Yours most penitentially.'

She went home that day, and continued to take the name of the Devil in vain in letters from Haddington,—" Nothing less than a Devil could have tempted me to torment you," until he humorously acquiesced : " I have very *nearly* forgiven you : we shall see what further can be done when we *come to settle accounts*. But remember your Bill payable at sight ! My own private idea is that you are a witch." Her absence speeded the translation work—ten pages a day in addition to proofs. He concentrated upon it till it became like a treadmill—" nothing but write and walk, walk and write, from morn to midnight." In one of his walks he called on Brewster to settle old accounts, and received from him details of the booksellers' tricks of trade. Boyd agreed to pay down £180 on the day of publication for the first thousand, £250 per thousand for the second edition, and after that the book was to be Carlyle's. He reckoned he might make £500 out of it, and was sure to be " paid sufficiently for all my labour," he told Jane, who did not care much for the work, as she read the proofs. She wittily said of Mignon that " she seems to play much the same part in the piece which the text does in the generality of sermons : is perpetually recurring without having any visible connection with what goes before or after. ' This is as good as anything Goethe said of Hamlet.

His love-letters were recreation, and pleased Mrs. Welsh, though the *Lovely Damsel of the Many Devices* who read them to her had to be wideawake to skip or paraphrase at times, and admonished him : " Remember ! no *darlings* or *anything of that nature—in English*." To this he answered in his text : " Bestes Liebchen," which might be " My Dear " to her mother, but said more than " Darling " to her

In March, Dr. Fyffe in desperation " tried another fit of illness," but neither Mrs. Welsh nor her daughter gave any sign of sympathy. So after a week he arose in perfect health and tried the effect of yellow leggings, a silver-headed whip and a fine white hat.[1]

[1] *Early Letters of J. W. Carlyle*, by D. G. Ritchie, pp. 87-9.

By the end of the month Carlyle had finished the second volume, and being more than abreast of the printers, went to Mainhill for April. In a letter Jane described to him the transfiguration of Fyffe—"Dr. Thumb," she called him—"in *one* day from a slovenly, muffled-up, snail-paced little man," about to die from love, into "the sprucest flourish of a creature." To Bess Stodart she was more explicit (18.4.1824) : [1] "I have run against the little gunpowder man of medicine, in the entry, several times. We 'mowe' (make mouths) to one another. I toss my head 'toploftically'; he looks as if he could eat me; and that is all." But his white hat set her thinking. She could not hope to make Carlyle reclothe himself to please her, but commissioned through Bess "one of the best gentleman's hats, of the most fashionable cut, *not* broad-rimmed, to be a present to my intended husband; so do see that they send a *Jemmy* one."[1]

Of course she had told him a man of such genius as his should not be doing translations. "One might as well set a mettled racer to draw in a dust-cart. The only thing that reconciles me to it, is the money it will bring." To which he answered :—

'It has often struck me as the most accursed item in men's lot that they had to toil for filthy lucre ; but I am not sure now that it is not the *ill-best* way it could have been arranged. . . . When I get that weary *cottage* erected, and all things put in order, who knows but it may be well with me, after all ? Will *you* go ? Will you ? "Not a hair's breadth!" Well, it is very cruel of you.

'It would edify you much to see my way of life here ; how I write and ride, and delve and muse on things new and old. On the whole, I am moderately happy. There is rough substantial plenty here : for me there is heart-felt kindness in the heart of every living thing, from the cur that vaults like a kangaroo whenever he perceives me, and the pony that prances when he gets me on his back, up to the sovereign heads of the establishment. Better is affection in the smoke of a turf cottage, than indifference amidst the tapestries of palaces ! Skiddaw and Helvellyn with their snowy cowls are more to me than St. Gothard and Mont Blanc : I often picture Jane and her mother, sometimes thinking of me, cheering this dull earth for me with a distant spot of life and kindliness !'

[1] *Ibid.*

Jane was thinking of him, assuredly. Her mother did not know what to think, though she liked his letters as yet. Dr. Welsh's sister Grace was with them as he was writing. She had come in March, but did not make Jane happy by her departure till 19.4.1824 ; and as often as her niece was out of hearing, she railed against learned ladies, and declared *the gentlemen* detested them. Mrs. Welsh repeated what she said to Jane and remained herself content to wait and see. " Let him make a position for himself " appeared a safe compromise.

" Like clockwork " he was turning out every day material for Edinburgh printers, and the translation was finished about Sunday (9.5.1824), when nothing remained to do but some proofs and the Preface.

The book had risen in his esteem as he re-read and translated it, and he told Jane in these concluding weeks : " I have not got as many ideas from any book for six years." So his Preface was as sincere as it was clever, in setting forth the greatness of the book. It was candid too—" the hero is a milksop " ; which was Goethe's own opinion in the end.[1] Carlyle wrote to Jane that she was right. " It is worth next to nothing as a novel. What a work ! Bushels of dust and straw and feathers, with here and there a diamond of the purest water ! "

[1] Bielschowsky's *Goethe*, II, VIII, p. 262 (English).

XVII

CARLYLE AND TOBACCO

AFTER finishing *Meister* (9.5.1824) he was about to pay calls for a week when he was tied to Mainhill by a sore throat. He blamed the north-east wind instead of the liver for that ; but was well aware his liver was none the better of the abstinence from tobacco, which had now lasted five months. His mother derided the doctor, and he used to admit : " I might as well have ridden sixty miles in the opposite direction and poured my sorrows into the long hairy ear of the first jackass I came upon." When saying so, he did not name the doctor, Bell, who would not take a fee from him, but accepted instead a copy of *Wilhelm Meister*. It may have been this May and at Mainhill and by the earthly providence of his mother that he found a long clay pipe and tobacco pouch handy when he lay down under a tree, and exclaiming, " I will endure this diabolical farce and delusion no longer," he had a good smoke there and then ; but he did not all at once revert. He seems to have left his pipe behind when he went away and restricted himself to occasional cigars in London and Paris, so that his vulgar pipe was not in full blast again till he returned to Mainhill next year.[1]

He never repented tobacco as much as he should. After the experience of fifty years more, he often said that it and brandy were the only two drugs he found useful. " Anodynes both," say the doctors now, admitting that the mercury their trade flung " into his system " may have damaged his stomach so much that an anodyne of some sort was needed if he was to live and work. It was once discovered by an intelligent doctor, superintendent of a big jail in Burma,[2] that most of the prisoners who had been brought there by opium had taken to it originally for relief from stomach

---

[1] *Edinburgh Sketches and Memories*, by David Masson, pp. 319–20, and Sir C. Gavan Duffy's *Conversations with Carlyle*, p. 69, etc., as well as *Reminiscences and Letters*.

[2] L. G. Fink, Myaungmya Jail, 1909.

pains ; and the same may be true of spirits, which is an excellent medicine, and only dangerous because too agreeable. Tobacco is safer ; but it hurt the nerves of Carlyle, and may have done harm by relieving pains which were danger signals and thus making it easier for him to exert himself too much. He never realised that, and overestimated what he owed to tobacco as much as what he owed to German. " He lauded it," said William Maccall, " as one of the divinest benefits that had ever come to the human race, arriving as compensation and consolation at a time, too, when social, political (and) religious anarchy and every imaginable plague made the earth unspeakably miserable."

" I can never think of this miraculous blessing from the gods," he is reported to have said, " without being overwhelmed by a tenderness for which I can find no words sufficient." [1]

The faithful Gavan Duffy told him what the doctors would say now that his smoking tended to make him sleepless. He admitted, " Some slight injury, but not much." It was a choice of evils. The damage to his nerves was more than he supposed, as Tennyson by and by insisted, declaring that Carlyle smoked too much and himself just enough : to which the reply was that Carlyle took only what was good for him, and Tennyson too much. [2] Each was right about the other. The sleeplessness of Carlyle and many other such " signs of genius " were the result of nicotine and tea, as well as overwork of the mind and underwork of the body, upsetting the balance of Nature. This he had by degrees to discover with little help from the doctors. His best adviser was a fine Birmingham man he met this year called Badams.

[1] Thomas Carlyle, "Table Talk," *Cope's Smoke Room Booklets, No. 5.*
[2] William Allingham, *A Diary*, pp. 237–8 ; amplified by Alexander Carlyle's verbal report to D. A. W. of his uncle's talk.

XVIII

HE GOES TO LONDON WITHOUT HER

(1824)

MEANWHILE at Missolonghi the surgeons were bleeding Byron to death (19.4.1824), and a month later (19.5.1824) the news was known in Scotland and Carlyle writing to Jane :—

'Poor Byron! Alas poor Byron! The news of his death came down upon my heart like a mass of lead ; and yet, the thought of it sends a painful twinge through all my being, as if I had lost a Brother! O God! that so many sons of mud and clay should fill up their base existence to its utmost bound, and this, the noblest spirit in Europe, should sink before half his course was run! Late so full of fire and generous passion, and proud purposes, and now for ever dumb and cold! Poor Byron! And but a young man ; still struggling amid the perplexities, and sorrows and aberrations of a mind not yet arrived at maturity or settled in its proper place in life. Had he been spared to the age of three score and ten, what might he not have done, what might he not have been! But we shall hear his voice no more : I dreamed of seeing him and knowing him. We shall go to him, he shall not return to us. Adieu, my dear Jane! There is a blank in your heart and a blank in mine, since this man passed away. Let us stand the closer by each other! I am yours for ever.'

Next day, before his letter could have reached her, she was writing to him—

'In the name of Heaven why don't you write to me? For God sake write the instant this reaches you, if you have not done it before. Wretch! You cannot conceive what anxiety I am in about you. One moment I imagine you ill or in trouble of some sort ; the next tired of me ; the next something else as bad. In short there is no end to my imaginings.

'To add to my perplexities, there have I had a letter from that stupendous ass the Orator (Irving), telling me such nonsensical things. I will tell you about my *visit to London*. I have no heart for it now. What an idiot I was ever to think that man so estimable! But I am done with his Preachership now and for ever.

'And Byron is dead! I was told it all at once in a roomful of people. My God, if they had said that the sun or the moon had gone out of the heavens, it could not have struck me with the idea of a more awful and dreary blank in the creation than the words, "Byron is dead!" I have felt quite cold and dejected ever since : all my thoughts have been fearful and dismal. I wish you were come. Yours for ever affectionately.'

He came to Edinburgh on Tuesday (25.5.1824), having written in advance to Jane : "I hope to spend a *day in peace* with you." Her mother approved ; but she forgot he had to write for her mother's eye, and exploded upon him :—

'Devil!—That I had you here to beat you with a stick! Such a fright you have given me! There is not a disaster under heaven, that I have not imagined to have befallen our commonwealth. May you come! My God! Haven't I been telling you to come for the last three months? "*A day* beside me!" You are provoking. I cannot tell you how many days I wish you to spend beside me. My wish in that matter will be *as things turn out ;* but do not go to fix any time for your journey, before we meet. You must stay longer than a day at all events.

'How happy I shall be. Thank God! I have you again : Byron's death made me tremble for all that I admire and love. My mother is waiting for me to walk with her. She is *good* still. God bless you, my Dearest. Despatch your business. Come! Yours ever.'

On Thursday he was telling her : "Angel, I had such a fight to-day with Brewster and a Gothic German for the memory of our poor Byron." But the point of his letter was that next night, Friday, he would be in Haddington. Her mother left them alone a good deal when he came, and he felt in "the third heaven." She had a hat to give him, and helped him in buying a shawl for his mother. After forty years, he remembered, he said, "the *gimp bonnet* she wore, and her anxious silent thoughts, and my own, mutually legible both of them, in part."

Never was his way of qualifying statements better justified. The publication of letters has revealed more than she told him then of her anxieties. When Irving was preaching at Haddington last year a few days before his marriage and living with the Welshes, he discovered Mrs. Welsh was standing between his old pupil and his friend Carlyle, and said to Jane—" Come to London and be my guest all next summer along with him—you'll have his company all the time."

It seemed to her " the happiest, happiest life that my imagination hath ever conceived," and she began to build upon the prospect of it. She had never seen the Miss Martin now becoming Mrs. Irving, but Carlyle's report upon her being favourable, all seemed well.

Her flirtation with Irving was a distant memory of four years ago. She took for granted at first that Mrs. Irving did not know it was for her sake that Irving had wanted then to cancel his engagement. But Irving's trade was utterance ; the very Christ he adored lived openly and bade His followers do likewise ; and Irving had lived so cleanly that he was heedless of appearances. He had no false shame about him, and less than the usual share of the other kind. So it soon appeared that Mrs. Irving knew who her rival had been, and steadily tabooed Jane Welsh, and the invitation to London did not come. Carlyle, a friend of her father as well as of her husband, and an old acquaintance of her own, was always a welcome guest, and in expensive summer quarters a paying guest ; but Jane Welsh indeed ! She had always sufficient reasons for not asking her, and left Irving to make his excuses as best he could.

He wrote to Carlyle about the beginning of May, reiterating the invitation to himself and explaining their house was " not in a condition to receive a lady." This was repeated to Jane, but she would not take the hint, and persisted in hoping against hope, till Irving wrote to her direct at last (10.5.1824), more than enough. He had abundance of excuses : house not all furnished, wife to be confined, her sister coming, and so on ; but he was also, as she said, " nonsensical " :—

' One thing more, my dear Jane, into your own ear. My dear Isabella has succeeded in healing the wounds of my heart, but I am hardly yet in a condition to expose them. My former calmness and piety are returning. I feel growing in grace and in holiness ; and before another year I shall be worthy in the eye of my own conscience to receive you into my house and under my care, which till then I should hardly be.

' Be assured, my dear Jane, the child of my intellect, of the same affection from me as ever, and as I have said, purer and more pure.

' Thomas Carlyle is to be with me this month ; and it is an inexpressible delight to me. I am, my dear Jane, Your most affectionate friend.'

His wife did not even send " her regards " till the risk of a visit was past for the year. Would she or anyone give Carlyle a hint of the old flirtation ? No wonder Jane was anxious. Pity she did not tell it to him at once, is easy to say when one knows the other man was blabbing ; but she was not sure of that as yet, and would feel it wrong to blab—it might sunder the best of friends. Give the woman her due !

A brother of the poet, *Gilbert* Burns, a land-agent living in Haddington, was by this time a familiar acquaintance of Carlyle, and a fragment of their talk survives. He " used often to say that his brother's conversation was never afterwards so delightful as when they two were working in the field, or digging peat together. Robert was full of poetry and enthusiasm." [1] Till Burns " left his father's house," he " was happy ; nay the gayest, brightest, most fantastic, fascinating being to be found in the world ; more so even than he ever afterwards appeared." [2]

The talk of Gilbert about his brother, Robert Burns, was always an addition to Haddington's attractions ; but on this occasion it was not needed. Jane kept him beside her without an effort—till Thursday morning (3.6.1824), when he had to go. The Bullers were expecting him in London, and James Johnstone was awaiting him in Edinburgh, having come from Broughty Ferry for two days of his company. Bookseller Boyd paid the £180 according to agreement. Brewster gave him letters to poet Campbell and engineer Telford, and promised many more. He had supposed the steamers went on Saturdays ; but found

[1] William Allingham, *A Diary*, pp. 283-4.
[2] *Essay on Burns.*

their day was Wednesday, and Saturday's boat was a smack. He decided to go on that day all the same, and on Saturday sent letters of farewell to Mainhill and Haddington, with a Shakespeare to Jane, and advice to read it as well as Milton and the histories and reviews. In the evening Thomas Murray escorted him on board. They sailed at seven, and were in sight of the Bass all Sunday. Of course he wrote to Jane he was thinking of her, and described the inside of the smack.

The voyage lasted nearly six days. The women passengers kept to their cabins. There were three other men. Sir David Milne was " one of the numerous baronets of the age," and dull. He shared a cabin with Carlyle, and snored all night and talked ineptitudes with much politeness. With a big face, pock-pitted and bristly, he was " courteous, solemn, yet awkward, dull; chewing away the ' r ' when he spoke, which indeed was seldom, and then mainly in the way of economic enquiry to passengers who knew London— what you could do there, see, eat, etc. ; and to every item, the farther question : ' And what is the cha-arge ? ' " He stood for many hours together steadying himself with his left hand clutching something on " the middle of the deck, and the thumb of his right hand stuck firmly with its point on the hip-joint ; his large blue rheumy eyes gazing on vacancy." Another passenger was a (military) Captain Smith, " brisk, lean, whisking, smart of speech and quick in bowing ; but if possible still more inane. These two demonstrated to me that sea-sickness was painful, that sea-captains ought to be expert, that London was a great city, that the Turks eat opium, that the Irish were discontented, that brandy would intoxicate," and so on. The third man was " Monsieur Dubois, a Strasburger, Lord Bute's fac-totum." He " with his flageolet, his *Valliant Troubadour*, and his *Es hatt' ein Bauer ein schönes Weib* (There's a peasant has a beautiful wife) alone contributed to save me. I laughed at him every day about an hour."

Laughed *with* him—would have been nicer. What Dubois thought of Carlyle is unknown, perhaps pitied his want of music. It is not likely that Milne gave him a second thought. Smith would notice his country clothes and perhaps recom-mend a tailor. At any rate one of the first things Carlyle bought in town was a suit of fine clothes and a good watch, too. The " Jemmy hat " was having the effect intended—he was dressing up to it. Tho six such days at sea may

do more for intimacy than years ashore, the Thames gave
them suddenly something to think about more interesting
than each other. As they moved up through a forest of
masts, the infinite sounds and movements, the bustle,
" the coal-heavers, the bargeman, the black buildings,"
made one feel like a drop in the ocean, as if " annihilated
in the immensity" of what seemed to be the "heart of all
the earth."   The fellow-voyagers separated soon after noon
on Friday at Tower Wharf, and never met again.

> " Nature by magnetic laws
> Circle unto circle draws ;
> But they only touch when met,—
> Never mingle—strangers yet ! "

XIX

IN LONDON

(1824)

CARLYLE was in time for early dinner with the Irvings, who welcomed him warmly at Islington. A son of Basil Montagu was lunching with them and was specially interesting at the moment as a sample dandy. Still more interesting was Kitty Kirkpatrick, who descended upon them while Carlyle's trunk was still in the hall. He noticed her switch from it the label to show to her cousin Mrs. Strachey, with whom she lived, the sister of Mrs. Buller. These ladies had themselves been Miss Kirkpatricks, and Kitty's mother was a rich Indian woman, and she was now herself an heiress, whom pious Mrs. Strachey was helping in the hunt for a good husband to endow.

Perhaps it was with some such thought that Mrs. Strachey had sought the acquaintance of Irving, when as a handsome bachelor and miraculous preacher he was brought to the notice of Society by Canning, mentioning in the Commons how his eloquence surpassed all that money could buy for the established Church of England. With delicate kindness Mrs. Strachey and Kitty had anonymously furnished the best room in his house; and here now in London was his literary friend, whom the Bullers thought so much of. No wonder Kitty called !

"A very pleasing creature," Carlyle confessed to Jane she was, with soft dark eyes and floods of auburn hair; and in the simplicity of his soul, for it hardly occurred to him till he was old to think of her in connection with love-making, as he had made his market, he held up her good qualities for imitation. "Though twenty-one, and not unbeautiful, sole mistress of herself and fifty thousand pounds, she is meek and modest as a Quakeress ; with a demure eye she surveys the *extravaganzas* of the Orator (Irving), laughing at him in secret, yet loving him as a good man, and studiously devoting herself to provide for the

establishment. Good Kitty! never I believe angry at any
creature. Would you or I were half as happy as this girl!"
To which the exasperated Jane retorted : " Miss Kitty
Kirkpatrick—Lord, what an ugly name ! ' Good Kitty!'
Oh, pretty, dear, delightful Kitty ! I am not a bit jealous
of her, not I indeed—Hindoo princess though she be !
Only you may as well never let me hear you mention her
name again."

One of his first visits in Irving's company was to the
Stracheys' house at Shooter's Hill in Kent. As they were
approaching, they caught a glimpse of Kitty among the
roses. Mrs. Strachey received the callers—a young matron
about twenty years younger than her husband, a retired
Anglo-Indian and now an official at the India Office ; but
unlike her more worldly elder sister, Mrs. Buller, she was
addicted to religion and serious. Both sisters were devoted
to their family duties ; but her preference for domestic
ideals made the younger the favourite of Carlyle—" the
only woman," as Jane Welsh soon told him, " to whom
I ever heard you give praise without some mixture of
sarcasm."

In old age he wrote about her :—" To this day, long years
after her death, I regard her as a singular pearl of a woman ;
pure as dew, yet full of love ; incapable of unveracity to
herself or others," and well deserving the love and esteem
she received from her husband. " It strikes me now," he
continued, " more than it then did, she silently could have
liked to see ' dear Kitty ' and myself come together, and so
continue near her, both of us, through life : the good kind
soul—and Kitty, too, was charming in her beautiful *Begum*
sort, and might have been charmed ? None knows." At
the time he was writing he had been told how she and the
Stracheys had for years been supposing her the model for
what is written in *Sartor* of Blumine, identifying the house
there with their own at Shooter's Hill. But he had confided
to Mrs. Strachey his adoration of Jane as soon as they were
on intimate terms, which made misunderstanding impossible,
and enabled her to be the " duenna cousin " between him
and Kitty with perfect kindness. In reality there never
was any love-making between them, and never any un-
pleasantness. The coincidences with *Sartor* were all external.
When Kitty was an old widow and the mother of many
children she told Carlyle he had alleged a kiss from Blumine
although he had never received one from her. He did not

say she had been mistaken all her life, and never once
mentioned Margaret Gordon. Her talk revived his recollections of her. He remembered : " She had one of the
prettiest smiles, a visible sense of humour (the slight merry
curl of her upper lip, *right side* of it only, the carriage of
her head and eyes on such occasions, the quiet little things
she said in that kind, and her low-toned hearty laugh, were
noticeable) ; this was perhaps her most spiritual quality ;
of developed intellect she had not much, though not wanting
in discernment. Amiable, affectionate, graceful ; attractive
(not *slim* enough for the title ' pretty,' not *tall* enough for
' beautiful ') ; had something low-voiced, languidly harmonious, placid, sensuous, loved perfumes, etc. : a half-
Begum in short ; semi-Oriental Englishwoman."

Another drawing-room to which Irving hastened to take
him was that of a lawyer, Basil Montagu, whose wife had
made their house the best equivalent in London of a Parisian
salon. She had taught Edward Irving to " rest," and liked
his friend Carlyle at once and " always made him very
welcome." [1] She and Montagu had both been married before,
and the flower of their household now was her daughter
Anne Skepper, about to wed the poet and lawyer, Procter
(Barry Cornwall), who thus described Carlyle : [2] " He had
grave features, a brown, florid complexion, and a simple,
manly manner, not depending on cultivation so much as
on the internal thoughts which gave it motion and character.
I found him very sensible and pleasant ; having some peculiar
opinions, indeed, with which, it must be owned, I did not
much disagree." In liberal politics and aversion to theology
they were alike, and in much else. Both had become devotees
of Shakespeare without a hint from any teacher. He was
eight years the senior of Carlyle, and had much to tell—
about his schoolmate Byron, for example. He gave him
a bit of a letter he had received from Byron, and it was
passed on to Jane Welsh, who rejoiced over it like a wor-
shipper over a relic of a saint. [3]

The friendship between Procter and Carlyle was never for
a moment clouded ; and Montagu himself was pleased with
the new-comer ; but not so his sons, including the " dandy "

[1] Preface by Mrs. Procter to *Carlyle Letters*, privately printed in 1881 :
copy in the London Library. The Letters there are reprinted in Moncure
Conway's *Thomas Carlyle*, pp. 227-55.
[2] E. W. Proctor, *Autobiographical Fragment*, etc., p. 164.
[3] *Early Letters of J. W. Carlyle*, by D. G. Ritchie, p. 101.

who met Carlyle at Irving's on the day of his arrival. They said nothing to their elders, but did not conceal from their step-sister that they " admired neither his dress, his uncouth manners, nor his dialect." [1]

Mrs. Montagu lost no time in telling him of how she encountered " My dear Robert Burns " at Dumfries, and how he had taken her out to walk " in the silent streets " in the intervals of dances there. One fine morning she and Irving took Carlyle to Highgate and presented him to Coleridge, who talked a little to him about Kant, when they were alone together " in narrow parts of the garden walks." Without success! The young man tried hard to revere the sage, as the rest were doing; but could not. He tried and tried again and again, resorting to the shrine with Montagu himself and Irving, worshippers both, and would gladly have joined in their Hallelujahs; but the feeling would not come—the Latter-day Saviour of the Church of England appeared to be hopelessly " sunk in putrescent indolence," like " a steam engine of a hundred horses' power with the boiler burst," and morally an awful warning instead of an example. His philosophic shibboleths seemed a mere hocus-pocus to hide that historical Christianity had become incredible.

When presently " protection " to the extent of gratis lodgings was proffered Carlyle himself, he explained to Jane: —

' It is very good in these people; but really their protection is a trouble to me. For their kind feelings, God knows I thank them from the bottom of my heart; but farther it is not suitable at present. As old Quixote said, and as I have often said after him, " if it were but a crust of bread and a cup of water that Heaven has given thee, rejoice that thou hast none but Heaven to thank for it! " A man that is not standing on his own feet in regard to economical affairs, soon ceases to be a man at all. Poor Coleridge is like the hulk of a huge ship : his masts and sails and rudder have rotted quite away.'

His arrangement with the Bullers had been to tutor the boys near London for some months. They expected then to winter in Cornwall, with him beside them; but by June Mrs. Buller had changed her plans and preferred to winter.

[1] Preface by Mrs. Procter to *Carlyle Letters*, privately printed in 1881: copy in the London Library. The Letters there are reprinted in Moncure Conway's *Thomas Carlyle*, pp. 227–55.

Kitty Kirkpatrick.

This is from a photograph of a miniature

[face p. 336

in Boulogne. Carlyle did not agree to go there, but said he would consider it, and consented to stay with Charles till October; but when they went into lodgings at Kew (22.6.1824), they found study under such conditions a sham, and said so. Then Mrs. Buller said that she must know whether he would go with them to France or not. If he would go, they must decamp for the country immediately. If not, the boy would be sent to prepare for Cambridge, He knew that was what she wanted, and answered that if he was required to decide at once, they were to count on his declining. They parted friends, Carlyle accepting only half of the twenty pounds Buller senior tendered " for his trouble," and the lady inviting him to attend her "rout" next night.

So by the first week in July he was back in Irving's, who welcomed him and pressed him to stay all the winter. Charles Buller and his father were grieved by the loss of such a tutor. Charles was " in a passion of sadness and anger." He met Carlyle by appointment, a few days after the parting, in Regent Square, on the occasion of an address by Irving to a great company assembled to see laid the foundation stone of a new " Caledonian Chapel." Some bricklayers' planks divided them from the crowd, and left them free to talk. Charles eagerly propounded " some new futility of a proposal," and looked very sad when Carlyle replied : " No, alas I cannot, Charles."

What Charles said to his mother that night is not on record. What the ex-tutor wrote to his mother was shaped to re-assure her :—

'Twelve months spent at Boulogne would have added little to my stock of cash, and fearfully diminished my remnant of spirits, health and affection. The world must be fronted some time, soon as good as *syne*' (by and by) ! 'Adieu, therefore, to ancient dames of quality, that flaunting, painting, patching, nervous, vapourish, jigging, skimming, scolding race of mortals.' (Which refers to the fashionable females that flooded Mrs. Buller's drawing-room, not to herself.) 'Their clothes are silk, their manners courtly, their hearts are *kipper*' (=dry fish, salted or smoked). 'I have left the Bullers' twelve months sooner than they would have parted with me had I liked. I am glad that we have parted in friendship ; very glad that we are parted at all. She invited me to a rout—a grand, fashionable affair—next

z

night. I did not go a foot length. I want to have no further
trade with her or hers, at least except in the way of cold
civility ; for as to affection, I do not believe that there is
one of them that even guesses what it means. Her sister,
indeed ' (Mrs. Strachey), 'likes me ; but she is as opposite
as day from night.'

(In another letter, there is more of the sister.) ' My chief
favourite is Mrs. Strachey, a sister of Mrs. Buller ; but
she is serious and earnest and religious and affectionate,
while the other is light, giddy, vain and heartless. She
and I will be sworn friends by and by.'

When he spoke to Mrs. Strachey about his sweetheart,
he was surprised to hear her say : " I respect Miss Welsh
for her conduct to Mr. and Mrs. Irving." He repeated this
to Jane in his next letter, hinting he was perplexed. She
was in no hurry to explain the riddle, but did at last remark,
apropos the failure of the Irvings to invite her : " The
Orator has only *one* voice in the matter ; his wife has the
other ; and his Wife I have obliged too deeply to hope for
kindness from her." And when at last she received a vague
invitation, she guessed it was not intended to be accepted,
and she did not come, but quoted Irving's sonnet to herself—
which was all she was willing Carlyle should ever know.

He had lost no time in seeing the sights, but the only
building in London he thought grand was St. Paul's. He
often spoke of it in later years. He had been coming west,
" hurrying along Cheapside into Newgate Street, when in
passing from the abode of John Gilpin " he looked through
the opening at the corner of the street, " and there stood
St. Paul's," he wrote to his brother, " with its columns and
friezes and massy wings of bleached yet unworn stone ;
with its statues and its graves around it ; with its solemn
dome four hundred feet above me, and its gilded ball and
cross gleaming in the evening sun, piercing up into the heaven
through the vapours of our earthly home ! It was silent as
Tadmor of the Wilderness ; gigantic, beautiful, enduring ;
it seemed to frown with a rebuking pity on the vain scramble
which it overlooked : at its feet were tombstones, above it
was the everlasting sky, within priests perhaps were chanting
hymns ; it seemed to transmit with a stern voice the sounds
of Death, Judgment and Eternity through all the frivolous
and fluctuating city. I saw it oft and from various points,
and never without new admiration."

On Monday (5.7.1824), Henry Crabb Robinson was taking tea at Charles Lamb's, and saw Irving there, " and his friend, Mr. Carlyle." [1] He found it " an agreeable evening enough," to his surprise, for between Irving and Lamb with his " incurable levity " there was room for " so little sympathy " that they " ought not to be intimate." [2] Wherein the judicious and handsome Robinson was right, tho Lamb, to his credit, had the sense to maintain that Irving was not a quack. [3] Carlyle had been described to Robinson by Irving a few weeks before this (10.6.1824) as " a friend of mine who has translated *Wilhelm Meister*. We do not sympathise on religious matters, but that is nothing," when a man is earnest—a very polite speech from the great divine, when addressed to one who did not pretend to be orthodox.

Carlyle did not return to Lamb's, but was drawn to Crabb Robinson, who was now a prosperous barrister of forty-nine, but mindful of the days of his youth, when he studied in Germany, and knew Schiller, and read Milton's *Samson* with Goethe. He had been a pioneer war-correspondent and his Diaries are still read. Perhaps his best service to good literature was taking down from an old woman the delightful story of *The Fisherman and His Wife*, the best of the *Household Tales* of Grimm. He was now frequenting the house of the Montagus, and often entertained Carlyle in his rooms in the Temple. On hearing which long afterwards, Espinasse enquired of him : " Was Carlyle modest when he was young ? "

" Well,, you know," was the reply, " Mr. Carlyle could *never* have been modest."

Away went Espinasse and repeated this to Carlyle, who laughed and told of a Mr. Southern he met at Robinson's —a writer and diplomat—who had been so much contradicted that " the next time he met ' Crabb ' he complained of the snubbing he had received from Carlyle," concluding pathetically, " Why, I couldn't have been always in the wrong ! " [4]

[1] *Life of Charles Lamb*, by E. V. Lucas, p. 529.
[2] *Diary, Reminiscences and Correspondence of Henry Crabb Robinson :* I, pp. 188–90 ; II, pp. 270–8 ; III, p. 486.
[3] *Life of E. Irving*, by Mrs. Oliphant, Chap. IX, footnote, quoting a letter of Charles Lamb to Leigh Hunt.
[4] *Literary Recollections*, by F. Espinasse, pp. 381–2.

XX

JOHN BADAMS OF BIRMINGHAM AND OTHERS

(1824)

MRS. MONTAGU had introduced Carlyle to John Badams, chemist, manufacturing sulphuric acid at Birmingham, and believed to be making a fortune. He was a " light-hearted and genially gallant kind of man," who fell into a sudden friendship with Carlyle, and hearing of his dyspepsia, told of his own, now happily abolished. He had studied medicine at Edinburgh, and cured himself and many another of chronic stomach troubles by diet and exercise, with a minimum of drugs. In fact he was in advance of the doctors of his day.

" Come and stay a month or six weeks with me," said he, "and I will cure you." He continued to repeat the invitation, which Mrs. Montagu reinforced, till at last Carlyle consented, astonished at himself. So at seven o'clock one bright Sunday morning (18.7.1824) he took his place beside the driver on the coach for " Brummagem."

It seemed the finest drive he ever had. It was his first in the south, and the speed, to which he was always partial, surpassed his expectations. The time for changing horses was ninety seconds. They went by Fenny Stratford and Stony Stratford, across the Ouse and to Coventry—it stayed like a panorama in his memory for two score years. The coachman was dressed like a gentleman and expressed the prejudices of one by calling any groundling he disliked " You Radical ! " Twelve hours after starting, Carlyle was set down at the west end of Birmingham near Badams' house and factory, and warmly welcomed.

It was a bachelor establishment. The housekeeper, Mrs. Barnet, " a friend of my mother," said he, occupied the ground floor with her family. In three days' time Badams had talked with Carlyle " about two folio volumes," and made him feel as if half the house were his, as if they had been " acquaintances of twenty years' standing." The talk was things in general, but dietetics were never forgotten. The treatment was : half-raw eggs and floods of weak tea, riding and good company, wine before dinner and early to bed. Mercury is not mentioned, but the castor-oil was copious, every four days. The patient soon was free from pain, but averse to hard exertion, and deliberately unbent with success.

Schiller was to be made into a book ; but there was no need for haste. He could do it in London. The unaffected kindness and geniality of Badams warmed Carlyle to the heart, and in 1866 he wrote as he looked back :—

'Seldom have I seen a franker, trustier, cheerier form of human kindliness than Badams's ; how I remember the laughing eyes and sunny figure of him, breaking into my room on mornings' (sometimes to waken him before six for two hours' gallop before breakfast) ; 'himself half-dressed—*waistband in hand,* and hair all flying. " What ? Not up yet—monster ! " The smile of his eyes, the sound of his voice, were so bright and practically *true.* A tight, middle-sized, handsome kind of man ; eyes blue, sparkling, soft, nose and other features inclining to the pointed ; complexion bluish, face always shaven bare ; essentially a gentleman ; and really looked well, and jauntily aristo-cratic, when dressed for riding, or the like. Slight rusticity of accent rather did him good.'

He was frank about his plebeian origin. His father had been a workman in Warwick ; and one of their rides was to see his native town and " the Castle," where, as a boy, he had copied a picture so well that Dr. Parr " the Whig Dr. Johnson " took notice of him and had him as a pupil. On other days the coal and iron works to the north and west of Birmingham engrossed Carlyle, alone or in company. Badams did not neglect his own work ; but contrived to keep his visitor well occupied and detained him twice as long as intended. Thus by his doing Carlyle was one of a party exploring the inside of the Dudley black country, which as yet he had seen on the outside only. " We in-spected blast furnaces," he remembered, " descended into coal mines ; poked about all day—with a short recess for luncheon." The historian of Birmingham region may find his letters useful. He felt its importance, saying : " It is in a spot like this that one sees the sources of British power."

'A space perhaps of thirty square miles to the north covered over with furnaces, rolling-mills, steam engines and sooty men. A dense cloud of pestilential smoke hangs over it, blackening even the grain that grows upon it; and at night the whole region burns like a volcano spitting fire from a thousand tubes of brick. But oh the wretched hundred and fifty thousand mortals that grind out their destiny there ! In the coal-mines they were literally naked, many of them, all but trousers; black as ravens; plashing about. In the iron-mills it was little better : blast-furnaces were roaring like the voice of many whirlwinds all around ; the fiery metal was hissing through its moulds, or sparkling and spitting under hammers of a monstrous size, which fell like so many little earthquakes. Here they were wheeling charred coals, breaking their ironstone, and tumbling all into their fiery pit ; there they were turning and boring cannon with a hideous shrieking noise such as the earth could hardly parallel ; and through the whole, half-naked demons pouring with sweat and besmeared with soot were hurrying to and fro in their red night-caps and sheet-iron breeches, rolling or hammering or squeezing their glowing metal as if it had been wax or dough. Yet on the whole I am told they are very happy ; they make forty shillings or more per week, and few of them will work on Mondays.

'In the town you hear the clank of innumerable steam-engines, the rumbling of cars and vans, and the hum of men interrupted by the sharper rattle of some canal-boat loading or disloading ; or, perhaps, some fierce explosion when the cannon founders are proving their new-made ware. I have seen their polishing of teapots, and buttons, and gun-barrels, and fire-shovels, and swords, and all manner of toys and tackle, their tubs and vats, as large as country churches, full of copperas and aqua-fortis and oil of vitriol.'

Badams kept two or three horses whereon to " ride for health," and when he could spare a day they galloped far. They went to Hagley one Monday morning, and after breakfast through the " Metallic Country " of Halesowen to the top of the Clent Hill for a view. They saw aristocratic roofs and many smoke pillars, spiral or straight, and in coming and going saw, thick by the roadside, little forges built of single brick, hardly bigger than sentry boxes, and in each of them, with bellows, stake and hammer, a woman busy making nails—it "seems as if all the nails of the world were getting made here."

He was introduced to several pleasant people ; and accidentally one evening heard a sermon from the then-famous Dr. Hall of Leicester, demonstrating that God did not lie— he "had no need to." "As good prove that God never fought a duel," sniffed Badams when told of it. In the shop of Jemmy Belcher, "a smirking little dumpy Unitarian bookseller," he took refuge from a shower one day, and in a magazine saw a hostile review of *Meister* by "De" Quincey, the son of Thomas Quincey, a Manchester merchant. The rain detaining him, he read it and noted some Scotticisms for correction, while consciously refraining from anger because the critic said the book was "morally detestable and artistically speaking rubbish."

"I will bring you into condition and set you on your feet," said Badams, persuading him to stay and persevere. "If he keep his word, I laugh at fortune ! " wrote Carlyle to Jane, in answering her assurance of fidelity. She had described to him the distracted devotion of a simple " Dugald G——," whom her mother now favoured and who had made a headlong proposal. The sight of him resorting to the house had made Fyffe furious, but their fate was the same. Mrs. Welsh had to allow her daughter to say she was engaged, and "dear Dugald" was disappointed. "A lovable creature" she called him to Carlyle, to make him feel how much she had sacrificed for him ; but Bess Stodart heard he was a "mooncalf" of the "Spaniel genus," and at last a liar.[1] What the young woman wanted was to be beside Carlyle in England, and that was why he tried to play her game in talk with Irving, who had come to Birmingham on business and was riding with him on the last day of August.

Irving complained that she wanted him to write letters, which he could not. "I am ever ready at a moment's warning to *do* everything in my power for my friends ; but I really have no time or topics to *write*."

Carlyle told him : " As to *doing*, none but Prime Ministers and Asiatic Monarchs can pretend to make or keep friends by that expensive method." He had no suspicion of what really made it impossible for Irving to correspond with Jane at all, in the way she wanted, and it is curious he did not see the difficulty about time was reasonable. He could not

---

[1] *Early Letters of J. W. Carlyle*, by D. G. Ritchie, pp. 99–100.

imagine that any man permitted to write to that wonderful young woman would let anything prevent him from doing it, and told her :—

'Doubtless, my Dearest, you will come to London. . . . I tell thee, our culture is but beginning ; there are regions of thought and feeling which have scarcely as yet loomed on the edge of our horizon ; thither let us tend unswervingly, never, never parting by the way ! What may we not accomplish ! In hours of happy musing, I figure myself as the interpreter of truth and manly integrity and imaginative beauty to thousands of my fellow men ; and Jane, my fair and pure Egeria, my inspiring Goddess of the Fountain, to originate, to perfect, adorn and recompense my labours ! Call this gasconading and vain dreaming: I know it is, my Dearest ; yet something of it *may* be realised ; and if we both live, *shall.*'

Mrs. Welsh may have been spared the perusal of this ; but even if she caught sight of it, would be mystified, not knowing how very intimate Numa, the Roman Solomon, had been with his Egeria. But her daughter knew ; and to be an Egeria was what she wanted. To combine the pleasures of a goddess and a woman is a natural ideal of an only child, who thinks it a kind of duty to please herself.

Carlyle was praying her to sanctify his *Schiller* by doing some translations he might insert, and praying without success. Her mother was striving to marry her quick to a man of means, any of several in sight, she hardly heeded which. Craigenputtock was without a tenant and the rent in danger—it might have to be reduced. Business was business. Recognising that Dr. Fyffe was out of the running, she warmly seconded Dugald G——, and when he failed took Jane a round of visits to country houses, in the hope that somebody needing a partner might yet cut out Carlyle —which was becoming more difficult than it would have been last year.

Perceiving her drift, her cousin, Captain James Baillie, sentimentalised with Jane. In age he was midway between his cousin and her daughter, a big and handsome clothes-screen in the Lancers, with glittering regimentals, four rings on his fingers and a private fortune of £1000 a year. He was hunting a rich widow at the moment, but Jane was good practice. She told Bess he was her beau-ideal, deficient

in nothing but genius. She accepted a ring with his hair
in it, and an invitation to stay in his house after his marriage,
as that would take her to London. But the marriage did
not take place, and none of the country houses could produce
a champion for Mrs. Welsh's purpose, so that between
worries of one kind and another, her daughter's tantrums
and her own, she appeared to Jane to be this autumn " not
once in the same humour for two hours at a time."

Meanwhile Carlyle was recovering as far as possible
from indigestion and mercury. The keen-witted Badams
was telling him, correctly, "There is no organ specially
deranged, only an over-worked system of nerves." That
was why even two months' castor-oil and the best of diet
and exercise had not made him well. Badams kept him to
the latest day he could, and made him promise to come back
to complete the cure.

Not far from the house and factory was the signboard of
WILLIAM SHAKESPEARE, maker and mender of boots
and shoes, which was a reminder that he had seen two Strat-
fords in coming, but not the one on Avon. They told him
Birmingham had a HOMER too, a button-maker. So
when on Thursday (23.9.1824) he left for London it was in
a coach which took the Avon route, and he was delighted
by the sight of the " grim-looking house of bricks " and
" beams of oak," where Willie Shakespeare toddled in and
out long ago. With a feeling like that of a pilgrim coming
to Jerusalem, he gazed upon the street where that wonderful
boy had played, and the hills and woods among which he
grew, and the church where he was buried. The canal was
new, but the town seemed little altered. The rippling
river was still the same.

XXI

WITH IRVING IN LODGINGS AT DOVER

(1824)

AFTER a few days in London he joined the Irvings and Kitty Kirkpatrick at Dover (30.9.1824), seeing Canterbury and its shrine on the way. The Stracheys came a week later.

Irving was feeling he needed rest and reflection. Tho his church was as crowded as ever, the crowds were no longer fashionable and powerful, and "the thought that the Christian religion was again to dominate all minds and the world to become an Eden by his means, was declaring itself to have been a dream. And he could never consent to believe it such." So wrote Carlyle long afterwards ; at present he was hoping for the best.

The divine took to nursing his baby to divert his mind, and spoke of "him" and his "operations" as if he were "the infant Lama" and wife and self "High Priestess and Priest of Thibet." On the beach might be seen "the giant with his broad-brimmed hat, his sallow visage, and sable-matted fleece of hair, carrying the little creature" in his hands, "tick-ticking to it and dandling it." "Is he not a pretty boy ? " the fond father asked, and maybe hoped Carlyle would notice a thing he did not like to mention but was glad to see, that baby had not the father's ugly squint. So no mere "Yes" could content him ; and he repeated the question scores of times, indoors and out, till at last Carlyle emitted an affidavit, so to speak, and finished that, but never suspected what was wanted.

Occasionally they took long walks together discussing religion and literature, men and things in general. These October weeks were more like old days in Kirkcaldy than any they ever saw again. Strolling on the beach one evening, they noticed the bricklayers finishing a house becoming noisy as they crowded round the gable-top. Irving was strangely moved and grasped the other's arm as he quoted

346

the scriptures : " See—they are going to bring out their topstone with shouting ! " Carlyle enquired of a by-stander : " What is it ? " Answered : " You see, sir, they gets allowance of beer." [1]

Carlyle sent his father a description of the farming methods of Kent and Warwick, neither equal to Dumfriesshire, but the people were better fed :—

' I have looked into the clean, brick-built, tile-flagged little cottages, and seen the people dining, with their jug of ale, their bacon, and other ware, and a huge loaf towering over it all. It is pleasant to see every one so well provided for. There is nothing like the appearance of want to be met with anywhere.'

In general Irving was spared contradiction, with his wife on one hand and Mrs. Strachey on the other. In the evenings, indeed, they were all together round the Strachey dinner-table or in the house of the Irvings ; and when he was reading aloud what Coleridge recommended he was liable to be quizzed by Kitty and Carlyle. But at other times Mr. Strachey gravitated to these two, and they left the saints alone. France was in sight and the weather fine. Kitty suggested to Strachey as the nights grew longer that they should visit Paris. They coaxed Carlyle to go with them. " It would be *so* pleasant—cost you little—do you *so* much good."

Mrs. Strachey ratified the project, wanting the Irvings more to herself. So Kitty's carriage was sent over, and one Thursday afternoon (21.10.1824) on the sands of Boulogne, she and her maid took their seats inside it and Strachey and Carlyle outside, and they started for Paris with the utmost speed of three lean post-horses.

---

[1] In the *Reminiscences*, T. C. dates this after the Paris visit ; but contemporary letters, etc., correct this.

XXII

TO PARIS AND BACK

(1824)

THEY took the common route, which history and Sterne's sentimental journey had made familiar—Montreuil, Noailles, Abbeville and so on. The second night on the road was spent at Beauvais. Strachey went inside occasionally, to let Kitty see the landscape, especially on the third day as they went through St. Denis, where Louis XVIII was lying in state. From there the drive was beautiful, yet hardly a vehicle or person met them ; which increased their surprise when they mounted Montmartre, and entered through the " iron-gate " of the custom-house, and suddenly beheld all Paris at their feet : " A deepish saucer of seven miles in diameter, not a breath of smoke or dimness anywhere, every roof and dome and spire and chimney-top clearly visible, and the skylights sparkling like diamonds." In spite of which the best remembered item between there and their hotel in town was the " curious speckled straw-hats " and dresses of the women in a fashionable street. With Kitty beside him, Carlyle had to see what interested her.

It was four o'clock on Saturday afternoon (23.10.1824) when they arrived. They roved about the boulevards till after dark, and then dined at a restaurant, their hotel providing bed and breakfast only. When the others retired Carlyle sat on the steps of the column in the Place Vendôme to enjoy the last cigar of the day. He heard martial noises round him as he was lighting up, and beheld with the pleasure of a schoolboy the military police of Paris parading to the sound of their drums, " clean, trim, handsome soldiers," in " blue-and-white." They swiftly separated into parties going in different directions, to " set the watch " in old-fashioned style, and the clangor of their drums faded in the distance.

There was more than the watch of the city old-fashioned

348

then. With few exceptions, the streets were dimly lit and narrow and crowded and unclean, and footpaths nowhere, so that there was " an everlasting press of carriages and carts and dirty people " in a hurry, shouting and jostling and stumbling.

Whether or not Mrs. Strachey had told her man about Jane Welsh, he played her game and was squire to Kitty most of their time in Paris, which gave Carlyle more leisure for sight-seeing. Together or singly, Strachey and he went out to purvey for dinners late and early. They were generally all together at table, occasionally joined by two young Irishmen, Emerson and Tennent, whom Carlyle had met in London, and another " favourite companion " of his, a half-pay officer, John Malcolm, better known in a year or two as a popular poet, but forgotten now. He had been in Wellington's army and received at Toulouse the wound that made him lame and was shortening his life. He had rushed into the army with the ardour of a boy ; and had strange things to tell. Here is one of his stories.

" No God, I tell you—and will prove it on the spot ! " shouted an older officer in the tent one evening. " How then ? " demanded Malcolm. The other turned his flask upside down. " Empty, you see ; we have no more rum." Then he held it up and prayed : " Fill us that ! " He paused and turned it bottom up again—" still empty you see," with a look of triumph.

There could not have been a more useful companion for Emerson and Tennent, who were on their way to fight for Greece, like Byron, and heeded little the opinions of those who like Carlyle considered the liberation of Greece no business of theirs. They did go on, but thanks to Malcolm maybe most of all, they came back soon and safe.

One evening Strachey took Carlyle to call on a Professor of Sanscrit, de Chézy, who had corresponded with him in India. He welcomed them heartily, but a language was lacking. Till lately Persian was in India like French in Europe, the language of gentlemen. So Strachey boisterously began with : " SALAAM," and a shrill-sounding string of words as mysterious to Chézy as to Carlyle. The Professor's Persian was as Parisian as Strachey's French was English. He politely tried it a little ; then dropped into French, addressing himself to Carlyle, who had to be interpreter. Strachey would not own to French at all in such company. It was an amusing twenty minutes. Chézy was

" glowing and emphatic " when he found a tongue. Strachey
said he had once described a rival as : " ce hideux reptile
de Langlès."

The opening lecture of Cuvier on Comparative Anatomy
was much admired by Carlyle, who " made out nine-tenths
of it " and wrote to his medical brother describing the
lecturer and his " look of sweetness and wisdom."

Legendre, " a tall, bony, gray old man," welcomed
Carlyle as the translator of his *Geometry*, and introduced
him to his niece who kept house for him. " How long are
you going to be in Paris ? " asked Legendre, and finding
it was to be so short a time, he " answered ' Diantre ! ' with
an obliging air of regret." He did what the time allowed—
took Carlyle along with him to the Institute, where he could
see many savants then famous, including the greatest,
Trismegistus Laplace, in " long blue silk dressing-gown,"
a fine model of elegant comfort as an indoor garment.
Laplace had " a dreamy smile," which was maybe due to
what there and then made " big Vauquelin the Chemist
fall sound asleep "—the session was " profoundly stupid "
—a paper was being read about silkworms by Majendie.
Legendre introduced the visitor to Dupin, " the famous
traveller," who was ready to introduce him to Laplace and
others, but he preferred to be a silent looker-on.

To another different Legendre he introduced himself
with success. He had a long talk about the Revolution
with the " solid butcher " Legendre, who had a handsome
share in it—the same who moved to hear Danton at the
bar of the Convention, when Robespierre arrested him, and
after the murder of Danton helped to finish Robespierre
and his Jacobins, and a few months later, Sansculottism
itself.[1]

At the Théatre Français he saw Voltaire's *Œdipe*, Talma
performing ; and when Talma said : " C'est nos craintes
qui ont formé les cieux " (our fears have shaped the heavens),
the audience rose up with a vehement shout of approval,
which was a sign of the times. " Unhappy France ! "
thought he, which was a sign of Carlyle. He never saw
Talma again, but did not forget him, declaring him in old
age : " incomparably the best actor I ever saw. Face like
a warming-pan for size," and expressive black eyes—" a
heavy, shortish, *numb-footed* man." This is his way of

[1] Carlyle's *French Revolution*, Part III, Book VI, Chaps. II and VII ;
Book VII. Chap. V.

describing the conscious composure traditional on the stage in Paris, perhaps. At any rate, his description of Talma might have been applied in every detail to Coquelin [1] seventy years afterwards.

With less admiration he saw two religious services—a " fool in hour-glass hat " at Ste. Geneviève's running about on his little stage, and in the Oratoire a Protestant performer equally hollow, on the death of Louis XVIII " Console-toi, O France " (France, be comforted) and so on.

Paris was placarded with official advertisements of a pamphlet by Châteaubriand—" Le roi est mort, vive le roi ! " (The King is dead, long live the King !) But Carlyle did not read it. He was much in the Louvre. One day he was alone there, " a row of wild Savoyards suddenly came storming past, with dishevelled hair and large besoms in hand, which they shoved out on any bit of paper or the like, distractedly proclaiming, ' Le Roi ! Le Roi ! ' and almost oversetting people to clear the way. Le roi, Charles X in person, soon appeared accordingly with three or four attendants : very ugly people, especially one who had blear eyes and small bottle-nose. Charles himself was a swart, slightish, insipid-looking man with the air of a gentle-man ; insipidly endeavouring to smile, and be popular, as he walked past ; sparse public indifferent to him, and silent nearly all. I had a real sympathy with the poor gentleman, but could not bring up the least *Vive le Roi*." He was going to look at a picture of a grandchild who might be heir to him one day, for indeed he was not young. He was not son but brother to Louis XVIII, and to Louis XVI also—the identical Monseigneur d'Artois " immortalised " in a history to be written ten years after now by the stranger watching him pass in the Louvre, wherein it is written how he did his country all the harm he could, as well as how he put his trousers on when he was leading the fashion. " He has breeches of a kind new in this world—a fabulous kind ; ' four tall lackeys,' says Mercier, as if he had seen it, ' hold him up in the air, that he may fall into the garment without vestige of wrinkle ; from which rigorous encasement the same four, in the same way, and with more effort, have to deliver him at night.' " Such was the divine being who ran away with the other divinities when the Bastille was taken ; and who was fated now after six years more to run away and cower into cover again. Meanwhile escorted by blear-

[1] Seen by D. A. W.

eyed bottle-nose and other ugly men he simpers through the picture gallery unheeded by the Parisian public, though to them of tragic importance.

To Carlyle he was a side-show. To walk about the streets was the best amusement. He felt like a boy at a fair, especially in such lively company as Tennent and Emerson, who were delighted to " do " the place with him. The Jardin des Plantes would interest anybody, and they often dined at the Palais Royal, where he bought a needle-case for each of his four sisters. He also got a present for Mrs. Welsh and a Molière for Jane, and doing as the rest were doing, would often drop into a tobacco shop and buy a cigar for a sou and walk out smoking. The mirrors in many public rooms amazed him. In writing to Jane, he described the hotel parlour : " About twenty feet square ; but glass and tinfoil spread it out into galleries like the Louvre ; and not one but twenty score of men are writing to you." He told his brother : " Looking glasses and trinkets and fricassees and gaming-tables seem to be the life of a Frenchman. I should think about fifty thousand dice-boxes are set a-rattling every night, especially on Sundays," in Paris.

One morning, Wednesday (27.10.1824), he was alone as he strolled about the famous Pont Neuf or old " New Bridge," where " jugglers and quacks, dandies and gulls and sharpers were racketing away." He went round by Notre Dame and turned aside into the Morgue ; and " there," he wrote to Jane, " lay the naked body of an old grey-headed artisan whom misery had driven to drown himself in the river ! His face wore the grim fixed scowl of despair ; his lean horny hands with their long ragged nails were lying by his sides ; his patched and soiled apparel with his apron and *sabots* (clogs) were hanging at his head ; and there fixed in his iron slumber, heedless of the vain din that rolled about him on every side, was this poor outcast stretched in silence and darkness forever. I gazed upon the wretch for a quarter of an hour ; I think I never felt more shocked in my life. To live in Paris for a fortnight is a treat ; to live in it continually would be a martyrdom."

So he was not sad to depart on Wednesday (3.11.1824). The weather was cooler, but still fine. There was much to see and nothing for Carlyle to do but to attend to Kitty. Strachey was factotum, though his French was threadbare. They reached Dover on the Saturday afternoon (6.11.1824). Mrs. Strachey and the Irvings by that time had gone home, and they waited only till their coach was ready. About nine or ten on Thursday Strachey and Kitty reached Shooter's Hill, where Carlyle caught a diligence which landed him for a shilling near the Irvings' house, in time to be welcomed before going to bed.

XXIII

THE SYMBOLIC HEN

(1824)

NEXT morning he was looking for lodgings, and in a day or two was settled in rooms, 25 Southampton Street, conveniently close to Irving's, where he often called and was always welcome, and where he was hoping he would soon see Jane Welsh as a visitor. Mrs. Strachey and Mrs. Montagu both knew better than to expect her, and Irving was embarrassed ; but to satisfy him Irving had sent her a kind of invitation. She knew better than to accept it ; and as he had said he was ready to " *help* " Carlyle " *to the uttermost* in his passage through life," she mischievously quoted this to Carlyle (10.11.1824),[1] and he answered :—

'Good Irving ! His thoughts are friendly, but he expresses them like a goose. "Help me to the uttermost !" If he can help himself to get along " the path through life," it is all that I shall ask of him. If his own shins are safe at the journey's end—a point on which there are many doubts—let him hang a votive tablet up, and go to bed in peace : I shall manage mine.'

The fears for Irving's future mentioned here were much in his mind. " Poor fellow ! He has his own trials awaiting him," he wrote some weeks later. These doubts were shared by other onlookers. Irving's popularity in the pulpit made other professional Christians envious and made anything dangerous which might give them a hold. More than usual he needed to be wary not to tolerate eccentricities in public performances or indulge in novelties of doctrine. His native fearlessness made him reckless, and his boundless belief in the Bible. A clever wife awake to danger might have saved him ; but he had no such good fortune. The next best thing Carlyle could see was to bring Mrs. Irving into closer communion with Mrs. Montagu, and to that he

[1] Printed in *Nineteenth Century Mag.*, January, 1914, p. 102.

applied himself in these later months in London,[1] with little but not altogether no success. Irving dedicated a volume of sermons to Mr. Montagu,[2] and Carlyle hoped his friend might be left to live and " cultivate his mind in peace and ray out a profitable mixture of light and darkness. There are many of warm hearts and half-cultivated heads who love him and admire him, and will stand by him," he wrote to a brother, declaring Irving " the best man I have met in England." To Jane, who was deriding the divine, he maintained :—

' He is a good man ; though he cannot speak or act one hour without cant, he really means to be sincere.

(As for himself he told her he did not want " a sinecure ") : —' It is no part of my plan to eat the bread of idleness, so long as I have the force of a sparrow left in me to procure the honest bread of industry. . . . I must divide my time between mental and bodily exercises ; if the latter could be turned to profit, I should regard the point as gained. Had I land of my own, I should instantly be tempted to become a— Farmer ! Laugh, but it is true. In one twelvemonth I should be the healthiest man in three parishes. This, you say, is Utopian dreaming. I am sorry that nothing half so likely to save me comes within the circuit of my capabilities : I must try to make the nearest possible approximation to it.'

When writing from Paris, he had asked her whether she would live with him in a country cottage. She now told him, No ! :—[3]

' All your faults are the effects of your isolated way of life. I am flattering myself that your *residence on the Continent* will have made you a bit of a Dandy. At least you will not speak Annandale, surely, after having *travelled*. It would be so delightful to find you about a hundredth-part as " elegant " as my amiable cousin (Captain Baillie) ! I am quite sure I should fall in love with you if you were.' (But she hastened to add a few days later, 18.11.1824) : ' I wish there was a glass window in my heart, that you might look into it. You can never know by words how much I love you.'

[1] Moncure Conway's *Thomas Carlyle*, pp. 227–33.
[2] Mrs. Oliphant's *Edward Irving*, at the end of Chap. IX.
[3] *Nineteenth Century Mag.*, January, 1914, pp. 101 and 103.

His letters to her reveal his mind undisguised :—

' If this pitiful book were off my hands' (which refers to
Schiller—he always tried to cultivate the habit of depre-
ciating his own performances to keep himself from pride)
' my fortune and circumstances shall be remodelled. ... The
want of health I am resolved to conquer. I *will not* sit
any longer with this infernal nightmare paralysing all my
faculties. A residence in the country, with quietness and
regularity, and fit succession of bodily and mental labour,
could not fail to set me quit of this quintessence of all curses.
... Life with all its difficulties and sickness is the problem to
solve. Occupation, the strenuous exertion of our faculties
in fulfilling the purposes of our conscience and will, I hold
to be the only panacea for the sufferings of a mortal. I
know it—strange that I should practise it so little ! ' . . .
' Freedom is the very life of man ! Let difficulties oppress
you as they please, do but satisfy your conscience that you
are straining every nerve to remedy them, and the very
search for peace, in some degree is peace.'

As soon as he was in rooms of his own, he set to work,
beginning by burning "all the trash of verses I could lay
my hands on." Then he gave three or four hours a day to
making a book of his articles on Schiller, for the first edition
of which he was to receive £90 on publication.[1] He read at
large for three or four hours more, and for the rest was
"walking about the dingy streets," paying calls and
meditating on Jane and the other items of his problem.
The fine French cooking had done his stomach no good,
and he returned without delay to the "rigorous practice
of the Badams system."

"A Magazine-hack" he said he would not be ; but
Wilhelm Meister was selling, and *Schiller* promised well.
Abundance of similar work appeared in sight. Good terms
were offered him for a *Life of Voltaire*, and he did not
worry about ways and means as much as Jane could have
wished.

"What is to hinder you settling yourself down within a
mile or two of London ? " she enquired,[2] ignoring his
suggestion for joint house-keeping.

[1] See *Early Letters*, 31.1.1825 ; II, p. 304 ; correcting *Reminiscences*,
II, p. 166.
[2] *Nineteenth Century Mag.*, January, 1914, pp. 101 and 103.

" If my beggarly health be improved, I may continue,"
he admitted, but explained in December :—

'I am sick, and must recover. Till then my mind lies
spellbound, the best of my talents (bless the mark !)
shut up even from my own view, and the thought of writing
anything beyond mere drudgery is vain. I must settle
within reach of Edinburgh or London.' . . .
    'If there be sleep and quiet and free air to be had on
earth, I will have them. The very sparrow earns for itself
a livelihood. Irving advises me to stay in London, not
knowing what he says. He himself has the nerves of a
buffalo, and forgets that I have not.'

One morning he was looking from his bedroom window
at the green and watched a pretty hen there going briskly
about and picking up whatever food was discoverable.
" See," he said to himself, " look, thou fool ! Here is a
two-legged creature with scarcely half a thimbleful of poor
brains ; thou callst thyself a man, with brain and reason,
and behold, how the one life is regulated, and how the other !
In God's name concentrate whatever reason thou hast,
and direct it on the one thing needful ! "
    He decided to take example from that " symbolic hen " and
go home to Annandale, and wrote to Jane (20.12.1824) :—

'Let us understand each other, if possible. I believe it
concerns the happiness of both that we do. My purpose is
to make *no* further changes in my situation, after the next
entire one, if I can by any means avoid them. *I would
labour for the sum-total of the future, though I commenced
at nothing, no longer for the day or the year that was passing
over me.*' [1]

It seems almost a shame to tell the rest of what is in
print—it was in German that he sent her " ten thousand "
kisses ; and how she translated that to her mother does not
appear. He had breathed the romantic air of Burns when
he was a boy, and now he was " returning to Nature."
    He outgrew ambition and wrote great books. But that
should not blind us to the comical self-conceit of the young
man resolving now that he would labour only " for the
sum total of the future "—as if any man could so direct

[1] Italics by D. A. W.

his actions ! It is easy to make too much of this. Such nonsense was in the air at the time even more than now. It was almost commonplace, and surely excusable in a love-letter. If a young fellow is not self-confident in handling a sweetheart who likes him, he is under par ; and that is the key to the voluminous love-letters still to come. He was like other young men, and might have sung Antonio's song in *Don Quixote.*

> " . . . Olalla, my Olalla !
> I praise you to the sky :
> When other girls abuse you,
> I give their beaus the lie.
> Let's to the church, Olalla !
> We'll make a happy two :—
> *The other girls will envy,—*
> *I'll wed and worship you !* "
> O Cock-a-doodle-doodle !
> O Cock-a-doodle-doo ! ! !

BOOK V

ROMANCE
1824–26

I

LONDON TOWN

(1824)

"AS a town," he wrote to Jane, "London is not worth looking at for above a week." He wrote to a brother :—

'Paris scarcely occupies a quarter of the ground, and does not seem to have the twentieth part of the business. O that our father saw Holborn in a fog ! with the black vapour brooding over it, absolutely like fluid ink ; and coaches and wains and sheep and oxen and wild people rushing on with bellowings and shrieks and thundering din, as if the earth in general were gone distracted. To-day I chanced to pass through Smithfield when the market was three-fourths over. I mounted the steps of a door, and looked abroad upon the area intersected with wooden pens for the cattle. What a scene ! Innumerable herds of fat oxen, tied in long rows, or passing at a trot to their several shambles ; and thousands of graziers, drovers, butchers, cattle-brokers with their quilted frocks and long goads pushing on the hapless beasts ; hurrying to and fro in confused parties, shouting, jostling, cursing, in the midst of rain and *shairn* [cattle-dung], and braying discord such as the imagination cannot figure. Then there are stately streets and squares, and calm green recesses, to which nothing of this abomination is permitted to enter. No wonder Cobbett calls the place a Wen. It is a monstrous Wen ! The thick smoke of it beclouds a space of thirty square miles ; and a million of vehicles, from the dog or cuddy-barrow to the giant waggon, grind along its streets for ever. I saw a six-horse wain the other day with, I think, number 200,000 and odds upon it !

'There is an excitement in all this, which is pleasant as a transitory feeling, but much against my taste as a permanent one. I had much rather visit London from time to time than live in it. There is in fact no *right* life in it that I can find : the people are situated here like plants in a hot-house, to which the quiet influences of sky and earth are never in their unadulterated state admitted. It is the case with all ranks : the carman with his huge slouch-hat hanging half-way down his back, consumes his breakfast of bread and tallow or hog's lard, sometimes as he swags along the streets, always in a hurried and precarious fashion, and supplies the deficit by continual pipes, and pots of beer. The fashionable lady rises at three in the afternoon, and begins to live towards midnight. Between these two extremes, the same false and tumultuous manner of existence more or less infests all ranks. It seems as if you were for ever in " an inn," the feeling of *home* is not known to one of a thousand. The necessaries of life are frequently adulterated, always' dear. . . . 'The blackguard population of the place is the most consummately blackguard of anything I ever saw. Yet the people are in general a frank, jolly, *well-living*, kindly people.'

He watched Mrs. Fry reading a chapter to females in Newgate, and saw two hundred male felons in their " stalls," of all kinds and ages, from sixty to eight. He remarked how like animals they looked, with their " gloating, callous, sensual countenances "—" they had never *thought* at all, they had only eaten and drunk and made merry." Their " sharpness was the cunning of a fox, their stubbornness was the sullen gloom of a mastiff. Newgate holds more human baseness than any other spot in the creation."

Mrs. Fry found goodness even there. He was only passing. The Londoners he had to look into closely were those in the trade he found himself drifting into—the men of letters, or the " Lights of London."

II

THE LIGHTS OF LONDON

(1824–5)

HAZLITT was absent on the Continent this winter. He had lately ceased to frequent the Montagus' *salon*, though much admired by Procter. Carlyle enquired about him from many ; but the anecdotes he heard in reply were like crackers, sparkling without giving light. He felt in the dark about Hazlitt. Procter himself on taking a wife this year was returning " in earnest " to his trade of Conveyancing, which seemed significant. Crabb Robinson, too, had lived upon the law.

Allan Cunningham and Carlyle had been drawn together whenever they met at Irving's. Though Cunningham was now a man of forty, successful in prose and verse, and " a genius of no common make," he was so modest that he seemed not to know that he was anything beyond a reading mason. He was a big man, straight and strong, " bright hazel eyes, open brow, sonorous hearty voice," and picked his way shrewdly through London life. Carlyle detested Scots ashamed of their country, would-be Cockneys ; and rejoiced to hear the accent of Cunningham, a Dumfriesshire man, who had been bred a mason, and as a child had witnessed Burns reading to his father " Tam O'Shanter." Except by reporting he had made little money by his writing, supporting a fine family by regular chisel work in Chantrey's studio and writing in hours of leisure.

Thomas Campbell was disappointing. But then, " he was my earliest favourite," Carlyle confessed, and perhaps he had expected too much. He found his hero at home " near the Edgware Road," a fashionable little dandy in blue frock coat and black wig, receiving him with a formal bow and " a belligerent expression " [1] in his " luminous " eyes. " He supposes I want him to help me in some way," thought Carlyle to himself, and quickly departed, which made

---

[1] W. Allingham, *A Diary*, p. 237.

their next meeting more agreeable. But they never unbent together. The " clipt accents " of the older man repelled the younger, and his air of fashion.

Nevertheless he may have been the " editor " who was one day walking with a " switch in his hand " down Regent Street in the company of Carlyle, and was thus addressed :—

' You poets have all of you mistaken the argument that you should treat. The past is too cool for this age of progress. Look at this throng of carriages, this multitude of men and horses, of women and children. Every one of these had a reason for going this way rather than that. If we could penetrate their minds, and ascertain their motives, an epic poem would present itself, exhibiting the business of life as it is, with all its passions and interests, hopes and fears. A poem, whether in verse or in prose, conceived in this spirit, and impartially written, would be the epic of the age.' [1]

This may have been told in kind explanation of the French Revolution book, by and by ; and at the time one can fancy how the older man was feeling shy. Carlyle was hurt and puzzled by the chilliness of his demeanour, but never suspected the likeliest reason. Campbell was quietly anti-clerical, and the intimacy between Carlyle and Irving would alone put the poet on the defensive. On this occasion he might have answered by the eastern proverb that none knows the feelings or thoughts of another. Anything said about these is a guess or a fiction. The passing crowd is as unfathomable as the abysms of space or time, and the man beside one moves away mysterious as a star.

Carlyle was comforted for Campbell's coldness by a letter from Goethe acknowledging his translation of *Wilhelm Meister*. " Conceive my satisfaction," he wrote to Jane at once (20.12.1824). " It was almost like a message from Fairy Land. But what says the letter ? Kind nothings, in a simple, patriarchal style. Transcribe my copy, and your own translation, that the same sheet may contain some traces of him whom I most venerate and her whom I most love."

He drew her attention now to a striking fact which bore

---

[1] *Cyclopedia of Literary and Scientific Anecdote*, by William Keddie (1854), p. 176.

upon their problem—the men of letters he could honour
were avoiding London :—

'Southey and Wordsworth have retired far from the din
of this monstrous city. So has Thomas Moore. . . . Leigh
Hunt writes "wishing caps" for the *Examiner*, and lives
on the lightest of diets at Pisa. But what shall I say of you,
ye—and all the spotted fry (small fish) that "report" and
"get up" for the public press, that earn money by writing
calumnies, and spend it in punch and other viler objects of
debauchery? Filthiest and basest of the children of men!
My soul come not into your secrets ; mine honour be not
united unto you! "Good Heavens!" I often inwardly
exclaim, "and is this the literary world?" This rascal
rout, this dirty rabble, destitute not only of high feeling
and knowledge or intellect, but even of common honesty.
The very best of them are ill-natured weaklings. They are
not red-blooded men at all. They are only things for writing
articles. But I have done with them for once. In railing
at them, let me not forget that if they are bad and worthless,
I, as yet, am nothing ; and that he who putteth on his
harness should not boast himself as he who putteth it off.
Unhappy souls! perhaps they are more to be pitied than
blamed. I do not hate them. I would only that stone walls
and iron bars were constantly between us.

'Such is the Literary World of London ; indisputably the
poorest part of its population at present. Among the
other classes of the people, I have met with several whom
I like considerably, and whose company still continues
to afford pleasure. The Montagus . . . the Stracheys . . .'
and so on.

One has to remember this was in a love-letter and bore
upon the practical question—where to live. There can be
no doubt of the truth of it. Even in public, Dickens and
Thackeray, Washington Irving and Balzac kept up the
chorus of curses on the "Garbages" who defiled their
"profession," which in public Carlyle did everything
possible to raise. But in writing to the woman he wanted
to marry him, he told her the truth, and the whole of it.

III

JANE WELSH'S ANSWER

(1825)

HER answer was womanly. She wanted him to stay in London, but did not say so till afterwards, and wrote now (3.1.1825) : " Tell me what plan you have *determined* on, and *then* I will tell you how I like it."

It was not convenient to be explicit. In spite of her love for Rousseau, she had none of Carlyle's eagerness to return to Nature, and accepted her mother's decision that he must make himself " a good match " before she could marry him. Her conscious ideal was vulgar ; it was to be a rich " lady " with a husband of genius ; and she was willing to wait indefinitely, dreaming of it ; but the only thing her young man was thinking of was what could be done in the immediate future. He was positively plebeian and matter-of-fact. The gist of much that passed might be put in the words of Burns—

> " Thou'rt aye sae free informing me,
> Thou hast nae mind to marry ;
> I'll be as free informing thee,
> Nae time hae I to tarry."

His warmth was not always screened in German. She had to skip occasionally in reading to her mother, or even mislay a letter now and then, which made her so emphatic in her admonitions to him to be reasonable that he sometimes destroyed a letter without sending it and wrote afresh.

At critical moments she referred to her mother before she replied ; but not so on this occasion apparently. She described how she had refused an invitation to " soothe and comfort " Captain Baillie, " the handsomest, most fascinating young man in England," who had abandoned the chase of a " rich widow," because she was to lose her income on remarriage. The Lancer remembered that his cousin's daughter had at least Craigenputtock, and might be a better match. So he wrote a letter of " fifteen pages " that was delivered at the same time as Carlyle's (20.12.1824),[1] to whom she reported :—

' You cannot think what an alarming whirl this Letter put my wits in. I was quite beside myself for about the space of one hour. In this critical situation I applied to Smith's *Moral Sentiments*, but the Devil was not to be cast out of me by abstract reasonings, and I was obliged to have recourse to Beethoven's most difficult Sonata, one of my last resources when I am fancy-possessed. It worked a miracle. I rose sound in mind, and wrote to my bewitching Cousin that I would not come. There now ! am not I a *prudent* creature after all ? If you knew what a dazzling host of temptations beleaguered the council-chamber of my thoughts, while the affair was in debate, you would wonder, I am sure, at the magnanimity of this decision.' [2]

Remembering what she had written about the eligible " Dugald G——," she reassured Carlyle about him too, and calculated this would keep him content awhile in London lodgings ; but he continued sick, and determined to finish *Schiller* and then go home, returning if not to Nature, at least to the country.

He was to stay awhile at Birmingham with Badams, whom he had been meeting occasionally at the Montagus' and who was eager to complete the cure. The best medical opinion now possible is that Badams was right in his treatment, prescribing warmth and exercise and a quiet country life. Carlyle's relatives seem to have felt sure of that from the first, and all along advised what in fact he did. One of the most welcome bits of news he ever sent to Mainhill was a letter (8.1.1825) to his farming brother Alexander, mentioning : " I am bent on *farming*, for the recovery of my health ; nay ' marriage ' itself is sometimes not out of my ulterior contemplation ! But I will explain when we meet."

He wrote to Jane next day.

[1] *Early Letters of J. W. Carlyle*, by D. G. Ritchie, p. 100.
[2] Letters, edited by A. Carlyle, *Nineetenth Century Mag.*, January, 1914, pp. 105–6.

IV

THE ENGAGEMENT BECOMES EXPRESS

(1825)

LOVE-MAKING is the commonest thing in the world, and there was nothing odd in what passed between Jane Welsh and Carlyle. The shabby use made of their letters by his biographer exposed their souls to critical dissection; but it was only by falsifying that curiosities could be produced. Inexperienced persons may long delight to dwell on these letters and see how he humoured his woman to the top of her bent, as any man may have to do and few have ever done better; but what concerns their history need not take long to tell. She had said Craigenputtock was without a tenant. So he wrote (9.1.1825) :—

'MY DEAREST,—

'I have somewhat to propose to you. You tell me, "*You* have land which needs improvement; why not work on that?" In one word then: Will you go with me, will you be my own for ever; and I embrace the project with my whole heart? Say Yes! And I send my brother Alick over to rent that Nithsdale Farm for me without delay; I proceed to it the moment I am freed from my engagements here; I labour in arranging it, and fitting everything for your reception; and the instant it is ready I take you home to my hearth, and my bosom, never more to part from me whatever fate betide us!

'If this scheme, the best for me and I think also for yourself, take effect, I look upon the recovery of my health and regular activity as no longer doubtful. I have lost them by departing from Nature. I must find them by returning to her. Depend upon it, Jane, this literature, which both of us are so bent on pursuing, will *not* constitute the sole nourishment of any true human spirit. Literature is the *wine* of life; it will not, cannot be its *food*. What makes Blue-stockings and Magazine-hacks? They neglect household

368

and social duties and enjoyments, and overlook the common blessedness laid out for *all*. So they become discontented and despicable, (like) Campbell, or wretched and dangerous, (like) Byron. Hinaus . . .! as the Devil says to Faust, (Out into the open field) ! There is no soul in these vapid "articles" of yours : away ! Be men before attempting to be *writers !*

'You, too, my Darling, are unhappy ; and ' unemployed, in short. 'O that I saw you, the model of wives, however widely your thoughts have wandered from that highest destination of even the noblest woman. I, too, have wandered wide and far ! Let us return, my Dearest ! Let us return *together !* Let us learn through one another what it is to live ; let us grow under the sunshine of Nature. . . . But I must leave these generalities, it is an earnest practical affair we are engaged in. The first point is funds. I have little to tell you that you do not know. My income though small might to reasonable wishes be sufficient ; were my health and faculties restored, it *might* become abundant. Shall I confess to you, my Dearest, this is a difficulty, which I imagine we are apt to overrate. The essentials of even elegant comfort are not difficult to procure : it is only vanity that is insatiable in consuming. And what is It to us, whether this or that Squire or Bailie be richer or poorer than we ?

'I will be a man in spite of the Destiny which so long has persecuted me. Yet it lies with you, my Dearest, whether I shall be a *right* man, or only a hard bitter Stoic. What say you, Jane ? Decide for yourself, and me ! Consent (and so on.)

'Speak, then, my Angel ! (And so on.) . . . Decide as you will, I am yours for ever,

'T. CARLYLE.'

The answer when it came was openly a joint epistle (13.1.1825.) :—

'MY DEAREST FRIEND,—

'I little thought that my joke about your farming Craigenputtock was to be made the basis of such a project. . . .

'You and I keeping house at Craigenputtock ! I would just as soon think of building myself a nest on the Bass Rock. Nothing but your ignorance of the place saves you from the imputation of insanity for admitting such a thought. Depend

upon it you could not *exist* there a twelvemonth. For my
part, I would not spend a month at it with an Angel. . . .
'You have sometimes asked me, did I ever think. For
once in my life at least, I have thought myself into a vertigo.
I will explain to you frankly. I love you, I have told you
so a hundred times ; but I am not *in love* with you. My
love is not a passion. It is a simple affection, a love which
influences, does not *make* the destiny of a life.
'Such temperate sentiments lend no false colouring, no
"*rosy light*" to your project. I see it such as it is' (as my
mother makes me see it, so to speak.) 'I do not wish for
fortune more than is sufficient for my wants ; my natural
wants and artificial ones. I will not marry on less, because
I conceive it a duty which every one owes to society, not
to throw up that station in it which Providence has assigned.
(And so on.)
'And now let me ask you, have you any *certain* livelihood
to maintain me in the manner I have been used to live in ?
Any *fixed* place in the rank of society I have been born and
bred in ? No ! Use the noble gifts which God has given
you ! Think of something else then, apply your industry
to carry it into effect, your talents to gild over the inequality
of our births ; and then—we will talk of marrying.' (As if
afraid she had gone too far, she hastened to add :) 'At
all events, I will marry no one else. This is all the promise
I can or will make. A positive engagement to marry I have
always considered ridiculous. . . . Such is the result of my
deliberations. You may approve or not ; but you cannot
persuade me. My decisions when I *do* decide are unalterable
as the Laws of the Medes and Persians. Write instantly
and tell me that you are content to continue my Friend
and Guardian—*and nothing more.*'

She concluded with the significant intimation that she
was writing with her " mother's sanction," and the assurance
she could never be happy without him.
This letter was handed in on Monday (17.1.1825), and
" pressing engagements " connected with *Schiller* kept him
busy till Thursday (20.1.1825), when he wrote a reply that
now overflows seven pages of print. By that time he had
mastered his wounded vanity, and was as cool as if he had
had a wife before, in telling her they must either part or be
engaged to marry soon. An admission that he had been
counting somewhat on her money can be explained by a

mistake of his when the love-letters are put under the intellectual miscroscope.[1] He supposed she and her mother were three or four times as rich as they were, living easily at the rate of about £700 a year, whereas they had barely £200 to spend, which shows how clever Mrs. Welsh had been in living up to the ideals of the Country-Town-Climbers or snobs on the social tread-mill. Her matrimonial manœuvring for her daughter was to that extent the usual game of bluff, a suspicion of which would explain why Rennie had shied off, and all the rich possibilities that sparkle through Jane's talk about the " offers " she had from Benjamin B——, Dugald G—— and Captain Baillie were subject to the proviso that the deal was carried through when the time came for settlements. Even Fyffe might have had an unpleasant surprise. It was no fault of Mrs. Welsh that no " settlements " were ever discussed. She seems to have meant the last letter to rid her of Carlyle, the interloper, and leave the way clear for a " better " match. He answered :—

' I must thank you for your candour. Your resoluteness I applaud. I also must be resolute. The miserable man is he who halts between two opinions, who " longs for the merchandise and will not part with the price."

' Your Letter shows that you have only an imperfect view of my present situation. For many months my conscience has been thundering : " Man ! thou art going to destruction. Thy nights and days are spent in torment. Up and rebuild thy destiny, if thou canst ! Up in the name of God who sent thee hither for other purposes than to wander to and fro bearing the fire of Hell in an unguilty bosom, to suffer in vain silence, and to die without ever having lived ! " Now I find my affection for you connected with whatever is holiest in my feelings or most imperative in my duties. It is necessary for me to know of you both what you will do and what you will not do. These settled, our line of conduct will be clear. I made this proposal deliberated for months and calmly decided on as the best for both of us. There was nothing in it of the love-and-cottage theory. . . .

' The maxims you proceed by are those of common and

---

[1] See *Love Letters*, I, p. 309. Taking "seven or eight thousand " as 7500, T. C.'s estimate of the household expenditure of Mrs. Welsh was between £625 and £750. Then see II, pp. 77, 111, and in particular 238-9, which gives T. C.'s summary on 26.2.1826 of the correspondence in the beginning of 1825.

acknowledged prudence, not unwise. But unless I adopt other than common maxims, I look upon my ruin as already sure. The stations from which we have looked at life are different. You have a right to anticipate excitement and enjoyment ; the highest blessing I anticipate is peace. You are bound to pay deference to others. I ' not so. ' This accounts for the wide discrepancy in our principles and intentions, and demands the serious study of us both.

' Now, my best friend, are you sure that you have ever formed to yourself a true picture of me, a man who has spent seven long years in *incessant* torture ? My patience with it is utterly gone, better to be dead than to continue it much longer. Even of my existing capabilities I can make no proper use till it is altered. These capabilities, I have long seen with regret, are painted in your kind fancy under far too favourable colours.' (One has to recall the habits of his pious childhood to realise this was sincere. Her exaggerated estimate of him was inconvenient in this argument, however agreeable in general. He went on :)

' I am not without a certain consciousness of the gifts that are in me ; but I should mistake their nature *widely* if I calculated that they would ever guide me to wealth and preferment, or even certainly to literary fame. As yet the best of them is very immature ; and if ever they should come forth in full strength, it must be to other and higher ends that they are directed. How then ? Would I invite a generous spirit out of affluence and respectability to share with me obscurity and poverty ? Not so. In a few months I might be realising from literature and other kindred exertions the means of keeping poverty at a safe distance ; the elements of real comfort, which in your vocabulary and mine I think has much the same meaning, might be at my disposal.

' Now this is what I would do. I would ask a generous spirit, of kindred to my own, to let us unite our resources, not her wealth and rank merely, but her judgment, her patience, prudence, her true affection, to mine ; and let us try if we could not rise above the obstructions that beset us both. *You* are such a generous spirit ; but your purposes and feelings are not such. Perhaps it is happier for you that they are not.

' This, then, is an outline of my fortune and principles. Both, I fear, are equally repulsive to you. I have thought of these things till my brain was like to crack. I do not pretend to say that my conclusions are indubitable ; I am still open to better light ; but this is at present the best I have.' (Here is a pretty touch of artless *natural* cunning, an invitation to parley, tempting to a woman.) 'Do you also think of all this ; not in any spirit of anger. Good God ! Why should we be angry ? Are we not alone in the world, each almost without a single counsellor save the other ? Let us, my dearest, unite our experience, and sit in judgment on the interests of both. And, if we must part (which may the God that made us both forbid !) let us part in tenderness, with the last kiss of love upon our lips. (And so on) . . . O my dearest, you *are* dear to me. (And so on). . . .

'Write what you think. But decide nothing rashly ; let us postpone it till I see you in Scotland. Why if we love each other, should not everything be well ? To your Mother, return my thanks. What I think of her, you know better than she does, and it is needless to repeat it here.' (Better not, indeed ! This is delicious, the only possible bit of humour in the letter, and maybe unintended. Mrs. Welsh was to discover next year how well he had taken her measure. He continues cheerfully :)

'I will not end in tragedy. Is that farm of yours *really* to be let ? And where is it, and who has the letting of it ? My brother and I have long had a scheme of conjoint farming ; and I feel more and more the essentialness of something like it to my recovery. You have no notion of my tolerance of places. After being every night for many years disturbed in my sleep by the noise of cities, and stunned and choked every day by their tumults and their smoke, *any* thing with green grass upon it and blue skies above it has the air of Paradise to me. Now, write, my Dearest ! Be good to me if you can. Yours wholly and ever,

'T. CARLYLE.'

Her reply was equally voluminous, and this time single-handed. Of course he had entirely failed to understand her letter, and there had never been any reason for him to feel hurt. She declined to believe he had been serious in talking of parting—it must have been metaphorical. "How could I *part* from the only living soul that understands me ? I would marry you to-morrow rather !" Of course her wishes were nothing but pure reason. "It certainly was not wealth or rank according to *my* views which I required you to attain. I merely wish to see you earning a *certain* livelihood, and exercising the profession of a gentleman," indifferent " whether you have hundreds or thousands a year." (Even that requirement he was now to understand figuratively.) " My tenderness for your feelings betrayed me into insincerity. I had some view towards an improvement in my sentiments towards you." (In short, though not in love I'm going towards it. More delicately perfect praise was seldom written than what follows.) " One loves you, as Madame de Staël said of Necker, in proportion to the ideas and sentiments which are in oneself ; according as my mind enlarges and my heart improves, I become capable of comprehending the goodness and greatness which are in you, and my affection for you increases. Not many months ago I would have said it was impossible that I should ever be your Wife ; at present, I consider this the most probable destiny for me. And in a year or two, perhaps, I shall consider it the only one." She concluded bidding him think no more of Craigenputtock, and write to her " immediately something to make me less unhappy."

Which of course he did, on the very day it came (31.1.1825), declaring it the best letter she had ever sent him, and " the most delightful piece of news " he could have got. He blessed the " sickening *cold* " which had kept him at home, because he thus received her letter a little sooner than if he had gone out with Irving as arranged that Monday. His work on Schiller had just been finished, and he must have given much of the day to his long epistle to Jane. It told her little she had not heard before, and might be summarised as : " Cock-a-doodle-doo ! " and " O, won't we be joyful ! " Yet it pleased her so well that she assured him that he was welcome to Scotland, though she had wished him to stay where he was. " Indeed, it would be difficult for you to do anything that could make me doubt the propriety of your judgment.

" Here am I blushing like an idiot whenever your name is mentioned, so that anybody who looks at me may read the whole matter in my face ; and then to be *half-engaged* ! I who have such a natural horror at engagements ! It gives me asthma every time I think of it. And yet, ce que j'ai fait, je le ferais encore (I'd do the same thing over again.) I cannot say this of much else that I have done in my day."

She used to date their engagement from the end of January, 1825.

V

WHY "SCHILLER" WAS PUBLISHED ANON

(1825)

HIS letters show he did not put his name to *Schiller* when it came out as a book from conscious modesty, holding himself back from the self-assertion and lust of glory which he saw around him, damaging even the good. His mother had to be reassured, and was told his authorship was no secret :—

'If any one lay it to my charge, I shall' admit it. 'Sometimes of late I have bethought me of some of your old maxims about pride and self-conceit : I do see this same vanity never fails to wither out the good and worthy parts of a man's character, and leave him poor and spiteful. There never was a wiser doctrine than that of *Christian humility*, considered as a corrective for the coarse unruly selfishness of men's nature.'

To Jane he was more explicit about the particular form of vanity which might be too tempting to themselves. Here is from the letter of 31.1.1825, rejoicing and praising her when she consented to become " engaged " :—

' "Fame! "—the very sound of it is distressing to my ears. O that I could show you the worshippers of it whom I have met with here ! To see how the shallow spirits of these Scribes are eaten up by this mean selfish passion ; how their whole blood seems to be changed by it into gall, and they stand hissing like as many rattlesnakes each over his own small, very small, lot of that commodity ! I swear to you I had rather be a substantial peasant that ate my bread in peace and loved my fellow-mortals, though I scarcely knew that my own parish was not all the universe, than one of these same miserable metre-ballad-mongers,[1] whose heart is dead or worse, for whom creation is but

[1] Shakespeare, *King Henry IV*, Part I, Act III, Scene I.

a mirror to reflect the image of his own sorry self and still sorrier doings ! '

Or, in other words, the seekers of fame subside into the stupid rabble who fail to enjoy the drama of the Universe because they take no interest in it beyond their own parts. The incidental quotation is from a favourite passage of Shakespeare—there was something of Hotspur in Carlyle. The letter continued :—

' There is a passage in this *Schiller* (by himself) which, if you make many words, I will force you to get by heart, Madam, and repeat every day along with your devotions ! *It is my very creed, expressed with Schiller's eloquence.'* [1]

And therefore worth quotation, at least as far as it used to be quoted in years to come. The reference to " devotions " was of course a joke :—

' The artist, it is true,' says Schiller, ' is the son of his age ; but pity for him if he is its pupil, or even its favourite ! Let some beneficent Divinity snatch him when a suckling from the breast of his mother, and nurse him with the milk of a better time ; that he may ripen to his full stature. And having grown to manhood, let him return, a foreign shape, into his century ; not, however, to delight it by his presence ; but terrible, to purify it. The Matter of his works he will take from the present ; but their Form from the absolute unchanging unity of his own nature.

' But how is the Artist to guard himself from the corruptions of his time, which on every side assail him ? By despising its decisions. *Let him look upwards to his dignity and his mission, not downwards to his happiness and his wants.*[1] Free alike from the vain activity, that longs to impress its traces on the fleeting instant ; and from the discontented spirit of enthusiasm, that measures by the scale of perfection the meagre product of reality, let him leave to *common sense*, which is here at home, the province of the actual ; while *he* strives from the union of the possible with the necessary to bring out the ideal. This let him imprint and express in fiction and truth, imprint it in the sport of his imagination and the earnest of his actions, imprint it in all sensible and spiritual forms, and cast it silently into everlasting Time.'

[1] Italics added.

Which shows that if Carlyle did not now fling himself into fictioneering like another Goethe or Schiller, Scott or Dickens, it was not because he thought it wrong, but for the very reason that prevented him writing poetry in imitation of Burns or Byron, namely, because he found on trial that he had not the knack of it.

How could he think it wrong ?   Fiction and poetry meant at first the same, and Sidney's *Defence of Poesy* would to-day be better described as a Defence of Fiction.   The truth of fiction lies in truth of type, illustrating right principles by examples and holding the mirror up to Nature.   The best of the Bible of the world, from the parables of Christ and *Æsop's Fables* to Shakespeare and *Don Quixote* and *Gulliver's Travels*, is what used to be called correctly the " true fiction " of it.

The best of all writing is where general truth is conveyed in types which are true in details.   Thus a reliable history or even book of anecdotes may be better than any " invention," and that was the kind of writing to which Carlyle was being led.   " If I can find nothing better to do," he wrote to a brother (14.2.1825), " I will write a whole string of such books " as *Schiller* or the *Life of Voltaire* proposed to him in London.   " Literary fame is a thing which I covet little ; but I desire to be *working* honestly in this business, which has now become my trade."

VI

EVENTS BY THE WAY

(1825)

IN February, as Irving was begging one "week of talk,"
he went to live in his house and was persuaded to make
the one week two. He had to abandon hopes of bringing
Mrs. Irving under Mrs. Montagu's influence, and delivering
her from fanaticism. He was made to feel instead that she
and it were separating him from his friend. They had
to taboo so much that they were drifting apart in spite of
themselves.

One day they called at the Admiralty Office in Parliament
Street, where Irving had an appointment not on Admiralty
business. An "Honourable Somebody" who had to attend
there for a salary wanted to expound to him a "sublime
new idea in Scripture Prophecy."

The "Honourable Somebody" eagerly talked away,
his wrinkled features "smiling and shuttling about at
a wonderful rate," polite but silly, as if crazed. Irving
responded in a lively style; but his companion sat apart
in silence, without even the affectation of interest, and as
they were walking home asked Irving:

"Do you really think that gentleman can throw any
light to you on anything whatever?"

Irving, stoutly: "Yes, I do." The Bible believer was
losing his way in the labyrinths of Revelations. They had
to agree to differ, and on Sunday (27.2.1825), in saying
good-bye to Carlyle departing in the coach for Birmingham,
Irving insisted on adding his "blessing."

Carlyle remained about a fortnight in Birmingham, but
he could not cheapen knives there, to oblige his mother.
He wrote to his brother to tell her (4.3.1825),—"I am a bad
merchant anywhere. The people seem to read in my face
that I cannot haggle or beat down their prices; so they
almost always overcharge me."

It is one of Nature's compensations that in proportion as we believe the gospel of grab, we grow blunter and blunter in brain. The man of great mind is instinctively careless about material needs and apt to disregard them overmuch, which is why Asia still adores the intellectual aspect of the ascetic ideal, and calls the European leaders—pigs. Thus it was that Carlyle, the acutest mind in Britain in 1825, might have been beaten in cheapening knives in Birmingham by the bluntest there, who was not even a member of the Exchange or a shopkeeper, but a neighbour of Badams, and survives in history anon, a lively and healthy but dirty man, half-idiot, half-beggar. He never washed, and his face was bristled like the hide of a boar. His breeches were slit at the sides, and flapping like aprons. Assailed one day by the eloquence of a critic, he responded superbly like a royal Adonis to the rabble, or, if permissible to say so, a Prime Minister to the Opposition, in words that floated through an open window to the quick ears of Carlyle who remembered them for fifty years : " Damn thee, I's an ornament to Society in every direction ! "

Carlyle had suggested to Jane that it would be good for them to " practice sincerity more and more towards one another." Accordingly on the day after reaching Birmingham (28.2.1825), he had written to her everything in his mind without reserve, and she now (13.3.1825) began to reciprocate in reply, deploring what she called " the miserable perversion of my own sentiments " which hindered her from letting herself go in frank affection. Soon she was writing in the style which makes her letters among the pleasantest ever printed, and all the more so because not meant for print.

Mrs. Montagu had given him a seal as a souvenir, and Mrs. Strachey a gold pencil. The kindness of these two ladies went to his heart and made him like London better than Edinburgh. The remark is as old as Erasmus that the sweetness of the women is the best of England's attractions. On his fourth day in Birmingham (3.3.1825), there came to him a *new* present from Mrs. Strachey—most likely cousin Kitty's, modestly sent in her name—the " most superb writing desk he had ever seen—which must have cost about twenty guineas." His name was engraved on one handle, and his favourite motto in Latin—Freedom, Truth, Poverty—on the other. There was no reason to suppose the gifts were intended as wedding presents, but nothing to prevent him using them as such. He gave them to Jane without delay. Poor Kitty !

On the way north, he stayed some days at Manchester, which was new to him ; and walked to Oldham, where he was welcomed by an old schoolfellow, a curate there, " very stupid but very kind." Then over the Yorkshire Moors he walked to Marsden, to see another " boy-and-college-friend," George Johnston, a surgeon. His youngest sisters, Jean and Jenny (14 and 11), were daily watching the coach from Carlisle as it came to Ecclefechan ; and on Saturday, (19.3.1825), they met him there, recognising him with radiant looks whenever he let down the coach window.

VII

THE CLEARING TIME

(1825)

HIS father had taken for him the farm of Hoddam Hill, on the Ecclefechan to Annan road and not far beyond his old school by Hoddam Bridge. His brother Alexander was to be farmer and his mother to attend to the women's side of affairs, with a maid and some of her younger daughters. The house was big enough to let him have two rooms for himself. Till the day of entry near the end of May, Mainhill was head-quarters, but in a week or two he was off to Edinburgh and Haddington.

He had a choice of work, and ended by agreeing to do for Tait some volumes of translations of German Romance, to be selected by himself. This meant reading scores of fictions in search of materials. Some forty volumes were collected in Edinburgh at once, and more requistioned from Germany. Perhaps he never read so much fiction in his life as in the year impending, 1825-6 ; but it suited him —there is a time for all things.

In commercial gambling there was a boom then, and Brewster was contemplating a periodical to be brought out by Tait, himself to do the Science of it, and Politics and Literature divided between Lockhart and Carlyle, who were to go equal shares with him ; but nothing was settled now, and Carlyle left everything to Brewster. The project might have taken shape, but that Lockhart before the year was out had become the well-paid editor of the Tory *Quarterly Review*. His father-in-law, Sir Walter Scott, who had helped to start it in 1809, was now at his highest point of glory, and Lockhart was as sincere a Tory as if he had been born a German King or English Lord. It is noticeable that Carlyle was nevertheless willing to go in harness with him and with Brewster, who was a simple creature in spite of his Science. The reason was that he trusted both and never made the modern mistake of personifying a periodical, and supposing it more than a means of publication. He felt responsible for no more than he wrote himself. It was now that he made acquaintance with Lockhart's friend, Sir William Hamilton,[1] a history professor he had long admired at a distance, and who broke the ice by speaking to him in the Advocates' Library. Another new acquaintance was a Dr. Julius (Yoolioos) of Hamburg, an official over on business about Quarantine and a man of letters, who almost embraced him as a son might a father because he had written a *Life of Schiller* and translated Goethe's novel, and handsomely undertook at once to write and soon was writing to him at length from Hamburg about the German books among which he was searching for stuff to translate.

He could only give the good Julius an hour, and had no leisure then for the country walks to which Hamilton invited him. Most of his time till the first week in May was spent in Mrs. Welsh's house in Haddington. Here is an accidental glimpse into it, in a letter from Jane Welsh to Bess Stodart, dated 11th April.[2] The Catherine named was a sister of the Dugald who had proposed to marry Miss Welsh. Last summer she had " finished " at an English boarding-school, and from the beginning of winter she had been staying with the Welshes, receiving lessons in music and drawing, French and Italian, to say nothing of needle-work and family life—a kind of paying guest, it is easy to guess. As for what follows, in the absence of other evidence, readers must discount to please themselves. Thus was it written :—

' Who do you think is living at the George Inn, and here every day ? *Himself!* Mr. Benjamin B——! Had anybody told me some months ago that this thing would come to pass, I believe I should have leaped over the moon for very gladness ; but " times are changed and we are changed in them." Oh ! It would have done your heart good to have seen how I received him.

' It was half-dark when he came ; my mother and Catherine were working at the window, and I was talking with Mr Carlyle by the fireside ; conceive my astonishment at so unlooked-for an apparition ! *Himself* suddenly stood before

[1] See, in addition to *Thomas Carlyle's Letters*, the *Memoir of Sir William Hamilton*, by John Veitch, pp. 113–26.
[2] *Early Letters of J. W. Carlyle*, by D. G. Ritchie, pp. 106–10.

me, all smiles and cordiality, and held out his hand. I
opened my eyes very wide, but my heart beat no faster ;
I rose deliberately from my seat, and made him such a
deliberately ceremonious curtsey that I almost threw myself
off my balance. He looked—just as *I* did when he passed
me on the Waterloo Bridge ; and I felt that I was
revenged !

'He was come, he said, to reside among us for some time,
to recruit his strength ; he had been ill—confined to bed
for three months. It was necessary that he should leave
town, and his acquaintance with us and Dr. Fyffe had induced
him to fix on Haddington as the place of his retreat. How
damned odd ! This curious annunciation was addressed to
my mother.

'I kept talking to Mr. Carlyle all the while about the Peak
of Teneriffe. Meanwhile the tea-kettle commenced a song
"*most musical, most melancholy,*" which quite distracted my
mother's attention ; she would not believe such sounds
could be produced by a mere tea-kettle. Mr. C. lifted it to
convince her of the fact ; he replaced it again. He tried
it in various positions, but the kettle would not be prevailed upon. "It was chagrined," he said, and so was
Mr. B——.

'He talked for two hours, however, with a miraculous
command of absurdity, and then departed, after promising
to be exceedingly troublesome to us. I behaved to him then,
and every time I have seen him since, in the most *pococurante*
manner imaginable. I suspect he will soon be convalescent
enough to return to the city. What a winding up of our
romance ! I would never have imagined that three years
could have so metamorphosed any human being ; from a
frank-hearted, tasteful, promising young man, he is grown
into a perfect personification of vanity and emptiness.
N'importe ! (No matter !) It is but one more bubble
melted into thin air !

'*Speaking of bubbles*, I do not go to London this season
either, for reasons which I have not room to explain. It
is not Mr. Irving's fault *this* time.'

This is enough to let us sympathise with Jane's difficulty
in writing to Carlyle sincerely unreserved, and everybody
in Haddington knew more than he did of the true story
of Dr. Fyffe, who eyed him askance whenever they met,
but was hardly noticed.

Carlyle was opener about past " affairs "—at least he had to promise he would love her more dearly than he had ever loved Margaret Gordon ; and when she told him what she thought fit to tell about her mother's financial worries, he made her promise that before they met again she should have delivered him from the painful thought of loving an heiress. She kept her promise. To please Carlyle, she gave her mother the Haddington house and everything there, and the life-rent of Craigenputtock. To please herself, she left Craigenputtock to Carlyle by a will, and told him so. She proudly said when all was done : " My money affairs are all arranged ; and now I am as poor as yourself." He thought he could reckon on affording £200 a year for their expenses. She said she was sick of Haddington and that would do ; and both of them as if by instinct minimised attention to money details, to an extent that those who mishandled their papers were never able to realise.

Another thing they settled before he finally returned to Edinburgh early in May. She was no longer to write to him under her mother's eye, or be required to read aloud his letters to her.

As she could not be always writing to Carlyle, however, and suffered from idleness, she begged him to start a correspondence between her and Mrs. Montagu. He could not refuse her ; and after going home, he wrote to Mrs. Montagu accordingly (20.5.1825) :—

(He confessed he despaired of bringing Mrs. Irving into her circle.) ' But ill-success in this attempt does not deter me from a new one. You know Miss Welsh of Haddington, if not in name, at least in character and from her friends. I was with her at her mother's when you wrote to me. Jane knew the writer by repute, in short, admired and liked the letter, and begged of me to let her keep it.

'She asked would you not write to *her*. I engaged to try, and now will you ? Can you ?

'This young lady is a person whom you will love . . . ardent, generous, gifted . . . but without models. (And so on.) It was Mr. Irving's wish, and mine, and, most of all, her own, to have you for her friend, that she might have at least one model to study. Separated by space, could you draw near to one another by the imperfect medium of letters ? Jane thinks it would abate the " awe " which she must necessarily feel on first meeting with you personally. She wishes it ; I also if it were attainable ; is it not ? ' [1]

Good-natured Mrs. Montagu was persuaded, supposing Miss Welsh to be young and plastic, whereas she was turning twenty-four and older than her years. The correspondence that follows gives a sober history the excitement of romance.

[1] *Thomas Carlyle*, by Moncure Conway, pp. 231-2.

2 c

VIII

PEACE AT HODDAM HILL

(1825–6)

JANE wanted to correspond with Mrs. Strachey too, but Carlyle knew better. Mrs. Strachey was religious, and Jane had been brought up to think so freely that she had had unalloyed enjoyment in reading Gibbon's mockery of Christian legends which once distressed Carlyle himself.

With her mother's consent she was to visit him at Hoddam Hill, which might become their home ; and his letters describe in loving detail its glorious surroundings :—

' " But then Society ? "—there is little of it on Earth, very little : and unhappy is the man whose own door does not enclose what is worth all the rest of it ten times told. My own Jane ! You cannot think how I rejoice that your tastes in this point correspond so completely with my own.

' James Johnstone, the meek pedagogue of whom you have heard me speak, wishes a school. Will you walk over any day and ask Gilbert Burns if there *is* to be a Parish School in Haddington, and when and how.'

In three weeks she had news for him (13.6.1825) : [1]—

' I have enquired about the Parish School. There is to be one ; but not for a twelvemonth. The house taken for the purpose will not be ready till then. If your friend is not settled by that time, there is little doubt of his getting it ; for Gilbert Burns, who has most to say in the business, has promised me to support any person recommended by you. God bless you, my darling. I am yours for ever and ever, JANE WELSH. Write *instanter*.'

As of course he did ; but let this suffice (24.6.1825), referring to the visit she was to pay :—

' I will take you to the top of Burnswark, and wander with

---

[1] *Nineteenth Century Mag.*, 1914, pp. 320-22.

you up and down the woods and lanes and moors, and talk of all things new and old. Earth, sea and air are open to us here as well as anywhere ; the Water of Milk was flowing through its simple valley as early as the brook Siloa, and poor Repentance Hill (or Hoddam Hill) is as old as Caucasus itself. There is a majesty and mystery in Nature, take her as you will ; the essence of all poetry comes breathing to a mind that feels, from every province of her empire. Is she not immoveable, eternal and immense, in Annandale as she is in Chamouni ? The chambers of the East are opened in every land, and the sun comes forth to sow the earth with Orient pearl ; Night, the ancient Mother, follows him with her diadem of stars ; and Arcturus and Orion call *me* into the infinitudes of space as they called the Druid Priest or the Shepherd of Chaldea. Bright creatures ! How they gleam like spirits, through the shadows of innumerable ages, from their thrones in the boundless depths of heaven !

> " Who ever gazed upon them shining,
> And turned to earth without repining,
> Nor wished for wings to flee away,
> And mix with their eternal ray ? "

(This was from their common favourite, Byron. He goes on :) '*I* have, twenty times ; though now and then also I have *not*. Would *you* go with me ? Come, and let us consult. It is many a weary year since I have been so idle or so happy. I have not done two sheets of *Werter* yet ' (and dropped it altogether presently, but did the *Travels of Wilhelm Meister*, and added now :) 'I read Richter and Jacobi, and like Basil Montagu am " a lover of all quiet things." '

He always remembered with unusual pleasure the time now passing. "These were among my happiest hours," he said to Espinasse, "spent in the company of poetic, genial men." [1] In his old age (12.10.1875), he told Allingham that he found Goethe's *sprüche* (weighty sayings) very hard to translate. " I found when I was translating from the German writers that each man has *a tune* : Goethe has his ; Richter has his, and, when I got into it, all went on well. That was the pleasantest kind of work I ever did. I could do it in any mood—like basket-making.

---

[1] *Literary Recollections* by F. Espinasse, p. 209.

Goethe's style is by far the most refined and difficult to render." [1]

His memory was not misleading him. The most intimate contemporary letters confirm what he wrote after forty years :—

'With all its manifold troubles, this year at Hoddam Hill has a rustic beauty and dignity to me ; and lies now like a not ignoble, russet-coated Idyll in my memory ; one of the quietest on the whole, and perhaps the most triumphantly important of my life. I lived very silent, diligent, had long solitary rides—on my wild Irish horse " Larry," good for the *dietetic* part ;—my meditations, musings and re-flections were continual ; thoughts went wandering, or travelling, through Eternity, through Time, and through Space, so far as poor I had scanned or known ; and were now to my endless solacement, coming back with *tidings* to me ! This year I found that I had conquered all my scepticisms, agonising doubtings, fearful wrestlings with the foul and vile and soul-murdering Mud-gods of my Epoch ; had escaped, as from a worse than Tartarus, with all its Phle-gethons and Stygian quagmires ; and was emerging, free in spirit, into the eternal blue of ether, where, blessed be Heaven, I have, for the spiritual part, ever since lived, looking down upon the welterings of my poor fellow-creatures, in such multitudes and millions, still stuck in that fatal element ; and have had no concern whatever in their Puseyisms, Ritualisms, Metaphysical controversies and cobwebberies ; and no feeling of my own, except honest silent pity for the serious or religious part of them, and occasional indignation, for the poor world's sake, at the frivolous, *secular* and impious part, with their Universal Suffrages, their Nigger Emancipations, Sluggard-and-Scoundrel Protection Societies, and " Unexampled Prosper-ities," for the time being ! What my pious joy and gratitude then was, let the pious soul figure. In a fine and veritable sense, I, poor, obscure, without outlook, almost without worldly hope, had become independent of the world ;— what was death itself, from the world, to what I had come through ? I understood well what the old Christian people meant by their " Conversion," by God's Infinite Mercy to them : I had, in effect, gained an immense victory ; and, for a number of years had, in spite of nerves and chagrins,

[1] W. Allingham, *A Diary*, p. 239.

a constant inward happiness that was quite royal and
supreme ; in which all temporal evil was transient and
insignificant ; and which essentially remains with me still,
though far oftener *eclipsed*, and lying deeper *down*, than
then. Once more, thank Heaven for its highest gift. I
then felt, and still feel, endlessly indebted to *Goethe* in
the business ; he, in his fashion, I perceived, had travelled
the steep rocky road before me—the first of the moderns.
Bodily health itself seemed improving; bodily health was
all I had really lost, in this grand spiritual battle now
gained ; and that too, I may have hoped, would gradually
return altogether,—which it never did, and was far
enough from doing ! Meanwhile my thoughts were very
peaceable, full of pity and humanity as they had never
been before. Nowhere can I recollect of myself such pious
musings ; communings, silent and spontaneous, with Fact
and Nature, as in these poor Annandale localities. The
sound of the Kirk-bell, once or twice on Sunday mornings—
from Hoddam Kirk, about a mile off on the plain below me—
was strangely touching, like the departing voice of eighteen
hundred years. . . .'

This recalls the best of the sayings of Buddha : " There
was nothing but misery in the Philosophies, and I did not
believe them. I sought only the Truth, and saw Peace
within me."

" Beware, O Teufelsdröckh, of Spiritual Pride ! " Beware, indeed ! It is not exclusively a Christian failing.
" Nothing is pleasanter," wrote Lucretius complacently,
" than to reach and remain upon the heights secure and
serene, which have been raised by the learning of the wise,
and from which you look down and see your fellows straying
in all directions seeking the path of life."

" There is no single path for all," say the wiser sages of
China, and Confucius carefully included this in their Bible,
in words as old as the oldest part of ours : " To have
learned that there is no one way is the way of the wise.
There is no invariable mark of Goodness, no eternal Model.
A superlative care for right-doing is the one thing needful.
You find it when behaviour is in harmony with the steady
voice of conscience. Heaven has given a conscience to
each of the crowd. If only they complied with it, their
conduct would show that the inner conscience was always
right. To make them quietly obey it is the business of

Government." There in a nutshell is the gist of all the teaching of Carlyle. That he had to disentangle and discover this for himself is the secret of his significance. On the spiritual plateau at Hoddam Hill, he found the hardest of his work was over. Most of the original thoughts in *Sartor* occurred to him as he looked around him there ; but none can trace the seeds of that spiritual garden. The Hebrews would have said " God spoke to him." Suffice it for us to know he now was filled with the peace which passeth understanding. " The Kingdom of Heaven is within you."

IX

MRS. MONTAGU INTERVENES

(1825)

MRS. MONTAGU had written to Jane Welsh whenever Carlyle suggested it. " What on earth did
you say to make her so good to me ? " Jane asked him,
reporting the correspondence begun. " She could not have
written more frankly and affectionately if I had been her
own child. I have never met with anything like this
from woman before." [1] She answered with effusion, of
course.

What emerges from *all* the letters is that Carlyle had not
told Mrs. Montagu the secrets of his heart and Edward
Irving had, so that she supposed she had to deal with an
enthusiastic girl, who had been in love with Irving, and
might be so still. Mrs. Montagu had no suspicion she was
writing to an experienced damsel of twenty-four, who had
been casting her bait about among eligible fishes for more
than half a dozen years.

In innocent simplicity Mrs. Montagu wrote to Carlyle
(30.5.1825) :—

' In writing to Miss Welsh I have had a task of considerable difficulty. " Her heart is in England, her heart is not
there," and I feared to be the means of stirring an old
flame. If Miss Welsh were to pass one week with me, she
might be satisfied that to be Mr. Irving's wife would—to a
spirit of her tone—be entire and unmixed misery : they
are not the least fitted to each other. Come back to us,
when you are well, for with all our faults we are not undeserving of you entirely.'

This led to an allusion in his last letter (24.6.1825),
alarming to Jane, who admonished him (3.7.1825) to keep
Mrs. Montagu's letter for her to read when she visited

[1] *Nineteenth Century Mag.*, 1914, p. 321.

him, "so take care you do not light your pipe with it,"
adding :—

'She will surely be satisfied *now* that there is no worm
of disappointment preying on my " damask cheek " ; for I
have told her in luminous English that my heart is *not* in
England, but in Annandale.'

In a hurried letter (19.7.1825) reporting complete the
legal circumlocutions whereby she divested herself of her
property in favour of her mother, Jane added a postscript :—

'I had *two* sheets from Mrs. Montagu, the other day,
trying to prove that I knew nothing at all of my own
heart ! Mercy ! How romantic she is ! Write presently to
Templand.'

Three or four days later she came to Templand with her
mother, and found awaiting her a letter from Mrs. Montagu
which made her miserable for a week, and has been so
much distorted [1] that the " operative part " of it must be
reproduced :—

'MY DEAR MISS WELSH,—
      'There is now before me on my table a beautiful
green Mandarin basin. It is to me *valueless ;* it will not
hold water. Notwithstanding its elegance, *it has a flaw in
it.* And this illustrates my feeling of the truth, entireness,
and integrity of friendship. Shall such a flaw be found in
my dear Jane Welsh ? No, my dear young lady, the past
as well as the present must be laid open ; there must be
no Bluebeard's closet in which the skeleton may one day
be discovered. You have received a new and dear guest
to occupy your heart, not as tenant at will, but as tenant
for life ; and if, with a noble show of friendship, you have
still only a show of it, what conclusion will that " soul of
fire " arrive at ? The wisdom that was before all time
hath said, " Perfect love casteth out fear " ; and till your
fears are all cast out, your love is still imperfect and your
cure incomplete. I could say much to you of the *policy*

---

[1] Compare the full text, *Love Letters,* II, pp. 148–50, with Mr. Froude's
Thomas Carlyle, I, pp. 305–6. A lawyer who in argument mis-stated the
gist of a letter as Mr. Froude has done would deserve reprimand and be
professionally discredited.

of a perfect integrity, but I scorn that base and grovelling word. You will think how easy it is to sit and dictate? Believe me, my love, I owe many peaceful days and nights to a similar disclosure poured into the ear of a passionate and jealous man ; a disclosure most painful, most humiliating—the particulars I will one day communicate to you. If this confession had not been made, how terrible would the evils have been, to which I might have been exposed ; and how could I have hoped to regain confidence, of which I should in that case have felt myself wholly undeserving? *Pride* is a paltry thing. *You* must stoop before you can be proud. Oh ! wear not the livery of fools whom you despise : in them it is excusable, but not in you.

'You see, my dear friend, what a terrible monitor you will find in me. The poor monk who puts on voluntarily a hair shirt will be but the type and shadow of your patient endurance,—if you do endure me,—and you must learn to do so ; for your wit will not overawe me, or your loveliness bribe me. I shall be the only friend you have out of the circle of your spells.

'Mr. Irving is here again; his Wife and Child are with her friends. He is now staying under our roof, where I so often entreated Mr. Carlyle to stay. We would have exorcised the bitter spirit that rends him, and have cast it out for ever. You will do this much more readily. I have a married daughter.' (Mrs. Procter, in short, and on account of her approaching confinement I will be in town till September, and then may go to Bolton Abbey, near Harrogate.) 'Will you come to Bolton ? And when you are safe under my protection, will Mr. Carlyle come too? "He hears me not, he minds me not " ; but he will answer and mind you. Your attached friend,

'D. B. MONTAGU.'

There was no suggestion in the letter that she had " no right to marry " Carlyle, but only kindly-meant advice not to hide from him the previous affair, which she might afterwards regret she had not told him. Mrs. Montagu did not know, and maybe never knew, that Jane had falsely told Carlyle she had never cared for Irving. What worried Jane was having to confess a fib. She did so, and sent him Mrs. Montagu's letter on Sunday (24.7.1825), declaring she had once loved Irving " passionately," a word which has been misunderstood by those who did not know that for fifty years it had been the fashion among young ladies who could appreciate *Werther* and Rousseau to talk like that. They could not speak of loving at all without loving " passionately," and it meant little more that Dominie Samson's " Prodigious ! " Receiving no reply, she wrote again on Saturday (30.7.1825), and this time " passionately " indeed :—

'Mr. Carlyle, do you mean to kill me ? Is it just of you to keep me so long in doubt ? Your displeasure I have merited, perhaps your scorn, but surely not this terrible silence ! Write then for Heaven's sake ! and kindly, if you can ; for I am wretched beyond all expression (and so on). O, I do love you above the whole Earth (and so on.) Be your answer what it may, I will love and venerate you to the last. You may be no longer mine, but I will be yours in life, in death, through all Eternity.

'JANE B. WELSH.'

Soon after writing thus, she was comforted by a letter he had written the day before, explaining how Sunday's letter had been delayed in delivery, and saying everything he could think of to make her happy, with such success that in a few days the matter passed out of her mind, as the shadow of a cloud passes over a field in sunshine and leaves no trace behind.

So completely was her mind set at rest that she did not hasten her visit though he pressed : " Come and see, and determine. Let me hear you, and do you hear me. As I *am*, take me or refuse me : but not as *I am not ;* for *this* will not and cannot come to good. When will you be here ? All are impatient for you here : I for many reasons. When will you come ? "

She wrote to Bess Stodart within a fortnight (13.8.1825),[1] making humorous use of a Scripture quotation in Carlyle's next letter :—

'MY DEAR, DEAR ANGEL BESSY,—
    ' (Don't be frightened, there is no commission in the wind). We were grieved to hear of your indisposition, and, as people have always most sympathy for the inflictions to which themselves are liable, we pitied you the more that your illness proceeded from bile. Think of me ! I have been

[1] *Early Letters of J. W. Carlyle*, by D. G. Ritchie, pp. 112-14.

engaged in this same warfare, now, several years, and have never been able to work out more than a few weeks of truce. " Perfect through sufferings," says the Scripture—a wholesome, comfortable doctrine for a bilious subject !

'My life is passing on here in the usual alternating manner. One day I am ill, and in bed ; the next, in full puff at an entertainment. It is difficult for a young person with *my attractions* to lead the life of a recluse, however much I wish it. I dined at a club dinner the other day, consisting —not the dinner but the company—of all the Justices (Just Asses) in the district with their wives. Mrs.—— of B—— was among them, a damned odd woman. She drank a bottle of wine during dinner, and was never a whit the worse for it. Speaking of " damned odd," James Baillie's match is entirely broken off, and himself on the road to Scotland ! ! At least so says Captain Gordon, a friend of his sister's and wholesale gossip in these parts. There was a letter from the dear gentleman to my Mother since we saw you. Your uncle will be glad to see some prospect of fingering the eighteen pounds.

'I purpose going to Dumfries in a week or two on a visit to my Grandmother, and afterwards into the lower district of Annandale to see—the country.'

It may have been in these very weeks that Carlyle's brother John brought him the *Edinburgh Review* for August, containing an astonishing essay on Milton which not only exalted Milton as Addison had done, but also glorified Cromwell as none had done before. He read it at once with enthusiasm. It was by young Macaulay, and dwelt in Carlyle's memory all his life as " the only thing of Macaulay's he ever read with lively satisfaction." It was so much applauded that the writer, like Byron, " awoke one morning and found himself famous."

X

VISIT TO HODDAM HILL

(1825)

JANE WELSH'S correspondence with Mrs. Montagu
went on flourishing, but little of it remains; and even
her letter of thanks to Carlyle on this occasion is lost.
His reply to it she had just been reading before writing
to Bess Stodart. It began : " My Dearest Little Ruth ! "
So she may have been calling herself Ruth. Assuredly the
humiliation had sweetened her spirit, and it was with some
sincerity that she followed Carlyle's example in applying to
bile the saying : " Perfect through suffering."

He said nothing to deepen her humiliation, being saved
by a lover's idolatry from fault-finding. " Oh Jane ! Why
should we murmur ? Are we not rich in better things than
silver or gold, or the vain babble of stupid men ? We have
found each other, and our hearts are one, our beings are
one ; for we love each other with a love not grounded on
deception but on *truth*, and no force can part us, or rob us
of that blessing ! Heavenly affection ! " (And so on, and
so on.) " I meant to write three lines, and behold my sheet
is full." (Nearly six pages of print !) He answered all her
questions about the Montagus. Bolton Abbey was an Inn,
and he would go with her to Bolton. He would fetch a pony
to Dumfries for her if she wanted it. He objected to nothing
but talk of her staying only " a day or two," as her mother
intended. " We will appoint no time—stay as long as you
can hold out." He offered her a choice of ponies, one to
amble, one to gallop, and said : " I do believe a week or
two of it would do you more good than all the doctors of
the county." So it may have been in order to lengthen
her visit that she did not come in August. She bade him
expect her on Thursday (1.9.1825).

It may have been on Saturday (3.9.1825) that she was
taken to Mainhill and offered his father a filial kiss.

" Na, na, Mistress Jean," said he, " I'm no fit to kiss the
like of you "—when fresh and muddy from the fields, he
implied.

396

" Hoot, James," said his wife, " you'll no refuse her when it's her pleasure."

" Na, na," said he, as he put the wondering young woman on one side and disappeared for a while ; but soon he came back clean-shaven and reclothed, and approached her with a smile : " If you'll give me a kiss *now* ! " he said.[1]

The weather was " set fair." The lovers roamed at random for two weeks—" Sabbath weeks," she called them, meaning a time of peace. They went together over the adjoining hill of Wood-cock-air, which he had explored as a boy. They may have done it on the same day as Kirk-connell Churchyard, renowned in song. She played chess at Hoddam Manse with old Mr. Yorstoun, Carlyle spectator. They dined with Irving's sister at Annan, whom she saw for the first time with curious interest. Their farthest ride was on a Saturday, nine or ten miles up the valley of the Milk to the north of Grange Fell and the house of a laird, ex-Glasgow merchant, Johnston. Carlyle had written to Mrs. Johnston in sending books to her lately (26.8.1825) :—

' I am still indolent ; a mere spectator of the " tragi-comic-pastoral farce " of existence, or at best but a candle-snuffer, snuffing a few German rushlights, to let the actors see better how to bear themselves. In Time, I doubt not, some secondary part may be given to me too, and I shall strut and bellow like the rest. For the present, the will of fate be done ! If it were not for the genius of sloth, I would visit Grange about twice a week.'

When he took Jane with him, they were easily persuaded to stay all night, and returning on the Sunday morning by way of Waterbeck, did their best to minimize offence to the Sabbath keepers, with success that was almost but not quite perfect. Nearing home, without a choice of routes, they passed on the way and disturbed, but as little as possible, some Ecclefechan worshippers on the way to Hoddam Kirk. One can hear with the mind's ear the muttered talk, and guess that it was not altogether for heretical opinions that Tom Carlyle was called an Atheist in the village.

On the third Monday (19.9.1825) as they rode to Dumfries

[1] Mrs. Oliphant's article in *Macmillan's Mag.*, April, 1881, p. 484 and footnote. The date required correction.

together she did not hide she was sorry to part. They left their horses at the Inn and he walked with her to the door of her grandmother's house.

She wrote to him next day that there was " nothing " there " but confusion and disquiet. My Grandmother and (three) Aunts have been lecturing to me at great length." Her uncles were bores at the best. A letter from her mother was " very kind. She makes no comment on my visit to Hoddam Hill, whatever ; but approves of the rest of my arrangements." One has to remember the young woman had made her visit so long that it was like a publication of her engagement.

XI

GENERAL SHARPE BECOMES IMPORTANT

(1825)

MISS WELSH needed all the sympathy her lover could give her. Her soul was struggling out of its entanglements of squalid snobbery. Their talk at Hoddam Hill had turned on where they were to live, for they had settled to marry soon, and she would doubtless let him know what a small house there was at Craigenputtock compared to where he was living ; and they decided that if they went to live there, they would have a good house in addition to one for the working farmer. This gives a suspicious significance to what Mrs. Welsh did in the beginning of October—she let Craigenputtock to another man, rejecting a bid from Carlyle's brother Alexander. " You may believe," wrote Jane reporting this (6.10.1825), " I never was more vexed and angry in my life."

There was no hope that they would be able to live at Hoddam Hill. It had to be vacated in May, 1826, and Mainhill in 1827, because of a dispute between James Carlyle and the landlord of both, " General " Matthew Sharpe, who had learned in the last ten years to trust his tenant, but did not understand him. They had settled about Hoddam Hill for £100 a year without thinking of £150 due to Mr. Blackadder, the outgoing tenant, who had been the factor for Sharpe and his father before him, but was retiring now and impatient to be paid. Who was to pay him ? Each thought the other should. Some farmers on other estates agreed to arbitrate ; but there was no debate about such sundries as the incoming tenant takes over. The claims of Blackadder were unusual, and the arbiters decided nothing. " Could not," they declared ; " would not," the parties thought, each sure of being right ; and certainly did not. The squabble lasted through the summer, and worried both sides. " The General " tried to bully his tenant without success. To every new proposal James answered " No," refusing to compromise beyond the limits of fair play. He was aware that the lease of Mainhill, which ended in 1827, would not be renewed if this were not settled ; but then, he did not think Mainhill was cheap, and was hoping to get something better, enquiring all around ; Miss Welsh assisting in Nithsdale. " I *will not* do it," said he once of something suggested. " I will rather go to Jerusalem, seeking farms, and die without finding one." Another time he said, " We can do without Sharpe, and the whole Sharpe creation." But this was at home and in private.

At harvest time the " General " with his friends and dogs came shooting over Mainhill Farm and trampled down the corn in a field near which James himself was trenching with an eye upon the reapers. By this time it was plain that " hard must come to hard," but the servants and the outsiders did not know that.

As the hunters were going through the corn, James straightened himself and without moving from where he stood demanded : " What right have you and your dogs to trample down my crops ? "

The farmer's men and the hunters moved aside, as if to be politely out of hearing while the " General " and his tenant spoke together. None ever heard from either what was said. An eager pair of listening young ears caught only this at the time : " . . . I won't renew your lease . . ." and, " I tell thee, Mathy Sharpe . . ." [1]

[1] Witness "Wull Wolls " or William Wells, cousin or father's cousin of John T. Wells, who took down his statement in the 'seventies, and in 1895 at Ecclefechan, heard it again not long before his death, and all the same, which seems to show the accuracy of William Wells.

XII

IN THE FARMER'S KITCHEN

THE youngster who ventured to stay where he was and heard all he could was "Wull Wolls" or William Wells, a boy of fourteen from the village, who had applied to James Carlyle for leave to fill the place of a shearer who had fallen ill and gone home. James let him start, but "I saw he hesitated," said Wull, "and felt him watching me sometimes."

At the first day's dinner, when all were sitting at table in the kitchen, Wull was "blate" or shy, and said "No" to a proposal for a second helping ; but his master from the head of the table said : "Thou'rt a Leviathan of a shearer," and so encouraged him that he took a second helping, and then a third—feeling that it was not grudged, and remembered the happy day with gusto after half a century.

"He sat at the head of the table and himself divided the midday dinner, and looked well to our meat," said Wull and everybody.[1] He was one of the "liberal" employers who killed a sheep for fresh meat to his harvesters, instead of giving them the salted stuff that made them thirsty. He was seen and heard on one occasion to be looking with loathing at some salted bull's heart and entrails on his own plate. "My soul abhors it," he said, and flung it on the floor for the dogs.

"There is nothing better," said his wife. "There is no fresh meat to-day, James."

"Then fetch us a goose from the stubble," said he, and what she thought the servants never heard. "He was aye a stiff old body and could bide no contradiction."

Porridge was the staple ; and skim milk was in most farms what the servants got to their porridge ; but James

[1] Including "Sam Wells" and John Wells, of Eaglesfield, the last survivor known to D. A. W. of those who had served James Carlyle, the father of T. C. Much that has been told by various authors was really about the second James C. of Scotsbrig, the son of the first. These statements were taken down by John T. Wells, Missionary, Edinburgh.

gave them fresh milk, and would often encourage them to drink more of it, saying : " If you don't get it good, it's your own fault. Keep up to her," meaning keep up to the cow, leave nothing and so make sure that the next milk supplied shall be fresh.

XIII

CARLYLE AT TEMPLAND

(1825)

MRS. WELSH'S silence about the length of Jane's visit to Hoddam Hill was eloquent ; but her father, Walter Welsh of Templand, and her sister " Jeannie " who kept house for him were now curious to see the young man they had heard about. He was invited and expected on the first Saturday of October, but sickness held him at home. " I am drowned in drugs," he wrote, excusing himself, which gave Mrs. Welsh another argument against him. But her daughter had long suffered from bile herself, and sympathised with emphasis (6.10.1825). " Sick too ! Oh me ! And I not near to nurse and comfort you ! Come, my Darling ! My Grandfather and Aunt will give you no freezing reception. I have prepared them to like you, and they *will*. On Monday we will look for you at dinner at three o'clock, Ever ever yours."

He came and stayed two days, and seemed satisfactory to everybody but Mrs. Welsh. Old Walter found only two faults in him—he smoked tobacco, and did not drink whisky, which seems an odd kind of " fault " to-day, but few in Scotland then suspected what a curse the politicians were bringing on the country in popularizing whisky in order to pick the people's pockets. Old Walter found his granddaughter's choice an excellent listener to anecdotes, with a sense of humour as keen as his own, which ensured their harmony. The old man was still tall and strong, hot-tempered, good-natured, and rather ripened than soured by many sorrows. Sometimes as he laughed " there was audible " what the young man now making his acquaintance recalled when old himself :—

'Something as of infinite flutes and harps, as if the van-quished themselves were invited—or compelled—to partake in the triumph. I remember one such laugh—quite forget about what—and how the old face looked suddenly beautiful

and young again. " Radiant ever-young Apollo," etc., of
Teufelsdröckh's laugh is a reminiscence of that. Walter
had an immense fund of inarticulate gaiety, a truly fine
sense of the ridiculous—excellent *sense* in a man, especially
if he never cultivate it, or be conscious of it, as was Walter's
case : and it must have been from him, then, that my Jane
derived that beautiful light of humour—*never* going into
folly, yet full of tacit fun—which spontaneously illuminated
all her best hours. Thanks to Walter ; *she* was of him in
this respect : my Father's laugh, too, is mainly mine—a
grimmer and inferior kind ; of my Mother's beautifully
sportive vein, a *third* kind, I seem to have inherited less,
though not nothing either, nay, perhaps at bottom not even
less, had my life chanced to be easier or joyfuller. " Sense
of the ridiculous "—worth calling such ; i.e. " brotherly
sympathy with the *downward* side "—is withal very indis-
pensable to a man : Hebrews have it not ; hardly any
Jew creature—not even blackguard Heine, to any real
length, hence various *mis*qualities of theirs, perhaps most
of their qualities too which have become *Historical*. This
is an old remark of mine, tho not yet written anywhere.'

It was the worst defect of Goethe too, witty though he
was, which Carlyle has never remarked anywhere ; but that
is another story. It was through the long-departed handsome wife of Walter, once a Miss Baillie, the daughter of
a Biggar doctor, that Jane used to claim connection with
the gypsies ; but the far-off collateral through whom she
claimed was not even a common gypsy, only a common
gentleman and thief. When Carlyle departed on Wednesday,
she went with him far enough to be able to kiss unseen, and
there was a tear hanging in her " long black eyelashes "
as he mounted and rode away.
        He noticed it, and the thought of leaving her behind
hung " like a black cloud " between him and the sunshine
as he went over the hills into Annandale, passing by the
farm where his mother was born and an old battle-field
(Dryfe Sands) where many Maxwells, Johnstones and
Carlyles mangled each other in 1593. He used to tell the
tale of pitiful slaughter there as he passed the place with
others, and when alone he saw again " with the mind's
eye " the unhappy spirits long ago departed.
        A week after reaching home, when the October winds
had wakened and were dashing the rain against the windows,

he wrote to her telling all his doings and his news in detail, and how his mother welcomed a gown she had sent her, and how dismal Hoddam Hill seemed without her compared to what she had made it. He wrote at length to cheer her :—

' If we have joy, we *must* have sorrow ; if we are not *wae* to part, how should we be *blithe* to meet ? There is a misery beyond the sharpest parting sadness ; the misery of a heart grown dead to sadness as to joy ; that loves not, fears not, hopes not, but sits amid utter desolation, reckless of all further ravages. This also I have felt ; I ought rather to rejoice that I feel it no longer.' . . .

' Fear not utterly, my Darling ! Life is yet all before us. I am far from regretting that you came. I never dared to love as now. Let us trust that these " Sabbath-weeks " were but an emblem of the long Sabbath-years we are to spend together for ever and for ever ! One would think that they might be made as happy ; but that were an error.' . . .

It would be easy to make too much of the melancholy " misery," wherein he was imitating their common favourite Byron more than he was aware, paraphrasing the lines which Byron called " the *truest*, though the most melancholy, I ever wrote " :—

" There's not a joy the world can give like that it takes away,
When the glow of early thought declines in feeling's dull decay. . . .
Then the mortal coldness of the soul like death itself comes down ;
It cannot feel for others' woes, it dare not dream its own. . . .
Oh could I feel as I have felt,—or be what I have been,
Or weep as I could once have wept, o'er many a vanished scene ;
As springs in deserts found seem sweet, all brackish though they be,
So midst the withered waste of life, those tears would flow to me."

In echoing this, Carlyle was sincerer than most—the sentiment abode with him. As great spirits go through all that men can know and end in a conscious ignorance as humble as when they started, so do such return to a second conscious spontaneity like that of children, as Byron sighed to do and might have done if he had been spared, as Carlyle did and Goethe, shaking off from them the sophistications of society.

The letter quoted (19.10.1825) reveals him outgrowing Byron, as if in spite of himself, and practising the maturer maxims of Goethe. " Since my return I have been taking some glimpses into the Books of Conscience, and find a weighty balance against me. If aught can be done, let us do it quickly. I have worked two days honestly at Tieck; in another ten I hope to be done with him, and perhaps attempting something better."

So said, so done. He soon had selected and arranged everything, but the work was not absorbing, and compatible with such diversion as he had the day after writing this letter.

XIV

IRVING AND OTHERS

(1825)

ON Thursday (20.10.1825) he went to Annan to meet Irving passing through on the way to London, where he was due on Saturday and to preach on the Sunday. Irving was found sitting with his father and mother in their parlour, among a crowd of cousins and admirers, but looking sad and sick, and "green" in hue, "sallow and careworn." No wonder! The little son he loved had died of whooping cough a week ago, and he was leaving his wife behind him ill in her father's house.

When he saw Carlyle he took leave of the rest, blessing sundry "by name in a soft low voice," and hitting the door lintel with the hat on his head as he turned round to go for a stroll in the fields with Carlyle. He had some hours to spare. He wrote to his wife that Carlyle "edified me very much with his discourse," [1] which would mean sympathy in his afflictions. Turning to other topics, he soon was "laughing with all his ancient vehemence" as he described in detail the conferences between Utilitarians and Christians over the new University for London. He had been on the "Committee" and said: "At one meeting poet Campbell was arguing loudly for a purely *secular* system when I entered, and on sight of me he very politely stopped short and sat down without another word on the subject. It will be *un*-religious, secretly *anti*-religious all the same," he concluded, saying he had left it "because religion was not cared for." Which made Carlyle hope that there might be some appointment suitable for himself there, as he reported to Jane, enclosing a letter from Irving to her, excusing himself for failing to pay an intended visit to her mother and her. "I hope in Heaven you may go to London," she answered. "I like the idea of it more than any scheme you have proposed to me."

[1] *Life of Edward Irving*, by Mrs. Oliphant, Chap. XI.

She was doing what she could to help his friend, James Johnstone, now a candidate for the Haddington Parish School, to which he was presently appointed, because Gilbert Burns and others relied on the recommendation of Carlyle ; and there Johnstone stayed for the rest of his life, to the satisfaction of everybody, himself included.

XV

AN ADVENTURE

(1825)

CARLYLE was pressing on with his translations, feeling
—the sooner they are done, the sooner we'll be
married, and over-exerted himself. So about the end of
October, on finishing Tieck, he rested half a week ; and at
once he found himself planning, he told Jane, a work of
Art to be an outlet for " the pictures and thoughts and
feelings " inside him " which *shall* come out, though the
Devil himself withstood it ! "

He was meditating thus while riding with snaffle bridle
his red horse, Larry, who loved to gallop and had also
just had three idle days, and was hankering as much as
his master for an outlet for the energy he felt within him.
They met a carrier's cart and Larry whirled round, and
getting the bit between his teeth, he let himself go, and
galloped down a steep place, like the swine beloved of
Huxley and Gladstone, by the lake-side of Galilee.

Larry was more lucky than the swine ; but his happiness
was equally short. The rider he jerked off was not detached
but trailed upon the road, and soon was standing beside
him, stunned, bemired and scratched. They went home
together like Don Quixote and Rozinante after an adventure.
There was no more thought that day of the masterpiece
unborn, and when they went out together again several
days later, Larry had his fill of galloping ; but there was
a heavy curb in his mouth, and his rider had a stick in his
hand, and was not thinking of his masterpiece. It may be
left to students to discover the passage in his writings
which is a reflection of this adventure. That was an after-
thought.

XVI

CAPTAIN BAILLIE INTERVENES

ON the day after Carlyle left Templand, Mrs. Welsh had exploded and said many "cruel unreasonable things" to her daughter with "bitter reflexions" against Carlyle, perorating: "he has bewitched and poisoned your mind."

Many a verbal victory had she had, but as the old hen cackles the young one learns, and Jane replied:

"You are unjust. My connection with so wise and honourable a man can be attended with no ill consequences, and any way such language is out of time—particularly since it was with your knowledge and consent that I" became engaged, in short.

Surprised by her defeat, the older woman "sulked for four-and-twenty hours," reported Jane to Carlyle. Her last hope was her rich cousin, whose visit was impending; and she did not want to fight at such a time; but she wanted to have her own way, and though living in the same house indited to her rebellious daughter "a long epistle":—

'Wherein she demonstrated—*not* by geometrical reasonings—that I was utterly lost to all sense of duty; and took much bootless pains to explain the inconsistency of her conduct towards *you*. "She had indeed given her consent to our union," she said, "when you should have made yourself *a name and a situation in life;* but only because I asked it, with tears, upon my bended knees' (which is not denied and is an interesting revelation) 'at a time, too, when my life seemed precarious."' (Whereupon Jane intercalates:) 'To the best of my recollection I was then enjoying tolerable health. "Afterwards, however, when you came to Haddington, and she watched your temper and perceived its *effect* upon me, it was then that her soul was torn," etc. etc. A pack of damned nonsense the whole of it! "Temper!" "Effect!" Truly, she has seen her own temper have a hundred times worse effects upon me than ever yours had.

Do we not love each other ? And what is love if it cannot make all rough places smoothe ? *Nein !* (No !) I am not afraid that my happiness will be wrecked upon this rock ; nor is my Mother, either, if the truth were told. I could lay my life this grand objection never entered her head till she was sitting with the pen in her hand, hunting after an excuse for so much caprice.

'Another cause of offence is my intimacy with Mrs. Montagu, " a woman whom I never saw, whom I know nothing about." (And so on.) But it is to no purpose ! I will go on corresponding with Mrs. Montagu as long as I have ink and paper ; and no man, woman or child shall prevent me from loving and admiring her as much as I please. You too, my dearest, I will continue to love and admire, tho the whole earth should blame my choice ; for I know in whom I have put my trust, and my resolution is steadfast as a rock. I have told this to my Mother, once for all, in a tone of decision, which should prevent further remonstrance.

'Nevertheless, I am anything but insensible to her displeasure. . . . Oh, it is heart-breaking, shocking, to live in this manner, with one to whom I am bound by the holiest tie ! . . . Alas, alas ! we understand each other no more.

'What will become of me till I have you again ? . . . O Lord ! '

She was here interrupted by a furious rapping at the door. Her mother's cousin, the handsome Lancer, Captain Baillie, had arrived in a fine emblazoned chariot with four horses, and " glittering in jewels, from the gold pendant of his rose-coloured cap, to the ruby buckles of his slippers." So she wrote, completing her letter next day (25.10.1825). On the day of arrival nothing could be done but attend to the visitors. He came not alone. Besides his valet and his big dog, he was attended by four little dogs and his sister Phœbe, to make Jane feel how much she would be welcomed and at home in a " higher sphere." The Lancer Captain was supposed to have besides his pay £1000 a year and a fine house, which seemed synonymous with happiness to Mrs. Welsh, who had taken such pains to make £200 a year appear like more. She hopefully recalled how much Jane used to appreciate Captain Baillie's attentions, and—was still wearing his hair in a ring on her finger.

"More Adonis-like, witty and elegant than ever," Jane called him now in writing to Carlyle, but the mother's hopes would have ended like snow-flakes on the river if she had read what followed : " I wish, in my heart, he were returned to the place whence he came. You have not the slightest cause to be jealous ! Jealous ! Oh mercy ! When I compare this fine gentleman with the *man* I love, what is he after all ? A mere painted butterfly, while he—my own— is like to the royal eagle, who soars." (And so on.) It is a prehistoric discovery that when a young woman can clearly see her duty and inclination agree, she becomes as irrepressible as the tides, an elemental force of Nature.

The Adonis of the day of arrival speedily seemed "Belial," and Jane did not amuse herself by flirting, as Carlyle suggested. She did not forget to thank him for his " obliging permission which doubtless I shall be right glad to avail myself of on some future occasion " with somebody else.

Meanwhile events were hurrying her. Here is a current item from a P.S. in her letter. " Have you heard of Mr. Gillespie's death ? He was married but a few weeks ago to a young lady whom he was engaged to for years. This is truly awful." It was a warning against a long engagement ; but there was no longer any danger of that. Mrs. Welsh's income from Craigenputtock had become irregular, and she was about to sell the house in Haddington and come to live at Templand, which made her want to capture Captain Baillie at once, and made her daughter want to marry Carlyle as soon as he could house her. He reciprocated her impatience so much that he was willing to do without the house ; but that was not needful.

In November Mrs. Welsh returned for the last time to Haddington, and Baillie descended there to complete his conquest, spreading out his decorations like a peacock his tail, with valet and dogs and sister in attendance. In vain, in vain ! Before December was a week old, even Captain Baillie could see the bird had escaped him. Whatever his income, he was sure to be exceeding it and needing cash. Perhaps a whisper of how Craigenputtock had been lately settled quickened his decision. At any rate he departed like a dream and was seen no more, leaving—Mrs. Welsh—lamenting ! And angry too ! Maybe she never knew how faithfully Carlyle was admonishing Jane to keep from quarrel with her. " In asserting your rights," he told her, " be meek. Do not cease to love your mother and to sweeten her days for her. . . . She cannot cease to love you. For me take no thought. Her aversion to me shall never be remembered against her." In another letter (29.12.1825) he wrote : " For your mother, do not let her unkindness afflict you : answer it by contrary conduct ; if you think it foolish and harsh, be you the more wise and gentle. This is to overcome evil with good, the only proper weapon to resist it with." Excellent advice, and he set her a good example of behaviour to her mother, in spite of provocations, whereof perhaps the worst was this January, 1826, when he came to Edinburgh (5.1.1826) to get more German books and correct proofs. He did not see Jane at all tho he was three weeks within sixteen miles of her. Many letters passed. In one (14.1.1826), wherein he mentioned the noises were spoiling his sleep, he told her he had thought of renting a cottage " in the middle of a walled garden " near Edinburgh, to be his home on leaving Hoddam Hill. His sisters might keep house for him ; but he asked :—

'Would you——? Professor Leslie has another plan. This tun-bellied philosopher met me on the North-bridge the other day, and wished me in the first place to write a Prize Essay on Comets for a gold medal and fifty guineas, which he had got to dispose of in that way ; a thing which I signified was a good way from my thoughts at that date ; and in the second place to go to Munich—in Bavaria—with a German Potentate, who wishes to be instructed in English Literature and Science, and is a courtier and apparently " a very good kind of a man." I told (him) I was ready to talk further, if the German Potentate inclined, when I heard his terms.'

She answered next day, Sunday though it was (15.1. 1826) :—

'MY DEAREST,—
'The announcement contained in your last letter bewildered my intellect. Last night I had serious thoughts of setting out for Edinburgh forthwith, in spite of all and sundry objections. I felt as if it would do me a world of good just to fall upon your neck and weep, and tell you once more what I have told you so often already, that you are dearer to me than aught on earth. But it must not

be ! Things are bad enough already ; I must not make them worse. And you will return to take up house *with Mary and Jane?* Indeed you will do no such thing. Nor go to Bavaria, unless the German Potentate would find room in his establishment for me also. Otherwise, you may tell Mr. Leslie that you have got a Wife to take care of at home. I am for ever yours.'

At the same time she was eagerly assisting, but in vain, his father's attempts to get a farm he wanted in Nithsdale ; and in a letter to his mother at Mainhill she compared her own patience in living through these three weeks without a sight of him to the Patriarch Job's : " for the *woman* who could undergo this thing, and yet not die of rage, could also survive, with a meek spirit, the carrying away of oxen and asses, the burning up of sheep, and even the smothering of sons and daughters."

From all which it is plain that though the handsome Captain Baillie made many mistakes in his life, he was right for once, when he went away ; and even Mrs. Welsh was beginning to see that now. Bess Stodart could have told her long ago.[1] When Carlyle was walking along Princes Street (about 19.1.1826) listening to the talk of Brewster, as full as ever of his literary newspaper and explaining his hopes of getting John Wilson, " Christopher North," to share the speculation, Carlyle observed Miss Stodart looking at him kindly as she was turning up a side street and pointing him out to another young lady, so that he turned away his head, explaining—to Jane, not Brewster who would not see it—" the pressure of etiquette was too heavy for me to bear. Tell Eliza that I saluted her in my heart." What old Walter Welsh had said, and Aunt Jeannie, is sure to have been helpful, but remains unknown except by the result. Mrs. Welsh could not fail to be aware rebellion was brewing—so many letters passing with contents unknown to her was ominous. So she gave over "sulking"[2] and resolved to make the best of what could not be helped. When on 25.1.1826 she saw Jane making a parcel of caps for her future mother-in-law at Mainhill, she brought her a little handkerchief, and said " with a sort of half-kind

[1] April, 1824. See *Early Letters of J. W. Carlyle*, by D. G. Ritchie, pp. 83-9 ; and to corroborate the editor's conjecture, 1824, see *Love Letters*, I, p. 337.
[2] *Nineteenth Century Mag.*, January, 1914, p. 109.

air," " You can put that in, if you choose, for Jane " (his sister). " You may believe," wrote her daughter to Carlyle, " I thanked her with all my heart for this small mercy, and hailed it as an indication of returning good-humour, with great joy."

His last letter from Edinburgh gave her the news of the bankruptcies of Scott and Constable and Ballantyne. On Friday (27.1.1826) he went home with translation work in hand for many months.[1]

---

[1] The statement, *New Letters and Memories of J. W. Carlyle*, I, p. 13, that he was at Haddington this month is shown to be a mistake of memory by contemporary letters.

XVII

GENERAL SHARPE DISAPPEARS FROM THIS HISTORY

(1825-6)

IN a letter to Johnstone [1] this winter, Carlyle reveals his feelings towards the laird who had upset his plans :—

'Sharpe has acted very like a knave, if not altogether as one in this matter. I meet him sometimes in my rides, but never without some slight desire to pull his nose. It is the itching of the unregenerate man in me this ; I ride on and think,—Is he not a son of Adam like thyself, with a squint in his eyes, great vanity, a young wife, a touch of villany, and a racked rent-roll, and nothing but one small fraction of a brain, to meet these many exigencies ? Let him fight his own battle.'

Soon after James Carlyle was sure he would not get the farm he wanted in Nithsdale, he heard that another which would suit him, Scotsbrig, two or three miles north-east of Ecclefechan, was to be vacant in May ; and he got a lease of it in March. The Hoddam Hill establishment was to go there in May, and for 1826-7 he would run Mainhill as well. After May (1827), Scotsbrig would be the only family head-quarters ; but till then, especially through the summer of 1826, it would be "our Tom's" alone as much as Hoddam Hill had been. That is to say, the house would be his to live in, and the farming business would concern his father and brother.

About this time (March, 1826) "the whole countryside" had a little excitement. The young "new-married wife" of General Sharpe was driving along a muddy road and "the tutor-fellow at Hoddam Hill" came cantering past her, a stranger yet well known ; and to the amazement of the gaping rustics beholding the miracle he did not even

---

[1] Unpublished letter.

draw bridle respectfully, much less bow or doff his hat.
He went by as if unconscious that the carriage—and
what was in it—belonged to " our only General," " the
Laird." [1]

The lady was sure he had splashed her ; but " that was
impossible," said witnesses ; " no drop of mud could have
reached above the lower part of her wheels." Whatever
it was that brought him, the " General " was well observed
as he strode soon afterwards to Hoddam Hill in a " boiling
rage," and the door was opened to him by Thomas Carlyle.

Unhappily there was no recording angel within hearing.
Any feminine complaints about splashing would be soon
dismissed.[2] A few words certainly spoken were in reply to
a lordly : " You ! What can you do about farming ? "

" Pay the rent," was the answer, " and all you have to
do is to get the rent. I'll use the land to feed larks on if
I like."

Assuredly the " boiling " laird departed in a minute or
two below the freezing point ; but he never would tell what
was said ; and though a day or two later Carlyle kept
Graham of Burnswark laughing " all the way from Annan
to Hoddam Bridge " by repeating it, we can hear them
laughing, little more. " The whole countryside " laughed
in chorus, and Scotsbrig having been secured, " my kindred,"
wrote Carlyle to Jane, " can now regard the ill-nature of our
rural Ali Pacha with a degree of equanimity much easier to
attain than formerly."

" The General's " tenants used to dine with him at Hoddam Castle when they came with their rents ; but the next
time money was payable, James Carlyle not only did not
go with it himself as he had always done before, he sent it
by the hands of his " youngest servant " " Wull Wolls."
Whereat the other tenants assembled whispered to each
other and Sharpe swore aloud.[3]

[1] Notes of John T. Wells of evidence of his " cousin " or cousin's son,
William Wells.

[2] " The lady was thoroughly bespattered with mud "—according to a
Border Magazine article, August, 1911. Maybe she said so, or was supposed
to say so—the report seems traceable to an Ecclefechan hotel-keeper, ex-
butler of the Sharpes. But the contemporary evidence is direct and credible
to the effect stated here ; and D. A. W. believes he proved this to the
satisfaction of the late G. McRobert, an excellent Edinburgh missionary,
who wrote the article in the *Border Magazine* and sent it to him.

[3] Notes of J. T. Wells : the witness being James Bell, farmer son of
the James Bell in whose service Mrs. Carlyle had been when she was Peggy
Aitken and James Carlyle was courting her, 1794.

The messenger looked innocent—" Wull Wolls " would be proud of his errand. Perhaps a doubt was hinted whether any insult was intended, and the matter mentioned to James himself by a friend. At any rate when Thomas Carlyle at Scotsbrig was completing his translation at ten pages a day, he had reluctantly to write for his father, who would not be denied, a polite conciliatory letter, which received no answer, maybe needed none, and left the quarrel ended with a minimum of ill-will.

This is all the more pleasant to remember because the father of Sharpe had been a Kirkpatrick of Closeburn, near Dumfries, and taken his uncle's name of Sharpe upon inheriting the Hoddam estate. He may have been akin to two Kirkpatrick brothers of Closeburn, one of whom begat Mrs. Buller and Mrs. Strachey, and the other a certain Kitty Kirkpatrick of this history. From 1815 to 1825 James Carlyle and his laird had been on the best of terms. It is a pity that the laird was too much in need of the £150 he only supposed to be due to him. He was poorer than he seemed, having to pay allowances to relatives, including a younger brother, Charles Kirkpatrick Sharpe, who loafed in Edinburgh Society all his life. " Besides," it may be said of our laird as of Count Zaehdarm, " his occupation being that of Owning Land, there might be faculties enough, which, as superfluous for such use, were little developed in him."

XVIII

ALL'S WELL THAT ENDS WELL

(1826)

IN the "Life of Richter" which Carlyle was now writing for his *German Romance*, he guessed that Richter had been led into literature by the pleasure of writing. This may be a clue to his own experience. Richter's *Quintus Fixlein* suggested much in *Sartor*. It was a masterpiece in the manner of Richter or Sterne that he was now meditating when Larry would let him, and the young woman in Haddington. Assuredly his haste to wed was partly prompted by the impossibility of serving two such masters—it is not easy to do a masterpiece and love-letters at the same time.

Both mother and daughter were tired of Haddington, they said to each other, and Mrs. Welsh said at once that Templand was the place for her. Aunt Jeannie's health was failing and old Walter Welsh needed a housekeeper. She generously proposed to give up everything to Jane and Carlyle ; but of course Jane would not hear of taking back the income she had assigned to her mother, and was confirmed in this by Carlyle.

In the first gush of reconciliation, Jane told her mother : "Wherever it is appointed *me* to live, you cannot surely intend we should ever live asunder." Her mother threw her arms about her neck and wept aloud. "Why have you never said as much before ? " As if it had been nothing but the fear of separation which had made her oppose so long the marriage now impending ! Jane believed this, and said she would propose to Carlyle that he was to hire the " nice little house " he spoke about in Edinburgh, and she and her mother would " hire one within some dozen yards of it ! so that we may all live together like one Family." The mother was aware this would never do, but yielded at last to " arguments, prayers, tears and kisses," and said : " I will do exactly as you please."

Carlyle had to explain it would never work. "It is impossible for two households to live as if they were one. Your Mother will *never* like me or find any pleasure in me. It will be her wisdom, therefore, and yours also, to keep me far from her." But the proposal had been humorously put, and he promised to consider it further "if you are *serious*."

What she called her "serious" answer is a mystery till one looks back and notices he had rashly let her know some weeks before that he had been dreaming all night about Mrs. Strachey and "Catherine Aurora—Miss Kirkpatrick." So now she retorted at great length in witty mockery : "You are the most tantalizing man in the world, and I the most tractable woman. Suppose we take different roads, and try how that answers. There is Catherina Aurora Kirkpatrick, for instance, who has fifty thousand pounds and a princely lineage, and ' never was out of humour in her life.' With such ' a singularly pleasing creature ' and so much fine gold, you could hardly fail to find yourself admirably well off. While I, on the other hand, might better my fortune in many quarters." She gave details of three other offers, concluding : " But what am I talking about ? as if we were not already married—alas, married past redemption ! . . ."

His answer filled seven pages of print, demonstrating how faultless he had been, and prosaically reminding her they were not married :—

' And do you hereby receive further my distinct and deliberate declaration that it depends on yourself, and shall always depend on yourself, whether we ever be married or not. Alas ! Jane, you do not know me ; it is not the poor, unknown, rejected Thomas Carlyle that you know, but the prospective rich, known and admired. I am reconciled to my fate as it stands. I have pronounced the word *unpraised* in all its cases and numbers ; and find nothing terrific in it, even when it means *unmonied*, and by the mass *neglected* or even partially *contemned*. I thank Heaven I have other objects in my eye than either *their* pudding or their breath. This comes of the circumstance that my Apprenticeship is ending, and yours still going on. O Jane ! Jane ! I could weep too ; for I love you in my deepest heart. Adieu, my heart's Darling ! I am yours, at your own disposal, for ever and ever.'

This hurt her, and she told him so at length, and said she had been jesting, declaring his " offers of freedom " to be " an outrage which I find it not easy to forgive." He was ashamed, and confessed it handsomely in a flood of words. " My Noble Jane! Thy heart has taught thee a philosophy better than all the schools will ever teach me." But he did not omit to come to the point, and asked whether she would marry him at once if he could get a house in the country.

She said she would, of course ; but explained it would break her mother's heart if they were separated, and— " O, my Husband, have you not told me a thousand times —and my conscience tells me also—that happiness is only a secondary consideration. It must not, must not be sought out of the path of Duty." And, in short, my Mother cannot come and live in Annandale. " I love you, Mr. Carlyle, tenderly, devotedly, as ever woman loved ; but I may not put my Mother away from me even for *your* sake. I cannot." So she suggested that she and her mother should take a house in Edinburgh, and asked : " Would you live with me in my Mother's house ? " She did not fail to insist that what had prejudiced her mother against him was " terror lest through your means she should be made childless."

He knew better ; but did not hurt her by saying so. He sent at once a note accepting joyfully her consent to marry soon ; but did not answer her question till he could write at length, and report he had got a house—he meant Scotsbrig. Then he urged that they should spend the summer there and make for Edinburgh in the winter. He quoted scripture about a wife leaving father and mother and cleaving to her husband ; and confessing he had been " selfish and thoughtless," he nevertheless told her frankly " the grand objection " to her project :—

' It may be stated in a word : *The man should bear rule in the house and not the woman.* This is an eternal axiom, the Law of Nature herself which no mortal departs from unpunished. It is the nature of a man that if he be controlled by anything but his own reason, he feels himself degraded ; and incited, be it justly or not, to rebellion and discord. It is the nature of a woman again—for she is essentially *passive* not *active*—to cling to the man for support and direction ; to comply with his humours and feel pleasure in doing so, simply because they are his ; to reverence while she loves him, to conquer him not by her force but by her weakness, and perhaps—the cunning gypsy !—after all to command him by obeying him.

'Your Mother is of all women the best calculated for being a *Wife*, and the worst for being a *Husband*. I know her perhaps better than she thinks.

'Now, think, Liebchen (Dearie), whether your Mother will consent in the spirit of Christian meekness to make *me* her guardian and director. If she can, *let* us all live together. If she cannot, the other thing must not be ; and for her sake, no less than yours and mine, we must think of something else.'

Mrs. Welsh was already doing so. Indeed, to do her justice, she had said all along that Templand was the place for her, and Jane reported joyfully (10.4.1826) :—

'My kind reasonable Mother views our romantic project with all the favour that heart could desire. And we will not be purchasing our happiness at the cost of hers ; for she will live, she says, at Templand, and visit us as often as may be.' (For the sake of her sister and father, she would soon have had to go to Templand, and) 'in going now, my Mother is only *anticipating* what *must* be her ultimate destination.

'The strangest thing has just occurred which I cannot but view as an omen that the gods are with us : a proposal is come to my *Mother* from Dr. Fyffe, *since I began writing*, to take this house off our hands upon any terms' (which seems to be) '*providential*.'

She ended with words in German that her mother was overlooking her letter, which made it cold and stupid. "I am shy of showing her my whole soul."

Mrs. Welsh wrote with her own hand :—

'MY DEAR SIR,—

'Jane has read to me what she has communicated to you respecting our future destination : which I trust will meet with your approval. This long perplexing emigration of ours draws to a close.' (Which is a touching way of talking, as if her heart was in the country after all, and Haddington where she had been so long had never been a home.)[1] 'May God grant that it' (this new arrangement, our return to the country and Jane's settlement there) 'may draw us all together in the bonds of love and happiness. With every good wish for your welfare, believe me in affection what you would wish the Mother of your Jane to be,

'G. WELSH.'

Of course he wrote and thanked her. There never was an unpleasant word between them ; and between her and Jane he continued to be the peacemaker. It was a delicate duty, and only possible when the ladies were much apart. It is the humour of reality that Jane shuddered at separation even for the sake of a husband, yet lived in a chronic condition of bicker with her mother. The curious conundrum remains for future casuists—why he did not use that in argument against her joint housekeeping proposal ? Was it sincere to write as if the only danger were of friction between Mrs. Welsh and himself ?

It is one of many instances in his life of a strange simplicity that seems stupidity but is seldom stupid, though it sometimes is, and may be so here. Any fellow is apt to feel the female of his choice infallible and shape his thoughts whatever way she wants. Perhaps it was a confused and distant recollection of such a state of mind that led theologians to formulate their fundamental maxim : " Believe a thing the more, the more it is impossible—there is no merit in believing what is true." Young women instinctively approve of that occasionally—in men.

[1] The meaning is sure. D. A. W. has heard a similar expression from an old Scotch lady, and enquired the meaning. Mrs. Welsh did not return to Haddington, and was buried beside her father at Crawford village.

XIX

HOUSES AND MARRIAGES

(1826)

CARLYLE intended the marriage to be "this very summer," as soon as *German Romance* was done. They would start at Scotsbrig. "The winter," he told his brother, "we may spend at Haddington: for her Mother goes to Templand to live; and I have just been persuading them not to let their house to Dr. Fyffe." But he soon found that Scotsbrig would never do. Alterations and repairs were in progress; and through the summer "plasterers and carpenters" were to be busy. This made him the more intent on their house at Haddington—"a sort of God-send expressly suited for our purpose," until a house in Edinburgh was ready, which he believed would not be possible before May, 1827.

He praised Mrs. Welsh's "generosity" in offering to furnish a house for them in Edinburgh; but explained to Jane that he could not afford the kind of house he feared she would get ready. "Such a house as the one where you now sit would cost, if furnished, somewhere about £150 a year: one very greatly inferior which I visited at Morningside was charged £60 for the bare unpapered and unfurnished walls. The humblest cottage costs between £30 and £40, to say nothing of taxes." In short, they must live cheaply. He would rather "live in a dog-hutch" than "in splendour and scarcity," and be "forced to *hawk* the laborious products of an aching head and heart for a piece of money, and become the drudge of some gross thick-sided booksellers." In other respects, his own "taste in houses" was "the easiest thing on earth to fit. Quietude by night, such that I can sleep in it—this is fully nine-tenths. In *all* other points, my toleration is boundless."

He insisted he was poor; and she offered to delay the wedding "if the thought of maintaining a Wife" were pressing on him; but he would not hear of that, explaining:—

'Wives are supported, some in peace and dignity, others in contention and disgrace, according to their wisdom or their folly, on all incomes from £14 a year to two hundred thousand: and I trusted in Jane Welsh and still trust in her for good sense enough to accommodate her wants to the means of the man she has chosen before all others, and to live with him contented on whatever it should please Providence to allot him, keeping within their revenue, not struggling to get without it, and therefore *rich*, by whatever arithmetical symbol, whether tens, hundreds or thousands, that same revenue might be expressed. This is not impossible or even very difficult, provided the will be truly there. Say what we like, it is in general our stupidity that makes us straitened and contemptible. The sum of money is a very secondary matter. One of the happiest, most praiseworthy and really most enviable families on the Earth at present lives within two bow-shots of me, that of Wightman the Hedger, on the produce of fifteen pence per diem (day), which the man earns peacefully with his mattock and his bill, not counting himself any philosopher for so doing. Their cottage on our Hill is tidy as a cabinet; they have a black-eyed boy whom few squires can parallel; their girnel (meal-chest) is always full; the man is a true, honest, most wisely conditioned man, an Elder of the Congregation, and meekly but firmly persuaded that he shall go to Heaven when his hedging here below is done. "What want these knaves that a King should have?" It is not miscalculation of expenses, then, that frightens me; the perplexity arises from other misunderstandings.'

Jane was adamantine against Haddington, but not explicit. How could she be explicit? It was hard enough that he had had to be told the truth about Irving. She had made up her mind that he would never know it about Fyffe, who still had hopes. Carlyle had not been seen in Haddington for a long time; and the exquisite Captain Baillie had lately been courting her openly and retired without success. And Dugald G——, the young highland laird, came there no more, and Benjamin B——, the moneyed amateur, had passed away from sight. The sympathies of Haddington gossips [1] were with Fyffe : "It's either you or the dominie—have another try." He was ready to clutch at any straw of hope; but had been held so much at a distance recently that he could not venture another direct proposal. There is much to be said for the expert opinion that his "providential" letter to Mrs. Welsh that he would "take the house off her hands upon any terms" had a double meaning. On the face of it, it was not business.

He was taken aback when he found she was willing to sell at once; but the house did suit him, and the front of it had long been his consulting-rooms, and Mr. Donaldson, who acted for Mrs. Welsh, found that a purchase on reasonable terms was in sight. But there was no reason discoverable by Carlyle—who lived "not by faith but by vision," as he wrote to Jane in this connection—why Fyffe should not be content with the rooms he was already using for a few months longer, and take over the whole of the house in May, 1827.

"Here, I have said, I *will* not live," she wrote to him, "and said it not without reasonable grounds and slow deliberation. But no other arrangement can you propose to me which I am not quite ready to acquiesce in. My Mother's project I would not have so much as laid before you, had I not believed it certain to meet *your* wishes and purposes. For Edinburgh, or any other great City, to *me* has no attractions. On the contrary I would prefer the Country much before it; because *there* I should have you more entirely to myself. But I much doubt if the Country be the fitter place for *you*, if the life of solitude and love, which would be heaven for me, would not for you become too soon a weariness. *That* do you determine."

"I confess my inability," he answered (13.5.1826), "with my present knowledge, to reconcile this very peremptory distaste with your usual good sense and love of me. *There must be something in the matter which I do not see.* [2] Your Mother and you are no unwise or uncalculating persons. Reconsider the business. Can you not procure a house in Edinburgh? Can you not revise your judgment in regard to Haddington? Can you devise no equivalent for it? My whole mind in one word is this : I think it were better for us both if we were wedded. Edinburgh I should greatly prefer, but see not how a footing in it is to be obtained."

[1] Reported to D. A. W. by persons who heard them direct.
[2] Italics by D. A. W.

In two or three weeks more Mrs. Welsh had taken 21
Comley Bank from a man she knew, exactly such a house
as he had specified : rent, £32 ; in the north-western
suburbs, within a few minutes of the west end of Princes
Street, yet away from smoke and noise.[1] She was even ready
to pay the rent, but was never allowed to do so. From
Haddington came furniture enough, and the house there
became Dr. Fyffe's, with entry as soon as he liked, and
Carlyle never discovered why the women had objected to
his living with his wife there after the marriage. But the
whole of Haddington would have wondered and blamed her
and her mother if they had acted as Carlyle had wanted,
for the newly married pair would have been in contact
" daily or oftener " with the agonized and disappointed
Doctor Fyffe.

Poor Fyffe, the rest of his history is no part of this, except
that the circumstances of his affliction, so interesting in
the county town of Haddington, must have been what made
Jane and her mother disappoint the gossips by not having
the wedding where she had been born and lived all her life.
They preferred to have it quietly at Templand Farm, Thornhill, which was now to be her mother's home and had long
been that of her grandfather, whose approval had helped
to make her mother agree to the wedding. To do Haddington justice, none of the gossips there was so foolish as Mr.
Froude. " You see, we knew too much," as one of them
modestly said. The word "misalliance" was never heard.
Such a notion never entered a head in Scotland about her
and him. On the contrary, the gossips who told a great
deal more than she knew herself about her shameful treatment of Dr. Fyffe, explained that she never had much and
that her richer suitors shied at her plainness and departed
on discovering how little of an heiress she was, and that she
had not only " led on " the unlucky young doctor, but really
preferred him and would have married him, if she had not
supposed the other man the better match. Wherein she
was mistaken, they maintained for more than a generation,
rejoicing to think Carlyle a fool or a failure and say : " It
serves her right." No part of Scotland was slower to admit
he was a great man—even Dumfriesshire was before it.

As soon as Carlyle heard a house had been got, he wrote
(18.6.1826) : " This Edinburgh arrangement is much better

[1] See letters in *Nineteenth Century Mag.*, January and August, 1914,
in addition to those in the *Love Letters*, in 2 vols.

than any other could have been " ; and he began to count how many weeks, five or six he made it, his translations would keep him too busy to go to town. Meanwhile Jane and her mother were making ready and getting a new rig-out. From grief—and economy—they had been wearing a kind of mourning ever since her father died.

Jane had also a good deal of sickness, so that her letters were hurried : " My head and heart are in an endless whirl," she told him, and he comforted her thus (19.7.1826) :—

' My own lassie, we will love one another not in *words* but in *deeds*—one of which is worth five thousand words— and front together all grievances. Here are two swallows in the corner of my window that have taken a house—not at Comley Bank—this summer ; and, in spite of drought and bad crops, are bringing up a family together with the highest contentment and unity of soul. Surely, surely, Jane Welsh and Thomas Carlyle, here as they stand, have in them conjunctly the wisdom of many swallows ! Let them exercise it then, in God's name, and live happy as these birds of passage are doing ! It is not Nature that made men unhappy, but their own despicable perversities.' (And their vanity, in short). . . .' They want to be happy, and by *happiness* they mean *pleasure*, a series of *passive* enjoy- ments : if they had a quarter of an eye they would see that there not only was not but could not be such a thing. I thank this distemper for having helped to teach me these things. . . .

' It is singular what a mockbird I am : I am writing here unconsciously in the very note of Jean Paul Friedrich Richter, on whose works I have been labouring for the last four weeks.'

He proposed to come and see them in Edinburgh, but she told him,—" Stay where you are till I am safe in Niths- dale " [1] ; and it was the last day in August before she was able to announce she was ready to see him at Templand, and had much to tell him " when we meet. And when will that be ? Mercy ! to think we have not seen each other for a whole year. O glorious instance of patience and long- suffering ! And the annals of our courtship afford many such. But in the other and better world we are about to enter, these Job-inflictions will be all forgotten, or remembered

[1] See letters in *Nineteenth Century Mag.*, January and August, 1914, in addition to those in the *Love Letters*, in 2 vols.

merely as a troubled dream. Write instantly what day I may look for you."

By the time that letter came, the *German Romance* was finished ; but he could not come at once, having made himself bilious by his over-eagerness in doing it. Nevertheless, on Monday night (4.9.1826), he and his brother John were drinking tea at the "nuptial feast" of James Johnstone, the new Parish Schoolmaster of Haddington, who was being married to Janet Carlyle. The feast was near Scotsbrig and ended with the formal wedding at four o'clock in the morning following, and Johnstone and his bride— a cousin of our Carlyles—rolled off in time to be at Haddington that same night. Honeymooning was not in fashion then in Scotland.

By Thursday (7.9.1826), Carlyle was at Templand, where Jane had plenty to tell him which concerned none but themselves, and a letter from Mrs. Montagu to show him, which it is likely she showed her aunt and grandfather as well. Part of it would interest them :—

' If Mr. Carlyle is near you, tell him that a lady, and a handsome one too, declared to Mr. Montagu and myself her "firm belief that the author of the *Life of Schiller* might have chosen as a wife, without the smallest chance of refusal, any unengaged lady in England." Is not this true fame ? '

Who the " handsome " woman was remains a mystery —she was no connection of Mrs. Strachey, it is safe to say ; for in a letter to Jane Mrs. Montagu " denounced Mrs. Strachey as an 'Arch-fiend !'" But she never drew Carlyle into her quarrels, though he was always loyal to herself.

By this time Jane had easily laid aside the wish for "fame," like a hat out of fashion. She never had it much at heart, whatever she supposed ; and could be as much amused as Carlyle at the " noble lady's " earnestness about it. To them it was merely a means of getting work and wages.

Carlyle went home on Saturday to Scotsbrig, " to expedite " what they had settled—getting clothes from a tailor in Dumfries was one of the items—and filled his vacant time by reading and " partially understanding " Kant's *Critique of Pure Reason,* so that he found himself " full of projects for instructing my benighted countrymen on the true merits of this sublime system, at some more propitious season." As for the journey from Templand to Edinburgh, she had only to say what she wanted. "Let me know your will," he wrote to her (27.9.1826), "and it shall be my pleasure. I shall only stipulate further that you let me, by the road, as occasion serves, *smoke three cigars*, without criticism or reluctance, as things essential to my perfect contentment! Yet if you object to this article, think not that I will break off the match on that account; but rather like a dutiful husband, submit to the everlasting ordinances of Providence, and let my wife have her way."

" Be always *so* good to me, and I shall make the best and happiest Wife," she answered (3.10.1826) :—

' When I read in your looks and words that you love me, I feel it in the deepest part of my soul ; then I care not one straw for the whole universe beside ; but when you fly from my caresses to—smoke tobacco, or speak of me as a new *circumstance* of your lot, then indeed my " heart is troubled about many things."

' I am going to be really a very meek-tempered Wife. Indeed, I am begun to be meek-tempered already. My aunt tells me she could live for ever with *me* without quarrelling—I am so reasonable and equal in my humour. There is something to gladden your heart withal ! And more than this ; my Grandfather observed while I was supping my porridge last night, that " She was really a douce peaceable body that *Pen!*" ' (A pet name for her.) 'So you perceive, my good Sir, the fault will be wholly your own, if we do not get on most harmoniously together. My Grandfather has been particularly picturesque these two days. On coming downstairs on Sunday evening, I found him poring over *Wilhelm Meister!* "A strange choice," I observed by way of taking the first word with him, " for Sunday reading." But he answered me quite sharply : " Not at all, Miss ; the Book is a very *good* Book : it is all about David and Goliath." But I must stop. And this is my last letter ! '

Though she had written that her mother was " dilatory and uncertain as ever," when at last he came to Templand on the appointed day (Monday, 16.10.1826), everything was ready. Next morning early they were married in her grandfather's house by the parish minister, Mr. Anderson, the only " other stranger " present being the bridegroom's brother John. They departed after breakfast, and like the Johnstones six weeks before, they were in their new home on their wedding day.

When they arrived about nine o'clock, Alison Greave, the maid from Haddington, was expecting them, and had a blazing fire and supper on the table. *Voilà tout!* (That's all) are the only words known to have been said by Mrs. Carlyle that night.[1] It was some days before the neighbours were aware a newly married couple was living at 21 Comley Bank.[2] So very quiet a wedding would be commoner if women knew how much it was preferred by men; but in this instance there is no trace of any such motive. Jane was thinking of nothing but her own convenience, and her young man was content to agree to anything but delay

[1] Unpublished letter. [2] Now spelled Comely.

INDEX

A

Abbeville, 348
Aberdeen, 150, 159, 311
Aberfeldy, 304
Adam, Dr., 73
Addison, 91, 110, 118, 395
Æsop, 377
Ætius, 146
Ailsa Craig, 190
Airdrie, 192
Aitken, Miss Carlyle, preface
Aitken, James, 216
Aitken, John, 8
Aitken, Margaret or Peggy, *Mrs. James Carlyle*, mother of T. C.
Aitken, Mrs. Margaret, maternal grandmother of T. C., 65
Aitkenhead, Thomas, 115
Akenside, 110
Alexander the Great, 25, 91, 214
Alison, Rev. A., 134
Allan, John, 50
Allen, Dr. Matthew, 204-6
Allingham, William, *Diary*, footnotes and 387
Allonby, 121
Anderson, Rev. Mr., 430
Anderson, Misses, preface
Andrew, "Son of Catgut," 80, 92, 114
Angus, Robert, 216
Annan, 34, 48, 49, 53, 59, 63, 68-71, 96-103, 107-11, 115, 129, 132, 137, 149, 177, 201, 241, 294, 381, 397, 407, 417
Anson's Voyages, 56
Anstruther, Mrs. James, preface
Archangel, 92
Archbishop of Canterbury, 28
Archimedes, 115
Arkwright, 9
Aristotle, 94
Armstrong, 81
Arthur's Seat, 207
Artois, Monseigneur d'Artois, 351
Astrakan, 149
Augusta, Miss, 208, 209
Augustine, St., 93, 122
Augustus, Fort, 255
Austerlitz, 63
Austin, Mrs., *Mary Carlyle*

B

Bacon, 145, 232
Badams, John, 326, 340, 345, 356, 367, 379
Bagdad, 146
Baillie, Capt. James, 344, 355, 366, 371, 395, 411, 412, 413, 425
Baillie, Joanna, 207
Baillie, Phœbe, 411, 412
Bailly, 135
Baine, 311
Baird, James, 216
Bajazet, 146
Ballantyne, 415
Balzac, 365
Bankton, 181
Bannockburn, 49
Barnet, Mrs., 340
Barthélemy, Abbé, 76
Bass Rock, 331, 369
Beattie, Jamie, 24
Beattie, Wull, 24
Beaumont and Fletcher, 266
Beauvais, 348
Beethoven, 367
Belcher, Jemmy, 343
Belfast, 69
Belisarius, 146
Bell, Dr. George, 308, 309, 325
Bell, Isabella, 42, 43
Bell, James, 40
Bell, John, 8
Benjamin B——, 248, 249, 371, 382, 383, 425
Ben Lomond, 196, 197
Bernouillis, 174
Berzelius, 168
Betty, 275, 300
Beveridge, 127
Bield, 143
Birmingham, 326, 340-5, 367, 378, 379
Birnam, 285
Birrens, see *Burrens*
Bismarck, 201
Blackadder, Mr., 399
Blacklock, Joe, 29
Blackwood, 173
Blair, 215
Blanc, Mont, 186, 323

2 F

433

2363   W. G. Board. CAR
            Nov. 1925
         ~,~